CAMBRIDGE

CW01649394

Commerce

for Cambridge O Level

COURSEBOOK

Deborah Malpas, Julie Whatford
and Sharon Elan-Puttick

Third edition with Digital access

CAMBRIDGE
UNIVERSITY PRESS & ASSESSMENT

Shaftesbury Road, Cambridge CB2 8EA, United Kingdom
One Liberty Plaza, 20th Floor, New York, NY 10006, USA
477 Williamstown Road, Port Melbourne, VIC 3207, Australia
314–321, 3rd Floor, Plot 3, Splendor Forum, Jasola District Centre, New Delhi – 110025, India
103 Penang Road, #05–06/07, Visioncrest Commercial, Singapore 238467

Cambridge University Press is part of the University of Cambridge.
It furthers the University's mission by disseminating knowledge in the pursuit of education, learning and research at the highest international levels of excellence.

www.cambridge.org
Information on this title: www.cambridge.org/9781009413299

First published 2010
Second edition 2016
Third edition 2024

20 19 18 17 16 15 14 13 12 11 10 9 8 7 6 5 4 3 2 1

Printed in Poland by Opolgraf

A catalogue record for this publication is available from the British Library

ISBN 978-1-009-41329-9 Coursebook with Digital Access
ISBN 978-1-009-41327-5 Digital Coursebook

Additional resources for this publication at www.cambridge.org/9781009413299

Endorsement statement

Endorsement indicates that a resource has passed Cambridge International Education's rigorous quality-assurance process and is suitable to support the delivery of a Cambridge syllabus. However, endorsed resources are not the only suitable materials available to support teaching and learning, and are not essential to be used to achieve the qualification. Resource lists found on the Cambridge International Education website will include this resource and other endorsed resources.

Any example answers to questions taken from past question papers, practice questions, accompanying marks and mark schemes included in this resource have been written by the authors and are for guidance only. They do not replicate examination papers. In examinations the way marks are awarded may be different. Any references to assessment and/or assessment preparation are the publisher's interpretation of the syllabus requirements. Examiners will not use endorsed resources as a source of material for any assessment set by Cambridge International Education.

While the publishers have made every attempt to ensure that advice on the qualification and its assessment is accurate, the official syllabus, specimen assessment materials and any associated assessment guidance materials produced by the awarding body are the only authoritative source of information and should always be referred to for definitive guidance.

Our approach is to provide teachers with access to a wide range of high-quality resources that suit different styles and types of teaching and learning. For more information about the endorsement process, please visit www.cambridgeinternational.org/endorsed-resources

Third-party websites and resources referred to in this publication have not been endorsed by Cambridge International Education.

Contents

How to use this book

Throughout this coursebook, you will notice recurring features that are designed to help your learning. Here is a brief overview of what you will find.

LEARNING INTENTIONS

These set the scene for each chapter, help with navigation through the coursebook and indicate the important concepts in each topic.

KEY TERM

Key vocabulary is highlighted in the text when it is first introduced, and definitions are given in boxes near the vocabulary, and in the glossary at the back of this book.

TIP

Tips are provided throughout to help with your learning. The tips might cover how to avoid common errors, advice on essay writing or guidance on how answers are arrived at.

ACTIVITIES

Activities give you an opportunity to check your understanding throughout the text in a more active way, for example, by creating presentations, posters or role plays.

REFLECTION

These activities ask you to think about the approach that you take to your work, and how you might improve this in the future.

WORKED EXAMPLE

Worked examples demonstrate chapter knowledge in practice, guiding you to the solution.

FORMULA

Key formulae are highlighted in boxes where they first appear in the text. A list of key formulae is also given at the end of the book.

Practice questions

At the end of each chapter you'll find more demanding practice questions, focusing on skills development and consolidation of your learning. Please note: * denotes that the question is from a past paper.

Knowledge check

The Knowledge check sections at the end of each chapter help you to check your understanding and recall of the chapter's content, without being formal practice questions.

SELF-EVALUATION CHECKLIST

The summary checklists provide you with a series of statements at the end of each unit outlining the content you should now understand. You will be asked to rate your confidence for each of these statements when revising. You should revisit any topics that you rated 'Needs more work' or 'Almost there'.

You should know about:	Needs more work	Almost there	Ready to move on

Introduction

Who is the book for?

The third edition of this coursebook is written for the updated Cambridge O Level Commerce (7100) syllabus for examination from 2026. If you are a learner following this syllabus, or a teacher guiding learners through it, you can be confident that the book fully covers the syllabus content to the appropriate level. The book may also be useful for taking other public examinations in commerce or business.

Structure of the book

The book is divided into six topic areas that reflect the subject content sections in the syllabus. Each topic area consists of one or more chapters. Chapters start by listing the learning intentions that will be covered. All chapters have several features to support learning, including activities to help develop skills, tips for avoiding common errors and opportunities for reflection on approaches to learning. Key terms are included in call-out boxes at relevant points and there are self-evaluation checklists to encourage consideration of how well the content is understood.

At the end of each chapter there are short answer questions and multiple choice questions to check your knowledge. There are also practice questions requiring longer answers. Some of these practice questions are taken from past Cambridge examination papers and are denoted by an asterisk. A few of the questions cover more than one topic. Coursebook answers are freely accessible to teachers on the 'supporting resources' area of our digital platform, Cambridge GO.

This coursebook contains a section on command words which provides guidance on each command word and aims to give you more confidence in the requirements of examination questions. The glossary at the end of the book provides a quick reference to aid revision of commercial terms and concepts.

Using the book

This book can be used to support and guide you as you progress through your studies. Following the Cambridge syllabus closely, it aims to help as you develop understanding of the purposes and functions of commercial activities and how these activities are influenced by changes in the commercial environment. You will develop knowledge and understanding of logistics and aids to trade, along with an understanding of the importance of communication and documentation and the impact of globalisation on commercial activity. You will also gain an appreciation of the nature and significance of sustainability and ethics in relation to commercial activities.

Completing the questions as you progress through the book will allow you to test your knowledge and understanding of basic commercial principles, techniques, facts and terms as well as commercial documents and the main functions and features of commercial activities. You will also have the opportunity to apply the commercial principles and ideas to given situations, analyse and evaluate problems and make reasoned judgements in an accurate and logical manner.

The Cambridge International Education syllabus is studied in many different countries. This coursebook aims to reflect the international nature of the syllabus by using examples and material from many parts of the world.

This coursebook comprehensively supports the revised Cambridge O Level Commerce syllabus; however, it should not be used in isolation. Commerce is an ongoing subject area and commercial activity is constantly changing. There is a need to keep up to date and to make use of resource material other than books. Much commercial activity surrounds us every day. It is important for every student of commerce to be receptive to the changing commercial environment.

Enjoy your Commerce studies and use this book as a valuable resource towards achieving success on your course.

Introduction to command words

The command words and definitions in this section are taken from the Cambridge O Level Commerce (7100) syllabus for examination from 2026. You should always refer to the appropriate syllabus document for the year of your examination to confirm the details and for more information. The syllabus document is available on the Cambridge International Education website at www.cambridgeinternational.org.

The purpose of using command words is to make it clear how you should approach answering a question. It is important that you understand what each command word is asking you to do.

These are the command words used in the Cambridge O Level Commerce (7100) syllabus and in the practice questions in this coursebook. In time and with practice, you will find that you can understand what skills you have to demonstrate in your answers to particular questions. The guidance provided below has been written by the authors to help you understand how to best respond to these command words.

Command word	What it means	Guidance
Analyse	examine in detail to show meaning, identify elements and the relationship between them	• The answer should show how the points/elements link together.
Assess	make an informed judgement	• Write about both sides of the particular issue/topic and then come to a supported conclusion about which, if any, is best.
Calculate	work out from given facts, figures or information	• The answer is likely to be a numerical figure. • It is important that you show your workings and that the final answer is clearly visible. Even if the final answer is incorrect, you may be able to gain some of the marks for the workings. • Don't forget to include the units involved in your answer, e.g. $US.
Compare	identify/comment on similarities and/or differences	• It is essential that you write about both items rather than just focusing on one of them. • Ensure that you compare the two or more items in terms of their similarities and differences; and not just state what they are.

Continued

Command word	What it means	Guidance
Consider	review and respond to given information	• Make a brief point that includes some evaluation.
Define	give precise meaning	• Always ensure that the definition is accurate.
Describe	state the points of a topic/give characteristics and main features	• Give appropriate knowledge of the topic or issue.
Discuss	write about issue(s) or topic(s) in depth in a structured way	• Give a balanced account of both sides, for and against, an issue or argument.
Evaluate	judge or calculate the quality, importance, amount or value of something	• Make a reasoned judgement and include a supported conclusion on the merits or otherwise of something.
Explain	set out purpose or reasons/make the relationships between things clear/ say why and/or how and support with relevant evidence	• The answer should include clearly identifiable reasons which could draw upon data or other information to make the explanation clear. • Sometimes the answer will state a point followed by some development – providing a reason (evidence) why the first point was made. • The answer may include words or phrases such as 'because', 'therefore' or 'this means that'.
Give	produce an answer from a given source or recall/memory	• The answer is likely to come from knowledge/theory from the course or a familiar source.
Identify	name/select/recognise	• Try to be precise about what has been identified.
Justify	support a case with evidence/argument	• Give good reasons or evidence for offering an opinion or reaching a judgement.
Outline	set out the main points	• Write a clear answer, avoiding a lot of detail.
State	express in clear terms	• Give the answer in clear terms. • The answer should be an uncomplicated, yet valid factual statement.

Unit 1

Commerce and production

> Chapter 1.1

Trade and commerce

LEARNING INTENTIONS

In this chapter you will learn:

- the differences between the terms trade and commerce
- the differences between home and international trade
- the six types of aids to trade
- the significance and elements of logistics in the supply chain
- the meaning of different types of commerce, including traditional commerce, ecommerce, mcommerce and scommerce
- how production, trade and commerce are codependent.

1.1.1 Trade and commerce compared

Trade means buying and selling of **goods** and **services** to earn a **profit**. Goods are tangible products that have a physical presence and can be touched. Services are intangible products with no physical identity. Profit is the amount of money that a business earns. Trading can only occur if money is involved in the exchange of goods and services. **Bartering** or swapping goods and services is not trade. Trade is central to all commercial activity.

Commerce focuses on supporting the exchange of goods and services. Commerce is about providing services to make the exchange of goods and services more efficient. These services improve the distribution of goods and services. They enable the right goods to be in the right place, at the right time, at the right price.

Trade can be at home or international.

> **KEY TERMS**
>
> **trade:** the buying and selling of goods and services to earn a profit.
>
> **goods:** tangible products that have a physical presence and can be touched.
>
> **services:** intangible products with no physical identity. They cannot be stored for later use and cannot be sensed through touch.
>
> **profit:** the amount of money that a business earns. It is calculated by subtracting the money it has spent from the total income.
>
> **bartering:** the exchange of goods and services without money.
>
> **commerce:** supporting the exchange of goods and services and providing services to make the process of exchange more efficient.

Home trade

Home trade pertains to the buying and selling of goods and services within the boundaries of one country. The buyer and the seller are located in the same country and the products are sold and purchased in local **currency**. Currency is a country's system of money used to buy and sell goods and services. For example, a seller based in Mumbai sells goods to a customer in Delhi. The customer pays the seller for the goods in Indian rupee. This avoids the needs to exchange currency. Home trade is a feature of many local businesses as they make/buy and sell to customers in the same country. Home trade usually supports personal relations between the business and customers as the owner is likely to have a good knowledge of the market. Methods of **transport** are likely to be road, rail or occasionally air (depending on the size of the country). Transport is the movement of raw materials, goods and other resources from one place to another place.

The growth of **ecommerce** has broken down the geographical restrictions that prevented many businesses operating outside their local area. Ecommerce involves the buying and selling of goods and services over the internet or through a website.

Home trade involves **wholesalers** and **retailers** (see Chapter 2.2).

> **KEY TERMS**
>
> **home trade:** the buying and selling of goods and services within the boundaries of a country.
>
> **currency:** a country's system of money used to buy and sell goods and services.
>
> **transport:** the movement of goods, raw materials, equipment and people from one place to another.
>
> **ecommerce:** the buying and selling of goods and/or services over the internet/websites. The term is short for electronic commerce.
>
> **wholesaler:** a person or business that buys products in large quantities from suppliers (often the manufacturer of the product) and sells them to retailers and/or other businesses in smaller quantities.
>
> **retailer:** a person or business who buys products from a manufacturer or wholesaler to sell on to consumers.

Wholesalers play an important role in the **distribution channel** for many products. The distribution channel is the path that a product takes from the initial **producer/manufacturer** (the business who manufactures the product) to the final customer. The distribution channel varies according to the product and manufacturer's choices, however, wholesalers support the distribution of many products. A wholesaler is a person or business that buys products in large quantities from suppliers (often the manufacturer of the product) and sells them to retailers and/or other businesses in smaller quantities. The wholesaler is the middle of the distribution channel between the manufacturer/producer (who manufactures the product) and **consumer** (the final user of the product).

Distribution channels focus on the path that the product takes from the initial producer or manufacturer to the final customer/consumer. The distribution channel could be simple as the product passes straight from the producer to the customer/consumer. However, some distribution channels are more complex and involve different businesses such as wholesalers and retailers which perform services to help the product reach the final customer/consumer. The distribution channel will form part of the supply chain for the product. The supply chain includes the whole system from obtaining the raw materials to produce the product through to receipt by the final customer/consumer.

A retailer buys products from a manufacturer or wholesaler to sell on to consumers. The retailer is therefore between the manufacturer/producer or wholesaler and consumer in the chain of distribution (Figure 1.1.1).

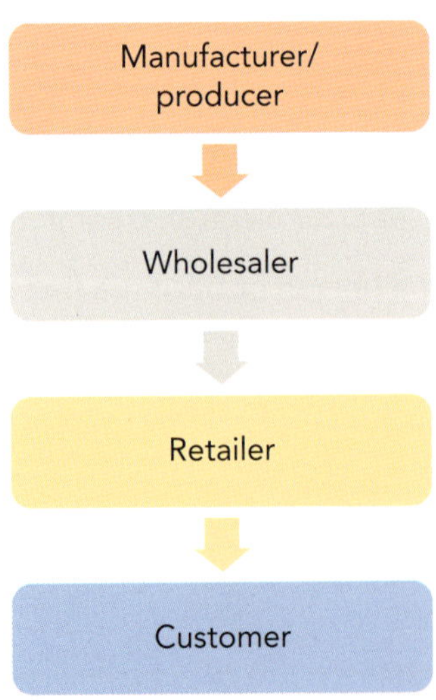

Figure 1.1.1: The wholesaler plays an important role in the distribution channel

Retailers sell products in different ways, including through:

- a physical shop
- face-to-face methods that do not require a permanent physical shop building, such as a:
  - **hawker** (a mobile salesperson who carries the goods they sell using a cart or the back of an animal)
  - **pedlar** (a mobile salesperson who carries the goods they sell door to door on their own head or back)
  - **kiosk** (a small structure with one or more open sides from which items are sold)
  - **tuck shop** (a small outlet located within another building that sells a limited range of goods)
- a website (operated by the retailer or a third party)
- an **online auction website**

KEY TERMS

distribution channel: the path that the product takes from the initial producer to the final customer. The distribution channel is made up of all of the businesses involved in movement of a good or service to the final customer.

producer: the business who manufactures the product.

manufacturer: the producer of the product.

consumer: the final user of the product.

hawker: a mobile salesperson who carries the goods they sell using a cart or the back of an animal.

pedlar: a mobile salesperson who carries the goods they sell door to door on their own head or back.

kiosk: a small structure with one or more open sides from which items are sold, such as newspapers, tickets or refreshments.

tuck shop: a small outlet located within another building, such as a school, that sells a limited range of goods, such as refreshments.

online auction website: where items are sold by auction over the internet. Sellers present the goods for sale on the online auction website, and individuals can bid the price for which they would purchase the product. The product is usually sold to the person who offers the highest bid to buy.

- **social media** – online communication channels, such as Facebook, that allow users to create, share and exchange information, pictures and videos
- **telesales** (the selling of goods and services over the telephone).

KEY TERMS

social media: online communication channels, such as Facebook, that allow users to create, share and exchange information, pictures and videos.

telesales: the selling of goods and services over the telephone.

International trade

International trade involves the buying and selling of goods and services outside the boundaries of the country to make a profit. The seller will be based in one country and the buyer will be located in another country. The currency used by the seller and buyer could be different and therefore international trade may be affected by currency fluctuations. For example, a business in London sells goods to a customer in New York. The customer has to exchange US dollars to pound sterling to pay the seller for the goods.

The methods of transport may include road, rail, air, sea and pipeline, depending on the physical distance between the two countries.

An **import** is a good or service produced in one country but bought by a customer in another country. An **export** is a good or service produced in one country but sold to a customer based in another country (see Figure 1.1.2).

Internationals are businesses that trade internationally, and are essentially **importers** (businesses that buy goods or services from other countries) and/or **exporters** (businesses that sell goods or services from other countries).

They have no investment, i.e., branches, offices or factories, outside the home country but buy and/or sell products to businesses/customers based in other countries. The operational facilities of internationals are within the home country only.

Some international businesses will only import or export whereas others import and export.

Figure 1.1.2: Imports and exports

Most countries are unable to produce all of the products that they need and so international trade is important.

A business may import raw materials that are then converted into products by its operations in the home country. Alternatively, a business may purchase finished products made in the overseas country, which it then sells to customers in the home country.

Conversely, a business may sell raw materials and components to customers in other countries which are then converted into finished products by the customer's operations. The business may also produce the finished product in its home country and then sell the complete product to customers in the overseas country.

As an international business has no operations in other countries, it is exposed to a number of risks, such as **trade barriers** (see Chapter 3.1), that affect profitability. The international business has no control over any of these factors. However they can influence the profitability of its trading operations by increasing/reducing the cost of trade and/or the work required.

KEY TERMS

international trade: the buying and selling of goods and services outside of the home country to make a profit.

import: a good or service produced in one country but bought by a customer in another country.

export: a good or service produced in one country but sold to a customer based in another country.

internationals: businesses that buy and/or sell products outside of the home country but have facilities only in their home country.

importer: business that imports goods or services.

exporter: a business that exports goods or services.

trade barrier: a restriction imposed by the government of a country to control international trade.

Increases in trade

Trade has increased greatly over the past 50 years. There are many reasons for the increase in trade, including:

- increased living standards. This has led to an increased demand for all types of products.

- improved communication, such as the launch of new digital communication methods. People and businesses can now communicate with others easier. Geographical boundaries are no longer an issue when communicating with trade barriers, as it is just as easy to communicate with people and businesses in other countries as it is with those based in the home country.
- improved transport links and transport methods. Goods can be delivered quicker and in larger quantities.
- mass **production** and use of the latest technology. This has increased the output of products, which increases the amount of surplus products that a business produces. The business may therefore seek to increase trade. Production facilities in countries around the globe benefit from improved production technology.
- trade is promoted by many governments to boost the country's economy.

KEY TERM

production: the process of making a good or service.

ACTIVITY 1.1.1

Trade has increased greatly over the past 50 years for various reasons as outlined in the previous section.

Carry out some research into the different reasons for the increase in trade and consider how they have affected a well-known business. You can choose a business that you are interested in for this activity.

Do you think the different reasons for the increase in trade have affected your business equally or have some reasons/factors had a greater influence than others? Have any of the reasons affected your business more than other businesses selling the same types of products? Would the reasons have the same impact on businesses in other industries? Why?

REFLECTION

Share your answers to Activity 1.1.1 with a partner or as part of a small group. Reflect on the activity as a pair/group.

Did your answers differ? Were you surprised by the answers that your partner gave?

Can you think of any ways to help you remember the different reasons for the increase in trade? You can add your ideas to your revision notes.

1.1.2 Aids to trade and logistics

Aids to trade are commercial services that support trade. There are many aids to trade, as shown in Figure 1.1.3.

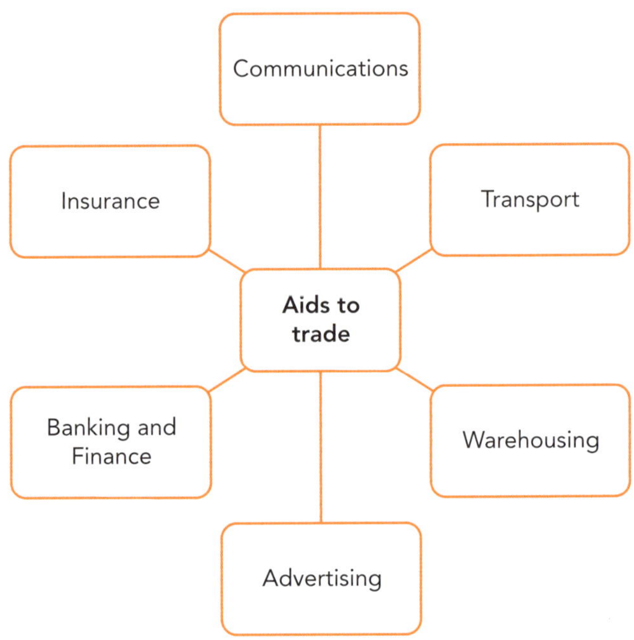

Figure 1.1.3: Different types of aids to trade

KEY TERM

aids to trade: commercial services that support trade.

Types of aids to trade

Table 1.1.1 describes the different types of aid to trade.

Aid to trade	Description
Communications	Communications are important to enable all of the parties involved in trade to contact each other. Communications are important for home and international trade, as the buyer and seller need to keep in touch. The methods of communication can vary and include face-to-face discussions, emails, SMS/text messages and more. Email is a method of communication to most places in the world using computers, smartphones and the internet. Technology has made trade communications quicker and has made trade over long distances easier. For more on communications, see Chapter 2.4.
Transport	Products need to move from one location to another. The products may be finished goods, raw materials, components or partially finished goods. People also need to travel to enable trade, e.g., travelling to work. The method of transport can vary depending on the type of trade but can include road, rail, air, sea and pipeline. For more on transport, see Chapter 4.1.
Warehousing	Warehousing provides storage for goods so they are ready for when the customer needs them. The goods include raw materials, part-finished products and finished goods. Other resources, such as machinery or vehicles, may also need to be stored. For more on warehousing, see Chapter 4.2.
Advertising	Advertising is part of marketing and is used to inform and attract people to buy the product and services. People are less likely to know about the product if it is not advertised and therefore would not be able to buy it. There are lots of different advertising methods – both physical and digital methods. Popular methods include television, radio, print (e.g., newspapers and magazines), websites, social media, vlogs/blogs and online banners. For more on advertising, see Chapter 5.1.
Banking and Finance	Banking facilities are needed to make and receive payments for the goods and/or services bought/sold. Banking facilities are offered to personal customers and business customers. Payment services can vary, including depositing coins/notes, cheque payments (written orders by a bank account holder instructing their bank to make a payment), electronic transfers (the direct transfer of money using electronic means) and card payments. The buyer and seller can also access a range of other banking services by visiting a physical branch of the bank, using automated teller machines (ATMs) and/or using online and telephone banking. Banking services can support the exchange of money into different currencies and can offer business banking guidance. Finance may also be needed to set up and/or expand trade operations. Finance is the money put into a business so that it can function. Banks offer a range of sources of finance including loans and mortgages. A loan involves borrowing of a set amount of money to be paid back to the lender in an agreed amount of time. A mortgage is a long-term loan used to buy a building or land. For more on banking, see Chapter 5.2.
Insurance	Insurance is a way of spreading risk among a group of people or organisations who contribute to a pool or common fund. Insurance services are important to protect the parties against potential losses from trade risks. The insurance services needed can vary according to the nature of trade but include cargo insurance, public liability insurance and trade credit insurance. Public liability insurance protects a business against claims made by members of the public. For more on insurance, see Chapter 5.2.

Table 1.1.1: Types of aids to trade

KEY TERMS

email: method of communication to most places in the world using computers, smartphones and the internet.

advertising: a type of promotion to consumers informing or persuading them to buy a particular product, service or brand.

cheque: a written order by a bank account holder instructing their bank to make a payment.

electronic transfer: method of payment allowing the direct transfer of money using electronic means without the need for paper-based or face-to-face transactions.

automated teller machine (ATM): a machine that can be used to access some banking services, such as withdrawing cash, using a bank card and changing a PIN (personal identification number).

finance: the money put into a business so that it can function.

loan: borrowing of a set amount of money to be paid back to the lender in an agreed amount of time.

mortgage: a type of loan used to buy land or property where the loan is secured against the property.

insurance: a way of spreading risk among a group of people or organisations who contribute to a pool or common fund. People obtain financial protection against losses that result from the occurrence of risks such as fire.

public liability insurance: insurance that protects a business against claims made by members of the public.

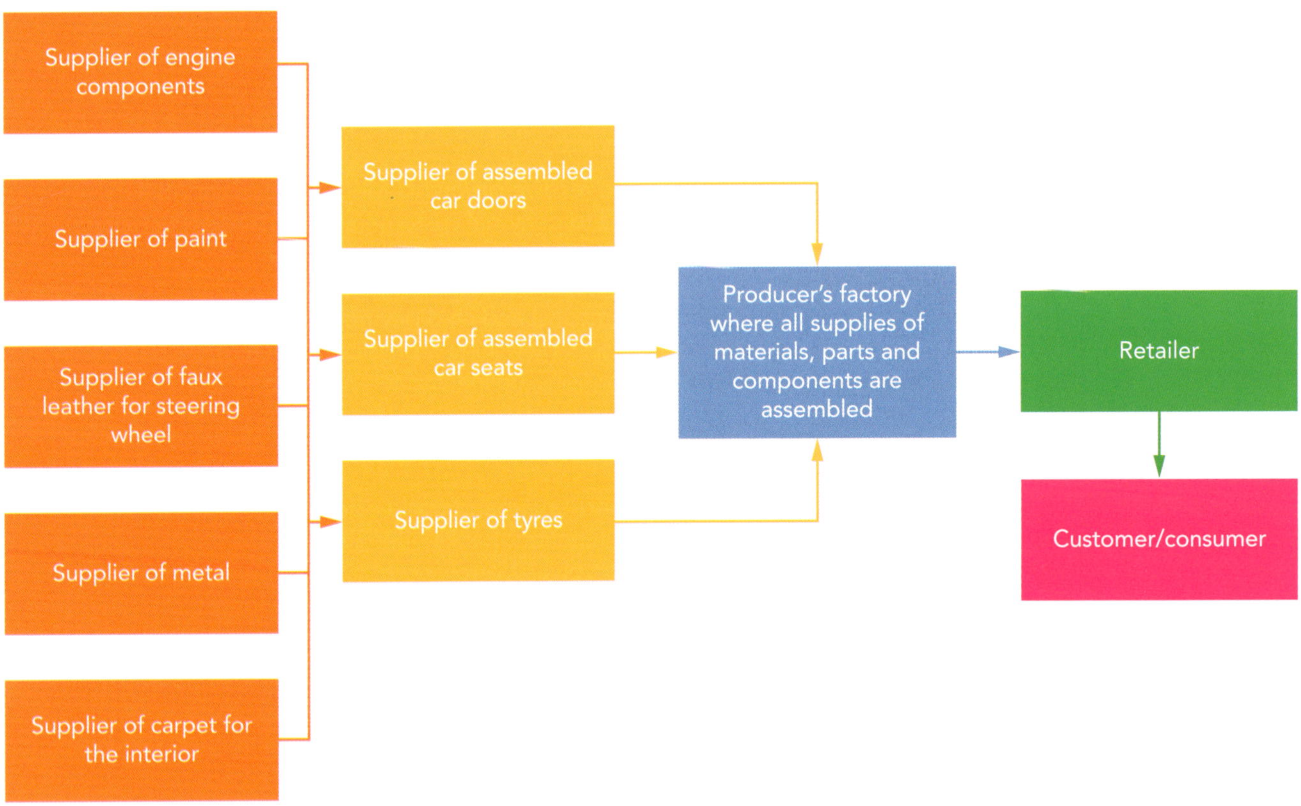

Figure 1.1.4: Example supply chain in the automotive industry

The meaning of logistics

Logistics is the planning and coordinating of the transportation and storage of goods throughout the **supply chain**. A supply chain is the complex logistics system that includes all of the steps in getting the finished good or service to the customer. Figure 1.1.4 shows an example of a supply chain from the automotive industry.

> **KEY TERMS**
>
> **logistics:** the functional area that plans and fulfils the efficient transportation and storage of goods from the manufacturer/warehouse to the customer.
>
> **supply chain:** a network of businesses and/or people who support the production of a product and delivering it to the consumer.

Logistics is important in commerce as the seller wishes to deliver the order to the customer in the most cost-effective way. The lower the cost the greater the profitability.

The elements of logistics in a supply chain

Most supply chains focus on two stages – production and distribution/logistics. In the production stage, the raw materials are produced into components and/or the finished product by the manufacturer. The number of stages in the production process depends on the complexity of making the product. Logistics focuses on moving the product for the customer.

Transport

Transport is essential to all types of business. The supply chain relies on transport to move goods and resources between the different stages of the supply chain. The nature of the product and/or type of commerce (i.e., home trade or international trade) will influence the appropriateness of different types of transport.

Raw materials need to be transported from the point of extraction to the producer/manufacturer to be converted into products and/or components. Transport is also used to transfer components and finished goods from factories to **warehouses**, wholesalers, retailers or to the final consumer. Whatever method of transport is used, it is important that it is reliable so that the item reaches the next stage of the supply chain on time and in good condition, i.e., undamaged. The journey may vary from a few miles to going from one side of the country to the other or even the other side of the world. Some goods are also needed urgently whereas others are less time dependent. The transportation may be performed regularly whereas others may be of a one-off nature. The transport system used by the business needs to be flexible for all needs.

> **KEY TERM**
>
> **warehouse:** a large building used to store raw materials or finished products ready for distribution for sale.

Transport can be divided into three categories:

- land, e.g., road, rail, pipeline
- water, e.g., sea, rivers/canals
- air.

Effective transport can help businesses expand trade by covering a wider geographic area. Transport can help businesses find new markets to support increased production.

Transport systems can affect the price of goods and/or services by ensuring that supply and demand are matched by avoiding surpluses and shortages.

Land

Road is one of the most popular ways of transporting materials and finished goods. The system of roads can vary greatly. In many countries, most main roads connecting towns and cities are well maintained with a tarmac surface. However, very remote rural areas and those with small populations may be connected by dirt and sand tracks.

Rail is another important part of the transport system in most countries. In landlocked countries such as Switzerland and Bolivia, rail links are a key way of moving goods from dry ports in other countries.

Pipelines may go over land, be buried underground or laid underwater. Pipelines are often used to carry liquids, such as water and oil, plus gases and some solids, such as sand, grain and sugar.

Water

Sea transport is important to transport goods between continents and islands. Large containers are often used.

Waterways such as canals, rivers and lakes can also be used, especially in countries such as Canada and the USA. The Nile River has been used to transport goods through eastern Africa for several thousands of years. Barges, **ferries** and other boats are used to transport products from a port at the mouth of a river along to the location they will be processed or stored.

> **KEY TERM**
>
> **ferry:** a ship that carries trucks that drive on and drive off without unloading.

Air

Air is a swift way of transporting goods between countries and major cities within a country. However, it is also relatively expensive. Air is used for transporting specific types of goods, such as perishable goods with a short lifespan (e.g., flowers) or valuable goods of a small size (e.g., jewels and stamps).

> **ACTIVITY 1.1.2**
>
> Read the short case study below and answer the questions that follow.
>
> *Kath runs a small business and imports T-shirts from five different countries that she then sells on to customers. The T-shirts are transported by sea to Kath's home country and then by road via lorry.*
>
> **a** Identify two reasons why Kath may have decided not to use air to transport the t-shirts from the supplier's country.
>
> **b** Explain two benefits of transporting the T-shirts by sea.
>
> **c** Explain two risks of using road transport to transport the T-shirts to Kath's business.

Freight forwarders

A freight forwarder is a person or business who moves goods (freight) for a fee. They provide the logistical services to support the movement of goods from the seller to the buyer. These services may be within a country or around the world. There are many freight forwarders including DHL, UPS and Sinotrans. Freight forwarders are often used by businesses exporting large volumes of goods or high-value goods by air or sea. However, some businesses prefer to use a **courier** if they are exporting smaller volumes. A courier is a business or person who delivers parcels on behalf of another business or individual in the supply chain, such as a manufacturer or retailer.

> **KEY TERM**
>
> **courier:** a business or person who delivers parcels on behalf of another business or individual in the supply chain.

Freight forwarders typically offer the following services:

- arranging transport, i.e., the delivery or moving of goods
- preparing, carrying and completing documentation, such as inspection certificates
- arranging insurance
- customs clearance
- unloading of goods
- arranging payment of freight
- inventory management
- packaging/labelling
- warehousing
- managing the security of goods
- logistics – planning the best routes and arranging the tracking of goods
- negotiating contracts with other organisations involved in the logistics of the goods.

Warehousing

A warehouse is a large building used to store raw materials or finished products ready for distribution for sale. They are often found on the edge of towns/cities and/or industrial parks. To support the efficient distribution of products to retailers/customers, they are often near to good transport links. Warehouses are sometimes called distribution centres. The warehouse ensures that stock is stored safely and securely. It protects the products from being damaged by severe weather conditions.

Modern warehouses rely on technology to support stock control and the efficient movement of goods. Stock management systems support the automatic reordering of stock, e.g., many warehouses set automatic reorder levels that send an order request to the manufacturer/producer via a shared network, without human intervention. Every time an item leaves the warehouse, the stock levels are immediately updated so that managers can instantly see what stock is in the warehouse at any time. These stock management systems are linked to the retailer so that customers receive accurate data about their orders.

Locating a product in a large warehouse can be challenging so the use of technology, such as robots to pick the order, is essential.

1.1.3 Types of commerce

Commerce can be delivered via traditional physical or digital platforms/methods. Digital platforms include ecommerce, **mcommerce** and **scommerce**. Mcommerce is the buying and selling of goods and/or services using mobile technology, e.g., a mobile phone, mobile application (known as a **mobile app** or just app), mobile device or the internet. Scommerce is the buying and selling of goods and/or services using social media channels.

KEY TERMS

mcommerce: the buying and selling of goods and/or services using mobile technology, e.g., a mobile phone, mobile app, mobile device or the internet. Mcommerce is short for mobile commerce.

scommerce: the buying and selling of goods and/or services using social media channels. The term is short for social commerce.

mobile app: an application that can be downloaded on to a mobile device such as a smartphone, e.g., a banking services app.

Traditional commerce

Traditional commerce is the buying and selling of goods and/or services at a physical location (Figure 1.1.5).

KEY TERM

traditional commerce: the buying and selling of goods and/or services at a physical location.

Traditional ways of selling goods and services include:

- shops, where the product is sold to customers through a physical shop, e.g., local independent shops, supermarkets or departmental stores.
- face-to-face, when a salesperson interacts directly with the customer in a range of possible locations, such as a showroom, office, salon, market stall, at the roadside, from a mobile shop/van, at home or in a pitch/demonstration. Services such as hairdressers and banking offer a face-to-face service.
- vending machines and other physical self-service facilities.

Figure 1.1.5: Fitting a new tyre is an example of traditional commerce

Physical or traditional ways of selling goods/services are expensive to operate as the business often has to pay a monthly rent or mortgage repayments (depending on whether the business is renting or buying the building). This can be a very large expense for the business to have to pay. There also needs to be a certain number of employees within the location at any one time to serve customers efficiently and safely. **Utilities**, such as gas and electricity, are required to provide a comfortable selling environment, which also adds to the **costs** of operating.

KEY TERMS

utilities: services used by the business to be able to operate, e.g., electricity, water, gas, broadband and telephone.

costs: the money that the business has to pay out to run the business. They are the expenses incurred by a business to produce and/or sell its goods and services.

Costs are the **expenses** incurred by a business to produce and/or sell its goods and services.

> **KEY TERM**
>
> **expenses:** the costs of running the business, e.g., insurance, wages and salaries.

A physical presence such as a shop front provides the business with instant publicity via the signage and window displays. Many shops are located on main streets in towns and cities or in retail centres alongside other retailers, and so benefit from passing trade in the area generally. Some customers prefer the experience of traditional commerce as they can enjoy a day out with friends/family while making their purchases. Many retail centres are developing activities/facilities to enhance the experience, e.g., the inclusion of tables and chairs, so people can socialise while shopping, and street entertainment.

Ecommerce

Ecommerce involves the buying and selling of goods and services over the internet/through websites. Ecommerce is short for electronic commerce. Ecommerce can be compared with mobile and social commerce, and in this context, ecommerce transactions take place on a desktop computer and/or laptop rather than other devices. Most ecommerce transactions take place via a website where customers can purchase goods through:

- the business's own website (e.g., Samsung has an online shop on its own website, and most banks allow customers to manage their accounts online)
- a third-party website, such as Amazon, that sells the product on behalf of the business.

Websites are often the first digital platform launched by a business. Most modern businesses have a website. Websites can reach a large audience. The internet is needed to access the website via a web browser. The website can normally be accessed on a range of devices but a desktop computer and/or laptop often provides the user with the best experience due to the amount of information and complexity of many web pages. Most businesses have introduced other digital access options to best suit other devices, such as mobile applications to target customers with a mobile and/or tablet. Commerce via mobile devices and social media are covered in detail under the mcommerce and scommerce sections later in this chapter.

Businesses can deliver a lot of content on a website, such as contact information, latest news, product information and blogs, in addition to purchase options. Ecommerce is the term that focuses only on the buying and selling of goods and/or services over the website (Figure 1.1.6). For many businesses, the ecommerce function is in addition to the information and advertising contained on the website.

Figure 1.1.6: Websites can be used for ecommerce

Some retailers have always operated a website but it may have been basic, with only information about the products offered. To operate ecommerce, the website has to be developed to enable payments to be processed. The website needs to be attractive to encourage customers to buy goods online. Clear images of all angles of the products should be included so customers have a clear idea of what they will buy as they cannot physically inspect the products online. Descriptions of the products should be detailed so that customers are fully aware of the features.

Once ordered, customers expect the product to be delivered swiftly. Retailers need to operate efficient distribution departments to fulfil the order quickly. The product needs to be picked from a warehouse (or the store) and packaged ready for dispatch. New job roles have been created to carry out these tasks. Warehouses are automated with use of technology, such as robots for picking and packing orders for customers. Technology specialists need to be employed to develop the IT systems used and maintain them. A fault can occur at any time, and it is important that technical support is available to fix the issue promptly. IT system problems could stop operations, and every minute that the system is down can cost the business thousands.

Many retailers work with courier businesses who deliver the goods to the customer. The courier represents the retailer and it is important that couriers are carefully selected. Some retailers focus purely on choosing the courier with the lowest price and quickest delivery. However, this approach may not be the best for the long term, as customers expect the highest service. The retailer will often have a contract with the courier to ensure that minimum service standards are followed. Customers may be located in different locations within a country, or even internationally, so the retailer is likely to work with different couriers. Not relying on one courier also helps the retailer to spread risk as there may be times when an individual courier is not able to deliver orders for the retailer, for instance, due to too much other work.

The growth of ecommerce has broken down the geographical restrictions that prevented many businesses operating outside their local area. This is important, as technology has enabled many businesses to expand by extending their geographical operations. Digital payment options, such as PayPal, and digital wallets, such as Google Pay and Apple Pay, have increased the security of paying for products online. This has made many customers more confident about buying products from an ecommerce website.

Mcommerce

Mcommerce is the buying and selling of goods and services through a mobile device such as a tablet or a smartphone. Mcommerce is short for mobile commerce. Many retailers have developed apps to enable customers to buy their goods or services. For example, fashion retailer H&M operates an app that customers can use to purchase clothing. Mcommerce is sometimes considered to be a subcategory of ecommerce. However, its growth and popularity have led many to consider it has a separate type of commerce. The percentage and share of digital commerce transactions that take place on a mobile device are growing annually. Part of this growth is due to the increased ownership of mobile devices. The number of mobile devices is expected to reach over 18 billion by 2025, a rise of over four billion devices compared to 2020 (Statista, 2021).

App users benefit from a simple user-friendly interface. The app interface is designed especially for the screen size of a mobile device, so using the app can be easier to navigate than using a mobile browser to purchase goods and services from the retailer's website (Figure 1.1.7). Users also benefit from a touch-enabled interface. An accelerometer is a tool that tracks different motions, such as shaking, tilting or rotating the device. Most app interfaces adapt to these changes in motion so that the screen/interface automatically changes according to the device's orientation. This provides users with a pleasant experience.

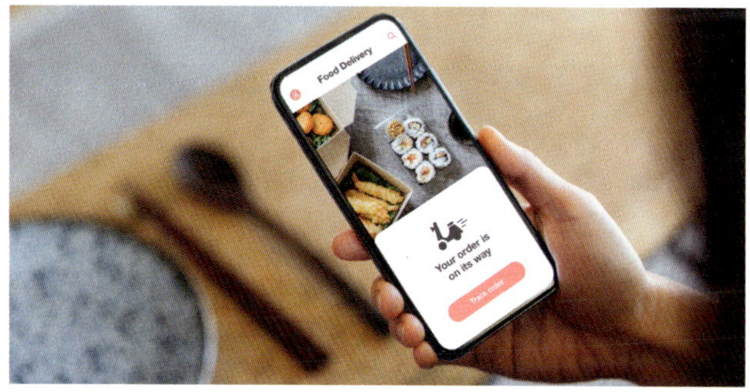

Figure 1.1.7: Ordering food via an app for home delivery

Mcommerce covers:

- in-app purchasing of goods and/or services
- **mobile banking**, i.e., using a mobile device such as a smartphone to carry out banking activities
- marketplace apps, such as Amazon. An online marketplace is a platform that supports customers to shop from different sources. This type of app does not own the products itself but works in partnership with the sellers (the sellers may be individuals or other businesses) to process buying, selling, payment and delivery services. The app is essentially a service to bring the buyer and seller together
- mobile ticketing
- digital wallets, such as Apple Pay and Google Pay.

KEY TERM

mobile banking: using a mobile device such as a smartphone to carry out banking activities.

Apps are developed for different operating-system requirements, such as iOS and Android, so that the app is compatible with a range of devices. Apps are not accessible until they are installed, unlike a website, which is generally accessible to anyone with an internet access and browser.

The content on many apps can be personalised to the user. Businesses can often track user engagement, which enables them to offer recommendations for other features/services. Mobile apps can also access other features on the mobile device, such as GPS or the camera. This can increase convenience for the user, e.g., by simplifying the process of uploading an image to the app. Similarly, using a phone's GPS means that information, services and content can be localised to the user's geographical area.

Table 1.1.2 describes key features of an app.

Feature	Description of feature
Downloadable onto device	Apps are downloaded onto the device. They do not rely on browsers so can be quicker to use depending on the connection. Many apps need an internet connection to access all functions.
Enhanced security	Apps can benefit from enhanced security so more functions can be offered to customers, e.g., banks often allow customers access to additional services via mobile apps compared to those offered via their websites. However, apps can take longer than a website for the business to develop due to their complexity, as they require extra programming. This can increase the cost for the business.
Simple to upgrade	Apps can be upgraded. Businesses push the updates to users and users download the update at a convenient time.
Access to downloads	Apps can enable digital products to be purchased by download directly onto the device, which is generally quicker than downloading from a website. Download is the main way of selling a digital product, such as a computer game or music. The app can make the product available to customers as a digital file to download either from its own app/website or through a download store (e.g., Apple Inc.'s App Store or the Google Play Store). The customer must investigate that the download site is legitimate, as there are many illegal download sites that can result in a computer virus or the customer being hacked.

Table 1.1.2: Features of apps

Scommerce

Scommerce is short for social commerce. Scommerce is the buying and selling of goods and/or services using social media channels, e.g., Instagram Shopping, which is linked directly to a business's Facebook Shop. The business can then sell products to customers via their Instagram account. The whole process, from seeing the product, researching its features and making the purchase, takes place on social media. There are many social media platforms, with new ones created regularly. Popular platforms include TikTok, Facebook, Pinterest and Instagram.

Social media channels can normally be accessed through links found on a business's website or the business's own social media account, such as Facebook. The business can share news and details of promotions via the social media account, such as details about a new product.

Potential customers may see products on their Instagram feed and can select the 'shop now' option to purchase. This enables customers to make a purchase without leaving the app. TikTok offers a similar feature. For instance, an individual may see a product as they are scrolling through TikTok and then click 'buy'. After buying, they can carry on enjoying their usual TikTok content.

Scommerce allows sellers to target customers more specifically, as different platforms tend to be used by different customer groups. Scommerce also allows more social interaction than ecommerce. Social media users/customers can contribute easily by offering likes, reviews, user ratings and referrals, and by sharing with other users. Users can consult other users on their purchases, which allows scommerce to incorporate some of the social benefits of a traditional retailer experience in a physical store. These aspects can support the marketing of the product to increase **sales** (the amount of goods or services sold) as an increasing number of customers look at reviews before making a purchase (via any method). Furthermore, the business can use the content of reviews to find out more about its customer's requirements (instant market research). The business can swiftly react to customer feedback to improve its products.

KEY TERM

sales: the amount of goods or services sold.

Scommerce is convenient for the customer, as the purchase is made without leaving the social media platform, which can improve the customer experience. It is relatively easy for sellers to set up a social media sales platform/shop, as social media platforms have simple tools for this.

Some social media platforms operate marketplace sites, e.g., Facebook marketplace allows businesses and individuals to sell new and pre-owned products and connect with potential customers in their local area. The seller can post a full description of the good or service and photos. Users can then send a direct message to the seller to find out more information and/or arrange to buy the product. The product can be sent to the customer using the post or a courier, or alternatively the customer can arrange to meet the seller and collect the item (if both parties live in the same area).

Multi-channel commerce

What is convenient for one customer to access may not be convenient for another, so, many businesses offer customers a variety of ways (or multiple channels) to purchase its products. For example, Levi's jeans can be purchased by customers in India via:

- its retail shops
- its own website
- third-party websites, such as Myntra.

Each type of commerce has relative advantages and disadvantages, so by using multiple channels the business is able to overcome any relative disadvantages. They can also appeal to diverse types of customers as certain market segments are likely to prefer each type.

Advantages and disadvantages of different types of commerce

Table 1.1.3 shows the advantages and disadvantages of different types of commerce.

	Advantages	Disadvantages
Traditional	Face-to-face contact builds customer trust. Customers can see or try the product they are buying (e.g., trying on a jacket to check the fit). Sales staff can demonstrate the features and benefits of a product. It can be a social experience, e.g., shopping can be a day out with friends and family.	It is more expensive than selling online, as businesses have to pay utilities, rent/mortgage and more staff wages. A wage is a payment to employees that varies according to the number of hours worked or their output. Customers have to travel to a shop, which takes time and may cause problems with parking. Opening hours can be limited.
Ecommerce	Reduces costs, such as rent, as businesses do not need physical premises. Prices online may be lower due to the lower operating costs. Some retailers offer cheaper prices for ecommerce customers compared to those buying from a shop/store. Customers can shop at any time of the day or night.	The development costs of creating an ecommerce website could be high. It is not as easy for the customer to speak directly to the business, e.g., if they have any queries about the product or need to make a complaint. Not all customers have access to the internet. Customers cannot see or touch the 'actual' product or try it on before buying it. Customers have to wait a few days to receive their goods. Logistical costs increase (delivery, staff training and larger warehousing space). The website, app and/or social media platform needs to be maintained. All product information needs to be kept up to date.

Continued

	Advantages	Disadvantages
Mcommerce	Reduces costs, such as rent, as businesses do not need physical premises. The app can be upgraded easily to fix bugs and offer new services/features. The app can be personalised to the customer. The app can use the camera or GPS on the device. Customers can shop at any time of the day or night.	The development costs of creating an app can be high. Mobile technology changes rapidly so the business needs to regularly upgrade its app. Not all customers have access to a mobile device, or the app may not be compatible with the device's operating system (especially if the customer has an older model device). Customers cannot see or touch the 'actual' product or try it on before buying it. Customers have to wait a few days to receive their goods.
Scommerce	There are fewer development costs than having to create a website or app. A business can target specific market segments according to the social media platform selected. Users can share content and reviews (more user interaction). Customers can shop at any time of the day or night.	Customers may leave inaccurate/misleading reviews, which may go viral. There is a large range of different social media platforms, so managing scommerce may be challenging. Not all customers use social media. Customers cannot see or touch the 'actual' product or try it on before buying it. Customers have to wait a few days to receive their goods.

Table 1.1.3: Advantages and disadvantages of different types of commerce

KEY TERM

wage: a payment to employees that varies according to the number of hours worked or their output.

24/7: 24 hours a day, 7 days a week.

ACTIVITY 1.1.3

Tick true or false in the box next to each of the statements in the table below to identify whether or not they are generally considered to be advantages of the different types of commerce.

Statement	True	False
Overhead costs are higher for retailers that use ecommerce.		
Customers can shop **24/7** using ecommerce, mcommerce and scommerce.		
Retailers can target specific customer groups using scommerce.		
Customers can easily speak face-to-face with the owner of an ecommerce site.		
Traditional commerce can be a social experience for customers.		
Customers can conveniently access a wider range of products via traditional commerce.		

REFLECTION

How did you decide on your answers to Activity 1.1.3? Discuss with a partner whether you think the answers are the same for all businesses involved in each type of commerce? Are there some questions that depend on the context or type of product?

1.1.4 The relationship between production, trade and commerce

Production, trade and commerce are interdependent. This means that each one is dependent on the others. Each element relies on services and functions from the others in order to provide an efficient service for the customer. Production is the process of making the good or service. Trade and commerce cannot take place until the good or service is produced.

Commerce helps businesses operating in the supply chain before, during and following production via the purchase of materials and the sale of the finished goods. Payments must be made as the product flows through the supply chain. Distribution is essential to ensure that the goods and services produced reach the customer. Trade, i.e., the buying and selling of goods and/or services, supports all the businesses in the supply chain. Key businesses provide the goods and services for distribution, which enables trade and commerce to operate and develop.

TIP

Take care to ensure that you understand the terms trade and commerce and the differences between them. Trade and commerce are related terms, but commerce is much broader as it includes all of the activities connected with buying and selling, such as production, marketing, insurance and distribution. Trade is just a part of commerce. Trade only involves the buying and selling of goods and/or services supported by the transfer of money.

SELF-EVALUATION CHECKLIST

After studying this chapter, complete this table.

You should know about:	Needs more work	Almost there	Ready to move on
the differences between the terms trade and commerce			
the differences between home and international trade			
the six types of aids to trade			
the significance and elements of logistics in the supply chain			
the meaning of different types of commerce, including traditional commerce, ecommerce, mcommerce and scommerce			
the relationship between production, trade and commerce			

Knowledge check

1. Describe the differences between home trade and international trade.
2. Identify two ways that banking services may be used to aid trade.
3. Explain two advantages of mcommerce.
4. Explain two disadvantages of scommerce.
5. Explain the difference between mcommerce and scommerce.
6. A warehouse will:
   - a advertise goods for sale
   - b design new goods
   - c manufacture goods
   - d store goods.
7. A benefit of ecommerce is:
   - a can sell products to a wider market
   - b customers can see products before buying
   - c high competition
   - d high operating costs.
8. Which of the following can provide cover against the risks of exporting goods?
   - a banking
   - b insurance
   - c logistics
   - d warehousing
9. Which of the following can help a business make customers aware of the products that it sells?
   - a advertising
   - b insurance
   - c transport
   - d wholesale
10. Buying and selling goods from a mobile device is known as?
    - a ecommerce
    - b mcommerce
    - c scommerce
    - d traditional commerce

Practice questions

1. a Define the term 'aid to trade'. [2]
   b State four types of aids to trade. [4]
   c State two services provided by a freight forwarder. [2]
   d Ali sells a range of clothing products in his home country. He is thinking of trading internationally. State three features of home trade and three features of international trade. [6]
2. a Define the term 'commerce'. [2]
   b State four benefits of traditional commerce. [4]
   c Clarko Fresh Foods sells its products through its 20 stores. The manager of Clarko Fresh Foods is considering closing the stores and selling via ecommerce. Should Clarko Fresh Foods move to ecommerce operations? Give reasons for your opinion. [8]

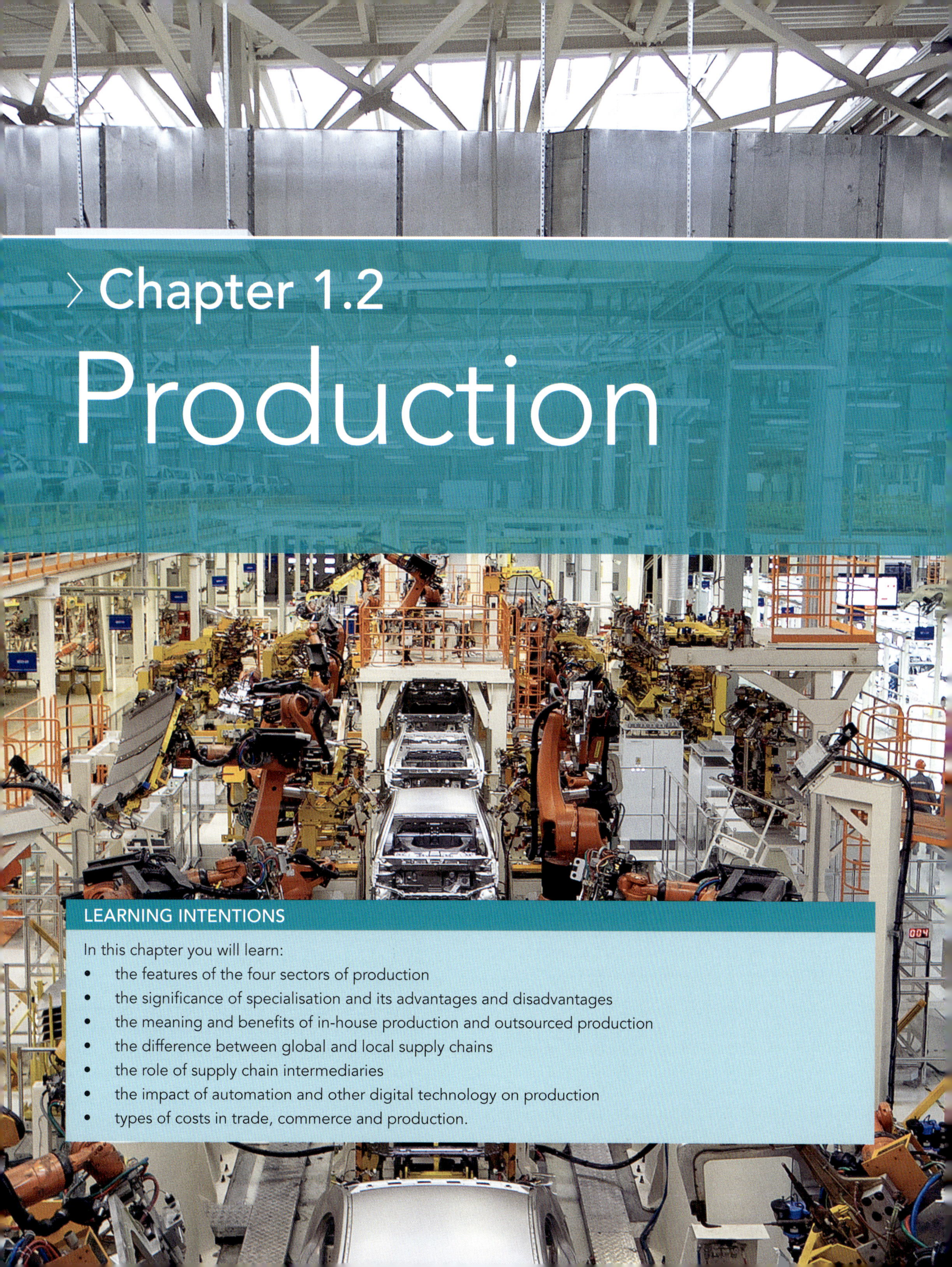

Chapter 1.2

Production

LEARNING INTENTIONS

In this chapter you will learn:

- the features of the four sectors of production
- the significance of specialisation and its advantages and disadvantages
- the meaning and benefits of in-house production and outsourced production
- the difference between global and local supply chains
- the role of supply chain intermediaries
- the impact of automation and other digital technology on production
- types of costs in trade, commerce and production.

1.2.1 The sectors of production

All organisations are involved in production when making a good or service. Production involves turning inputs into outputs. It is the process of combining different components or raw materials and turning them into a different product. Production of goods and services enables a business to satisfy people's **needs** (things that human beings require for survival) and **wants** (things that people would like to have as they make their lives more pleasant).

KEY TERMS

needs: things that human beings require for survival, such as water and shelter.

wants: things that people would like to have as they make their lives more pleasant, such as a mobile phone.

Production can be divided into four different sectors:

- primary
- secondary
- tertiary
- quaternary.

Primary industries

Businesses that operate in **primary industries** are involved with extracting **natural resources**. They are often referred to as **extractive industries**, as the activities involve removing natural resources from the ground, such as metals, oil, coal, food and stone (Table 1.2.1). Often the natural resources are used by another business for further processing or manufacturing to make them into a final product. However, sometimes the natural resources are extracted in a format ready for the final consumer, e.g., fresh fish or some fruits.

Figure 1.2.1: Fishing is an example of a primary industry

KEY TERMS

primary industries: industries that extract or obtain natural resources from the earth.

natural resources: resources or materials taken from nature, such as sand or stone.

extractive industries: industries that involve removing natural resources from the ground.

Industry	Type of product/resource extracted
Mining	Coal, limestone, chalk, metals, clay
Drilling	Oil, gas
Quarrying	Stone, rock, minerals and gravel
Forestry	Timber, wood
Farming	Crops such as grain, wheat, maize, rice, vegetables
Fishing	Fish

Table 1.2.1: Examples of primary industries

Some industries are exhaustive and others are non-exhaustive.

- Exhaustive industries are those that take resources that are not replaced, e.g., quarrying and drilling.
- Non-exhaustive industries are those that take resources that can be renewed, such as forestry and fishing.

The nature of primary industries in a specific country often depends on its climate and geological conditions.

There are plentiful oil supplies in the Middle East; so, countries in this area dominate the supply of oil globally. Brazil is one of the world's leading producers of coffee as its climate is ideal for growing Robusta and Arabica coffee beans. A producer is the business who manufactures the product.

Secondary industries

Secondary industries convert the raw materials into finished goods. They take the natural resources that were extracted by businesses in the primary sector and change their form using technology, machinery and labour.

> **KEY TERM**
>
> **secondary industries:** industries that convert natural resources/raw materials into finished goods.

Secondary industries include:

- manufacturing
- construction
- processing.

Manufacturing

Manufacturing involves the production of goods with the help of equipment, labour, machines, tools and chemical or biological processing or formulation. Manufacturing often takes place in a factory and may involve many processes. Some manufacturers are **multinational**, which means they operate in several countries, and therefore specific processes may take place in different countries. Different branches of a multinational manufacturer may specialise in a specific process. For example, many car manufacturers are multinational. The engine may be built in a factory in one country whereas the body panels may be produced in a factory in another country. The engine and body panels may then be transported to a factory owned by the multinational in another country to assemble the car.

> **KEY TERM**
>
> **multinational:** operating in several countries. The operations may involve the manufacture and/or selling of products in the various countries.

Manufacturing businesses often cluster in specific geographic areas, e.g., a number of car manufacturers are located in Germany whereas China has an established manufacturing sector producing electronics. Often workers with specialist skills for a particular industry are based in geographic areas where several businesses are located. This is due to the increased number of employment opportunities in the area for people with those skills. These employment opportunities attract people to relocate to the area to develop their careers. Local education providers, such as colleges and universities, will also offer specialist training and qualifications to equip people with the skills demanded by businesses in the locality.

Construction

Construction involves constructing something such as a building, road or bridge. Workers use materials that were extracted by primary sector businesses to construct the project.

Construction projects vary significantly in size, ranging from building large buildings (such as hospitals or factories) and large housing developments to small-scale domestic projects, such as a house extension. There are a range of different roles within construction, including:

- specific trades, such as bricklaying, plumbing, carpentry and welding
- professional jobs, such as architect and civil engineers.

Construction projects are often medium- or short-term, as once the building is complete it is used for its main use, e.g., living accommodation or the operation of a business. Construction workers often have to move geographic areas as they work on a range of construction projects. Construction has been significantly affected by new technology. Technological advances enable projects to be constructed at a lower cost and sometimes off-site so that adverse weather conditions do not delay the project. Technology also helps the industry operate in a more sustainable manner and construct buildings that are more sustainable to operate.

Processing

Processing involves carrying out a number of actions to achieve a specific result, e.g., smoking salmon fillets.

Processing involves carrying out an operation to preserve or change the original material in some way. Many foods are processed so it stays fresh for longer and/or to improve the taste. Pharmaceuticals is another major processing industry that transforms materials/ingredients into medicines.

Tertiary activities

Tertiary activities involve the provision of services. These services can be described as commercial service and/or direct services.

- Commercial services support the distribution of raw materials from primary products and goods from secondary production, e.g., stock control, or commercial insurance services to protect any potential risks.
- Direct services are those that are given directly to the person receiving them, for instance, hairdressing services or healthcare services by a doctor.

It can be challenging to distinguish between commercial and direct services. A train driver provides a tertiary service. Sometimes the train driver will drive a passenger train and so perform a direct service for the people travelling on the train. However, on another day they may drive a cargo train. In this instance they are performing a commercial service as they are transporting goods.

KEY TERM

tertiary activities: industries that are involved in the provision of services.

Quaternary activities

Businesses operating in this sector provide intellectual and knowledge-based products. This sector also provides services, but **quaternary activities** tend to be intellectual rather than repetitive in nature. Tertiary services tend to be more repetitive, such as taxi driving or insurance services. People who work in the quaternary sector tend to be very highly educated. Quaternary activities often drive innovation and competitiveness in the economy, and highly educated people are required to innovate and find new ways of working.

Examples of industries in the quaternary sector include:

- **research and development (R&D)** – the process of innovating new products to introduce to the market
- **consultancy** – services and/or advice provided by a professional
- **generation of information** – the creation of information that can be used within businesses
- digital technology.

These industries produce a range of innovative goods and services, such as robotics, the **internet of things**, autonomous vehicles, 3D printing, artificial intelligence and **quantum computing**. The internet of things describes the growing number of appliances/devices that are connected to the internet. For example, many homes have a number of smart devices, such as a television, security camera or video doorbell. Quantum computing is an area of computing that uses quantum mechanics to solve complex problems faster than a traditional computer.

KEY TERMS

quaternary activities: industries that provide intellectual and knowledge-based products.

research and development (R&D): describes the process of innovating new products to introduce to the market.

consultancy: services and/or advice provided by a professional. The professional providing the services and/or advice is known as a consultant. They will be very knowledgeable and experienced in the area of work. Businesses can pay a lot of money for specialist consultancy services.

generation of information: information generation relies on three activities – data input, processing and output. These three activities create information that can be used within businesses.

internet of things: describes the growing number of appliances/devices that are connected to the internet. Many homes have a number of smart devices, such as a television, security camera or video doorbell.

quantum computing: an area of computing that uses quantum mechanics to solve complex problems faster than a traditional computer.

The work of the quaternary sector affects each of the other three sectors. For example, the use of modern fertilisers and machinery have automated primary activities such as agriculture. **Artificial intelligence (AI)** helps to automate routine tasks in the secondary sector, which reduces the labour force in these areas. The work of the quaternary sector is also improving living standards globally – for instance, the development of medicines to treat serious illnesses so that they are no longer life threatening, and the creation of vaccinations in response to the COVID-19 pandemic.

Figure 1.2.2 summarises the different sectors of production.

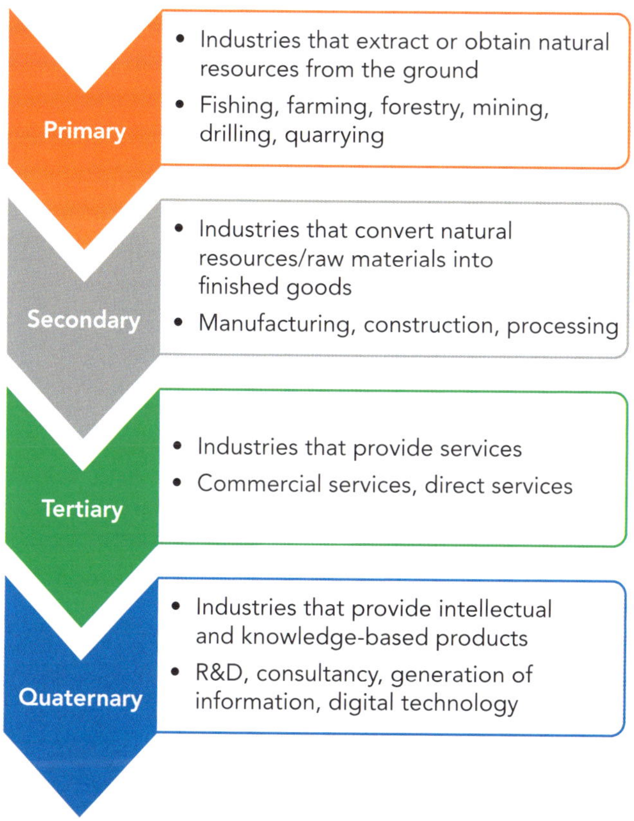

Figure 1.2.2: The different sectors of production

Categorising the activities of the sectors of production

It can sometimes be challenging to categorise the sector of production that an individual is operating within. Sometimes one individual carries out several activities and in doing so operates in multiple sectors of production. For example, a farmer may grow strawberries on their land. Growing fruits is an example of a primary industry. However, they may also operate a farm shop on their farm. Retail is an example of a tertiary activity. The farmer may also make strawberry smoothies on their farm. Making the smoothies from the strawberries that were picked from the crops is an example of an activity within the secondary sector.

KEY TERM

artificial intelligence (AI): the programming of computers to perform tasks that require the intelligence of humans. AI is becoming increasingly sophisticated and applications include visual perception, speech, decision-making, and translation between languages.

TIP

Always think carefully about the operations of the business to help you categorise the sector of production. What is the business's role in the production of the final good or service? For example, if the business converts a range of raw materials into a final product, they will operate in the secondary sector as they are producing.

ACTIVITY 1.2.1

Create a poster to show the four sectors of production with examples of businesses in your local area for each one. Use images to show the range of activities and include key terms. You can use the poster to support your revision of this topic.

Stages of industrial development

Different countries are at diverse stages of industrial development. Most countries have businesses operating in each of the four sectors of production. However, the proportion in each sector will vary according to how developed the country is industrially. In some countries, the primary sector is still the dominant sector accounting for the largest proportion of employment. In other countries, the secondary or tertiary sectors may be more significant than the primary sector. International trade means that countries rely on each other for provision of raw materials and the manufacturing/selling of goods. This concept supports **specialisation**, where people focus on what they do best, and which is considered later in the chapter.

KEY TERM

specialisation: where people focus on what they do best. Individuals may concentrate on one task or activity.

The proportion of businesses within each of the four sectors can change over time as the country becomes more developed. This is shown by the Clark Fisher model (Figure 1.2.3), which identified three phases as described in Table 1.2.2.

Phase	Outline
Pre-industrial	A large proportion of businesses will operate in the primary sector, for instance, agriculture.
Industrial	During this phase, the secondary and tertiary sectors become more important. Primary sector activities start to decline.
Post-industrial	In the third phase, manufacturing starts to become less significant and the tertiary sector becomes the dominant sector. Quaternary industries also become more important. The primary sector will become smaller, with only a relatively small number of businesses involved in primary industries.

Table 1.2.2: Stages of industrial development

De-industrialisation is a feature of the post-industrial phase as the country's economy focuses mainly on the service sector rather than secondary activities.

Industries in the secondary sector have declined in many developed countries such as Germany and the UK. This is because developing countries such as South Korea, India and Pakistan can supply goods more cheaply due to lower wage rates and less employment legislation.

The tertiary sector grows in countries as people living in the country become better educated, have higher paid jobs and more leisure time. People want to spend more money on travel, tourism, education and entertainment, which supports the growth of tertiary industries to satisfy the increased demand.

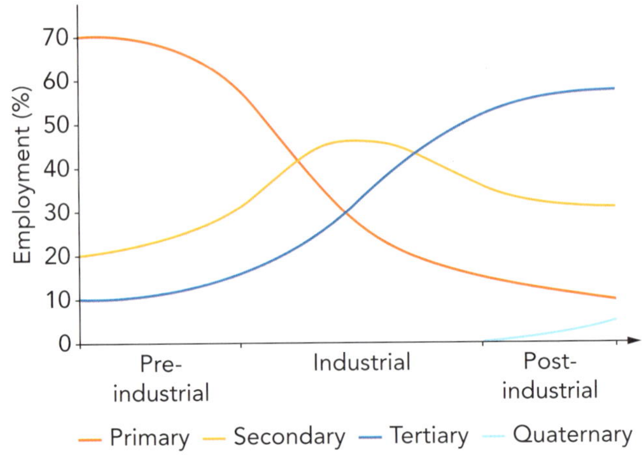

Figure 1.2.3: The Clark Fisher model

The changes to the importance of the sectors of production in a country can have many social effects. The decline of primary and secondary industries in many countries has led to unemployment. Businesses move operations to other countries and/or close completely. When the business closes they no longer need the employees who have highly specialised skills. These skills are not demanded by the growing tertiary and quaternary industries and so the employees are forced to learn new skills to gain further employment (Figure 1.2.4). This can be significant for employees who may have worked for the secondary industry since leaving school 40 years earlier.

Figure 1.2.4: Many unemployed adults return to college or university to learn new skills to help them find new employment

Often, secondary industries move to less developed and newly emerging economies. Nigeria is an example of a country moving to the industrial phase. Tertiary industries are developing in the country and the money generated is used by the government to develop schools, hospitals and infrastructure, which provides more jobs for the area.

Countries may also experience environmental effects from the changes. Leather manufacturing in India has negatively affected the environment. **Waste** (unwanted or unusable) water and chemicals from the factories are released into rivers and lakes, contributing to **pollution** in the River Ganges. Pollution is the release of harmful materials into the environment.

Many less developed countries continue to rely on the export of raw materials to more developed countries. For instance, chocolate manufacturers in developed countries import cocoa beans from poorer countries such as Brazil. The poorer countries can be exploited by richer countries, which is unethical and not desirable.

KEY TERMS

waste: unwanted or unusable substances or resources. It is something that is no longer required.

pollution: the release of harmful materials into the environment.

Specialisation

Specialisation is focusing on what people do best. Many businesses divide production activities up and employ people to concentrate on doing the same job over and over again. This is known as division of labour. Countries may also specialise in particular industries as clusters of businesses operating in the industry develop.

Before the industrial era, many families were **self-sufficient** and produced everything they needed to satisfy their basic needs. However, today most people specialise in one type of work to earn a living. Specialists create surpluses of a product, which can be sold to others who do not have the skills or resources to create the product themselves. Specialists also buy products from others that they cannot make themselves. They earn money from performing their job role, which is used to buy the products they need. This is known as trade. As you learned in Chapter 1.1, trade exists within a country and internationally between countries.

KEY TERM

self-sufficient: able to satisfy one's basic needs without the help of anyone else.

Specialisation may take place at different levels as shown in Figure 1.2.5:

Figure 1.2.5: Levels of specialisation

Table 1.2.3 describes the different levels of specialisation.

Level of specialisation	Description
Occupation	Individual people may become well known for a specific skill or personal quality. Individuals in a team will have their own personality, skills and experiences and often concentrate on the tasks that they are most suited. For example, a school may employ eight maths teachers. However, one may work best with younger pupils whereas another may prefer supporting older pupils with their revision. It makes sense for each teacher to specialise in teaching the classes that best meet their skills, personal preferences and experience.
The workplace	The production process is divided so that employees or departments within the business specialise in a particular task or activity. This is known as division of labour. Employees will focus on one or a few narrow tasks on each product. The product will then move between the different employees to work on subsequent tasks. The final product is the combined effort of many workers.
Firms or factories	Most companies or factories specialise in making a particular product. This is because different equipment/resources are needed to make specific types of product. Microsoft is a large multinational company that operates in the computing industry. It creates computer software and apps, and produces computer hardware products, such as laptops and gaming devices. Microsoft has offices in many countries globally.
Within areas of a country	Often regions, cities or towns within a country specialise in the production of specific goods or services. The region may have natural resources, climate factors or another geographical factors that support this specialism. For instance, many businesses in the fashion industry are located in the Italian city of Milan. Milan is often regarded as a global fashion capital due to links with respected fashion designers such as Giorgio Armani and Gianni Versace. The city hosts global fashion events and is a hub of leading fashion boutiques.
National	Many countries become well known for specific industries. They specialise in what they do best or most economically. People in the country develop specialist skills and expertise targeted at the industry. For example, Germany specialises in the production of cars whereas New Zealand specialises in lamb and dairy products. The impact of this type of specialisation is comparative advantage, where a country who has specialised is likely to create a surplus of the type of good or service and will export the surplus quantity to other countries.
Regional	A number of countries in a region (area) may collectively specialise in a specific type of product. For instance, countries in the Gulf states are rich in oil and so countries in the region, such as Iraq, Abu Dhabi and Saudi Arabia, specialise in oil production.

Table 1.2.3: Overview of the levels of specialisation

KEY TERM

comparative advantage: when a country specialises in producing specific goods and services, they become most efficient at producing them or can do so at a lower opportunity cost than other countries. The country is likely to create a surplus of the type of good or service and will export the surplus quantity to other countries.

Advantages and disadvantages of specialisation

There are many advantages and disadvantages of specialisation, which can be considered from the view of the individual, factory and country (Table 1.2.4).

	Advantages	Disadvantages
Individual	The employee will become better skilled at the narrow range of tasks that they carry out. They may work faster, which can lead to higher pay if piece rate payment systems (where an employee is paid a certain amount for every item produced) are used. If the work is automated, the amount of physical labour will reduce. Training focuses on one task, so is quick and less demanding. Unskilled workers can be quickly trained to do the specific task.	Boredom may occur as the worker does the same task over and over. This may negatively affect motivation, leading to poor quality and lower output. The employee does not have a range of skills, which may make it difficult to find alternative employment. The employee does not have the satisfaction of completing a product from start to finish.
Factory	The factory can focus on one product. Division of labour can be used, which leads to increased efficiency (achieving a task or goal with no waste or effort) and productivity (rising output per employee hour). An increased output of standardised products can often be produced at a lower unit cost, which leads to higher profits. Unit cost is the cost per unit produced, i.e., the cost of buying or making one product. Automated methods of production can be used, as it is worthwhile to invest in the technology needed due to a narrow product range, e.g., robotics, machinery and technology. Specialist workers can be employed, which helps the business gain a competitive advantage. Unskilled workers can also be employed and trained to do the specific task that they will specialise in. Economies of scale – as a business grows and produces an increased number of units, the average unit cost of a product falls.	It may be challenging to motivate workers due to the lack of task variation. Interdependence, where each part of the factory depends on the performance of other areas. If one area underperforms or is affected by employee absence, the next process cannot be completed.

Continued

	Advantages	Disadvantages
Country	Businesses in the country can export the surplus of a product, which can provide an injection into the circular flow of income. Clusters of businesses within an industry are attracted to the country. This means that workers with the specialist skills for the industry and relevant suppliers are also likely to cluster in the area. This makes finding new employees and suppliers easier for the business.	There is a risk of structural unemployment due to occupational immobility. Structural unemployment occurs when there is a mismatch between the skills needed by employers and the skills that employees can offer. Occupational immobility is when an employee finds it difficult to change jobs within an industry, as the skills between jobs and industries are not transferrable. It may lead to the over-extraction of a country's natural resources. The country's economic performance may be negatively affected if global demand for the product falls.

Table 1.2.4: Advantages and disadvantages of specialisation to an individual, factory and country

Limits to specialisation

There are limits to specialisation, such as the size of the market. Mass production using division of labour is suitable for products that are highly demanded. However, if more products are supplied than are demanded, there will be a surplus, which can increase wastage and reduce prices (due to supply and demand). There must also be an appropriate infrastructure to allow the products to be distributed globally to meet demand.

KEY TERMS

piece rate: where an employee is paid a certain amount for every item produced, e.g., a payment for every pen produced, rather than the time taken to produce them. It is a way of calculating an employee's wages.

efficiency: achieving a task or goal with no waste or effort. It is about producing more output from less inputs (i.e., resources).

productivity: the efficiency of the production of goods or services. It can be measured in different ways, e.g., labour productivity measures the amount of goods or services produced per employee.

unit cost: the cost of buying or making one unit of the product.

interdependence: where two or more tasks/activities rely on each other. For example, Task 3 cannot be completed until Task 1 and Task 2 are done.

economies of scale: as a business operates on a larger scale it will benefit from cost savings. The average cost of producing the product will reduce as the number of products increases.

structural unemployment: a type of unemployment that occurs because there is a mismatch between the skills needed by employers and the skills that employees can offer. Many factors, including technological developments, can mean that the skills needed by employers change, which can make the skills that the employees can offer obsolete.

occupational immobility: when an employee finds it difficult to change jobs within an industry as the skills are not transferrable between jobs and industries. For instance, a doctor may find it hard to transfer to a job as a vet.

1.2.2 In-house production and outsourced production

Production can be performed in different ways. Some businesses use **in-house production** to make its products, which means that all tasks/activities are completed internally within the business itself. **Outsourced production** is when the business carries out the tasks/activities with the support of another business. The other business will complete the tasks/activities on behalf of the business that is paying for the outsourcing.

KEY TERMS

in-house production: all tasks/activities are completed internally within the business itself.

outsourced production: when a business hires another business that completes the tasks/activities on behalf of the business that is paying for the outsourcing.

Some businesses use a mix of the two types of production, for instance, a car manufacturer may outsource the production of the seats to another business but produce all other parts and components in-house. The other business delivers the seats to the manufacturer and they assemble the final car in-house. The decision as to whether to produce in-house or outsource depends on:

- cost
- access to the required skills and resources
- factory capacity
- time
- quality of the output produced
- management effort
- risk.

ACTIVITY 1.2.2

Think about the various factors to consider when deciding whether to produce a product in-house or outsource. Which factor do you think is the most important and why? Discuss your argument with a partner.

REFLECTION

Think about your answer to Activity 1.2.2. Is the most important factor the same for all businesses? Why? What have you learnt about production decision-making from this activity?

In-house production

Many businesses produce core products and services in-house (Figure 1.2.6). If the product or service is an essential part of the business's operations, it is more likely to be produced in-house.

Keeping production in-house allows the business to have full control of operations. They can choose the employees to recruit and coordinate operations. Quality standards can be closely monitored, which can help the business to ensure customer satisfaction.

Some businesses have to consider confidentiality, for instance, if the product is unique and subject to an exclusive recipe or design. Outsourcing the production would involve sharing details of the recipe or design, which the business may feel is not worth the risk. Other tasks may rely on confidential customer data, which the business may not wish to share outside the business.

Figure 1.2.6: Many businesses keep production in-house to maintain control and monitor quality standards

Internal employees often have a better understanding of how the business operates. They will be familiar with the culture and how managers expect tasks/activities to be carried out. They know the business's core strategy, aims and objectives, which they align with. This can ensure that the task/activity is carried out in line with the business's preferences.

The quality of output will influence the business's reputation and they may feel that it is not worth the risk to the reputation and image. A contractor may work with many different businesses, including competitors, so they are not focused on the business's reputation. They will only focus on meeting the contractual terms.

If a business's internal resources are not used to full capacity throughout the year, the business may decide to take on contracts from other businesses itself, such as producing products for another business. These contracts will provide an additional income stream for the business. By keeping production in-house, the business will maintain the required equipment, technology and employee skills, and so will be in a good position to take on additional work if it has spare capacity.

Outsourced production

Sometimes a business may be offered a one-off order or find a sudden increase in demand from regular customers. If the business is operating at full capacity, it may not have the resources to increase production. The additional output could therefore not be satisfied without the help of another business. The business may feel that it is worth the effort of finding another business to meet the additional demand and/or one-off order, as it could lead to more work in the future. Further, as the need to increase capacity is not constant throughout the year, the business's managers may feel that it is not worth expanding the factory as the resources would be under-utilised for the majority of time. The one-off order or increased demand may be linked to seasons and last for two months of the year. The resources would be under-utilised for most of the year, which would be inefficient.

Different functional areas are needed to operate a factory or office, such as human resources, marketing, catering, cleaning and technical support. Sometimes businesses may decide to outsource some functional areas if they feel they do not have the expertise to do it, or to the required standard in an efficient manner (Figure 1.2.7). Often specialists in the functional area can deliver the product or service cheaper and to a higher quality. An example is cleaning of the factory and/or offices each day. All buildings must be cleaned regularly to provide a pleasant working environment for employees. However, if the business is a food product manufacturer, its managers are unlikely to be cleaning experts. Managers may find that it is too time consuming to recruit cleaners, especially if **labour turnover** (the rate at which employees leave) is high among the cleaners. Managers may also lack the specialist knowledge to support the cleaning team. No in-house training can be offered as it is not a core part of the business's operations. They may therefore hire a specialist cleaning company to carry out the cleaning services on its behalf.

> **KEY TERM**
>
> **labour turnover:** the rate at which employees leave an employer (and are replaced by new employees) over a period of time. Low labour turnover means that the workforce is stable and many employees are likely to have worked for the business for a long time.

Figure 1.2.7: Many schools outsource catering services

Cleaning companies may have the contracts to clean the buildings of a number of businesses and can provide a specialist high-quality service for the businesses that employ them.

Sometimes the prices charged by the contractor are higher than in-house production. This is because the contractor needs to make a profit from the goods or services supplied. The business may be prepared to pay the higher price due to the higher quality that the contractor can offer and/or because outsourcing avoids the need to coordinate/manage the task in-house.

However, sometimes the prices charged by the contractor are cheaper than the cost of producing the goods or services in-house. This is because of the benefits of economies of scale. The contractor is likely to be a specialist in the production of the good or service, so will have access to specialist equipment, technology and skilled employees. All of these factors increase the efficiency of the contractor's operations, reducing the cost of production. The contractor may only offer the good or service. They will therefore benefit from lower prices from their supplier due to the high quantity of raw materials that they buy from the supplier for the contracts for the different businesses that they serve.

Successful outsourcing relies on a detailed contract to outline the responsibilities of each partner. This is important because the quality of the products produced will impact on the reputation of the business appointing the contractor. The types of information included in the contract may include:

- price paid to the contractor
- quantity of products supplied
- quality of products required
- deadline for delivery of products
- delivery instructions.

Table 1.2.5 highlights the benefits of in-house and outsourced production.

Benefits of in-house production	Benefits of outsourced production
It gives the business the ability to maintain control of operations, including quality standards. It ensures that information remains confidential. It may be cheaper than employing a contractor who wishes to make a profit from the outsourced work. Employees will be more familiar with the business's operations, culture and standards. The work will be carried out in line with the business's strategy, aims and objectives. There is less risk of damage to the business's reputation. The business may be able to take on external contracts itself if it has spare capacity. The business can earn additional income from the external contracts. There is no contract to issue to the contractor.	It enables the business to meet an expected increase in demand and/or one-off order if it does not have spare capacity internally. The contractor is likely to specialise in the good or service outsourced, so the quality may be higher. The contractor will have the expertise to deliver, for instance, by employing specialist employees. The contractor may produce the good or service more cheaply than the business could internally due to economies of scale. Employing a contractor may be less time consuming for managers as they do not have to coordinate and manage production.

Table 1.2.5: Benefits of in-house and outsourced production

1.2.3 Global supply chains

A supply chain is the network of businesses and/or people who support the production of a product and its delivery to the consumer. Supply chains can be domestic or global. **Domestic supply chains** are where the businesses and/or people who support the production and delivery of the product are based in the same country such as Pakistan, for instance raw materials from a supplier in Hub are delivered to a producer's factory in Badin. Domestic supply chains are chosen by some producers as they reduce the potential risks as the businesses are closer geographically. The language and currency is also the same. However, **global supply chains** are increasingly common due to **globalisation**. Globalisation is the development of world trade into a single **global market**. Cross-border transactions can add to the complexity of the supply chain due to different time zones, currencies and languages. The time for the product to pass through

KEY TERMS

domestic supply chain: a network of businesses and/or people based in the same country who support the production of a product and delivering it to the consumer.

global supply chain: a network of businesses and/or people based in different countries who support the production of a product and delivering it to the consumer.

globalisation: the development of world trade into a single global market.

global market: one market where goods and services are sold worldwide.

the various stages may also be longer due to the greater distance involved. Sometimes the supply chain has to be global as the materials needed to produce the product are not available in the producer's country, e.g. due to the required climate or the availability of suitable suppliers.

The product will move through various stages as it moves through the supply chain, e.g., from the producer or manufacturer to the consumer. Several businesses may support the product's journey to the consumer and perform key activities, including storage, advertising and transport (Figure 1.2.8). These businesses include the retailer, who typically sells the product to the consumer. Often the retailer is different to the producer, although in some cases it can be the same business. **Agents**, who provide a link between two parties (buyer and seller), can also form part of the supply chain, especially if it is long and/or complex. **Regional distribution centres**, which are large warehouses that store products bought by a business to allocate between branches in the region, are another example of a business supporting the distribution of the product.

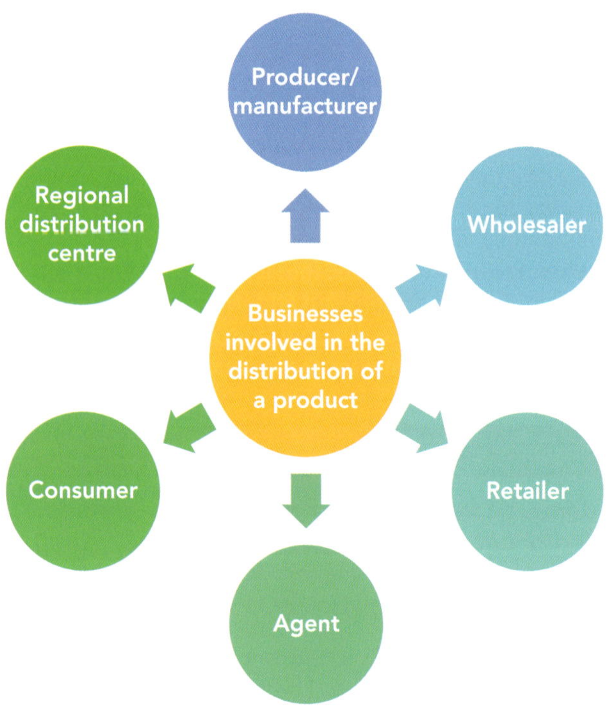

Figure 1.2.8: Businesses supporting the distribution of products to the consumer

KEY TERMS

agent: a person who provides a link between two parties (buyer and seller). They earn commission by acting on behalf of one of the parties.

regional distribution centre (RDC): a large warehouse for storing products bought by a business to allocate between branches in the region.

1.2.4 Intermediaries in a supply chain

An **intermediary** is a person or business who acts between two parties to try to reach an agreement or complete a task. Wholesalers and retailers are examples of intermediaries in a supply chain. They act between the producer/manufacturer and the consumer.

KEY TERM

intermediary: a person or business who acts between two parties to try to reach an agreement or complete a task.

The role of home trade intermediaries in a supply chain

Wholesalers and retailers are examples of two home trade intermediaries in a supply chain.

Wholesalers

Wholesalers play a vital role in the supply chain for many products. A wholesaler is a person or business that buys products in large quantities from suppliers (often the manufacturer of the product) and sells them to retailers and/or other businesses in smaller quantities. This is known as **breaking bulk**. The wholesaler is the middle of the supply chain between the producer and consumer.

KEY TERM

breaking bulk: taking a large quantity of goods and dividing them into smaller quantities.

Although the wholesaler carries out important tasks, their services are not free. Wholesalers are businesses and need to make a profit. This can make the price paid for the product by the consumer more expensive to enable the wholesaler to make a profit. Many products are sold in competitive markets and consumers want the cheapest price possible. Wholesalers are being removed from many channels of distribution to try to keep the price low.

Retailer

A retailer buys the products from a manufacturer or wholesaler to sell to the consumers. The retailer is therefore between the manufacturer or wholesaler and the consumer in the supply chain.

Retailers sell products in different ways including:

- **itinerant retailers** with no fixed location, such as a hawker, pedlar or street market trader
- vending machines
- physical shops
- online.

The nature of retail is changing due to the increased popularity of online transactions.

KEY TERM

itinerant retailer: a retailer with no fixed location that will move location periodically.

The role of international trade intermediaries in a supply chain

Agents and factors are examples of two international trade intermediaries in a supply chain. Agents and factors are often used because they may have specialist knowledge of the country and/or international trade that the seller can benefit from.

Agent

An agent operates on behalf of other businesses/people (known as the principals). The agent's role is to bring sellers and buyers of goods together. The agent does not own the goods and they earn a **commission** for the service provided. This means that they receive a percentage of the value of the goods sold.

KEY TERM

commission: a percentage share of the value of the goods sold.

Factor

A **factor** is a type of agent in international trade. The factor brings the sellers and buyers of goods together, but also has possession of the goods. This makes factors different to agents, who do not take possession of the goods. The service the factor provides is called a factorage, and the factor takes commission for this.

KEY TERM

factor: a type of agent who has possession of the goods. They bring sellers and buyers of goods together in return for a commission.

Future role of intermediaries

Increasingly, however, the role of the intermediaries is reducing in importance. Supply chains are becoming shorter with fewer people and businesses involved. This means that there are fewer people and businesses looking to make a profit and the consumer benefits from lower prices and/or the producer has higher profits.

The producer has more control if the supply chain is shorter. They are closer to the consumer and able to build a better relationship with them. Some producers may not want to be close to the consumer whereas others believe that it is a useful way of gaining feedback from the consumer, which can be used to develop new products and improve current ones. The producer also has control over the level of service that the consumer receives, which helps to maintain its **brand** image and reputation. A brand is the name of a business's products or services that is used for marketing purposes. Some intermediaries may distort the information between the producer and the consumer and/or exaggerate the features of the product. This can lead to consumer dissatisfaction.

KEY TERM

brand: the name of a business's products or services that is used for marketing purposes, such as Coca-Cola or Toyota.

1.2.5 Effects of digital technology on production

Technology has affected all aspects of production. Technology is changing all the time and producers/manufacturers regularly invest in new equipment to increase the efficiency of production.

The impact of automation

Automation is the range of technology that makes a process, system or series of activities operate automatically. Automation increases the efficiency of the production of goods and/or services.

Robotics has automated many routine and repetitive tasks in production. Tasks can be completed quicker and more accurately than with human labour. Productivity can be increased. Robotics are used in many different areas, such as assembly of products, welding, shipping and picking products in a warehouse. Robotics are often customised to the task performed, such as three- or six-axis arms used for picking. Robotics are often most appropriate in large-scale production environments, as small volumes do not warrant the large **capital** investment required. Capital investment is spending on **assets** for long-term use in the business, such as robotic equipment, machinery and vehicles.

KEY TERMS

capital: money invested in a business by its owner(s).

assets: items that a business owns that have monetary value.

Robots can be used to support the transfer of materials, such as machine loading and unloading of materials. The robot will move the materials or components from one location to another, e.g., from one conveyor to another. Parts can also be placed onto pallets in an arrangement determined by the robot. Transferring heavy and bulky parts can be challenging and dangerous for humans, so using robots can help businesses provide a safer environment for the workforce.

Many processing operations also use robots. The robot uses a tool to perform a process, such as spot welding or spray painting. Spot welding is a common task in the automotive industry, and the robot can position a spot welder against the vehicle panels and frames to assemble the car body. Automated welding processes are faster and produce a better weld quality, in addition to reducing labour costs. Using robots is also safer, as employees no longer have to be concerned about injuries such as burns. Using robots for spray painting can be more precise and can produce a more even finish without paint marks or drips. The robots can be slim enough to reach small areas that may be challenging for human employees.

Robots can assemble products efficiently. They can select the product from the conveyor belt to position it in the desired location. They can also inspect the quality of products. Robots can position a sensor to determine if the part meets the quality specifications. Table 1.2.6 discusses the advantages and disadvantages of using robots in production.

Advantages of using robots in production	Disadvantages of using robots in production
There is better quality work as robots can be more precise. It can result in quicker production/increased productivity. Robots can work 24/7. Safety increases as dangerous and harmful tasks can be assigned to robots. It can result in different work opportunities for employees, e.g., more technical job roles that employees may find more interesting. Less floor space may be needed for the task as the robots may be compact in size.	Fewer human employees are needed, which can lead to redundancies. The work of the remaining employees may change. For example, it may be more repetitive, which can demotivate employees. High capital investment is needed to purchase the equipment. Robots may break down. Robots are not appropriate for all tasks, e.g., complex one-off tasks are less suitable for robots to carry out than repetitive tasks.

Table 1.2.6: Advantages and disadvantages of using robots in production

Production management software

Production management software is used to help coordinate the production of products. Modern manufacturers use software to design and manufacture products. Computer aided design (CAD) includes the use of software to design new products and adapt existing products. The software is often more accurate than sketches created by humans as the dimensions can be more precise. The software allows the designer to view the new product in a 3D format from a range of angles. Computer aided manufacturing (CAM) covers the use of software to automate manufacturing. Many tasks can be automated using CAM, which can reduce the number of employees needed for a process, reducing the business's costs.

The impact on production of digital communication with suppliers

Modern businesses communicate digitally with suppliers. Regular and fast communication with suppliers is important, as many businesses need supplies quickly to complete new orders from customers. Many businesses also keep the amount of stock held to a minimum to operate efficiently, so, they rely on reliable suppliers.

Email is often used to transfer messages to suppliers on a daily basis. Detailed reports, images and information can be shared quickly with suppliers using email. Many organisations have also created specific systems to communicate with suppliers digitally.

Electronic data interchange (EDI) is where information is exchanged electronically from one business to another business. EDI removes the need for paper communications. Many businesses develop EDI systems to communicate with suppliers.

EDI can be used for many tasks, such as automating the issue of purchase **orders**, **invoices** and **delivery notes**. A purchase order is a document sent from the buyer to the seller giving details of what the buyer wishes to order. An invoice is the bill sent by the seller giving details of an individual transaction. A delivery note is a copy of the invoice sent with the goods to the buyer.

KEY TERMS

order: a document sent from the buyer to the seller giving details of what the buyer wishes to order. Also known as the purchase order.

invoice: the bill sent by the seller giving details of an individual transaction.

delivery note: a copy of the invoice sent with the goods to the buyer. It is signed by the buyer when the buyer receives the goods.

Stock management systems support the automatic reordering of stock. For example, in production, an automatic reorder level can be set so that when the stock of materials reaches a specific point, an order request may be sent to suppliers without human intervention. As an order for a product is received by the business, the EDI may place an order to the suppliers to ensure that all materials/components are delivered in time for the order. The production plan can be shared with the supplier. EDI systems support just-in-time (JIT) manufacturing systems that rely on efficient deliveries at the time that they are needed within production. EDI helps the producer/manufacturer develop a better relationship with its suppliers. Suppliers also like EDI as the producer/manufacturer is less likely to go to a different supplier without EDI. This therefore makes the business a loyal customer of the supplier. Table 1.2.7 lists the advantages and disadvantages of digital communication with suppliers.

Advantages of digital communication with suppliers	Disadvantages of digital communication with suppliers
Quicker processing of tasks Can support efficient production operations Can help the supplier offer the producer/manufacturer a better service	Fewer human employees needed, which can lead to redundancies High cost to purchase the hardware and develop the system Technology may break down

Table 1.2.7: Advantages and disadvantages of using digital communication with suppliers

1.2.6 Costs involved in trade, commerce and production

There are many costs involved in trade, commerce and production, which are summarised in Table 1.2.8. Businesses work hard at reducing the costs as much as possible to increase the profitability of operations.

Costs are the money that a business has to pay out to run the business. They are the expenses that a business has to incur to produce and sell its goods and services. All businesses need to be aware of the different costs incurred to operate, so they can produce accurate budgets and also take action to reduce costs where possible.

Cost	Description
Advertising	Advertising can help to attract customers and inform them about the features and benefits of the product offered. Without advertising, the business is likely to sell only a limited number of goods and/or services. Advertising can be expensive, depending on the medium used. Options such as television can be very expensive due to the number of customers that can be reached. Other methods are lower cost, such as social media or posters/leaflets. A poster is a large printed sheet that often contains pictures and is used to promote something in public places.
Bank charges	Banks often charge business customers to operate their bank account. The bank charges vary between banks but could include a monthly or annual fee for having the business bank account, plus transaction costs, for instance a fee for paying in cash, transferring money or sending/receiving international payments.
Commission	Agents and factors may charge commission for their services, which is a cost for the business employing them. The commission will vary according to the amount of product sales that they support – the more work that they generate, the higher the cost.
Customs duties	Customs duties are a tax charged on products shipped across international borders. These duties are set by the government to promote fair competition with domestic businesses.
Inventory	Inventory is another word for stock. All businesses need to keep a certain amount of materials/products in stock to meet production schedules and customer demand. Inventory held needs to be purchased from the supplier, which can tie up working capital (the capital available for the day-to-day running of the company) in the business. The stock then needs to be managed by employees, which incurs a labour cost, insured against any risk and also stored in the correct conditions, which may also cost if the product is perishable or needs hot/cold temperatures. There is also the risk that the inventory may go off or be damaged before it can be sold.
Labour	Employees are needed to support trade, commerce and production. Employees need to be paid a wage or salary for the work that they do. A salary is a payment to employees that does not vary according to the number of hours worked or the employee's output. Employees may carry out roles directly involved in trade, commerce and production, or work in support functions such as human resources.
Packaging	Packaging is needed at the different stages of the supply chain. Raw materials may need packaging to transfer from the point of extraction to the producer/manufacturer, e.g., sugar or flour may be packed in bags. Packaging is needed to protect the products for sale and display them in an attractive manner for sale to the customer. Packaging must be durable to offer appropriate protection.

Continued

Cost	Description
Renting/ leasing a building or equipment	Many businesses choose to rent or lease assets (such as a building, machinery or a vehicle) rather than own them. Renting is where the business can use the asset, normally for a fixed period of time. They will agree to make a regular payment to the asset's owner to compensate them for the use of the asset. Leasing or hiring are alternative words for renting.
Transportation	The supply chain relies on transportation to move between the different stages of the supply chain. The nature of the product and/or type of commerce (i.e., home trade or international trade) will influence the appropriateness of different types of transport. The cost of transport will vary depending on the method used, i.e., land, air or water.
Utilities	Utilities are the services used by the business to be able to operate, e.g., electricity, water, gas, broadband and telephone.
Warehousing	A warehouse is a large building used to store raw materials or finished products ready for distribution for sale. Warehouses are sometimes called distribution centres. The warehouse ensures that stock is stored safely and securely. It protects the products from being damaged by severe weather conditions. Warehouses are very expensive to operate. Often a business will rent the warehouse, so the business will have to pay rent to the landlord. The stock also needs to be insured to protect it against the risk of damage, theft or other issues. Insurance premiums, which are the payment(s) that a customer makes to the insurer for the insurance cover, can be high if the stock held is of a high value. The stock also needs to be maintained. Some products need to be stored at a specific temperature, which may be costly, e.g., refrigerated conditions in the warehouse are needed for perishable products to be stored. Employees will work in the warehouse and so the business will have to pay labour costs.

Table 1.2.8: Costs involved in trade, commerce and production

KEY TERMS

poster: a large printed sheet that often contains pictures and is used to promote something in public places.

customs duty: a type of taxation that the consumer must pay on imported goods.

working capital: capital available for the day-to-day running of the business.

salary: a payment to employees that does not vary according to the number of hours worked or their output. A salary is usually an annual amount which is divided into twelve equal monthly instalments that the employee receives for their work each month.

leasing: a method of having the use of assets by renting them rather than buying them.

insurance premium: the payment(s) that a customer makes to the insurer for the insurance cover.

Calculating different types of costs

It important to accurately calculate costs to find the profit earned.

Labour costs

Labour is a large cost for many businesses, especially if it employs a lot of people. Labour costs can be either wages or salaries. A wage is a payment to employees that changes according to the number of hours worked or their output over a period of time. Wages may be paid on a weekly or a monthly basis. Many production workers or non-managerial employees receive wages. A salary is normally paid to employees who are more senior in the business, such as a supervisor or manager. The payment is fixed and does not vary. The employee receives the same amount of salary regardless of the number of hours that they work or their output. The salary is usually an annual amount that is divided into 12 equal monthly instalments. The employee will then receive their salary payment on a set day every month.

Here is an example of a labour cost calculation.

WORKED EXAMPLE 1.2.1

Calculating labour cost

A business employs three people. They are all paid on a monthly basis. Two employees receive an hourly wage of $12 per hour. One of the employees worked 140 hours during the month and the other employee worked 100 hours. The manager receives an annual salary of $30 000.

Required

What is the monthly labour cost for the business?

Answer

Employee 1 = 140 hours × $12 per hour
= $1680

Employee 2 = 100 hours × $12 per hour
= $1200

Manager = $30 000 ÷ 12
= $2500

Total labour cost = $1680 + $1200 + $2500
= $5380

Bank charges

Most banks charge a fee to carry out transactions for businesses, e.g., a fee to convert money to a different currency or a transaction fee for each transaction made. Some banks also charge a monthly fee on the account.

Here is an example of a bank charge calculation.

WORKED EXAMPLE 1.2.2

Calculating bank charges

A bank charges a fee of 0.3% for each international payment. An importer paid their international supplier $45 000.

Required

How much did the bank charge the importer?

Answer

= $45 000 × 0.3%

= $45 000 × 0.003

= $135

Warehousing costs

Businesses often rent warehouse space to store products and/or materials. The owner of the warehouse will charge the business rent which is often paid on a monthly basis. The rent may be calculated in different ways but could depend on the area of the building used by the business.

Here is an example of a warehousing cost calculation.

WORKED EXAMPLE 1.2.3

Calculating warehousing cost

A business rents 8000 square metres of warehouse space. The rent is $3.50 per square metre per month with operating expenses of $0.35 per square metre per month.

Required

Calculate the total monthly rent.

Answer

Cost of 1 square metre per month = $3.50 + $0.35
= $3.85

Total cost of warehouse space = $3.85 × 8000
= $30 800 per month

Delivery costs

Some retailers offer home delivery services for customers. For instance, supermarkets may deliver a customer's food purchase to their home, or a restaurant may deliver orders so customers can enjoy the food at home. Large and bulky items, such as furniture or electrical appliances, are often delivered, as customers would struggle to fit their purchase into a normal size car. Sometimes the customer may be charged a delivery fee, but other businesses may offer the delivery service free of charge.

Here is an example of a delivery cost calculation.

WORKED EXAMPLE 1.2.4

Calculating delivery costs

A furniture retailer offers a free home delivery service to its local customers. An average of 160 home deliveries are made every month. The average monthly cost of petrol for the delivery vehicles is $3000. The driver receives a salary of $2000 per month.

Required

Calculate the average monthly cost of delivery per household.

Answer

Total monthly cost for the delivery service
= $3000 petrol + $2000 driver salary

= $5000

Cost of delivery per household = $5000 ÷ 160 households
= £31.25 per household

Commission

Commission is a payment based on the number or value of items sold. It is usually calculated as a percentage of the money generated from the sale.

Some employees who work in sales receive a commission payment to motivate them to sell more of the business's products. The business will earn more **revenue (turnover)** if more products are sold, and the business shares some of this extra income with the employees. The commission payment will be paid in addition to the basic salary or wage.

KEY TERM

revenue (turnover): the money received from selling goods or services.

Some businesses may sell products on behalf of others, e.g., an art gallery may sell an artist's paintings. The majority of the money paid by the customer purchasing the painting will go to the artist, but the art gallery may also receive commission for helping to sell the painting. Estate agents often charge the seller of a house or building a commission for its services. The higher the price of the property sold, the greater the commission that the estate agent will earn. This motivates the estate agent to sell the property for the highest price possible. The commission fee will pay for the estate agents costs in selling the property, e.g., administration, advertising the property, showing people around the property, etc.

Here is an example of a commission cost.

WORKED EXAMPLE 1.2.5

Calculating commission

An estate agent sold a property for $250 000. The estate agent charges the property seller a commission fee of 1%.

Required

Calculate the commission fee.

Answer

= 1% × $250 000

= 0.01 × $250 000

= $2500

Customs duty

Many businesses that import goods and services have to pay customs duty based on the value of the products sold. Customs duties are a tax paid to the government.

Here is an example of a customs duty calculation.

WORKED EXAMPLE 1.2.6

Calculating customs duty

Mayur sells 500 kettles at a unit price of $10 each. The customs duty is 15%.

Required

Calculate the amount of customs duty that Mayur will have to pay.

Answer

Value of products sold = 500 × $10
= $5000

Customs duty = $5000 × 0.15
= $750

Solving problems

Sometimes the cost calculations need to be rearranged to find a missing figure. For instance, a business may know the amount of wages paid to an employee for a week's work and the employee's hourly wage rate. The manager can use this information to calculate the number of hours that the employee worked that week.

Here is an example of finding missing information.

WORKED EXAMPLE 1.2.7

Finding missing information

Glora was paid \$320 last week. Glora receives an hourly wage of \$16 per hour. The manager wants to find out how many hours Glora was paid for.

Required

Calculate how many hours Glora was paid for.

Answer

= \$320 ÷ \$16

= 20 hours

The cost figures often relate to a specific time period. When calculating costs, it is important that the costs all relate to the same period of time, for instance, all costs must be for a period of a month or a week. This may involve covering some costs to a different time period, e.g., a monthly cost into a weekly cost or a monthly cost into the cost for the entire year.

Here is an example of converting cost information into different time periods.

WORKED EXAMPLE 1.2.8

Converting cost information into different time periods

a A business pays \$950 rent per month.

Required

How much rent does the business pay over the whole year?

Answer

= \$950 × 12 months

= \$11 400 per year

b Kai receives a wage of \$2000 for the month of July. There are four working weeks in July.

CONTINUED

Required

Calculate the average wage that Kai earned per week in July.

Answer

= \$2000 ÷ 4 weeks

= \$500 per week

ACTIVITY 1.2.3

Calculate the costs that the following businesses have to pay.

a A bank charges a fee of 0.2% for each international payment. An importer paid his international supplier \$15 000. How much did the importer pay in bank charges?

b A company has found a warehouse to rent. It has 3000 square feet of warehouse space. The rent is \$2.50 per square foot per month with operating expenses of \$0.30 per month. Calculate the total monthly rent.

c Stella is importing 1000 T-shirts at a unit price of \$5 each. The customs duty is 18%. Calculate the total amount of customs duty that Stella will have to pay.

d A supermarket offers a free home delivery service to its local customers. On average, 600 home deliveries are made every month. The monthly cost of petrol for the delivery vehicles is \$2000. The driver's salary is \$1300 per month. What is the average monthly cost of delivery per household?

e An art gallery sold Raj's painting for \$5000. Raj paid the art gallery a commission of 10%. Calculate the art gallery's commission.

f A business employs one employee and a manager who are paid each month. The employee receives an hourly wage of \$10 per hour and has worked 150 hours during the month. The manager receives an annual salary of \$30 000. What is the monthly labour cost for the business?

SELF-EVALUATION CHECKLIST

After studying this chapter, complete this table.

You should know about:	Needs more work	Almost there	Ready to move on
the features of the four sectors of production			
the significance of specialisation and its advantages and disadvantages			
the meaning and benefits of in-house production and outsourced production			
the difference between global and local supply chains			
the role of supply chain intermediaries			
the impact of automation and other digital technology on production			
types of costs in trade, commerce and production			

Knowledge check

1 Describe the features of the four sectors of production.

2 Identify two examples of industries that would operate within each of the four sectors of production.

3 Analyse two advantages of specialisation to a factory.

4 Analyse two disadvantages of specialisation to an individual.

5 Describe the difference between in-house and outsourced production.

6 Grace owns a sandwich shop and incurs the following costs to operate the business:

- rent of the shop: $1000 per month
- average cost of raw materials per sandwich: $0.80 per sandwich
- packaging: $0.30 per sandwich
- insurance: $2500 per year
- advertising: $2300 per year.

Grace estimates that she sells 8500 sandwiches each year.

Work out the annual cost to operate Grace's sandwich shop every year.

7 A benefit of specialisation to a country is:

a division of labour

b high unemployment

c repetitive tasks may be boring for employees

d surplus products can be exported.

8 Which of the following is essential for successful outsourcing?

a appointing the cheapest contractor

b high pricing

c issuing a contract

d making a quick decision

9 As a business grows and produces an increased number of units, the average unit cost of a product falls. This is known as:

a comparative advantage

b economies of scale

c increased productivity

d specialisation.

10 Which of the following is not a benefit of in-house production?

- a increased sales
- b increased control
- c increased cost
- d increased quality monitoring

Practice questions

1 a Define the term 'specialisation'. [2]

b State two disadvantages of specialisation for a factory. [2]

c Anytown School is experiencing problems recruiting cleaners. The principal is thinking of outsourcing the cleaning of the school to an external contractor. Recommend if the principal should outsource the cleaning of the school. Give reasons for your opinion. [6]

d State four types of business cost. [4]

2 a Define the term 'in-house production'. [2]

b State four industries within the tertiary sector. [4]

c The operations director of Weldz Engineering is thinking of introducing robots in production. The employees are not happy due to the impact on their jobs. Should Weldz Engineering introduce robots in production? Give reasons for your opinion. [8]

Unit 2

Commercial operations

› Chapter 2.1

Different types of enterprise and outsourcing

LEARNING INTENTIONS

In this chapter you will learn:

- the distinction between private and public sector enterprises
- the features of different types of private sector enterprises
- the key aspects and aims of public corporations
- the suitability of different types of ownership in given situations
- the features of multinational companies
- why multinationals exist in the global economy
- the impact of multinational companies locating in a country
- the features of franchises
- the pros and cons of franchises
- physical and ecommerce location factors
- the suitability of physical and ecommerce location factors in different situations
- the development of outsourcing, including contract manufacturing and logistics.

2.1.1 Types of enterprise

Businesses vary in size. Some are very small and owned by just one person whereas others are very large with operations around the globe, such as Apple and Sony. Some businesses are owned by the government. In this chapter you will learn about the different types of business and their operations. You will consider how they are funded and what their aims and objectives are.

A business can operate within just one country or in a number of different countries.

As you learned in Chapter 1.1, home trade is the buying and selling of goods and services within the boundaries of one country. Home trade is a feature of **local enterprises** (businesses serving a specific geographic area), as they make/buy and sell to customers in the same country. Home trade usually supports personal relations between the business and customers as the business owner is likely to have a good knowledge of the market. The growth of ecommerce has broken down the geographical restrictions that prevented many businesses operating outside of their local area. However, despite this change, many businesses choose to offer their goods and services to a specific geographic area only.

Changes to the nature of retail may benefit local retailers. Many national and international businesses are moving away from physical shops in favour of online operations and ecommerce. This means that many local businesses are able to take their place physically, and are therefore able to compete by offering something different to the mass-produced offerings. Local businesses may benefit from financial assistance in the form of **grants** and **subsidies** from local councils that are keen to promote **enterprise** in the area. A grant is a sum of money given to a business or individual for a specific purpose. A subsidy is financial assistance offered by national/local government to support economic and social policy. Local businesses can support **economically sustainable communities**, as they enable residents to purchase items within the community, thereby creating jobs for local residents and reducing travel out of the area. Economically sustainable communities are communities that have adequate financial resources to survive and operate in the future.

KEY TERMS

local enterprise: a business serving a specific geographic area.

grants: a sum of money given to a business or individual for a specific purpose. Often the business or individual needs to satisfy certain criteria to receive the money. The money does not have to be repaid.

subsidies: financial assistance offered by national or local government to support economic and social policy.

enterprise: a business managed by one or more individuals who can take the initiative to make decisions and take calculated risks.

economically sustainable communities: communities that have adequate financial resources to survive and operate in the future.

2.1.2 The public and private sectors

Many economies are **mixed economies**, with enterprises within two sectors, which are:

- the **private sector**
- the **public sector**.

KEY TERMS

mixed economies: economies with organisations in both the public and private sectors.

private sector: enterprises in the private sector are owned by individuals or groups of individuals. They are not owned by the state or the government.

public sector: organisations that are owned and controlled by the government. They are state-owned.

Organisations in the public sector are owned and controlled by the government, i.e., they are state owned or **nationalised**. These organisations may be owned by the national government and/or local councils. They exist to offer goods and services to benefit the public. Enterprises in the private sector are owned by individuals or groups of individuals.

Mixed economies can be contrasted with communist countries, such as China, North Korea, Cuba, Laos and Vietnam, where most business activity is provided and controlled by the government. The businesses operate for common good and not profit.

KEY TERM

nationalised: owned by the state, i.e., government.

KEY TERMS

sole trader: a business owned and run by one person.

shareholder: a person who owns shares in a company by investing money. They become an owner by buying a share in the company.

shares: a security that represents the fraction of ownership that the shareholder has in a company. The holder of a share is a known as a shareholder.

stock: also known as equity. Stock is the term to describe all of the shares in a company. Units of stock are known as shares.

cooperative: a type of business owned by its members.

The private sector

Many organisations belong to the private sector. Enterprises in the private sector may vary in size from just one owner, such as a **sole trader**/proprietor, or large public limited companies owned by hundreds of **shareholders**. A shareholder is a person who owns **shares** in a company by investing money. Shares represent the fraction of ownership that the shareholder has in a company. Shares are a unit of **stock**, which is the term used to describe all of the shares in a company. The private sector also includes **cooperatives** which are owned by members.

Private sector enterprises often aim to make a profit, alongside other objectives. Figure 2.1.1 outlines the different types of private sector enterprises.

Sole traders (sole proprietors)
- Businesses owned by one person

Cooperative
- A type of business owned by members

Partnerships
- Ordinary partnerships
- Limited liability partnerships

Limited companies
- Private limited companies (Ltd)
- Public limited companies (PLC)

Figure 2.1.1: Private sector enterprises

Table 2.1.1 describes the features of each form of business ownership.

	Who owns the business?	Type of liability	Who is responsible for decision-making?	Who receives the profits made by the business?
Sole trader	One owner (i.e., the sole trader)	Unlimited liability (responsible for all business debts)	The sole trader	The sole trader keeps all profits.
Cooperative	Members	Limited liability (not personally responsible for the full debts of the business)	The board of directors, who are appointed by the members. A director is a person who runs the business on behalf of the shareholders/owners.	Members receive a cash payment or a share of the profits known as a dividend at the end of the year.

Continued

	Who owns the business?	Type of liability	Who is responsible for decision-making?	Who receives the profits made by the business?
Ordinary partnership	Two or more owners (partners)	Unlimited liability	Each partner will have equal responsibility for decisions unless agreed differently in the partnership agreement/ deed of partnership (a written document that details the contract between the partners).	Generally, each partner receives an equal share of profits unless agreed differently in the partnership agreement.
Limited liability partnership	Two or more owners (partners)	Limited liability	Each partner will have equal responsibility for decisions unless agreed differently in the partnership agreement.	Generally, each partner receives an equal share of profits unless agreed differently in the partnership agreement.
Private limited company	Shareholders	Limited liability	The board of directors, who are appointed by the shareholders	Shareholders receive a share of the profits (i.e., a dividend) equal to the value of the shares that they bought.
Public limited company	Shareholders	Limited liability	The board of directors, who are appointed by the shareholders	Shareholders receive a share of the profits (i.e., a dividend) equal to the value of the shares that they bought.

Table 2.1.1: Features of each form of business ownership

KEY TERMS

unlimited liability: the owner(s) of the business is liable for the full debt of the business. If the business gets into debt or fails, the owners may be forced to sell their personal possessions to repay the business's debts.

limited liability: the owners of the business can only lose the amount that they originally invested into the business if the business gets into debt or fails. The owners cannot be forced to sell their personal possessions to pay for the business's debts.

board of directors: a group of people who are appointed by the shareholders/members to set strategy and run the business on their behalf. They represent the shareholder's or member's interests.

director: a person who runs the business on behalf of the shareholders/owners. They are usually responsible for a specific area or function within the business.

dividend: a share of the profits paid to shareholders to reward them for investing in the business.

partnership agreement/deed of partnership: a written document that details the contract between the partners. The partnership agreement includes key information about how the partnership will operate, such as how profits and losses are shared, how decisions are made and the name/purpose of the partnership business. The document can be referred to for future reference and in the event of disagreement.

Sole trader

A sole trader, or sole proprietor, is an enterprise owned and run by one person (i.e., the sole trader/proprietor). It is one of the most common forms of ownership for **start-up businesses**. Many local businesses, such as plumbers, stall holders and gardeners, are sole traders.

Sole traders have to complete all the tasks related to their business even if they are not experienced in those tasks. For example, a car mechanic may be very knowledgeable about repairing cars but may have less experience of marketing their business or managing the financial aspects, such as doing the accounts. This could affect the quality of decisions taken.

A sole trader can keep all the profits that they make but they have to make all business decisions on their own.

Sole traders have unlimited liability, which means that they are responsible for all business debts. So, if the business gets into debt, they may have to sell some of their personal possessions, such as their car or home, to repay the business's debts.

KEY TERM

start-up business: a business that has just been created. It is only just starting to trade.

ACTIVITY 2.1.1

Discuss the advantages and disadvantages of running a business as a sole trader with another student.

Create a short presentation to explain the advantages and disadvantages that you identified.

At the end of the presentation, summarise if you would like to run a business as a sole trader and the reasons why. Does the type of good or service sold affect the appropriateness of operating as a sole trader?

REFLECTION

Think about the presentation task that you have just completed. How did you approach the activity? Did you learn any additional advantages and/or disadvantages after your discussion with the student you worked with? Did you share the same opinion about running a business as a sole trader or did you have different opinions? Why do you think your opinions were similar or different?

Cooperatives

A cooperative is a type of business owned by its members. The members may be customers, employees, suppliers, residents, farmers, etc. The type of members can vary depending upon the type of cooperative and how it is set up. Cooperatives focus on delivering their mission to their members rather than maximising the financial return to investors.

Each member has one vote regarding all important decision-making. This means that membership is democratic and everyone has an equal say in how the cooperative operates. There are no majority shareholders. Membership is open and voluntary, so anyone who meets the criteria should be able to join.

A cooperative is not a charity so each member contributes something and receives something in return. The contribution can vary depending upon the type of cooperative, for instance, it could be that the person works for the cooperative or shops there. Any surplus made from the income generated after all costs are covered are shared between the members or reinvested into the cooperative. The reward received by members is often referred to as a dividend.

A board of directors is often selected by the members to run the co-operative and make operational decisions on their behalf.

Partnership

A partnership is a business owned and run by two or more people who are known as partners. The partners usually draw up a legal contract, a partnership agreement (Figure 2.1.2), which states each partner's role and share of profits. Many businesses operate as partnerships, including solicitors, accountants and estate agents.

Figure 2.1.2: A partnership agreement can help the partners to avoid disagreements and misunderstandings

The partners jointly share responsibility for decision-making, which can lead to disagreements if the partners want different things or feel the business should develop in different ways.

The profits are shared equally by the partners (unless the partnership agreement states differently).

Each partner invests capital into the business and may also bring different skills and experiences to the partnership. This allows each partner to specialise in specific tasks or areas of the business. For example, one partner may be responsible for marketing the business whereas another may do the financial tasks.

Most partnerships have unlimited liability, so the partners are responsible for the business's debts and may have to sell some of their personal possessions to repay them.

It is important to choose partners carefully as all partners are liable for decisions made by the others. For example, if one partner makes a bad decision that loses a lot of money, all of the partners are jointly liable, even if they were not consulted about the decision.

Some partnerships are set up as limited liability partnerships. A limited liability partnership is similar to a traditional partnership except that the partners (i.e., owners) benefit from limited liability. This means that each partner (i.e., owner) is not personally responsible for the full debts of the business. They only risk losing the amount of money that they invested into the business. Many solicitors and accountants operate as limited liability partnerships.

Private limited company

A private limited company is usually a small- or medium-sized business that is owned by shareholders, although some larger businesses continue to operate in this way. Private limited companies can be identified by the abbreviation after the company name, which varies according to the country (Table 2.1.2).

Abbreviation	Country
(Pty) Ltd	South Africa
LLC	United States
Ltd	United Kingdom, Mauritius, Hong Kong
Pvt. Ltd	Pakistan, India, Zimbabwe, Bangladesh, Sri Lanka
Sdn Bhd	Brunei, Malaysia

Table 2.1.2: Private limited company abbreviations in select countries

Each shareholder invests capital into the business by purchasing a share. In return for their investment, each year the shareholder receives a share of the profits, called a dividend. A board of directors is employed by the shareholders to run the company and make decisions on their behalf.

Shareholders benefit from limited liability. This means that they are not responsible for the full debts of the business. They only risk losing the amount of money that they invested in the shares. Many private limited companies are small, family-run businesses. Shares in a private limited company are not sold on the **stock exchange** (a place where shares and stocks are bought and sold), and can only be bought and sold with the permission of the other shareholders, which ensures that the shareholders maintain control of who is an owner. For this reason, the shareholders of many private limited companies are friends and family members of the individual that set the business up initially. Some financial information must be publicly available for anyone to view, for instance, the profit/loss made and the value of the business's assets and liabilities. This can cause issues, especially if competitors access the information.

KEY TERM

stock exchange: a place where shares and stocks are bought and sold.

Private limited companies have their own legal identity and can sue and be sued, separate to the shareholders and owners.

Public limited company

A public limited company is usually a larger business that is owned by shareholders. They can be identified by the abbreviation after the company name, which varies according to the country (Table 2.1.3).

Abbreviation	Country
Bhd	Malaysia
Inc. or Corp.	United States
JSC	Pakistan
Ltd	South Africa, India, Zimbabwe, Bangladesh
PLC	United Kingdom

Table 2.1.3: Public limited company abbreviations in select countries

Shareholders invest capital into the business by purchasing a share, similar to a private limited company. However, the key difference is that the shares are sold on the stock exchange and the permission of other shareholders is not required to buy and sell shares. This means that the owners have no control over who can buy shares and there is a risk of **takeover** if one shareholder buys 51% or more of the shares. This would mean that the majority shareholder has control of all decisions, as they have more voting power than other shareholders.

KEY TERM

takeover: the taking of control of a company by purchasing more than half of its shares, i.e., 51% or more, to become the majority shareholder. The majority shareholder has control of all decisions as they have more voting power than other shareholders.

Shareholders receive a share of profits, called a dividend, in return for their investment and also benefit from limited liability and have a separate legal identify. A board of directors is employed by the shareholders to run the company and make decisions on their behalf.

Advantages and disadvantages of different private sector enterprises

Table 2.1.4 outlines the advantages and disadvantages of the different private sector enterprises.

Type of private sector enterprise	Advantages	Disadvantages
Sole trader	The sole trader can make all business decisions. They can keep all profit earned. They are relatively cheap and easy to set up (i.e., no complex paperwork). The sole trader can usually choose their own working hours and holidays etc.	They have unlimited liability. They may lack experience in some areas of business. The sole trader may have to work long hours. They are not paid when they are unwell or take time off for a holiday. The owner's capital is limited to the sole trader's savings. There are no other owners to contribute savings. It may be challenging to secure external finance due to perceived high risk. Business decisions cannot be shared.

Continued

Type of private sector enterprise	Advantages	Disadvantages
Cooperative	Members have equal voting rights. Members receive the personal satisfaction of contributing to business decisions. They have limited liability. There is no limit on the number of members.	They are more complex and costly to set up due to legal requirements. There can be slower decision-making as all members must be consulted.
Partnership	They are relatively cheap and easy to set up (i.e., no complex paperwork). There is greater capital. Partners can offer different skills and experience. Decision-making and work can be shared according to experience and strengths. There is shared responsibility for business risk.	They have unlimited liability. There may be disagreement and conflict amongst partners regarding business decisions and workload. It may take longer to make business decisions. Profits must be shared among the partners.
Private limited company	Additional capital can be raised by selling shares. There is limited liability. Shares can only be bought and sold with the permission of the other owners.	They are more complex and costly to set up due to legal requirements. Certain financial information needs to be publicly available. There can be slower decision-making as all shareholders have to agree.
Public limited company	Additional capital can be raised by selling shares. There is limited liability.	They are more complex and costly to set up due to legal requirements. Certain financial information needs to be publicly available. There can be slower decision-making as all shareholders have to agree. There can be a risk of takeover.

Table 2.1.4: The advantages and disadvantages of different private sector enterprises

Liability

To understand the features of the different types of ownership, it is useful to recap on the definitions and review the advantages and disadvantages of the two types of liability (Table 2.1.5).

Type of liability	Definition	Advantages	Disadvantages
Limited liability	The owner of the business can only lose the amount that they originally invested in the business if the business fails/goes into debt. They cannot be forced to sell their personal possessions to pay for the business's debts.	The amount that the owner can potentially lose is limited, so they cannot lose any more money than they originally invested. The owner cannot be forced to sell any of their personal possessions, such as their house or car, to repay business debts.	Some people and organisations that the business owes money to may never recover the full value of the debt.
Unlimited liability	The owner of the business is liable for the total debts of the business. If the business fails/goes into debt, they may be forced to sell their personal possessions to repay the business's debts.	There is less paperwork to complete when setting up the business.	The amount that the owner can potentially lose is unlimited, so they could lose more money than they originally invested. As the amount is unlimited, they may be forced into bankruptcy. The owner can be forced to sell their personal possessions, such as their house or car, to repay business debts.

Table 2.1.5: Definitions, advantages and disadvantages of the two types of liability

The public sector

Public sector enterprises are funded by the national and/or local government via taxation and government grants, loans and money generated from any trading activities/fees charged. The enterprises do not aim to make a profit, but generally aim to cover the costs of operation. Any money that the enterprise makes is known as a surplus and is usually reinvested to support future operations and development.

Table 2.1.6 describes the advantages and disadvantages of public sector enterprises.

Advantages of public sector enterprises	Disadvantages of public sector enterprises
Some industries are unattractive to private investors and so public ownership is the only way of operating.	Lack of competition may prevent value for money and choice for the consumer.
The government can keep control of essential services and protect their long-term provision in the public interest, e.g., telecommunications. Some essential services may not generate a sufficient profit/income to be offered by any other private organisation.	There is no incentive to operate efficiently, which means an enterprise may operate with too many staff or maintain a declining industry.

Continued

Advantages of public sector enterprises	Disadvantages of public sector enterprises
They provide employment. Some industries are so expensive to set up and operate that government investment is the only option. The government may stop an underperforming private sector organisation from failing by transferring it to public ownership (nationalisation). The UK government took this action during the banking crisis in 2008 to maintain trust in the banking system and prevent economic problems.	Too much bureaucracy can lead to inefficiency and slow operations/decision-making due to government interference.

Table 2.1.6: Advantages and disadvantages of public sector enterprises

Public corporations

Public corporations belong to the public sector.

The features of public corporations

Public corporations are typically owned by the national government and are expected to **break even** (reach the point where they are not making a profit or a loss) or make a profit. Public corporations are an example of a public sector organisation. A large proportion of a public corporation's income will come from service charges or taxation rather than directly from government. Profits are reinvested into the organisation. An example is the British Broadcasting Corporation (BBC), which provides television and radio services in the UK. The BBC is answerable to government departments, which set financial targets and budgets.

TIP

Public corporations are different from public limited companies, which are part of the private sector. Public corporations are answerable to the national government, which sets its financial targets and budgets, whereas public limited companies are answerable to shareholders (i.e., owners) and run by a board of directors. Public limited companies do not receive funding from the government and/or taxation.

Public corporations tend to operate on a large scale and so benefit from economies of scale. Over time, the number of public corporations in many countries have reduced as governments have privatised them. **Privatisation** is the transfer of an organisation, industry or service from public to private ownership. Privatisation is the opposite of nationalisation and often aims to increase efficiency and reduce the government financial support required.

KEY TERMS

public corporations: organisations that are owned by the government/state to provide a specific service but aim to break even and generate a large proportion of income from fees and/or taxation.

break even: reach a point where the business is not making a profit or a loss. The total costs are equal to the total revenue generated.

privatisation: where an organisation, industry or service transfers from public to private ownership.

Reasons for public corporations

Public corporations provide important public services in the country that they operate. Sometimes the services would not be financially viable to offer in any other way, since a private sector enterprise would not be able to make enough profit. Public corporations are large organisations and often benefit from economies of scale. The cost savings from the large-scale operations can be passed on to the public in competitive pricing and/or improved services. Operating as a public corporation can also protect the public interest by ensuring that they operate in an unbiased way. Shareholders cannot influence decision-making for financial gain. Planning and coordination of services can be easier as the government will oversee the operation.

The appropriateness of different types of ownership in given situations

Section 2.1.1 has introduced a range of different types of private and public sector enterprises. Each type of ownership has specific advantages and disadvantages and no types of ownership is best for all situations. The appropriateness varies depending upon the context, including:

- aims and objectives of the business, i.e., to provide a public service or make a profit for owners
- the number of owners and their attitude to risk
- the type of product sold and/or industry
- the size of the business and scale of operations.

The appropriateness can also change over time, for instance, someone may set up a new business as a sole trader, but as the business grows the **entrepreneur** (an owner that sets up a new business) may feel that a partnership or a private limited company is more appropriate. When choosing a type of ownership, it is important to think about the context and the relative advantages and disadvantages of each type of ownership to help identify the most appropriate type.

KEY TERM

entrepreneur: an owner that sets up a new business.

ACTIVITY 2.1.2

You and three of your classmates have decided to set up a small café business as an ordinary partnership. Discuss the answers to the following questions with three of your classmates.

a Agree a type of business to set up and describe the goods/services that you will offer.

b Identify three decisions that you need to agree on before you start the business.

c Explain two advantages of setting up the café as a partnership.

d Analyse two disadvantages of running the café as a partnership.

2.1.3 Multinational companies in the global economy

Multinational companies – also known as multinationals – typically have a head office in one country with operational facilities in other countries. They have investment, i.e., offices or factories, outside the home country.

Multinationals tend to be large public limited companies, often with thousands of employees in multiple countries.

Key decisions and operations are managed from the head office. This is known as a centralised structure. Multinationals have to operate in accordance with the laws of the countries where they are located. However, often they are so large that they can influence the government of that country, with implications for local businesses who compete with them in the country. This influence is often viewed as unfair by local businesses and many multinational companies have received negative coverage as a consequence.

However, the investment made by multinational companies can also be beneficial for the host country as they may enable infrastructure improvements to support the operation of their business, with benefits for other businesses and local residents. They often employ large numbers of local people who may be trained by the multinational company, which upskills them (i.e. teaches them additional skills). Local businesses may also form part of their supply chain, which may help them to expand and boost performance. The additional work means that the businesses that supply the multinational will need to employ more people. These employees can then spend their salaries to buy goods and services from other businesses. These businesses will then benefit from increased sales and expansion. In this way, the multinational company's investment helps businesses and the area generally. The investment will lead to greater economic prosperity in the country.

Often multinationals adapt their products to meet the local needs of customers in other countries. McDonald's is a well-known multinational company. McDonald's menus are often customised to the needs of the various countries it operates within. For example, it adapts its menu to suit the tastes of its Chinese market, as it recognised that Chinese customers have different preferences to those of the US and Europe. Having operations in different countries enables multinational companies to adapt to local customer needs, as the products for that specific market can be produced in that country. This benefits the business with higher sales. Operations in each country can run independently to those in other countries if required.

Alternatively, some multinationals organise manufacturing across several countries by concentrating one aspect of production in each country. For example, raw materials may be supplied in one country, while various components could be made in other countries, before assembling the final product in another country. This product may then be sold in other countries. The multinational business will make decisions about the best country to focus on for each aspect of production, according to:

- the type of raw material (as some materials can only be grown in certain climates)
- the skills of workforce in each country
- whether the product is bulk gaining or bulk reducing.

Some products are known as bulk-gaining as they become larger, heavy and bulkier as they are produced, so the producer may wish to carry out the final stages of production near to the final customer, to reduce transportation of the final product, e.g., cars (Figure 2.1.3). Other products are bulk-reducing, which means that the product becomes smaller, lighter and less bulky as it is produced, so it is better to locate production nearer to the suppliers of raw materials and transport the finished product to the customer, e.g., beer.

As the multinational business has operations in the other countries, it can protect itself from risks such as **exchange rate** fluctuations and trade barriers, which can affect profitability. An exchange rate is the price of one country's currency expressed in terms of another country's currency. To protect itself from these risks, the multinational business will make and sell products within the host country to avoid importing and exporting. However, if the multinational organises manufacturing across many countries, it will still be exposed to the risks. Many transactions involve converting currencies. For example a German company purchases equipment from a British supplier for GBP500 000. If the exchange rate is GBP1 = EUR1.20, the cost to the German company in euros would be EUR600 000 (GBP500 000 × 1.20).

Figure 2.1.3: Cars are an example of a bulk-gaining product

KEY TERM

exchange rate: the price of one country's currency expressed in terms of another country's currency.

There are numerous well-known multinational companies that operate in lots of industries (see examples in Table 2.1.7).

Industry	Examples of multinationals
Accountancy	Ernst & Young, KPMG, PricewaterhouseCoopers
Automotive	Toyota, Ford, Volkswagen, Honda
Confectionery	Mars, Nestle, Cadbury
Household products	Procter & Gamble, Unilever
Mobile technology	Nokia, Samsung, Apple, Huawei Technologies
Oil	British Petroleum, ExxonMobil, Royal Dutch Shell
Pharmaceuticals	Pfizer, AstraZeneca
Soft drinks	Coca-Cola, Pepsi
Sportswear	Adidas, Nike, Puma
Technology	Facebook, Google, Microsoft

Table 2.1.7: Examples of multinational companies and the industry that they operate in

The positive and negative impacts on a country of multinational companies locating there

Multinational companies can affect the **host country** in lots of ways. Some impacts are positive but others are negative. Table 2.1.8 summarises the positive and negative impacts.

How multinationals benefit the host country	Potential drawbacks from multinationals for the host country
Jobs are created for local people to work within the multinational's operations in the country. This can reduce unemployment in the country and/or create different jobs with the opportunity to learn new skills. The new jobs will boost the spending power of the multinational's employees and they will be able to buy more products from other businesses in the country. This creates indirect benefits from the investment. Taxes are paid by the multinational to the host country's government, which it can use to enhance public services within the country. Local businesses may form part of the multinational business's supply chain, which provides more business for the local enterprises, which could result in further job creation. The infrastructure surrounding the multinational's operations may be enhanced, e.g., new roads built and improved telecommunications. Other businesses and local residents will also benefit from the enhanced infrastructure and new short-term jobs will be created to build the infrastructure.	Multinationals may hire existing employees/managers from operations in other countries, which limits new job creation for local workers. Any jobs that are offered to local workers may be lower paid. Often multinationals receive incentives from the host government to encourage them to locate in the specific country, e.g., grants and subsidies. Once the incentives end, the multinational may decide to relocate elsewhere, which could leave unemployment and deprivation, i.e. people not being able to afford to buy items that are necessary to live. The multinational may move capital and profits around the world via their complex accounting systems, which may reduce the tax paid to the host government. Some multinationals ensure that their tax liability falls in the country with the most attractive tax rates. The multinational will have operations in different countries and its supply chain may be limited to trading with its subsidiaries/operations in other countries. This will limit the benefit for local suppliers. Some multinationals are accused of consuming local resources and exploiting local employees with low wage rates. There have also been examples of the use of child labour and polluting the local area, which harms the local environment. The multinational may be larger than the government of the host country and can influence decision-making unfairly. This influence may disadvantage local businesses in the country. The multinational will create competition for local businesses, which may struggle to compete. The multinational may operate on a larger scale and benefit from economies of scale.

Table 2.1.8: The positive and negative impacts on a host country of multinational companies locating in the country

> **KEY TERM**
>
> **host country:** the country where the multinational company locates. The country hosts the multinational company.

2.1.4 Franchises

Franchising is a popular type of private sector enterprise. A **franchise** is where one business (known as the **franchisee**) buys the right to operate under the brand name of another business (the **franchisor**). For instance, the franchisee pays McDonald's a fee to operate its business under the McDonald's brand name.

KEY TERMS

franchise: an arrangement where one business buys the right to operate under the brand name of another business. Franchises are operated in the private sector.

franchisee: the business that has bought the right to operate under the brand name of another business.

franchisor: the business that owns the franchise and grants a licence to the franchisee to operate under its brand name and use its business format in return for a fee.

Many well-known fast-food restaurants, such as Subway, Taco Bell and Burger King, are franchises (Figure 2.1.4). Although fast-food franchises are very common, franchises also operate in a range of other industries, such as hairdressing (Toni & Guy), coffee shops (Costa Coffee) and convenience stores (Spar). While some franchises, such as the examples mentioned here, are large international businesses with franchises in different countries, others are very small and might only operate in one country, or in one town or area.

Figure 2.1.4: Pizza Hut is an example of a franchise

Operating a business as a franchisee

Many entrepreneurs choose to become a franchisee and run a business under the brand name of the franchise business. It involves running a business using an existing idea and brand name. A franchisor (the owner of the brand/business idea) sells the right to operate the business/business idea under their brand to the franchisee (entrepreneur/another business).

The franchisee typically pays the franchisor a fee to set up the franchise, which can be expensive depending upon the type of franchise. They also have to follow the rules set by the franchisor. These rules often cover many aspects of running the business, such as décor of the premises, staff uniforms, prices and product range, to ensure a 'standardised' experience for customers. This means that the franchisee has less freedom to make their own operational business decisions than they would if running an independent business. For this reason, franchising is not suitable for all people looking to start their own enterprise, especially those doing so for independence. The franchisor is responsible for making all the key business decisions. Every year, the franchisee has to pay a percentage of their profits, known as a **royalty fee,** to the franchisor. This can reduce the amount of profits available for the franchisee business and/or **retained profits** for future investment. Retained profit is profit kept back for use in the business and not paid out to the owners or shareholders as dividends.

The franchisee is an independent business in its own right. The franchisee has to set up its own business and needs to choose the type of ownership that it feels is most appropriate, such as a sole trader, partnership or private limited company.

KEY TERMS

royalty fee: the share of profits made by the franchisee that is paid each year to the franchisor.

retained profit: profit kept back for use in the business and not paid out to the owners or shareholders as dividends.

TIP

Remember: a franchise is not a true form of business ownership as it can be owned and run as a sole trader, partnership or private limited company.

In return for the set-up fee, the franchisee will receive training from the franchisor to learn how to operate according to its business model. They will also be able to access support from the franchisor if any problems arise.

Many entrepreneurs choose to start a franchise if they have not run a business in the past, as the franchisor will guide them through the process of starting the business so they are less likely to make mistakes.

Most new businesses find the first few years of trading challenging as customers are unaware of their brand name and products. It can take years to gain loyal customers. Starting a new business is very risky and a high proportion of new businesses fail to survive the first five years. However, starting a franchise reduces the risk of failure because the brand name is already known by customers. There will be loyal customers who will support the new franchise business from the opening. This means that the franchisee is likely to make more sales revenue than they would if they had operated under a new brand name.

Operating a business as a franchisor

Many successful businesses have quickly expanded by selling franchise opportunities to other businesses. The franchisor will have developed a profitable business model and popular brand name over time. Franchising enables the business to expand quickly by offering the franchisee the opportunity to operate under its brand name. The franchisee must pay the set-up costs so the franchisor does not have to generate the capital needed to expand. The franchisee will also pay a set-up fee to the franchisor to buy the right to operate under its brand name and instructions of how to operate the business model. Receiving this set-up fee will increase the income into the franchisor's business.

Selling franchise opportunities is a less risky way of expanding overseas. The franchisee will typically be based in the overseas country and will have detailed knowledge of the market, culture and customer preferences. The franchisee will also be responsible for carrying out market research and developing a business plan to apply to become a franchisee, so the franchisor will know the financial projections and likely success of the proposed franchise business. The franchisor will only accept applications from franchisees who demonstrate that they can operate a successful and profitable business.

The franchisor will receive a share of the profits made by the franchisee's business each year. The royalty fee paid will provide a source of additional income for the franchisor.

However, trusting a franchisee to operate the business appropriately can be risky. The franchisor's business name is at risk if the franchisee is unsuccessful or makes a bad decision. The franchisor's business reputation could be damaged by the actions of the franchisee. It is therefore important to carefully review applications from franchisees to ensure that they will operate the franchise business appropriately. Many franchisors have strict criteria for becoming a franchisee.

The franchisor also has to provide training and support for the franchisee, which can be time consuming and expensive.

The advantages and disadvantages of franchises

There are many advantages and disadvantages of starting a business as a franchisee, which are summarised in Table 2.1.9.

Advantages of operating an enterprise as a franchisee	Disadvantages of operating an enterprise as a franchisee
There is a greater chance of success as the business brand/name is already known.	Many important decisions will be made by the franchisor.
The franchisee is supported by the franchisor, e.g., advice and activities coordinated by head office, such as national marketing.	The franchisee has to follow the rules of the franchisor, e.g., using specific suppliers.
The franchisor may offer training.	It can be expensive to set up.
Limited business knowledge is required by the franchisee as they follow the franchisor's business model.	A proportion of the profits made each year must be paid to the franchisor (royalty fee).
The franchisee may be able to network and liaise with other franchisees.	
After paying the royalty fee, the franchisee can keep the remaining profit.	

Table 2.1.9: Advantages and disadvantages of operating an enterprise as a franchisee

Table 2.1.10 summarises the advantages and disadvantages of expanding an enterprise by selling franchise opportunities. The advantages and disadvantages are from the perspective of the franchisor.

Advantages of expanding an enterprise by selling franchise opportunities (becoming a franchisor)	Disadvantages of expanding an enterprise by selling franchise opportunities (becoming a franchisor)
It is a less risky way of expanding into new countries as they can benefit from the franchisee's local knowledge. The franchisee is responsible for paying the start-up costs so less capital is needed. It can be a quick way to expand a business. The franchisor can charge a high set-up fee. They will receive a share of the profits each year (royalty fee). They maintain control of how the business is run as important decisions are made by the franchisor.	It can be high risk if the franchisee makes a decision that damages the franchisor's business reputation/brand name. The franchisor has to provide training and support.

Table 2.1.10: Advantages and disadvantages of expanding an enterprise by selling franchise opportunities

2.1.5 Physical and ecommerce location factors

The decision of where to locate a business is one of the most important. Finding the right location will help the business to prosper and become very successful. However, choosing the wrong location can lead to the business failing. **Business location** decisions can affect the amount of revenue generated and the costs of operating the enterprise. Globalisation means that businesses can now choose to locate anywhere in the world, as many of the barriers that once restricted location decisions no longer apply. The removal of these barriers has encouraged businesses to move to different countries.

KEY TERM

business location: a place or structure occupied by an enterprise to run its operations. This includes any building or site used in the operation of the business.

There are many factors that can influence the location of a business. Often a combination of factors must be considered when choosing a business location. The factors can be divided into two groups:

- physical location factors
- ecommerce location factors.

Physical location factors

Figure 2.1.5 summarises some of the physical location factors.

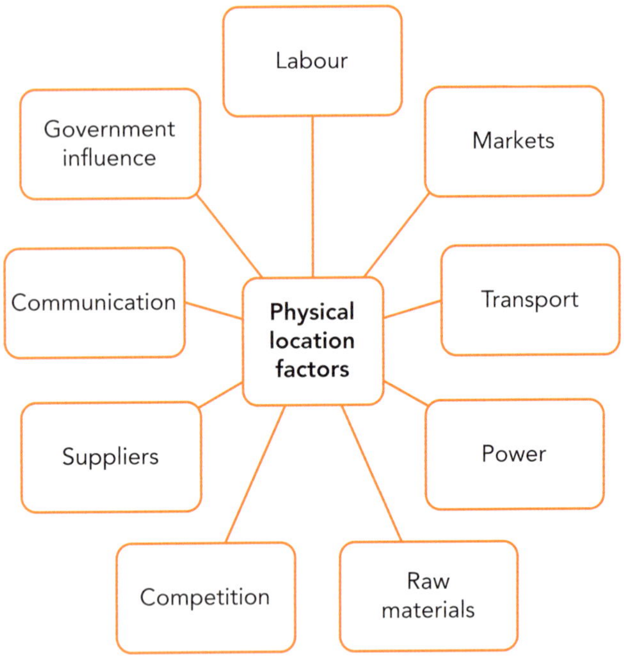

Figure 2.1.5: Physical location factors

Labour

Most businesses need to employ people to operate the business. The business needs to consider if there is an adequate supply of suitable employees in the area to employ. Unemployment levels can affect the supply of labour. In areas of high unemployment there will be more people looking for work so it may be easier to employ workers. However, the people looking for work may not be suitable. Many businesses need skilled labour to produce their products. The business therefore needs to consider if there are enough people in the area with suitable skills, qualifications and experience. Sometimes businesses locate in areas where similar businesses are already based because there are more likely to be people in the area with the required skills. This is one of the reasons why businesses in certain industries cluster together in some areas.

The business may train people in the local area with the skills needed. They could work with local colleges or other education providers to develop courses. This may take time but will increase the supply of suitable labour. Some multinationals transfer employees from other locations to help set up and manage new branches. They may employ a mix of existing employees and new employees. The existing employees can develop the new employees by sharing their knowledge and experience.

However, the impact of technology has reduced the importance of people living near to their employer. Some job roles can be performed by people who work from home. Home-based employees may rarely visit the work location and can live long distances away. They could even work for a business located in a different country. This can help businesses find employees with highly specialist skills who may not live in the area that the business is based. The relative importance of whether qualified people live near to the business or not can vary depending on the nature of work.

A high proportion of the costs to operate a business are often labour costs. Salary levels in the area also need to be considered. Salary levels can vary significantly across the regions of a country. Likewise, average salaries differ in different countries. For instance, average annual salary levels in Mexico, Slovakia and Hungary are about one-quarter of the levels in countries such as the United States, Iceland, Luxembourg and Switzerland (OECD, 2022). The business may decide to locate in an area where labour costs are cheaper to reduce the costs of production.

ACTIVITY 2.1.3

Use the internet to research how wage and salary levels vary around the world. Investigate how the salary levels in your country compare with another five countries of your choice. Present your findings in a chart and explain how the findings may influence a business's location decisions.

Markets

Being near to potential customers is important for many businesses, especially a retail business. Retailers need to consider if the people in the area are likely to buy the products that they sell. For instance, a luxury retailer selling high-priced non-essential products is unlikely to do well in an area of high unemployment and deprivation. People living in the area are less able to afford to buy the products sold. When choosing a suitable location, many businesses think about the demographics and local economic conditions to predict the number of potential customers. They may use data and statistics to evaluate the profile of the area.

However, retailing is increasingly being made online, so the importance of location to retail businesses is changing. Rather than placing a shop in the correct location to attract customers in the local area, it is often more important for retailers to locate their warehouses close to good transport facilities so that goods ordered online can be delivered promptly to customers.

Proximity to the market is also important for other service providers, such as care homes and hairdressers, so customers can easily and conveniently access the services.

Bulk-gaining manufacturers also need to locate near to customers to reduce transportation costs. It is cheaper to transport the less bulky raw materials and components to the factory than it is to transport the bulkier finished product.

Transport

The business needs to consider the roads, railways, airports and ports in the area. Depending on the nature of the product, some transport types will be more important than others. Transport links are important to keep the costs of transporting raw materials and finished products as low as possible. The ease of accessing the transport systems is very important. Locations close to good transport links are highly demanded, which can affect the cost of land/buildings.

Good transport links are essential for businesses. Many businesses locate their warehouses close to good transport facilities so that goods can be delivered promptly to stores and/or customers. Delivery times are important, and delivering the product quicker than competitors can give the business a competitive advantage.

Transport links to support employees to access the business location should also be researched. Good road links and public transport is needed if a large number of employees are required to access the business premises each day. Some businesses operate minibuses to get their employees to the workplace each day if the location is rural and/or inaccessible.

Power

Electricity is important to operate all equipment needed to run any business. Power is needed to light the building and operate any machinery/technology. The cost of energy varies across the world. Utilities such as gas and electricity prices are different in different countries. The utilities needed to operate businesses can vary according to the product and type of operation. For instance, aluminium smelting, the process of extracting aluminium, consumes a lot of energy. Businesses involved in aluminium smelting may be forced to locate in countries with inexpensive sources of energy.

Raw materials

Many businesses rely on specific raw materials to produce products, especially manufacturers. The cost of transporting some raw materials to a factory for processing may be very high, especially if they are bulky raw materials. Bulk-reducing manufacturers often locate near to suppliers of raw materials to reduce the cost of transporting. It is cheaper to transport the finished product to the customer as the final product is less bulky.

The waste products of one business may be the raw materials for another. To support **sustainability**, the business may locate close to businesses that can make appropriate use of its waste products to reduce waste disposal costs. For instance, some of the waste from Unilever's manufacturing processes can be reused as animal feed. Sustainability is about maintaining an ecological balance by avoiding the exhaustion of natural resources.

KEY TERM

bulk-gaining manufacturer: a business that manufactures a product that becomes heavier and/or larger as it is made. The final product is heavier and/or larger than the materials/components used to make it.

sustainability: the long-term goal of maintaining an ecological balance by avoiding the exhaustion of natural resources.

Competition

Competition can have a direct impact on the likely success of the business. Setting up a retail business near retailers selling similar items should be avoided unless the business can offer something different. Areas of high competition are less desirable for a retailer as they will find it challenging to attract customers. The competitors may be established with loyal customers, so entering the market may be difficult.

However, some manufacturers may prefer to locate near to competing businesses as there will be a greater number of people in the area with the skills that they need. The colleges and education providers in the area may offer courses to equip people with relevant specialist skills.

Suppliers

Suppliers are critical to the operations of many businesses. Suppliers offer raw materials and components for production. The cost of transporting some raw materials to a factory for processing may be very high, especially if they are bulky raw materials. Bulk-reducing manufacturers often locate near to suppliers of raw materials to reduce the cost of transporting. It is cheaper to transport the finished product to the customer, as the final product is less bulky. In contrast, bulk-gaining manufacturers are less concerned about locating near to suppliers and try to locate close to customers instead.

Some businesses operate just-in-time (JIT) manufacturing systems whereby supplies are ordered to arrive just as needed for production. JIT manufacturers do not hold stock (or only hold limited stock) of raw materials. This system relies on a close relationship with suppliers, and locating close to suppliers is beneficial to enable materials to be delivered quickly if required. JIT manufacturers may choose to locate near to suppliers for this reason.

Communication

Communication systems include Information and Communication Technology (ICT) infrastructure, such as broadband links and other telecommunications networks. These are important for communications with other sites and businesses they work with. Mobile coverage must be researched, as the mobile signal strength can vary within and between countries.

Government influence

Often the national or local government may wish to influence where businesses locate. They may encourage new businesses in areas of high unemployment and low incomes to improve the local economic conditions. The government may offer grants and/or subsidies to businesses locating to certain areas. This gives the businesses a financial incentive to locate there. This type of government intervention is common in areas where a large employer may have closed and there are high numbers of former employees looking for work. The skills and experiences of these employees may be specialised and only relevant for the type of work that they previously carried out.

Most businesses need to gain planning permission to set up a new business. This can be a lengthy process and local residents have the opportunity to object. However, the government may speed up planning application procedures in certain areas. This can reduce the time and cost of setting up a new business.

The government may also invest in upgrading the infrastructure in the area to attract new businesses. Businesses need fast broadband, so installing superfast broadband can make it easier for them to operate.

The government may offer financial incentives to businesses that employ people who may struggle to find employment. These incentives make these people more attractive to employers and support them to become financially independent to boost the economy. For instance, some governments offer grants to businesses who employ people who have been unemployed for a long period of time.

Ecommerce location factors

Ecommerce businesses are increasing rapidly in number and they have different location considerations that include:

- Wi-Fi
- warehousing
- technology specialists
- logistics.

Wi-Fi

Wi-Fi is important as many ecommerce enterprises rely on it to operate. Superfast broadband is needed in the area, so businesses must consider this when choosing where to locate. Broadband problems could stop operations, which could cost the business a significant amount of money. Broadband speeds must be researched before making a location decision to ensure adequate speeds and reliability.

Warehousing

Many ecommerce retailers have large warehouses to stock all of the products offered. The warehouses are sometimes called distribution centres, but they perform the same function. Ecommerce retailers sell products 24/7. It can be challenging to predict future demand, so most retailers keep a certain level of stock of each product to be able to fulfil orders efficiently. Customers want products to be delivered quickly after ordering. Quick delivery of items is an important competitive advantage.

Once the customers place the order, the details of the product go straight to the warehouse so that it can be picked. Customers can only order products that are in-stock as the warehouse stock levels are checked by the order system. Locating the product in a large warehouse can be challenging, so using technology, such as robots, to pick the order is essential. Order picking has moved from a **labour intensive** (where production relies mainly on labour) to a **capital intensive** (where production relies mainly on capital) process in many ecommerce businesses.

> **KEY TERMS**
>
> **labour intensive:** where production relies mainly on labour, i.e., employees.
>
> **capital intensive:** where production relies mainly on capital, i.e., technology, machinery, robots.

The warehouse ensures that stock is stored safely and securely. It protects the products from getting perished by severe weather conditions.

Ecommerce warehouses can be large. One of Amazon's many distribution centres is at Tilbury near London and occupies an area of 2 million square feet. Gaining planning permission for such large buildings can be challenging as local people may fear that it will spoil the local landscape. Warehouses are typically located near to good transport links, including roads, rail, airports and ports to support the distribution of orders. Warehouses often have lorries arriving and leaving 24 hours per day, so are often located away from residential areas.

Technology specialists

Warehouses are automated with use of technology such as robots to pick and pack orders for customers. Modern warehouses employ relatively few employees as the work is capital intensive. Thousands of robots navigate the warehouse aisles using QR codes on the floor, helping employees pick items ready for dispatch.

Technology specialists need to be employed to develop and maintain the IT systems used. A fault can occur at any time, and it is important that technical support is available to fix the issue promptly. IT system problems could stop operations, and every minute that the system is down can cost the business thousands in lost revenue.

Logistics

Logistics is the functional area that plans and fulfils the efficient transportation and storage of goods from the manufacturer/warehouse to the customer. Logistics is important for ecommerce enterprises to deliver the product to the customer. Some businesses operate the logistics function in-house whereas others outsource to external contractors.

The ecommerce enterprise may wish to locate near to the external contractor's depot so that parcels can be collected quickly to dispatch to customers. Sometimes the contractor may set up a base at the business's premises so that it can work in close partnership.

Logistics is important as enterprises wish to deliver the order to the customer in the most cost-effective way. Delivery routes are carefully planned to help drivers move through the addresses efficiently by reducing the miles travelled.

The appropriateness of physical and ecommerce location factors

This section has covered a range of location factors. The relative importance of each location factor varies according to the context, including the:

- type of product sold and/or industry
- type of work carried out by employees
- operating environment of the country.

The different factors will affect the appropriateness of the business's location. Choosing a location is a key decision for all businesses. However, the relative importance of the factors can vary depending upon whether the business trades via ecommerce. Businesses that sell products online only do not have to consider the proximity to the market and accessibility for customers has much as a business that sells products from a shop. Ecommerce businesses often choose cheaper premises away from busy urban areas. Whereas proximity to the market is an important consideration for a business selling from a physical shop as if the shop is not easily accessible for customers it is unlikely to sell many products.

Communication factors, such as ICT infrastructure, are likely to be more important for a business operating via ecommerce. The business will rely on broadband to communicate and sell its products to customers. If the broadband is unreliable the business would not be able to sell any products during that time. The business may lose sales as customers may buy from more reliable competitors instead. However, communication factors are less important for businesses that sell from a shop as transactions are done face-to-face; so, even if the broadband did not work, the business could still sell products.

The relative importance of each factor can also change over time. For instance, a physical retailer may start to sell products online, which means that many of the ecommerce location factors become more important.

2.1.6 The growth of outsourcing

As you learned in Chapter 1.2, production can be performed in different ways. Some businesses keep the production of products in-house, which means that all tasks/activities are completed internally within the business itself. Alternatively, some businesses use outsourcing, which means that another business carries out the tasks/activities on behalf of the business.

Businesses are increasingly outsourcing aspects of production and operations.

Contract manufacturing

Contract manufacturing is a type of outsourcing. Sometimes a business is offered a one-off order or faces a sudden increase in demand for regular customers. However, the business may be operating at full capacity and may be unable to increase production. The business may therefore decide to find another business that can meet the additional demand and/or a one-off order. Outsourcing manufacturing in this way is called contract manufacturing.

KEY TERM

contract manufacturing: where a manufacturer contracts with another business for the production of components or products. It is a form of outsourcing.

The need for increased capacity may be seasonal or of a one-off nature, so the business's managers may feel that it is not worth expanding the factory as the resources would be under-utilised for the majority of the time. For example, increased demand may be linked to a season and last for two months of the year. The additional resources would be under-utilised for the other ten months, which represents 83% of the year (10 months out of the 12 months the resources will be under-utilised), which would be inefficient.

Instead of outsourcing the manufacturing of the product, some manufacturers may outsource the packaging or other element of the preparation of the final product for sale. In this instance, the manufacturer will produce the product in-house and then outsource the final packaging to another business.

Logistics

Logistics are outsourced by a growing number of businesses, especially ecommerce enterprises. Ecommerce enterprises can receive orders from customers globally and they may work with a network of delivery companies/couriers to deliver the order to the customer efficiently and quickly.

The company employed represents the business. If the product is delivered late or is damaged, it can negatively affect the business's reputation. The customer knows that the delivery company/courier is employed by the business they ordered from and expects them to oversee the quality of the delivery. Poor delivery experiences from appointed contractors is the source of many online post-purchase customer reviews.

Cost considerations

Sometimes the prices charged by the contractor are higher than in-house production, since the contractor needs to make a profit from the goods or services supplied too. However, the business may decide to pay the higher price as the quality that the contractor can offer may be better, or it might be that outsourcing avoids the need to coordinate the task in-house, which will save the business time, resources and effort. However, sometimes the prices charged by the contractor are cheaper than the cost of producing the goods or services in-house. This could be because of the benefits of economies of scale. The contractor may be a specialist in the production of the good or service so will produce a high volume of the good. They could also have access to specialist equipment, technology and employ skilled employees, which can help lower the unit cost. All of these factors increase the efficiency of the contractor's operations, reducing the cost of production. Additionally, the contractor may benefit from lower prices from their supplier due to the high quantity of raw materials that they buy.

Successful outsourcing relies on a detailed contract to outline the responsibilities of each partner. This is important because the quality of the products produced will impact on the reputation of the business appointing the contractor.

SELF-EVALUATION CHECKLIST

After studying this chapter, complete this table.

You should know about:	Needs more work	Almost there	Ready to move on
the distinction between private and public sector enterprises			
the features of different types of private sector enterprises			
the key aspects and aims of public corporations			
the suitability of different types of ownership in given situations			
the features of multinational companies			
why multinationals exist in the global economy			
the impact of multinational companies locating in a country			
the features of franchises			
the pros and cons of franchises			
physical and ecommerce location factors			
the suitability of physical and ecommerce location factors in given situations			
the development of outsourcing, including contract manufacturing and logistics			

Knowledge check

1 Identify three advantages for the franchisor of expanding its business by selling franchise opportunities.

2 Explain two features of a cooperative.

3 Analyse three disadvantages of operating a business as a public limited company.

4 Explain the difference between a private and public limited company.

5 Explain three drawbacks to a host country of a multinational business locating a factory in the country.

6 Which of the following is an advantage of operating the business as a partnership?

a It may take longer to make decisions.

b Profit must be shared amongst partners.

c Workload and decision-making shared.

d There is unlimited liability.

7 Who is the owner of a public limited company?

a dividend

b government

c partner

d shareholder

8 Which of the following location factors is most likely to be of greatest importance for an ecommerce enterprise?

a competition

b raw materials

c suppliers

d warehousing

9 An organisation owned by the government belongs to the:
   a public sector
   b private sector
   c shareholders
   d mixed economy.

10 A product is packaged for a manufacturer by a contractor. This arrangement is known as:
   a a cooperative
   b contract manufacturing
   c franchising
   d logistics.

Practice questions

1 a Define the term 'multinational'. [2]
   b State two reasons for public corporations. [2]
   c Jason runs a small website-design business as a sole trader. The business is very successful and Jason would like to expand. He enjoys operating as a sole trader due to the benefits that this type of enterprise offers. However, he is thinking of converting to a partnership with his friend Remi. Recommend if Jason should convert his business to a partnership. Give reasons for your opinion. [6]
   d State four positive impacts of a multinational company on a host country. [4]

2 a Define the term 'limited liability'. [2]
   b State four benefits of running a business as a private limited company. [4]
   c Nasreen has always wanted to run her own business and is thinking of starting a vegan food restaurant. She has not run a business in the past. She can either set up a restaurant on her own or become a franchisee of Fresh Vegan Food. Which option is best for Nasreen? Give reasons for your opinion. [8]

Fresh Vegan Food

Want to start your own restaurant?

Run your own Fresh Vegan Food restaurant.
900 000 INR

Royalty fee of 25% of annual profits made

Support provided

Visit our website for more information

Chapter 2.2

Retailing and wholesaling

LEARNING INTENTIONS

In this chapter, you will learn:

- the different types of retailers, both small scale and large scale
- the features, advantages and disadvantages of each retailer type
- why small-scale retailers survive
- selling techniques used in retail
- digital retail trends
- the effects of ecommerce on traditional commerce
- the purpose and significance of wholesalers
- why independent wholesalers survive.

2.2.1 Supply chain

A product will move through various stages as it moves through the supply chain, e.g., from the producer or manufacturer to the consumer. Several businesses may support the product's journey to the consumer and perform key activities, including storage and providing guidance to the customer regarding the product. These businesses include the retailer, who typically sells the product to the consumer. Often the retailer is different to the producer, although in some cases it can be the same business. Wholesalers also form part of the supply chain. A wholesaler is a person or business that buys products in large quantities from suppliers (often the manufacturer of the product) and sells them to retailers and/or other businesses in smaller quantities.

2.2.2 Retailing

A retailer buys products from a manufacturer or wholesaler to sell on to consumers. The retailer is therefore between the manufacturer or wholesaler and the consumer in the supply chain.

Retailers sell products in different ways, including:

- itinerant retailing with no fixed location
- vending machines
- physical shops
- online stores.

Itinerant retailers

Itinerant retailers are retailers with no fixed location, such as hawkers, pedlars or street market traders. The retailer will move around periodically, sometimes several times during a day. They sell their products in relatively small quantities to the final consumer. As they move location, they usually have limited stock for logistical reasons. It is not practical to move large quantities of inventory.

Pedlars and hawkers

Pedlars and hawkers are mobile and carry the goods they sell (Figure 2.2.1). Pedlars and hawkers are similar, but a pedlar will carry the goods they sell on their head or back whereas a hawker will carry the goods using a cart or the back of an animal. They sell in the street, from house to house or at busy locations such as a railway station. The types of goods sold are limited as they need to be easy to carry, such as household goods and toys. Most countries have laws that control their operations although people often work illegally. Laws can help to ensure that the retailer is not selling in an unsuitable location or likely to cause problems for other people or businesses in the area. The laws aim to prevent illegal activity, such as the sale of dangerous or banned products.

Figure 2.2.1: Pedlars and hawkers are mobile and sell their goods in a range of different locations

Roadside services/traders

Some people work outside shops to provide services to customers such as cutting hair (Figure 2.2.2), repairing/cleaning or making clothes. These retailers are most common in African, Asian and Eastern European countries.

Figure 2.2.2: Barber services may be provided by a roadside trader

Mobile shops

Mobile shops bring their products to the consumer in specially adapted vans, buses or small trucks (Figure 2.2.3). This type of retailer travels to different locations, such as housing developments, car parks or festivals and events. The type of good sold varies. Examples of mobile shop retailers include ice cream and fast-food sellers; milk sellers making daily deliveries to households in the UK or butchers in Italy and Germany. Sandwich vans serving employees who work on industrial estates in the UK are popular.

Figure 2.2.3: Many mobile shops sell food and drinks at a range of locations

Street market/retail market traders

Markets are popular and may be permanent or held at a regular time, such as a weekly market in a town centre. Some markets are annual events, such as the Christmas markets in many European countries. Markets can be open-air or covered. A range of stall holders will operate in the market, so customers can choose from a variety of products, which are often different from those sold in the shops. Foodstuffs such as vegetables (Figure 2.2.4), bakery, meat and fish are often popular alongside handmade items, clothing and household goods.

Figure 2.2.4: Buying fruit and vegetables from a street market stall

ACTIVITY 2.2.1

Carry out research into the different types of itinerant retailers in your area that do not operate from a fixed location.

You should present your findings as a poster or a set of slides. Illustrate your work with pictures/photos to show the different types of itinerant retailers.

What are the advantages to the retailer and consumer of not operating from a fixed location?

Pop-up retail

Pop-up retail is a growing trend where displays or small stalls operate for a short period of time in a variety of places, including vacant shop premises, the centre of a town/city or inside a shopping mall. These pop-up displays/stalls may run from one day up to a couple of months. They are temporary in structure. They may sell seasonal items, such as calendars or Christmas stock, or may coincide with another event/activity occurring. For example, a clothing retailer may have a pop-up stall in a shopping mall while the mall hosts a fashion event.

Vending machines

Goods can be sold from self-service machines, which are known as vending machines. The machines are found in busy areas with lots of people walking by, including airports, railway stations, schools/colleges and leisure centres. The range of goods sold are often convenience items, such as hot/cold drinks, chocolates, sweets, crisps and toiletries (Figure 2.2.5). Vending machines that sell tickets are often found in railway and bus stations, so customers can buy tickets without having to visit the cashier. Stamps are also sold from vending machines outside some post offices.

Figure 2.2.5: A range of different products are sold from vending machines

Physical shops

Many retailers sell goods and services from shops. The shop building can vary. The following sections consider a range of different retailers with shops.

Independent retailers

An independent retailer is a retailer that is responsible for their own business. They are not part of a franchise or chain with other branches of the same brand. Independent retailers are often **small-scale retailers** with only one branch. They may be run by a family and operate as a sole trader or partnership. These retailers are increasingly popular as consumers seek unique alternatives to the mass-market products sold by larger retailers.

> **KEY TERM**
>
> **small-scale retailer:** a retailer selling goods and/or services from one outlet, branch or base.

In the UK, high streets are changing, with many large retailers moving out of the high street and relocating to larger stores in out-of-town complexes. Small-scale retailers are moving to the vacant shops, as increasingly customers are looking to support local, independent stores. Many customers are growing bored of shopping complexes and town centres looking the same and instead want the unique experience that independent retailers can often offer.

Speciality shops

These retailers sell a restricted range of goods aimed at a particular market. The goods sold will vary but could include computers, jewellery, sports equipment or art supplies. The retailer will offer personalised service. The employees will be very knowledgeable about the product type and therefore able to offer advice to customers. Specialist retailers may be independent or part of a chain of stores with multiple branches, such as Truworths and Apple.

Multiple chain stores

A multiple chain store has ten or more branches.
A chain store has less than ten branches.

There are two types of multiple chain store:

- variety chain stores, which sell a selection of different goods, such as Kingstons in Zimbabwe.
- specialist multiple chain stores, which focus on one type of product, such as Clarks, which sells footwear in many countries.

Some chain stores only operate in one country whereas others have branches in different countries.

As the retailer operates multiple stores, they can benefit from economies of scale. The retailer can buy stock in large quantities direct from the manufacturer. Due to the size of orders, the manufacturer is likely to sell goods for a lower price. Sometimes the manufacturer will produce goods just for that specific retailer, which they can sell under their own brand label.

Supermarkets

Supermarkets are large stores that sell food and other household goods. Customers can buy a variety of goods, which typically include own-brand items alongside branded goods. Supermarkets are often considered to cover at least 184 square metres, with three or more checkouts. Supermarkets offer customers a convenience as they can buy all types of goods in one store. This saves them the time of having to visit a number of specialist stores. Supermarkets often group similar products into different departments, such as fruit and vegetables, bakery products, delicatessen items, sushi and healthcare products. They also stock an increasing range of non-food items, such as clothing, household goods and electrical items.

Customers walk round the supermarket, put goods they wish to buy into a trolley or basket and pay at the checkout. Many supermarkets have introduced more self-service options in place of personal service. Technology allows customers to go to self-service checkouts to scan and pay for products without seeing a human cashier. This reduces the number of employees required and therefore labour costs.

Many supermarkets allow customers to purchase goods online. Employees then select the goods ordered from the shelves, and a delivery service delivers the items to the customer's home.

KEY TERM

self-service: the customer's selected goods are scanned and paid for by the customer themselves on unstaffed electronic tills.

Hypermarkets

Hypermarkets are similar to a supermarket but are larger in size. They typically cover a floor area of over 5000 square metres. The range of goods sold is similar to a supermarket but larger, to offer customers more choice. Hypermarkets aim to generate a high turnover of goods to make profits. Due to the volume of goods sold, hypermarkets benefit from economies of scale.

Departmental stores

These stores are large in size and provide a wide range of goods in different departments. Famous departmental stores are Meikles in Zimbabwe, Hua Ho in Brunei and Harvey Nichols in the UK. The goods are displayed in different departments or sections with dedicated staff who work in that area: for instance, cosmetics, furniture or electrical goods.

In some countries, departmental stores are becoming less popular. Large chains, such as Debenhams in the UK, have gone out of business. The cost of operating the stores is high due to the large size of store. The retailers struggle to compete with online retailers with lower operating costs.

Online retailers

Online retailers sell goods and/or services via digital methods over the internet. Some online retailers only sell goods and/or services online, whereas others sell online alongside other methods, such as through many supermarkets or speciality shops. Online retailers may be involved in different types of commerce including ecommerce, mcommerce and scommerce.

Online retailers rely on different marketing strategies. Relationships with customers can be built face-to-face with many other types of retail. Different methods are used for online operations. Many retailers set up a mailing list and email updates/latest news messages to customers so the customer stays up to date with offers and product updates. The email addresses can be collected when the customer places an order. The retailer is likely to hold a lot more personal information about their customers when they buy online than if they purchased in-store. This can be used to give the retailer a better understanding of customer behaviour and buying habits. This knowledge can help marketing staff to plan and introduce effective marketing. Data protection laws must be followed, so the retailer needs to ensure that the customer gives permission to receive the marketing emails.

Customers often do an internet search before choosing a product or retailer to buy from. Search engines are usually used to support this process, such as Google or Yahoo. Retailers are keen to be listed near the top of the search list as this will increase the chances of the customer visiting their website. Retailers focus on search engine optimisation to support ecommerce. Search engine optimisation describes actions that a business takes to improve the visibility of the website.

Due to the reduced costs of operating as an online retailer, customers may benefit from lower prices.

KEY TERMS

search engines: computer programs, such as Google, Bing and Yahoo, that help people to find specific websites or information online.

search engine optimisation: techniques to make it more likely that a particular website will appear at or near the top of the results list from an internet search.

TIP

The trends in retailing are changing rapidly. Keep up to date with changes by looking at media reports and news articles about the changes in the retail sector. There will be stories covering both a national and local area.

Advantages and disadvantages of each type of retailer

Table 2.2.1 describes the advantages and disadvantages of different types of retailer.

	Advantages	Disadvantages
Itinerant retailers	They can move location, so are able to reach a large number of customers. They can offer the goods close to the people – increased convenience. They can offer unique products.	They can only maintain a limited stock of each item and a limited range of products. They may only accept cash. They may lack after-sales service as the customer will not be able to locate them after they move.
Vending machines	They are relatively small, so can fit in small spaces, e.g., reception areas. They can advertise. Brands/products. They have limited overheads as customers serve themselves.	There is no interaction with customers so the retailer is unable to gain feedback. The business/building hosting the vending machine needs to pay rental fees for the machine, which increases costs. They may break down, leaving customers dissatisfied. Prices can be higher than other retailers.
Independent retailers	They can offer unique alternatives to the mass-market products sold by larger retailers. Customer service is normally good. They are able to react to local needs/wants.	Prices may be higher due to lack of economies of scale. The brand name will not be known outside the area. They may struggle to compete with larger retailers.
Street markets	Markets can attract large numbers of people. They can move location, so are able to reach a large number of customers. There are lower overheads than operating from a permanent building.	It is time consuming to set up and pack away the stall each day. They can only maintain a limited stock. Stock may be exposed to extreme weather if stall is outside.
Speciality shops	The retailer will be well known for the product specialism. The retailer is able to develop expertise in that area. There may be several shops under the same brand, e.g., Apple.	There is a limited product range. The retailer may target one market segment (type of customer) only, e.g. one gender or age group.

Continued

	Advantages	Disadvantages
Multiple chain stores	They can develop a well-known brand as customers may shop at different branches of the store. There are economies of scale due to the high volume of sales, which can lead to lower prices. All stores may be served from a central warehouse. Stock may be transferred between stores to meet demand.	It can be challenging to ensure a consistent service experience across branches. Customer needs may differ across a country, e.g., regional and local differences.
Supermarkets	They offer a wide range of products. There are economies of scale due to the high volume of sales, which can lead to lower prices. They may offer exclusive ranges due to relationships with producers. There are long opening hours, which offer more convenience for the customer and may result in more customers for the retailer. They may offer on-site customer car parking and/or public transport to the store, which is convenient for the customer and may mean more customers can visit the store, leading to more sales.	They are normally located in towns/cities, which means customers living outside towns/cities have to travel to the supermarket, which may be inconvenient. Customer needs may differ across a country, e.g., regional and local differences.
Hypermarkets	They offer a very wide range of products. They offer convenience, as the customer can buy a large range of products during their visit. There are economies of scale due to the high volume of sales, which can lead to lower prices. They may offer exclusive ranges due to relationships with producers. There are long opening hours, which offer more convenience for the customer and may result in more customers for the retailer. They may offer on-site customer car parking and/or public transport to the store, which is convenient for the customer and may mean more customers can visit the store, leading to more sales.	They are normally located in towns/cities, which means customers living outside towns/cities have to travel to the hypermarket, which may be inconvenient. Customer needs may differ across a country, e.g., regional and local differences. Some customers may find the store too large to navigate, especially if they only need a few items. There are high operating costs due to the size of the store.

Continued

	Advantages	Disadvantages
Departmental stores	They can offer a wide range of products – convenience for the customer. Different departments may target different market segments. They are often located centrally in the town/city. There are economies of scale due to the high volume of sales, which can lead to lower prices.	There are high operating costs due to the size of the store. They may struggle to compete with online retailers.
Online retailers	There are reduced operating costs, such as rent, as the retailer does not need physical premises. Prices online may be lower due to the lower operating costs. Some retailers offer cheaper prices for ecommerce customers compared to those buying from a shop/store. Customers can shop at any time of the day or night.	There can be high development costs for creating the website/app. It is not as easy for the customer to speak directly to the business e.g., if they have any queries about the product or need to make a complaint. Not all customers have access to the internet. Customers cannot see or touch the 'actual' product or try it on before buying it. Some products cannot be sold online, e.g., a haircut. Customers have to wait a few days to receive their goods.

Table 2.2.1: Advantages and disadvantages of each type of retailer

ACTIVITY 2.2.2

Supermarkets are found in most towns and cities. You probably have a supermarket close to where you live.

What are the advantages of buying from a supermarket for the customer and also the supermarket (retailer)?

Are there any disadvantages of buying from a supermarket for the customer and the supermarket (retailer)?

Make a list of the advantages and disadvantages in your revision notes.

REFLECTION

Think about Activity 2.2.2. What did you learn from completing the activity? Did it encourage you to think about your local supermarkets? Why is it important to think about local examples of retailers that relate to your learning? Why did the activity encourage you to relate your learning to the local retail environment – what is the benefit of applying your learning to a practical example?

Small-scale retailers' survival

Many retailers operate on a small scale. They serve a local market, in a specific geographic area.

Small-scale retailers are those with one branch or base, such as a pedlar, market stall, tourist gift shop in a seaside town or a small coffee shop. They often operate as a sole trader or partnership and are sometimes run by a family. These retailers are increasingly popular as consumers look for alternatives to mass-market products sold by larger retailers.

Small-scale retailers are able to offer personal and friendly services for customers. Customers are often loyal to the retailer and most customers are local. The retailers may offer **informal credit** to regular customers, where items bought during the week are paid for at the end of the week after the customer receives their wages. The retailer may stock specific items for particular loyal customers whom they know well. These retailers are popular with people who find it difficult to travel to larger shopping complexes, such as some elderly people or those with young children.

Small-scale businesses are often part of the community that they operate within and develop good relationships with customers/community (Figure 2.2.6). These businesses may offer **niche products** to meet the individual needs of the locality served, e.g., local food products.

KEY TERMS

informal credit: credit given by small-scale retailers to trusted customers.

niche product: a good or service aimed at a small group of customers within a market.

Figure 2.2.6: Customers buying refreshments from a local café business

The opening hours of a small-scale retailer may be flexible according to local needs. For instance, there may be a regular event in the area one evening each week and so the retailer may open late on that day to meet customer demand. Larger-scale retailers may not be able to respond to local needs in this way as employees are employed on a standard employment contract, and opening hours are decided centrally by the head office.

Small-scale retailers often struggle to compete on price with larger national and international businesses. Large-scale retailers often benefit from economies of scale, meaning that more goods can be produced at a lower cost per unit. Large-scale retailers can often reduce their prices to levels that would be unprofitable for local businesses. Small-scale retailers rarely offer the lowest price to customers. However, small-scale retailers compete by offering good customer service as they get to know their customers well, and by offering a range of specialist products that retailers operating on a larger scale cannot offer. Many customers choose to pay a higher price for the enhanced customer service. The services can be more personalised as the small business can get to know customers well and adapt products to meet the needs of individuals.

ACTIVITY 2.2.3

Research a small-scale retailer in your area.

Identify the businesses that the small-scale retailer competes with and create a mind map to summarise how they compete:

- How are its goods/services different from competitors' good/services?
- How do its prices compare?
- How does it attract customers?

REFLECTION

Think about the skills that you used to research the small-scale retailer. Identify the different skills that you used to complete the task. Why are these skills important to help you succeed with your commerce studies?

2.2.3 Retail selling techniques

Retailers use a range of different techniques to sell products to customers. Many of these techniques support the marketing of the product.

Branding

Many products are branded. A brand is a name and image of a retailer or product to help it stand out from others offered by competitors. A brand can influence how customers see a product or a retailer and represent what the retailer stands for. The brand can add value to the product as customers are more likely to trust a brand.

Many well-known products are known by their brand name. Bounty is a chocolate brand produced by Mars. Bounty chocolate bars are coconut covered in chocolate. There are other similar products sold under different brand names, but customers may stay loyal to Bounty.

The name of the retailer is likely to be a brand. Lidl operates supermarkets throughout the European Union (EU) and also the UK, USA, Switzerland and Serbia. The retail brand is known for offering low prices.

Own brands

Many larger retailers sell own-brand products. These products carry the name/**logo** (a graphic or symbol to represent a product or business) of the retailer that sells them and are often cheaper than the well-known branded versions. Many supermarkets and multiple chain stores sell own-brand products, as they sell a sufficient volume of products to make it worthwhile to produce their own range. Sometimes the own-brand products are produced on behalf of the retailer under contract by a leading producer. Some larger supermarkets offer different own-brand versions of a product line, for instance, 'finest/luxury' own-brand biscuits alongside 'value/economy' own-brand biscuits.

KEY TERM

logo: a graphic or symbol to represent a product or business. A logo is part of the brand.

Logos

A logo is part of the brand. Many retailers and products use a logo as part of their brand. Spar's logo is a distinctive green tree image within a green circle that is used alongside its name. Apple's logo is an image of an apple with a bite out of it, and Nike uses a tick. The logo is often used on signage, digital marketing material, traditional advertising, product packaging and on the actual product itself.

Packaging

Packaging is the materials used to present or protect the product. Most products are sold with packaging. The packaging often includes branding, such as the logo and product name/description. The barcode – a graphic made up of lines (bars) and spaces with a product number underneath – is also part of the packaging, to make it easy to scan and manage stock.

Packaging should be designed to appeal to the target customer so that they are attracted to buy the product. Packaging often changes over time to extend the life of the product. New packaging often makes customers think that the product has changed (even if the product inside is the same) and therefore attracts additional sales.

Many producers are evaluating their use of packaging to become more environmentally sustainable. Unnecessary packaging can increase the cost of producing the product and create more waste to dispose of. Many producers actively look for ways of reducing packaging. Only the minimum amount of packaging needed to protect the product should be used. Different materials can also be used to limit the **environmental impact**, for instance, using recycled material to package products and making the packaging from materials that can be recycled for future uses. Environmental impact is the effect human activity has on the environment.

KEY TERM

environmental impact: the effect human activity has on the environment.

Self-service

Many retailers offer more self-service options, including self-service checkouts to scan and pay for products, which you learned about in the section on supermarkets.

Some supermarkets now allow customers to use special scanners to scan their items as they put them in their trollies. This avoids the need to scan all of the items one by one at the checkout, as the scanner will tell the customer the final amount to pay.

Many customers prefer using the self-service options as they can be quicker. Some customers also prefer not to interact with human employees. The customer is also in greater control of their expenditure as they can see the price of each item that they scan and how the total bill increases. This can help the customer to budget, as they can avoid buying items that may take them over the amount that they wish to spend.

However, some customers are reluctant to use the technology and prefer the human interaction with the cashier at the end of their shop. Retailers have to install additional security measures to reduce the risk of customers walking out without paying for the products, e.g., additional closed-circuit television (CCTV) cameras that monitor all self-service transactions or employees to oversee the process and provide assistance as required.

Retailers also employ staff to offer help to customers at the self-service options. This can increase customer confidence when using these options for the first time, as they know that support will be available if they are unsure about anything.

Retailers are increasingly installing self-service options as they find it attracts many customers who prefer this option. It also reduces the retailer's operating costs as they no longer have to employ employees at each checkout. Often one employee supervises a number of self-service checkouts to offer help to customers, for security reasons and to sort any technical problems. This can reduce the retailer's costs, and therefore increase profitability.

After-sales service

The relationship with the customer does not stop when the customer pays for the product. After-sales service is often needed after the time of purchase. After-sales service covers all of the support and resources given to the customer after purchase. Examples include repairing or replacing the product if it develops a fault within a certain period after purchase, product upgrades, obtaining feedback from customers (customer satisfaction surveys), technical helplines and loyalty offers.

After-sales service helps to ensure that the customer is completely satisfied with their purchase and helps to develop the relationship with them. A positive relationship can build customer loyalty, as it increases the chance of the customer buying from the retailer again in the future.

Barcoding

Most products have barcodes. Barcodes are often black and white and can be read by scanners. In retail, the use of barcodes at the time of purchase supports stock management systems. Barcodes are scanned at the checkout/till when the product is sold. Scanning the product will confirm the price. Every time an item is sold, the stock levels are immediately updated so that managers can instantly see what stock remains at any time.

Direct mail

Direct mail is where advertising materials (such as letters, brochures, leaflets and postcards) are sent directly to customers. Traditionally, printed material was sent to the customer by post. Today, however, many businesses use email or SMS text messages instead. Direct mail may be used to make customers aware of current offers/promotions and new products.

> **KEY TERM**
>
> **direct mail:** personally addressed advertising, including catalogues and leaflets sent by post.

Direct mail helps the retailer target specific customers. However, often customers receive direct mail from lots of businesses, which can limit its effectiveness. Customers may become annoyed by the amount of direct mail that they receive. Direct mail is often referred to as 'junk mail' as some people put the material straight into the bin, often without reading. This means that the resources put into sending the material to the customer are wasted, e.g., wasted cost of printing the material, postage costs and time/effort. The retailer also needs to maintain the up-to-date contact details of its customers, as otherwise the direct mail will not go to the correct person. This can be costly and time consuming to maintain. The retailer can only use this method to target existing customers or anyone who has expressed an interest in the business. Direct mail is not an appropriate way to attract new customers.

Loyalty programmes

Some retailers offer loyalty programmes, including many supermarkets, such as Imtiaz, which operates stores in Pakistan. Some coffee shops, for instance, offer customers a card or an app through which they can collect points. They may earn one point each time they order a drink, and once they collect ten points they are rewarded with a free drink. Loyalty rewards encourage customers to return to a retailer, rather than go to a competitor, to 'earn' points that lead to discounts, in-store **coupons** or free products. It is also cheaper for a retailer to keep a customer loyal than to attract a new one. Loyalty programmes are not only offered by large businesses. Many small businesses also offer loyalty schemes. Independent retailers in some small towns and cities group together and operate a loyalty programme where customers receive points when they spend in any participating retailer.

KEY TERM

coupons: documents that can be used in part-payment of a future purchase of the product.

Loyalty programmes also allow a retailer to collect useful data on customers' buying patterns and habits, which it can use to target them with products, services and promotions. Some retailers analyse the data collected from loyalty programmes to give customers money-off coupons on products that they buy frequently. This targeted approach increases the likelihood of extra sales. The retailer can also gather a large amount of personal data about the customer when they apply to join the loyalty programme, such as name, address, email address and telephone number. The retailer can then use this information for marketing purposes, e.g., sending an SMS text message to a customer to make them aware of weekly offers on products that they normally buy. Customer addresses can also help the retailer know where their customers live, which could be used when planning new store locations. If there are a lot of customers in one area of the country, the retailer may choose to open another store there.

As lots of retailers offer loyalty programmes with similar rewards, it is difficult to create a scheme that stands out. A large number of loyalty programmes in a specific market can limit the effectiveness of individual schemes.

Informal credit

Informal credit may be offered by small-scale retailers to customers who are known to them and/or have a good record of paying on time. Informal credit is based on trust, so the retailer needs to be sure that the customer will return to pay for the items. With informal credit, items bought during the week are paid for at the end of the week after the customer receives their wages. The retailer is less likely to offer informal credit to other customers if they do not know them, if the customer wants too much credit or if they have reason to believe that the individual will not pay the money owed.

Informal credit can help to build a relationship with the customer and keep them loyal to the retailer as they are less likely to receive informal credit from other retailers. However, there is an increased risk that the customer will not pay and the retailer will lose the value of the goods taken by the customer. If this keeps happening, the retailer is unlikely to continue trading.

Cash-on-delivery

Cash-on-delivery, or COD, is where the delivery payment is made when the retailer (or courier) delivers the package to the customer. This system means that the customer does not have to pay for the item before the parcel is sent. COD can help build trust between the retailer and customer as payment is not made until the product is seen and delivered. This reduces the risk for the customer. However, the main risk in COD is that the customer refuses the delivery, which can cost the retailer. The retailer will have spent money delivering the product to the customer and will then have to pay to return it.

2.2.4 Digital retail trends

Technology is impacting retail. This section considers a range of different digital retail trends.

Omnichannel retailing

Omnichannel is where the retailer aims to offer customers a seamless shopping experience across all channels. This is a business strategy that means that customers benefit from links between stores, online channels and mobile channels. For example, a customer may see a clothing retailer's window display. After seeing the store window display, the customer decides to buy the product. The customer goes home and orders the product via the retailer's app. The product is delivered to the customer's home address.

An omnichannel strategy will help the retailer to strengthen its brand and develop a closer relationship with customers.

Omnichannel is used by a growing number of retailers as they look to offer **multi-distribution channels** to customers. Customers increasingly want a convenient and personalised shopping experience, and offering a range of different channels allows them to meet the needs of a wider number of customers.

Many retailers with physical stores offer customers 'click-and-collect' services. The customer can order the goods online but the order is delivered to a local store instead of being delivered to their home. This may be more convenient for the customer if they are not at home at the delivery time or do not want to wait at home for the delivery.

KEY TERMS

omnichannel: where the retailer aims to offer customers a seamless shopping experience across all channels.

multi-distribution channel: where a retailer sells its products to customers using a range of different methods, e.g. store, website, app.

Cashless stores

There is a growing trend for cashless transactions. The use of notes and coins to pay for purchases is reducing globally in preference for other methods, such as **credit cards**, **debit cards** and digital payment systems, such as Apple Pay, Google Wallet, Samsung Pay and PayPal. A debit card is a plastic card issued by a bank that can be used to make immediate payment for goods and services up to an agreed limit. A credit card is a plastic card that is used to obtain goods and services without making payment at the time of the purchase. Digital payment systems allow the user to add funds on their phone or other device. They can then spend the money in-store and online at businesses that accept digital payment methods. Digital payment transactions may be viewed as more convenient by the customer as they only have to remember to carry their phone, as all of the details are stored on the phone. The systems may also be considered as more secure, as phones have in-built security features, such as personal identification numbers (PINs) and finger/voice recognition systems, which prevent unauthorised use. Cash and notes can be easily lost, and once mislaid, you cannot trace them or prevent someone else spending them. Most credit/debit card transactions are contactless, using **contactless cards**. This is more convenient for customers, who do not have to worry about forgetting a PIN.

Many retailers are now asking customers to pay by card or digitally as it is more convenient for the retailers too – they do not have to spend time counting the cash/notes and to deposit the money at the bank. There is also no risk of counterfeit notes/coins.

KEY TERMS

credit card: a plastic card that is used to obtain goods and services without making payment at the time of the purchase. It can also be used to obtain cash.

debit card: a plastic card issued by a bank. It can be used to make immediate payment for goods and services up to an agreed limit.

contactless card: a debit, credit or gift card that can be used to make payments without having to touch a card reader. Users tap the card over the top of the reader and the payment is made using the card details read by the card reader.

Electronic point of sale (EPoS)

Electronic point of sale (EPoS), a computerised system of monitoring stock, recording sales and taking payments, is used by many retailers. This system supports automatic stock control and reordering of items.

> **KEY TERM**
>
> **electronic point of sale (EPoS):** a computerised system of monitoring stock, recording sales and taking payments.

EPoS systems involve product barcodes being scanned at the checkout at the time of purchase. When an item is sold, the retailer's stock is reduced by one. When the stock level is low and reaches the point when reordering is required, the system automatically places an order for new stock. Managers can look up the stock levels of a specific product instantly. EPoS systems are more accurate and less time consuming than someone manually managing the control of stocks.

Modern systems utilise internet technologies so that orders are automatically sent to suppliers without any human intervention. This ensures that stocks of items are always available to meet customer needs. These systems are not only used by retailers but have been extended to warehouses and factories to support the ordering of raw materials and/or supplies.

Stakeholders such as suppliers, both within and outside of the business, can collaborate and share data easily using cloud systems. Cloud systems run via the internet and enable data to be shared with stakeholders with compatible systems. Sharing data in this way reduces the labour involved with stock management and speeds up the process. Suppliers can offer retailers a more efficient service, which then allows the retailer to satisfy customers better, as they are able to arrange new stock quicker.

Click and collect

As you learned in the omnichannel section, many online retailers operate physical stores and offer customers 'click-and-collect' services. The customer may be planning to visit a retailer's store that does not stock the product that they need, so click and collect can enable customers to access the full product range offered by the retailer even if the local store is small in size with limited product lines. As mentioned, click and collect is also convenient for customers who do not want to wait at home for an order to arrive.

Variations of click and collect are now operated by retailers who only operate online. Some have partnered with physical retailers who will handle parcels on their behalf. Others have installed customer collection or pick-up points, where the courier will leave the parcel in a secure locker that the customer can access at a convenient time using a security code sent to their phone.

Self-service checkout

In response to these trends, many stores have introduced more self-service options in place of personal service (Figure 2.2.7). This can create a competitive advantage for retailers as self-service is more convenient and preferred by some customers. It also enables the retailer to reduce its operating costs, which can increase profit margins and/or enable the retailer to lower its prices. Advances in digital technology have facilitated this retail development.

Figure 2.2.7: Customer scanning their shopping using a supermarket self-service checkout

Subscription commerce

With a subscription, the customer will make a regular payment to a retailer to access a product or service. This arrangement is common for certain types of product, such as Netflix or provision of mobile/broadband services. The customer will sign a contract for the product, which could commit them for a fixed period, e.g., 12 months. If the customer no longer needs the subscription, they may have to pay to leave the contract.

A benefit of subscription commerce is that the retailer 'ties' the customer into their products. The subscription will generally not allow the customer to switch to a different business during the fixed term. The regular income can help the retailer to plan and budget. Often customers forget about a regular payment from their bank account each week/month and so may continue to pay for the service even if they no longer use it.

Subscriptions can also help develop a relationship with a customer. As part of the subscription, the retailer may offer the customer incentives to remain loyal. For instance, subscriptions generally run for a fixed period, e.g. 12 months, and the customer may be offered a reduced subscription price at the end of the fixed period to encourage them to renew for a further 12 months. The subscription may also involve regular communications from the retailer, e.g., a monthly email that includes the customer's statement and/or invoice. Many retailers include other marketing messages within the communication to try to make the customer aware of other goods and/or services, prize competitions and positive news stories about the retailer. All of these messages can help the retailer to develop a positive relationship with the customer, which may encourage them to buy other goods or services from them again in the future.

QR codes

A QR code (Figure 2.2.8) is a variation of the barcode. A QR code is made up of black squares and dots that represent different pieces of information. The code is scanned and translated into human-readable data. QR codes are used by people in lots of situations but can be used in shops for speedy payment at the checkout. Users can scan the QR code at the checkout and the amount due can be automatically deducted via a digital payment system.

QR codes can also be used as part of a loyalty programme. The loyalty card issued to customers may include a QR code that customers scan at the checkout to link their purchase with their loyalty account to earn points. They can also be used as part of a marketing campaign where customers are asked to scan the QR code to obtain a discount or enter a competition, for instance.

Figure 2.2.8: QR codes are increasingly used by retailers

Virtual reality (VR) showrooms

Virtual reality showrooms enable customers to benefit from a showroom experience without physically entering the retailer's premises (Figure 2.2.9). Virtual reality is a computer-generated environment with scenes or objects that seem to be real, making the user feel like they are actually there. Virtual reality showrooms enable retailers to demonstrate products across a wider geographic area. Ikea uses virtual reality showrooms to provide an innovative 3D product experience to customers so they can visualise an Ikea product prior to purchase. Without this feature, Ikea's online customers would have to wait until the product is delivered and assembled to visualise the product. Virtual reality showrooms can reduce the risk of the purchase as the customer is better informed before buying. Virtual reality showrooms can be used by many different types of retailer, including car retailers or kitchen/bathroom suppliers. This feature is relatively new for some retailers but likely to be increasingly used in future as supported by technological developments.

Figure 2.2.9: Virtual reality helps retailers to demonstrate products to customers

Dropshipping

Dropshipping is where the retailer does not keep the products it sells in stock. The storage, distribution and delivery of the products are outsourced to an external contractor. The external contractor is known as the dropshipper. Dropshipping has developed from the growth in ecommerce transactions. Figure 2.2.10 offers an overview of the dropshipping process.

KEY TERM

dropshipping: a business model that allows the retailer to sell its products online without needing to own or operate the physical location where those products are stored and processed.

1. The seller signs an agreement with the external dropshipper contractor.
2. The customer orders the product online.
3. The order is received by the seller and processed.
4. The customer receives confirmation of the order.
5. The details of the order are forwarded to the dropshipper.
6. The dropshipper picks and sends the order to the customer.
7. The customer receives the product that they ordered.

Figure 2.2.10: The dropshipping process

Dropshipping is used by many small entrepreneurs as it enables them to start a business with low overheads and less capital needed. It can also help them to serve customers over a wide geographic area.

Mobile phone/smartphone apps

As you learned in Chapter 2.1, mcommerce (short for mobile commerce) is the buying and selling of goods and services through a mobile device such as a tablet or a smartphone. Many retailers have developed apps to enable customers to buy its goods or services. The percentage and share of digital commerce transactions that take place on a mobile device is growing annually due to increased ownership of mobile devices and the increased convenience that they can offer. This trend is predicted to continue in the future.

Multi-channel retailing

Something that is easy for one consumer to access may not be convenient for another. For this reason, many retailers offer customers different methods (or multiple channels) for buying its products. For example, many clothing retailers allow you to buy in store, online and through third-party retailers.

Each type of channel has relative pros and cons, so by using multiple channels, a business is able overcome any relative disadvantages. Businesses can also attract a variety of customers, as certain market segments are likely to prefer each type. Retailers can therefore adapt marketing activities for each channel used to maximise sales. For example, **social media advertising** may be used to encourage some customers to purchase online, whereas television advertising may be used to promote products available in stores. The product range may also be adapted so specific products may only be available online, to reflect the profile of customers who typically purchase online. Social media advertising is the use of social media channels to promote a product, service or brand to consumers.

KEY TERM

social media advertising: using social media channels to promote a product, service or brand to consumers.

2.2.5 Effects of ecommerce on traditional commerce

Traditional retailers have had to change their business operations to respond to the growth of digital channels. Some retailers have always operated a website, but it may have been basic, with only information about the products offered. Many traditional retailers offer click and collect services whereby customers can purchase the product conveniently from the website but collect it from the shop. This can be more convenient than having the product delivered to the home, especially if the customer may not be at home when the delivery is made. Click and collect enables the retailer to offer the benefits of ecommerce ordering with the convenience of collecting from the shop.

Traditional retailers have also focused on offering a personal relationship with customers to compete with ecommerce competitors. For instance hosting special events for loyal customers or providing personalised demonstrations of products in-store such as showing a customer how to use a new laptop or allowing a customer to test drive a car before purchase. The demonstrations can give the customer the confidence to purchase the product as they have seen and/or tested the product. This is more challenging for ecommerce retailers to offer.

Traditional retailers also use websites to market products. The retailer can include a lot of information about products on the website so customers can then make an informed decision when they visit the shop to purchase. Traditional retailers often use email and SMS text messages to promote products and encourage customers to visit the shop.

Ecommerce relies on a more advanced website to support payment of products purchased. Detailed product descriptions and clear images of all angles of the products should be included. This is so customers have a clear idea of what they will buy, as they cannot physically inspect the products online. To maintain customer satisfaction, the website must also be robust so that it does not break down often.

Once ordered, customers expect the goods to be delivered swiftly. Retailers need to operate efficient distribution departments to fulfil the order quickly.

Many retailers work with courier businesses who deliver the goods to the customer (Figure 2.2.11). This is an example of outsourcing. The courier represents the retailer, so couriers must be carefully selected to ensure customers receive high-quality customer service. A negative experience will reflect badly on the retailer. Customers may be located in different locations within a country, or even internationally, so the retailer is likely to work with many couriers.

Figure 2.2.11: A courier delivers an order to a customer

2.2.6 Wholesalers

Wholesalers play an important role in the distribution of products to the final consumer in many cases. This section will consider the importance and role of the wholesaler.

As you learned in Chapter 1.2, wholesalers play an important role in the supply chain for many products. When wholesalers buy products in large quantities from suppliers and sell them to retailers and/or other businesses in smaller quantities, this is known as breaking bulk. The wholesaler is the middle of the supply chain between the producer and consumer.

Types of wholesaler

There are different types of wholesaler:

- **general wholesalers** – wholesalers who offer a wide range of goods in large warehouses
- **specialist wholesalers** – wholesalers who stock a specific type of good, such as electrical items

> **KEY TERM**
>
> **general wholesalers:** these wholesalers offer a wide range of goods in large warehouses.

- **cash-and-carry wholesalers** – wholesalers who accept cash payments and often do not offer delivery services
- intermediaries – factors and brokers operating in international trade. A broker works in many industries such as insurance and the buying/selling of property and shares. A broker supports transactions between sellers and buyers. They help the transaction run smoothly and ensure that the buyer and seller have all of the information that they need. Often brokers work independently of the seller and can advise the buyer. A broker does not take possession of the product sold. A factor is similar to a broker except they will take possession of the product sold. The factor will often sell the product on commission. They operate in their own name and do not disclose the name of the principal
- **voluntary chains** – a group of retailers formed by a wholesaler.

Find out more about the different types in Figure 2.2.12.

General wholesalers	• Stock a large variety of goods in large warehouses • Operate on a national, regional or local area
Specialist wholesalers	• Stock a specific type of good, such as electrical goods
Cash-and-carry wholesalers	• Operate for cash payments • Often do not offer delivery services
Intermediaries or 'middlemen'	• Factors and brokers operating in international trade
Voluntary chains	• A group of retailers formed by a wholesaler • The group of retailers work together on a non-contractual basis to achieve economies of scale in advertising and buying

Figure 2.2.12: Types of wholesaler

The wholesaler still needs to make a profit on these important tasks, and their services are not free. This means that their presence in the supply chain may increase the price that consumers pay for goods. Many products are sold in competitive markets, and consumers want the cheapest price possible. Some manufacturers are removing wholesalers from their supply chains to try to keep the price low.

The retailer may buy products from a wholesaler in different ways, such as:

- visiting the wholesaler's warehouse
- placing an order online through the wholesaler's website
- through a visit from one of the wholesaler's travelling sales representatives
- placing an order by post, email or telephone.

KEY TERMS

specialist wholesalers: these wholesalers stock a specific type of good such as electrical items.

cash-and-carry wholesalers: these wholesalers accept cash payments and often do not offer delivery services.

voluntary chains: a group of retailers formed by a wholesaler. The group of retailers work together on a non-contractual basis to benefit from economies of scale in advertising and buying.

The functions and services provided by the wholesaler

Wholesalers offer a range of services that often simplify the distribution of the product to the consumer. These functions can help both the manufacturer and retailer in different ways.

Services that wholesalers offer to manufacturers

Wholesalers offer a range of different services for manufacturers (Figure 2.2.13).

Buying raw materials

The wholesaler is able to sell a range of raw materials to manufacturers. These raw materials may be sourced in the home country or imported. Examples of raw materials may include wool, oil and wheat.

Purchasing in bulk

The wholesaler purchases the goods including raw materials in large quantities, i.e., bulk. This often means that the goods are bought at a lower cost, which may mean lower prices for the manufacturer than if they had bought in a smaller quantity from the producer. Buying from the wholesaler also means that the manufacturer will not have to work with many different suppliers/producers and also retailers. This can save time and reduce the administration involved.

Figure 2.2.13: Services provided by a wholesaler for the manufacturer

Clearing production lines

Once the goods are sold to the wholesaler, the production line is cleared. The large quantities of goods purchased are stored by the wholesaler until they are sold on. This means that the manufacturer does not have to operate storage facilities for the stock, which saves expenses such as warehouse rent, insurance and wages of warehouse employees. Less working capital will also be tied up in the unsold stock.

Reducing storage

As wholesalers store the goods until they are sold, the manufacturer does not have to operate storage facilities for unsold stock, which saves the manufacturer expenses such as warehouse rent, insurance and wages of warehouse employees. Less working capital will also be tied up in the unsold stock.

Supporting production in advance of demand

The demand for many goods changes throughout the year. Some goods are seasonal in demand. However, manufacturers may prefer to produce the products at a constant rate or during quieter periods if the goods are not perishable. The manufacturer does not have to store the goods, so can manufacture beyond the capacity of their warehouse storage.

Offering knowledge of the market

Wholesalers will work with many manufacturers and retailers and may specialise in a specific market/product. The wholesaler will therefore have a lot of knowledge of the market and industry, and can advise the manufacturer about changes in consumer demand. This can help the manufacturer plan future production and new product development.

Paying

Wholesalers traditionally pay cash for the goods bought from manufacturers, but offer **trade credit** to the retailers for the goods they buy. Cash payments will help the manufacturer's working capital and enable them to use the cash to finance future production. Increasingly, however, manufacturers supply the wholesaler on a trade credit basis. Trade credit allows a business to buy goods from a supplier without paying straight away. This helps the wholesaler's cashflow as they can try to sell the goods to the retailer. The retailer will then pay the wholesaler, which the wholesaler can use to pay the manufacturer.

KEY TERM

trade credit: selling goods and services and expecting payment for them after an agreed period of time.

Preparing goods for sale

Wholesalers play an important role in preparing the goods for sale. The manufacturer will send many goods pre-packed to the wholesaler. However, when breaking the bulk, the wholesaler will divide the goods into suitable numbers to sell on to the retailer, e.g., a manufacturer may deliver a batch of 10 000 packets of biscuits to the wholesaler. The wholesaler will then divide them into the quantities of 1000 packets to sell on to 10 retailers.

Supporting a reservoir of goods

Wholesalers support a reservoir of goods. Some goods are seasonal and so only in demand at certain times of the year, e.g., winter clothing or fireworks. Other goods are only produced at certain times of the year and can be stored by the wholesaler so that they can be supplied to retailers throughout the duration of the year. For example, fruit and vegetables may be placed in cold storage until required. This saves the manufacturer from having to store the goods until sold. The wholesaler can therefore balance supply and demand for the goods, which can help stabilise prices.

Bearing risk

Wholesalers also bear risk, which reduces the risk to the manufacturer of products not selling. Wholesalers generally purchase before the orders are placed for the goods. The wholesaler therefore orders in anticipation of demand, and if they assess the demand accurately, they will make good profits. However, the wholesaler will then bear the risk of losses if consumer demand falls, e.g., due to economic changes or fashion changes. The wholesaler may be left with large stocks of goods that are not in demand and may have to sell them off at a loss, or waste the products if they are perishable.

Services that wholesalers offer to retailers

Figure 2.2.14 lists services provided by a wholesaler for the retailer.

Figure 2.2.14: Services provided by a wholesaler for the retailer

Breaking bulk

Manufacturers often produce products in large quantities and prefer to sell on to the wholesaler in these large quantities to increase efficiency. Larger quantities involve less administration, time and cost for the manufacturer. However, many retailers only wish to purchase a small quantity of a variety of products. The wholesaler will help to meet the needs of the manufacturer and retailer by dividing bulk purchases into smaller quantities for the retailer. This saves the retailer having to hold large stocks, which could be a problem if they only have limited storage facilities.

Offering a large range of goods

Most retailers like to sell a range of products to meet the needs of all customers, e.g., three different brands of rice. Wholesalers generally stock a wide range of different products and/or brands of products. This means retailers can purchase a range of different products from one wholesaler. This saves retailers having to place orders with lots of different manufacturers, which can save time and administration, and is more convenient. Some manufacturers may only accept orders of a specific size, so may refuse to supply small orders. The wholesaler may also make the retailer aware of different types of products that they had not even thought of selling.

Advising retailers

Wholesalers work with many manufacturers and retailers and often specialise in a specific market/product. The wholesaler will therefore be very knowledgeable about the market and industry, and can advise the retailer about changes in consumer demand. This can help the retailer decide which product to order.

Displaying and marketing goods

Some wholesalers allow the retailer to visit their warehouse and physically inspect products, especially in cash-and-carry warehouses.

Storage

Some retailers only have limited storage facilities. Manufacturers may only supply a specific quantity of goods, which is too much for the retailer. By buying from a wholesaler, the retailer can buy a smaller quantity of the good, which reduces storage.

Delivery

Many wholesalers offer a delivery service to supply the goods to the retailer. This saves the retailer the cost and time of having to collect the goods. Delivery services can often be arranged at short notice, which allows retailers to quickly restock if customer demand suddenly increases.

Supporting a reservoir of goods

Some goods are seasonal and so only in demand at particular times. Other goods are only produced at certain times of the year and can be stored by the wholesaler to enable steady supply, e.g., fruit and vegetables may be placed in cold storage until needed.

This ensures that retailers can rely on a constant supply of these products to meet customer demand throughout the year. Most retailers like to offer customers a full range of products throughout the year if in demand.

Bearing risk

Wholesalers order from the manufacturer in anticipation of demand from retailers in the hope of making a profit. However, the wholesaler will then bear the risk of losses if demand from retailers falls, e.g., due to fashion changes. The wholesaler may be left with large stocks of unwanted goods and may have to sell them off at a loss or waste them if they are perishable.

Offering trade discounts

Wholesalers offer trade discounts to customers, which allows the retailer to buy the product at a lower cost. Often wholesalers offer larger discounts if the retailer buys larger quantities. This allows the retailer to either offer customers lower prices, which may be lower than competitors, or leave the price at the same level, enjoying a higher profit margin. Retailers can often buy goods from a wholesaler using trade credit, which benefits working capital.

Why independent wholesalers survive

Wholesalers are important intermediaries in a supply chain. They act between the producer and the consumer. Increasingly, however, the role of the intermediaries – including wholesalers – is reducing. Distribution channels are becoming shorter, with fewer people and businesses involved, especially with the growth of ecommerce. Reducing the number of intermediaries means that there are fewer businesses that need to make a profit, which can help to reduce the price for customers. This can make the product more competitive on the market. Ecommerce also means that it is easier for manufacturers to sell directly to the customer.

However, despite this trend, independent wholesalers, such as cash and carry wholesalers and voluntary chains, continue to survive and offer vital services. A key reason for their survival is that their services help maintain a stable and secure supply of products for customers. Customers are increasingly looking for convenience, so maintaining stock levels is critical.

SELF-EVALUATION CHECKLIST

After studying this chapter, complete this table.

You should know about:	Needs more work	Almost there	Ready to move on
the different types of retailers, both small scale and large scale			
the features, advantages and disadvantages of each retailer type			
why small-scale retailers survive			
selling techniques used in retail			
digital retail trends			
the effects of ecommerce on traditional commerce			
the purpose and significance of wholesalers			
why independent wholesalers survive			

Knowledge check

1 A wholesaler is an important part of the distribution channel for many products. Describe three services that a wholesaler offers to a manufacturer when distributing their products to retailers.

Selling through wholesalers

2 Describe three digital retail trends.

3 Analyse two positive effects of ecommerce on traditional commerce.

4 Explain the difference between a mobile shop and a street market stall.

5 Explain two features of a departmental store.

6 Which of the following is an example of an itinerant retailer?
- a chain store
- b hawker
- c hypermarket
- d supermarket

7 Which of the following is most likely to deliver goods to the consumer?
- a courier
- b pedlar
- c retailer
- d wholesaler

8 A customer looking for value for money may do which of the following before choosing which product to buy?
- a look at online reviews
- b buy the first product they see at a shop
- c visit the closest retailer that sells the product
- d buy the product online

9 Breaking bulk means:
- a damaging a product during delivery
- b dividing the product into smaller quantities
- c offering good value for money
- d reducing the supply chain.

10 The final person in a supply chain is the:
- a agent
- b consumer
- c retailer
- d wholesaler.

Practice questions

1 a Define the term 'wholesaler'. [2]

b State two reasons why small-scale retailers survive. [2]

c Gifts Galore sells a range of items for celebrations throughout the year. The business is thinking of using a wholesaler to distribute its products to customers. Recommend if Gifts Galore should use a wholesaler. Give reasons for your opinion. [6]

d State four features of a supermarket. [4]

2 a Define the term 'itinerant retailer'. [2]

b State four reasons why a retailer may introduce self-service checkouts. [4]

c Bianca operates a small shop selling clothing products, but is keen to expand the business. She is thinking of launching an ecommerce website. Do you think Bianca should expand by launching an ecommerce website or opening a second shop. Give reasons for your opinion. [8]

Chapter 2.3

Trading documents

LEARNING INTENTIONS

In this chapter you will learn:

- documents used in home trade
- documents used in international trade
- the different steps of the online ordering process
- digital technology used in trading documents.

2.3.1 Why are commercial documents used in trade?

Commercial documents are used in trade for various reasons. They enable trade on credit with customers who purchase regularly. Trade on credit is an agreement to buy goods or services on account, therefore no immediate payment is made. They facilitate contact between the buyers and the sellers. They are also used to compare prices and terms between suppliers of the same goods or services.

Commercial documents provide a written record of any transaction and are used to avoid mistakes when doing business with other companies. Companies buying and selling are likely to make many transactions in a day. Having written documentation helps to make sure that the transaction has been successfully completed. Commercial documents inform buyers about the quality and quantity of goods, pricing, delivery arrangements, payment terms and other transaction details.

Commercial documents help to settle disagreements over the goods supplied or the prices that have been agreed. If there is written evidence of the transaction, problems can be solved.

Commercial documents are used for accounting purposes – to show the amount of business done, to calculate sales revenue and to help calculate profit. The seller's accounts staff issue some documents to ask for payment from the buyer.

Commercial documents help to provide legal evidence or proof in the case of disputes. They help to prevent fraud and to provide information for tax purposes. They provide information for duties calculations and provide information for customs clearance purposes. Duties are a form of taxation on certain goods or services. Customs clearance is the act of taking goods through the **customs authority** to assist the progress of goods into a country (import) and out of a country (export). A customs authority is an organisation that is responsible for controlling a country's imports and exports, collecting trade statistics, preventing smuggling and collecting tariffs.

Commercial documents serve as a contract for carriage between the buyer and seller and a letter of guarantee for a payment to be made to a specified person. Carriage is the transportation of goods from one place to another. Commercial documents provide evidence of products purchased and paid for, and provide evidence of tickets purchased for an event, concert or airline.

KEY TERM

customs authority: an organisation that is responsible for controlling a country's imports and exports, collecting trade statistics, preventing smuggling and collecting tariffs.

2.3.2 Documents of home trade

The documents used in home trade vary from business to business, but most commercial transactions follow the stages described in this chapter. Some of the documents shown are used by the buyer, and some are used by the seller. A summary of who uses which document is shown in Table 2.3.1.

Documentation in order of use	Buyer uses	Seller uses	Use
1 Enquiry	✓		To find out about the seller's goods or services
2 Quotation		✓	To provide the buyer with the information requested
3 Order	✓		To place an order for the seller's goods
4 Invoice		✓	To show the goods, their prices and the total amount of the bill
5 Delivery note		✓	To list the goods delivered to the buyer
6 Credit note		✓	To correct an overcharge on a bill

Continued

Documentation in order of use	Buyer uses	Seller uses	Use
7 Statement of account		✓	To show all the transactions between the buyer and the seller for a trading period
8 Payment/ receipt	✓	✓	To prove payment has been received via electronic transfer, credit transfer or cheque

Table 2.3.1: Commercial documents summary

KEY TERMS

enquiry: formal request for information about the goods and services offered by the seller.

quotation: a reply to a potential buyer giving details of goods and services requested in an enquiry.

credit note: a receipt given to a customer who has returned goods, been overcharged, received goods not ordered or received damaged goods.

statement of account: a document sent at regular intervals to buyers purchasing on credit. It gives details of all the transactions between the buyer and the seller during a trading period and the balance that still needs to be paid.

receipt: a document showing that payment has been made.

Enquiry

An enquiry is a formal request for information about the goods and services offered by the seller (Figure 2.3.1).

An enquiry takes the form of an email or letter with the buyer's letterhead. The reasons a business enquiry may be sent include asking for a catalogue, pricing, information on a product, availability, delivery dates and terms of payment, such as discounts and credit terms.

Enquiries may be sent to several companies so that the buyer can compare the prices and terms of payment.

BEACHWEAR
57 Sunsheel Center
Curepipe
Mauritius

1 June...

Clothing Warehouse
86 Dr Edwards Street
Port Louis
Mauritius

Dear Sir/Madam,

We would like to request a copy of your current catalogue of the goods on sale together with the price list. We would also like to request a quotation for the following:

100	T-shirts in assorted colours
100	Hats in assorted colours

Please send through your terms of sale and delivery dates.

Yours faithfully,

Marie Gopaul
Purchasing Manager

Figure 2.3.1: An example of an enquiry letter sent from Beachwear to Clothing Warehouse, asking for a catalogue and a quotation for specific items

Quotation

A quotation is a letter or email reply sent to the potential buyer giving details about the goods or services described in the enquiry.

A quotation should give full details of:

- the goods
- their description
- catalogue number
- size or weight
- number or quantity of goods to be ordered
- time and method of delivery
- packaging

- price (unit price – the price for one – and total price)
- any discount
- terms of sale (how quickly payment is required). A quotation usually has a time limit before which it should be accepted, often expressed as 'for acceptance within x days'. This is to protect the seller against sudden rises in costs that would affect the price given in the quotation. The quotation gives the information necessary to form a sales agreement.

In Figure 2.3.2, '5% 30 days' means that if payment is received within 30 days, a 5% discount will be given on the amount due. This is known as a **cash discount**. Cash discounts are deductions that aim to encourage customers to pay their bills within a certain time frame.

KEY TERM

cash discount: a deduction from the price of goods shown on an invoice to encourage customers who bought goods on credit to pay promptly. For example, offering a 5% discount on an invoice due in 30 days if the buyer pays within the first ten days of receiving the invoice.

CLOTHING WAREHOUSE
86 Dr Edwards Street
Port Louis
Mauritius

Quotation No. 664
3 June…
To: Beachwear
57 Sunsheel Center
Curepipe
Mauritius

For the attention of Marie Gopaul

In reply to your enquiry dated 1 June, we have the pleasure of quoting you for the following:

DESCRIPTION	CODE	QTY	UNIT PRICE	TOTAL
T-shirts, various colours	BG12	100	$20	$2000
Hats, various colours	MF56	100	$25	$2500
			Subtotal	$4500
			Discount	20%
			Subtotal less discount	$3600
			Shipping/handling	$120
			Quote total	$3720

Delivery time: 10 working days
Cash discount: 5% 30 days
Acceptance required within 2 weeks.
We look forward to receiving your instructions, which will receive our prompt attention.

Jean Bundhoo
Sales Manager

Figure 2.3.2: An example of a quotation sent from Clothing Warehouse to Beachwear in response to their enquiry

Order

The order, also known as the purchase order, is a letter, email or order form supplied by the seller or on a webpage. The buyer sends it to the seller to show details of what the buyer wishes to order (Figure 2.3.3).

The order gives full details of the goods required, such as quantity, description, catalogue number and price. It will also state the terms of delivery (any delivery charge), terms of payment (discounts) and the expected delivery date, as well as the address to which the goods should be sent. The order is signed and dated by the buyer or someone authorised to purchase on behalf of the buyer – such as the purchasing manager if the buyer is a company. If a new client places an order on credit, the seller will check the buyer's creditworthiness – the ability to pay for what is bought. The seller will ask for a reference to see if the buyer conducts their financial affairs properly and pays their bills.

BEACHWEAR
57 Sunsheel Center
Curepipe
Mauritius
ORDER

No.2861

Date: 10 June...
To: Clothing Warehouse
86 Dr Edwards Street
Port Louis
Mauritius

Please supply:

DESCRIPTION	CODE	QTY	UNIT PRICE	TOTAL
T-shirts, various colours	BG12	100	$20	$2000
Hats, various colours	MF56	100	$25	$2500
			Subtotal	$4500
			Discount	20%
			Subtotal less discount	$3600
			Shipping/handling	$120
			Quote total	$3720

As per Quotation Number 664 dated 3 June...
Deliver to: Clothing Warehouse at the above address

Marie Gopaul
Purchasing Manager

Figure 2.3.3: An example of an order sent from Beachwear to Clothing Warehouse with details of what Beachwear wishes to order

Invoice

An **invoice** is a list of items provided or work done, with their cost, for payment at a later date, i.e., for goods bought on credit (Figure 2.3.4). It shows the details of an individual transaction.

An invoice shows the details of the products, including catalogue number, quantity, the unit price (price for one) and the total price of each item, the order number and the terms of payment. It shows the **trade discount** (if any) deducted and the total price. The trade discount is a reduction in the catalogue or list price of a product given to businesses within the same trade. An invoice also lists the terms of payment and any tax, e.g., sales tax, that is payable. An invoice may have **errors and omissions excepted (E&OE)** printed at the bottom of the form. This means that the seller has the right to correct any mistakes on the invoice or to add any information to the invoice.

If a customer has been undercharged or overcharged, these adjustments are dealt with by issuing another document, such as a credit note, which is a receipt given to a customer who has returned goods, been overcharged, received goods not ordered or received damaged goods. The invoice is not normally a request for payment. There are several copies of the invoice. One copy goes to the buyer of the goods. Other copies may be used as advice notes, delivery notes and as an accounting record.

In Figure 2.3.4, '3% 30 days' indicates that 3% discount will be given on the amount due if it is paid within 30 days.

KEY TERMS

trade discount: a reduction in the catalogue or list price of a product given to businesses within the same trade.

errors and omissions excepted (E&OE): a statement printed at the bottom of a commercial document. If an error is made on the commercial document, the seller reserves the right to correct the error.

INVOICE

No. 6347

CLOTHING WAREHOUSE
86 Dr Edwards Street
Port Louis
Mauritius

Date: 16 June…

Order No.: 2861

To: Beachwear
57 Sunsheel Center
Curepipe
Mauritius

Delivery note: 1256
Terms: 3% 30 days

DESCRIPTION	CODE	QTY	UNIT PRICE	TOTAL
T-shirts, various colours	BG12	100	$20	$2000
Hats, various colours	MF56	100	$25	$2500
			Subtotal	$4500
			Discount	20%
			Subtotal less discount	$3600
			Shipping/handling	$120
			Invoice total	$3720

E&OE

Figure 2.3.4: An example of an invoice sent from Clothing Warehouse to Beachwear giving the details of the transaction that has taken place

Delivery note

The delivery note is a copy of the invoice (Figure 2.3.5). It is sent with the goods to the buyer. The delivery note is used when a supplier uses his or her own transport to deliver goods. The buyer uses the delivery note to check the goods. If satisfied, the person receiving the goods signs the delivery note to show that all the goods have been received and are in good condition. If the buyer is unable to check the condition of the goods (e.g., because he or she cannot unpack them while the delivery person is present), they should sign the delivery note and state that the goods have not been examined. If some or all of the goods are damaged, the buyer should contact the seller as soon as possible. If possible, the delivery note should be marked to show that some of the goods received have been damaged. A copy of the delivery note is handed back to the person delivering the goods as proof of delivery, and a copy is kept by the person receiving the goods. It shows the buyer's and seller's names and addresses and full details of the goods supplied, but usually not the prices.

Credit note

A credit note is a receipt given to a customer who has returned goods, been overcharged, received goods not ordered or received damaged goods (Figure 2.3.6). The buyer may have also submitted gift vouchers or coupons (used by manufacturers to attract customers) to the seller, so the buyer needs to be compensated. The credit note decreases the amount the buyer owes to the seller and will be shown as a credit on the statement of account.

A credit note is usually printed in red or pink to distinguish it from the invoice and because it represents money going out of the business. If trade discount has been deducted from the price of the goods on the original invoice, that trade discount must also be deducted from the price of the goods returned, and should appear on the credit note.

DELIVERY NOTE **No.** 782

CLOTHING WAREHOUSE
86 Dr Edwards Street
Port Louis
Mauritius

Date: 17 June…

Order No.: 2861

To: Beachwear
57 Sunsheel Center
Curepipe
Mauritius

DESCRIPTION	CODE	QTY	UNIT PRICE	TOTAL
T-shirts, various colours	BG12	100		
Hats, various colours	MF56	100		

Received by .... **Date** ....

Print name ....

E&OE

Figure 2.3.5: An example of a delivery note sent from Clothing Warehouse to Beachwear with a description of the items being delivered

CREDIT NOTE   **No.** 65

CLOTHING WAREHOUSE
86 Dr Edwards Street
Port Louis
Mauritius

Date: 20 June...

To: Beachwear
57 Sunsheel Center
Curepipe
Mauritius
Invoice number 6347
Invoice date 16 June...

Quantity returned	Description	CODE	Cost $
2	T-shirts	BG12	40
5	Hats LESS 20% trade discount	MF56	125 33
		CREDIT VALUE	$132

Clothing Warehouse
Authorised signature ....

Figure 2.3.6: An example of a credit note from Clothing Warehouse to Beachwear showing the amount to reduce their account by

Statement of account

A statement of account is a document that shows all the transactions that have taken place between a business and customer for a given period of time (Figure 2.3.7).

A statement of account is prepared by the seller at the end of a trading period, usually a month. It is sent to the buyers who buy on credit, and shows all the transactions for the month – the purchases made, the payments made, any credit notes issued and any discount given.

A statement of account lists the balance owing at the beginning of the month and the outstanding balance at the end of the month. There may also be a section that shows any overdue payments. It does not give the details of actual goods bought. Each line of the statement is one transaction.

The statement of account serves as a reminder to the buyer to pay the balance owed. It enables the buyer to check their accounts and to notify the seller if there is an error. It confirms the transactions made during the month.

The statement of account shows the amount of cash discount given, e.g., 5 %, 30 days, if prompt payment is made. Cash discounts are deductions that aim to encourage customers to pay their bills within a certain time frame. Cheques, credit notes and cash discounts are entered in the credit column because they reduce the amount owed. Invoices are entered in the debit column because they increase the amount owed.

The buyer will pay the balance shown as the last figure in the balance column on the statement less any cash discount due if payment is made within the time stated. Note that previous cash discounts applied after prompt payments may also be included in the statement, e.g., \$21 in Figure 2.3.7. If Beachwear pays the remaining balance (\$4368) within 30 days, they will only have to pay \$4236.96 (\$4368 less a 3% discount). Payment is made using credit (bank) transfer, **direct debit**, cheque or even cash. A direct debit is a bank service that enables variable amounts to be paid from a bank account at varying times, when requested by the creditor.

KEY TERM

direct debit: a bank service that enables variable amounts to be paid from a bank account at varying times, when requested by the creditor.

If previous payments are overdue, a statement of account may also show overdue amounts and how overdue the amounts are (see 'Current', '30 days', '60 days' and '90 days' in Figure 2.3.7 – there are currently no overdue payments so the statement just shows the balance in the 'Current' column). 'All cheques should be crossed' means the cheque may only be deposited into a bank account. The cheque may not be cashed over the counter.

TIPS

- Make sure you know the differences between debits and credits on statements of account. A debit is what is owed by the customer, e.g., invoices for ordered goods. A credit is any payment made to reduce the debt, including any credit notes issued by the supplier.
- A cash discount does not mean someone has to pay in cash in order to receive the discount. A cash discount is used to encourage payment within a time period, but payment can be made by any method e.g., electronic funds transfer (EFT), card payment or cash.

STATEMENT

CLOTHING WAREHOUSE
86 Dr Edwards Street
Port Louis
Mauritius

Terms: 3% 30 days

Date: 30 June…

To: Beachwear
57 Sunsheel Center
Curepipe
Mauritius

Date	Particulars	Debits $	Credits $	Balance $
1 June	Balance owed			700
5 June	Cheque no. 643612		679	21
	Cash discount		21	0
16 June	Invoice no. 6347	3720		3720
20 June	Credit note 65		132	3588
26 June	Invoice no. 6520	780		4368

CURRENT	30 DAYS	60 DAYS	90 DAYS
$4368			

All cheques should be crossed and made payable to Clothing Warehouse
E&OE

Figure 2.3.7: An example of a statement of account sent from Clothing Warehouse to Beachwear, stating the amount owed

Receipt

A receipt is a document that shows that a payment has been made (Figure 2.3.8). A receipt acts as the proof of money received and is issued by the seller to the buyer. It is useful to the buyer for record purposes.

CLOTHING WAREHOUSE
86 Dr Edwards Street
Port Louis
Mauritius

Date: *5 June...*
No.: 921
Received from: *Beachwear*
The sum of: *Six hundred and seventy-nine dollars*

Cheque	*679*	*00*
Cash		
Discount	*21*	*00*

....
CLOTHING WAREHOUSE

With thanks

Figure 2.3.8: An example of a receipt sent from Clothing Warehouse to Beachwear showing the amount paid for goods

ACTIVITY 2.3.1

a Divide into groups of three to four students.

b Each group should cut out a series of cards. Each card needs to be approximately 6 cm by 6 cm. You will need at least nine cards. Write the name of a document of trade on each card. Write 'cash discount' on another card. On another nine cards, preferably cards of a different colour, write the purpose of each of the documents of trade and the meaning of cash discount.

c Shuffle all the cards together. Use as a revision tool to extract the documents of home trade in the correct order for a transaction, and to match each document with its purpose/definition.

2.3.3 Documents of international trade

As you learned in Chapter 1.1, international trade is the import and export of goods and services between an individual or business in one country and an individual or business in another country. This section looks at the commercial documents used in international trade.

Certificate of origin

A **certificate of origin** is a document that declares that products in a shipment were produced, manufactured or processed and obtained in a particular country (Figure 2.3.9). The document contains information on the product, its destination and the country of export. Their main purpose is for customs clearance procedures, to determine duties or legitimacy of imports. The certificate of origin is filled out by the exporter of the goods.

In Figure 2.3.9, 'Forwarding agent – References' refers to the name of the company or individual organising the transporting of the goods. 'Notify Party' refers to the person or company who needs to be notified of the arrival of the goods. 'Marks and Numbers' is an optional area used to identify different pieces of the cargo to ensure there are no problems identifying the goods at the port. The section at the bottom is an example of what the signatory area could look like at the bottom of a certificate of origin.

KEY TERM

certificate of origin: a document certifying that goods in the shipment are from a particular country.

CERTIFICATE OF ORIGIN	
Shipper name and address Orion Ltd 784 Brightside Brooklyn	**Forwarding agent – references**
Consignee name and address Punjab Enterprises 569 New Lahore Road Pakistan	**Notify party**
Exporting carrier	**Country of manufacture** USA
Total number of packages	**Date of export** 1 September…

Marks & numbers	Commodity description	Quantity/unit of measure	Weight (kg)	
			Gross	Net
OL567	Lawn mowers	10 crates	450 kg	450 kg

These commodities, technology or software were exported from the United States of America in accordance with the Export Administration Regulations. Diversion contrary to US law prohibited.

Dated at ____________ on the ___________ day of ____________ , 20……
Signature of Notary: ____________________

Sworn to before me this ___________ day of ____________ , 20…..
Signature of notary: _____________________

The _______________________ , a recognized Chamber of Commerce under the laws of the State of _____________________ has examined the manufacturer's invoice or shipper's affidavit concerning the origin of the merchandise and, according to the best of its knowledge and belief, finds that the products named originated in the __________________________.
Secretary: __________________________

Figure 2.3.9: An example of a certificate of origin created by Orion Ltd for goods being sent to Punjab Enterprises

Bill of lading

The **bill of lading** is the most important export document when goods are transported by ship (Figure 2.3.10). It gives details of the type, quantity and destination of the goods being transported. It is issued by the shipping company, usually as a set of three original documents. One is kept by the shipping company, one goes to the consignor (the person or company who delivers the goods) and the last is sent to the consignee (the person or company who receives the goods).

KEY TERM

bill of lading: a document used when goods are transported by ship that gives details of the type, quantity and destination of the goods being transported.

A bill of lading contains the name of the shipping company, the name and address of the consignor, the name of the ship carrying the cargo, the name and address of the consignee, ports of shipment and where the cargo is unloaded, the date of issue of the bill of lading, a description of the goods, the number of packages/containers, the signature of the ship's master and freight charged.

If a bill of lading is classed as 'clean', there is no damage to the goods; if it is classed as 'dirty', there is damage to the goods. A bill of lading provides evidence that a contract for the carriage of the goods has been made between the consignor and the shipping company. It is a **document of title**, which is a formal commercial document that proves ownership of goods. Whoever has possession of the bill of lading can claim ownership of the goods. It is, therefore, important to make sure that the importer receives the bill of lading before the goods arrive.

A bill of lading is a negotiable document – ownership can be transferred to another person by endorsing it before the goods arrive at the port. The importer can, therefore, look for a buyer while the goods are still at sea. The shipping company can endorse the transfer.

A bill of lading may be used as a document in support of an insurance claim. When goods are carried in containers, the traditional bill of lading is replaced by combined transport documents covering different methods of transport. These will cover the cargo from the point of departure to the destination.

KEY TERM

document of title: a formal commercial document that proves ownership of goods.

BILL OF LADING — **No.** J654

FAISAL SHIPPING LINE
22–44 Dock Street
Brooklyn

Consignor/Shipper
Orion Ltd
784 Brightside
Brooklyn

Consignee
Punjab Enterprises
569 New Lahore Road
Pakistan

Ship: Ocean Maid — **Voyage no:** 2098 — **Freight charges:** prepaid
Port of loading: Brooklyn — **Date of sailing:** 15 September...
Port of discharge: Pakistan — **Date of arrival:** 22 September...

Marks and numbers	Numbers of packages and Descriptions	Gross weight
OL567	10 crates – lawn mowers	450 kg

Date: 1 September — **Place of issue:** Anyport
Signature of Ship's Master ....P Khan ....

Figure 2.3.10: An example of a simplified bill of lading sent by Orion Ltd to Punjab Enterprises describing the goods in the shipment

Air waybill

The **air waybill** is used when goods are transported by an aircraft (Figure 2.3.11). The air waybill is used as evidence of a contract of carriage and as a receipt to be signed by the consignee when the goods are delivered. It may be used by customs for import purposes, such as assessing import duty.

KEY TERM

air waybill: a document used when goods are transported by air.

An air waybill contains the:

- name and address of the consignor
- name and address of the consignee
- name of the airline
- flight number and date of flight
- description of the goods
- freight charged
- number of items sent and
- signature to show goods received by the airline.

It should be remembered that the air waybill is not a document of title. The delivery of the goods is not dependent upon the presentation of the air waybill by the consignee. Goods will be delivered to the consignee when the consignee provides proof of identity. Possession of the air waybill does not mean that the person can sell the goods and does not confer ownership of the goods. Documents in international trade need to be different from those used in home trade because there is more chance of loss over longer distances. Greater detail needs to be given so that duties payable can be assessed, and documents need to be provided so that the exporter can be paid.

AIR WAYBILL **No.** B4671

AIRWINGS AIR CARGO LTD

2345 OFFICE Block H

Brooklyn Airport

Consignor: Orion Ltd, 784 Brightside, Brooklyn

Consignee: Punjab Fashions, 569 New Lahore Road, Pakistan

It is agreed that the goods described below are accepted for carriage. They are received in good order and there are no dangerous articles contained in the packages.

Consignor: L. Franks **Airline's representative:** P. Wang

Flight no.: AW124 **Date of flight:** 15 September…

Airport of departure: Brooklyn **Airport of destination:** Pakistan

Number of packages	Description of goods	Weight
2 boxes	Red satin trousers 'Buzz' range	6 kg
3 boxes	Olympic T-shirts	9 kg

Issued: Anytown Airport **Date:** 1 September… **Freight charges:** Prepaid

Received by: …………………… **Date:** ……………………

Figure 2.3.11: An example of an air waybill sent by Orion Ltd to Punjab Enterprises describing the goods received by the airline

Documentary credit

A **documentary credit** (letter of credit) is a method of payment that protects the exporter and importer in a sale contract. It gives a guarantee to the exporter that they will receive payment after the shipment of goods has been fulfilled (Figure 2.3.12). The importer gets a guarantee that the goods ordered will be delivered. The exporter guarantee is usually issued by the buyer's bank on their request.

The exporter usually requests the documentary credit to check the credit worthiness of the importer. Documentary credit is also known as a letter of credit.

> **KEY TERM**
>
> **documentary credit:** a letter issued by a bank and sent to another bank, usually in a different country, which acts as a guarantee for payment to be made to the specified person. Documentary credit is also known as a letter of credit.

LETTER OF CREDIT

$15 000

Applicant: Punjab Fashions, New Lahore Road, Pakistan

Issuing bank: National Bank of Pakistan, Lahore, Pakistan

Beneficiary: Orion Ltd, 784 Brightside, Brooklyn

Receiving bank: Northfield Bank, Brooklyn, New York, USA

Date of application: 3 September…

This letter of credit can be drawn from the Lahore branch of the National Bank of Pakistan as long as you provide two of the following documents:

- bill of lading
- air waybill
- insurance certificate
- certificate of origin
- invoice
- receipt.

Figure 2.3.12: An example of a letter of credit drawn up between Punjab Fashions and Orion Ltd

ACTIVITY 2.3.2

a In pairs, decide on a real-life scenario of an international trade transaction, including the type of products being traded, the countries involved and the shipping method.

b Create a set of documents that would be needed for this transaction.

c After completing the documents, discuss the importance of each document and how they work together to ensure a smooth international trade transaction.

REFLECTION

Does looking at a real-life example of an international trade transaction help you understand the concept better? Do you still struggle to understand the purpose of some international commercial documents used?

2.3.4 Digital use of trading documents

The documents used in commercial transactions are processed using computers. Using a computer is cheaper, quicker and often more accurate than completing the documents by hand. Documents can be easily completed, amended and checked on a computer. They can be stored in the computer's memory and easily retrieved when required.

The stored documents can form the basis for future orders and invoices. Statements of account can be assembled using a computer program that groups together all the invoices and other transactions for a particular customer. Records of regular customers can be kept in the electronic files, enabling automatic mailing lists to be assembled. Names, addresses and other details of these customers can also be held on a computer database.

The stages of the online ordering process

When a customer browses and then orders a product from a website, the following steps in the ordering process occur:

1. The customer finds the items they would like to purchase and adds them to their cart.
2. The customer enters their personal details, e.g., name, address and email address.
3. The customer selects a delivery method.
4. The customer chooses their payment method e.g., Mastercard, Visa, American Express or PayPal.
5. Once the order is placed, it is sent to the company's fulfilment centre where it can be processed.
6. The products are picked, which means physically locating the items that were ordered. Once the products have been located, they need to be inspected for quality-control measures.
7. The products are then packaged for delivery. Packaging refers to putting them into boxes or bags so that they are ready to be delivered. Fragile items may be wrapped in Bubble Wrap or foam before they are placed in a box.
8. The products are shipped, which means getting them to the customer's doorstep. This can be done through many delivery methods, which the customer will have selected when placing their order.
9. The customer receives their product and signs a delivery note on receipt of their product.

Identifying digital technology in trading documents

Digital technology has enabled a lot of international trade documents to become paperless (Figure 2.3.13). This section discusses a few examples.

Figure 2.3.13: Technology has enabled international trade documents to become paperless

Digital signature

A digital signature is like an electronic 'fingerprint'. It is a code attached to an electronically transmitted document to confirm the information originated from the signer and has not been altered. Digital signatures are used as a stamp of authentication on digital documents such as email messages. Another term used for a digital signature is e-signature.

Courier services also make use of handheld devices, such as tablets, smartphones and scanners, to reduce the amount of paper waste. Handheld devices can capture signatures of customers on delivery and store them for future reference (Figure 2.3.14).

Figure 2.3.14: A handheld device being used for digital signing purposes

Secure access

Secure access is a security feature that provides a user with secure access to a network. Secure access provides an additional layer of security to internet web applications. It acts as a digital intermediary between the requests of users and the servers of corporate web applications.

Secure access is a cloud-based infrastructure, which means you can implement and deliver security services such as threat prevention, credential theft prevention and data loss prevention. Businesses make use of secure data to minimise or prevent data breaches or misuse, ensuring that only authorised individuals can have access to the business's trading documents.

Cloud-based storage

Cloud-based storage is a mode of computer data storage where digital data is stored on servers in external locations. It saves a significant amount of space and money for a business by eliminating the need for data storage facilities on the business premises. The cloud storage provider is the owner of the hardware and software, and is responsible for hosting, managing, maintaining and securing data stored on the system. Businesses purchase cloud storage and are able to scale up or down depending on their needs.

The cloud enables employees to collaborate with colleagues and work remotely and after business hours.

Electronic receipts

An electronic receipt is a digital document that a salesperson provides after they have received payment for an item. It can be sent via email or downloaded from the payment management system.

Another term used for electronic receipts is an e-receipt. It contains the invoice number, payment date, seller's name, buyer's account details, how payment was made and amount. E-receipts have a positive impact on the environment, leading towards a paperless commerce environment.

Electronic tickets (etickets)

An eticket is an electronic document used for ticketing purposes, such as for events, concerts or airfare admission. Etickets are stored in a database and can be printed at home or at the ticket counter of the venue. Etickets are emailed to the buyer as a PDF file or stored in an online ticketing system. They contain information such as the customer's name, flight number, seat number and other relevant details about the purchase.

Customers must show their eticket when they arrive at the venue or airport to be permitted entry. Each eticket is unique and contains a barcode or QR code that can be scanned for verification. Etickets also serve as proof of purchase.

ACTIVITY 2.3.3

a Research online and find an article that covers the digitalisation of documents.

b Analyse the benefits and challenges of the shipping world moving to digitalisation of documents.

c Identify any opportunities for further improvement in the digitalisation of documents.

REFLECTION

Think about what you learned while studying this chapter. What was more important: what you learned or how you learned it?

SELF-EVALUATION CHECKLIST

After studying this chapter, complete this table.

You should know about:	Needs more work	Almost there	Ready to move on
documents used in home trade			
documents used in international trade			
the different steps of the online ordering process			
digital technology used in trading documents			

Knowledge check

1 The diagram shows part of an invoice paid by a retailer.

		$
30 boxes	bottles of instant coffee @ $50 per box less 20% trade discount	1500 300
	TOTAL	1200

If two damaged boxes of coffee are returned, what should the supplier send to the retailer?

a a credit note for $100

b a credit note for $80

c an invoice for $100

d a receipt for $1200

2 Which document gives a summary of a customer's transactions over a period of time?

a delivery note

b invoice

c statement of account

d order

3 What is the purpose of an invoice?

a to estimate the cost of goods
b to give proof of payment
c to order goods
d to show the amount due

4 Which is the correct sequence of using commercial documents when buying on credit?

a statement → quotation → order → invoice
b order → quotation → invoice → statement
c order → statement → invoice → quotation
d quotation → order → invoice → statement

5 A buyer ordered 200 books. The seller sent 210 books and charged for this amount. The seller later credited the cost of ten books to the buyer's account. In what order should the commercial documents be used?

a receipt → order → credit note → statement
b invoice → order → credit note → statement
c order → invoice → credit note → statement
d statement → credit note → invoice → order

6 Microwaves are sent from China to Australia using sea transport. Which document is completed as evidence of the contract of carriage when these microwaves are transported by sea?

a letter of credit
b air waybill
c bill of lading
d delivery note

7 Provide one difference between cash discount and trade discount.

8 Which commercial documents will the buyer in a departmental store complete to obtain goods?

9 Why would a seller use multiple copies of invoices?

10 How does giving cash discount assist a trader's available cash?

Practice questions

1 *State **two** items of information that are contained in an invoice sent from a wholesaler to a retailer. [2]

Cambridge O Level Commerce 7100, Paper 22, Q4b, June 2020

2 *Fig. 3.1 shows an invoice that has been used in a commercial transaction between a wholesaler and a retailer.

INVOICE No. 832

BB Wholesalers
Mumbai

CC Retailers
Mumbai

28 September 2018
Terms: 5% 21 days

Your Order No. 596

Code	Description	Quantity	Unit Price $	Amount $
J490	Jeans	40	30	1200
MJ628	Jackets	25	80	2000
S952	Sweaters	24	35	840
T637	Ties	100	10	1000
			Sub-total	5040
		LESS Trade Discount 20%		(i) ………
		Invoice Total		(ii) ………

Figure 3.1

Use Fig. 3.1 to help you answer the following questions.

a Complete the invoice in Fig. 3.1 by entering
 i Trade Discount and
 ii Invoice Total [2]
b Explain what is meant by *Terms: 5% 21 days*. [3]
c Explain **one** difference between an order and an invoice. [2]

Cambridge O Level Commerce 7100, Paper 23, Q3a, b, c, June 2019

› Chapter 2.4

Communication

LEARNING INTENTIONS

In this chapter you will learn:

- the difference between written, oral, electronic and visual communication
- different methods of communication
- factors affecting the choice of communication method.

2.4.1 What is communication?

From the time you wake up until you go to bed, you communicate with many people, making use of different communication methods. Before leaving for school, you speak to family members at home. At school you listen to and talk to teachers and chat to friends. You send messages to friends via **phones**, listen to TV programmes and read books, magazines and online articles. In all of these situations a form of communication is taking place.

Communication is a two-way process – the sending and receiving of a message from one person to another or from one organisation to another.

People communicate with one another for different reasons. In the field of commerce, communication occurs within businesses, between businesses, between businesses and the public, between members of the public and among businesses situated in different countries.

> **KEY TERM**
>
> **phone:** a means of communication that enables a conversation to take place without people being visible to one another.

2.4.2 Types of communication

Communication methods can be divided into four main types:

- oral
- written
- electronic
- visual.

Oral communication

This is the exchange of information, thoughts and ideas through the spoken word. It can take the form of face-to-face interaction or an interaction through an electronic device, such as a smartphone or tablet device, using **videoconferencing**. Videoconferencing is a system of linking people in different locations with sound and (usually) visuals so that a meeting can take place. The best way for businesses to transfer information verbally is through oral communication, such as a staff meeting, webinar or workshop.

Oral communication can take place in the following situations:

- face-to-face conversations, such as discussions in offices
- individual contact using a phone, teleconferencing or videoconferencing
- interviews for jobs
- meetings, both formal and informal
- giving instructions, e.g., from manager to employee
- staff appraisals – one-to-one discussions between employees and managers to assess employees' work performance
- conferences or seminars – formal occasions with speeches or lectures to a number of people
- training sessions, either within a company or in specialised colleges or training centres
- press conferences – organised events to officially distribute information and answer media questions or to make company announcements
- public address systems, using loudspeakers connected to microphones to make public announcements in large areas.

> **KEY TERM**
>
> **videoconferencing:** a system of linking people in different locations with sound and visuals so that a meeting can take place.

Table 2.4.1 discusses the advantages and disadvantages of oral communication.

Advantages	Disadvantages
Personal contact between sender and receiver can be enhanced by non-verbal communication, such as tone of voice, facial expression or body language. People listening to the speaker can ask questions and receive feedback immediately. Language used can be adjusted to the receiver's needs. For example, if the receiver speaks a foreign language, the speaker can use simple language to explain a topic to the receiver. If the receiver does not understand the terminology used regarding a topic, the speaker can explain the terminology to the receiver. It can develop into a discussion so points can be clarified.	There is no written record. The receiver might not listen. It may take a long time, especially if many people are involved. There may be misunderstandings as the information may lack details if the conversation is not planned correctly ahead of time. The listener might ask questions the speaker cannot answer. Noise may disrupt the message and cause the receiver to hear incorrectly. Non-verbal signals may conflict with the message (eye contact or gestures), which may cause confusion. Some people are better communicators than others and may dominate a conversation.

Table 2.4.1: Advantages and disadvantages of oral communication

Written communication

Written communication is a written message that two or more people exchange. It provides a permanent record of a message and can be looked at more than once to check understanding. Written communication is usually more formal but less effective than oral communication. Oral communication is more convenient and less time consuming than written communication.

Oral communication delivers an immediate answer whereas written communication does not. Examples of written communication include emails and text messages.

Written communication can be used in the following situations:

- letters – these are used to communicate internally and externally, and are usually produced on the firm's letterhead. Examples include circular letters and letters asking for debt settlement. Individuals can also send letters to businesses, such as a job application letter (Figure 2.4.1).
- company magazines and newsletters – these are produced at regular intervals to provide staff and customers with a review and pictures of past events and to give details of future events.
- forms – these are designed to make sure that all the information required is included in one document. Examples of forms include invoices, purchase orders and job applications.
- notices and noticeboards – used for communication within a company. These are usually placed in prominent positions where they can be seen, are easy to read, concise and eye-catching.
- memoranda (memos) – these are short notes used to communicate within an organisation.
- press releases – these are announcements to the press and other media, concerning important events in an organisation.
- reports – these comment on a particular topic and are a response to a demand for information.
- meeting documents – these include notices of meetings, agendas and minutes. A notice of meeting informs company shareholders, directors and any interested parties of the time, date and place of a company meeting. The agenda is a list of items to be discussed in a meeting. Minutes are the official record of items discussed in a meeting, decisions made in a meeting and the people present.
- catalogues, brochures and leaflets – these are publications that are sent to customers or prospective customers, and give detailed information on the company's products or services.

Figure 2.4.1: Example of a job application letter as an instance of written communication

Table 2.4.2 discusses the advantages and disadvantages of written communication.

Advantages	Disadvantages
It is a permanent record for future reference, which cannot be changed. It allows time for planning a response. It is enforceable by law, so it can be used as evidence in a dispute. It enables technical and complex information to be communicated accurately. It can be supplemented by visual or numerical data. It can be sent to several people. There is less chance of misunderstanding between the writer and the recipient, and it can be checked more than once.	It can take time to produce. There is no personal contact. It can receive a slow response. It may be badly written, e.g., with poor use of language, being too wordy or having lots of mistakes, which may mean the message is not received correctly. It may not be read in full or may not be understood by the reader. It may be costly to produce. It may be difficult to explain complex points.

Table 2.4.2: Advantages and disadvantages of written communication

Electronic communication

Electronic communication is information sent between people over a phone line or internet connection. Businesses communicate with customers, suppliers and other businesses by email, fax, text messages, video messages and internet messaging. Videoconferencing reduces the need for people to be physically present at a meeting. It allows businesses to work with experts from all over the world, and problems can be solved and projects completed without physically being together. This can lower costs, increase job satisfaction and improve collaboration.

Electronic communication is useful because it can be used when someone is travelling or away from the office. It can also be used in emergency situations, e.g., if an office needs to close due to bad weather conditions. Businesses can send brief text and email messages from a mobile phone.

Table 2.4.3 discusses the advantages and disadvantages of electronic communication.

Advantages	Disadvantages
It is very quick. Messages can be sent to many people at the same time. Some methods are a permanent record and can be viewed more than once. The cost is low. It is easily accessible for those with internet access/ mobile phones. It offers long-term storage. Creative messages can be created with visual, audio and text. Consumers have access to websites all day, not just during working hours. A business can communicate with people far away.	Not everyone has access to the equipment required, e.g. internet, mobile phones. There might be security threats, such as viruses and hacking. The cost of equipment and software is high. There is the potential for addiction to electronic devices, which can become a distraction and lead to lower productivity. Confidentiality may be threatened as unintentional recipients may see the message.

Table 2.4.3: Advantages and disadvantages of electronic communication

Visual communication

Visual communication uses visual components to communicate information or ideas (Figure 2.4.2). Types of visual communication include videos, pie charts, bar charts, diagrams, maps, photographs and slide presentations. Getting a clear message across with just words can be difficult. Adding visual content can help ensure a message is understood correctly.

Examples of businesses using visual communication include:

- using narrated screencasts to train new employees. Screencasts capture a series of actions taking place on a computer screen or mobile device over time, such as the steps required to use a piece of software. A company can then add audio or text narration to these to help instruct the employee watching it.
- recording a conversation (with permission) in place of taking notes.
- recording audiovisuals explaining visual graphs to reduce misinterpretation in a presentation.

Table 2.4.4 describes the advantages and disadvantages of visual communication.

Advantages	Disadvantages
Complex information can be simplified to be understood.	People might interpret the information differently.
Visual content might attract the attention of the viewer.	Some elements might be lost through visual communication, e.g., cultural etiquette may be lost through a visual stimuli but could be explained through written communication.
People often remember visual stimuli more than they do written because the visual memory links the visual to emotion, which makes it easier to remember.	

Table 2.4.4: Advantages and disadvantages of visual communication

Figure 2.4.2: A slide-show presentation with bar and pie charts for visual communication

ACTIVITY 2.4.1

a Divide into groups.

b Choose a scenario from the following types of communication or adapt as necessary:

  i oral communication: a sales representative negotiating a deal with a client

  ii written communication: a manager providing instructions to an employee

  iii electronic communication: a manager communicating about a new product launch through email by providing the product name, launch date, target market (who the product is aimed at), the marketing strategy (deciding what channels to use to reach your customers), a detailed description of the product and product images

  iv visual communication: a marketing team presenting sales data to their colleagues.

c Present your communication and explain how you used your assigned type of communication to achieve the objective.

d Share your thoughts on which types of communication you prefer to use and why.

REFLECTION

Which part of this activity did you find most useful? Did you find by sharing your thoughts on which type of communication you prefer to use that you learnt something about yourself? Does this information help you understand your learning method better?

2.4.3 Methods of communication

People use communication on a daily basis. The way you communicate depends on who you are communicating with and the purpose of the communication. Different communication methods are suited to different situations. This section looks at the different methods of communication.

Letters

A letter is a message conveyed from one person or business to another through written, typed or printed communication. There are many types of letters that may be sent from a business to customers, including circular letters, letters confirming orders or prices, letters providing information, letters of apology or letters asking for the settlement of debts. Letters are usually word-processed so that they can be saved and amended if necessary. These days, emails are often used instead of letters.

Table 2.4.5 describes the advantages and disadvantages of letters.

Advantages	Disadvantages
A permanent means of communication More precise and explicit Enforceable by law and can be used as evidence in a dispute Less chance of misunderstanding between the writer and the recipient	Takes time to produce May be badly written May be difficult to explain complex points No personal contact Can be a time lag between being sent and being received

Table 2.4.5: Advantages and disadvantages of letters

Telephones: mobiles and smartphones

A phone is a means of communication that enables a conversation to take place without people being visible to one another (Figure 2.4.3). Many companies have landlines but also make extensive use of mobile phones. Cordless phones are popular and offer features such as stored numbers, caller identification and telephone answering.

Landlines use electrical currents to send the sound of your voice to the receiver. Mobile phones use wireless technology. Mobile phones can be held and you can move around with a mobile phone, whereas a landline is fixed to a wire in a specific spot.

Figure 2.4.3: Discussing business with a colleague via phone

Table 2.4.6 describes the advantages and disadvantages of a phone.

Advantages	Disadvantages
Immediate contact and instant feedback is received, unless you get voicemail. It enables discussion to take place and decisions to be made, unless you get voicemail. The conversation is private. You can speak to someone anywhere in the world.	The person being called might not be available. There is no record of the conversation. Time differences may cause difficulty with international calls. Reception is not always available in all places. Smartphones have a high risk of loss or theft. Calls can be expensive.

Continued

Advantages	Disadvantages
Calls can be made any time of day or night. Internet calls may be free – you are paying for the internet usage but not charged for the call. A voicemail message can be left if the person is not available to take your call. Smartphones can send text messages and connect to the internet and social media. Mobile phones can be used in an emergency situation. Smartphones are small and portable.	When used in public places, noise nuisance might be a distraction on smartphones. Voicemails might not be clear. Body language and non-verbal cues are missed.

Table 2.4.6: Advantages and disadvantages of phone

TIP

Make sure that you can explain the reasons why a method of communication is advantageous, e.g., a phone is fast to use as the caller can make immediate contact.

Face-to-face communication

Face-to-face communication is when two or more people can physically see each other while communicating (Figure 2.4.4). Face-to-face communication can be more effective than written communication, as people are able to see each other and judge body language and facial expressions.

KEY TERM

face-to-face communication: when two or more people physically see and interact with one another.

Table 2.4.7 describes the advantages and disadvantages of face-to-face communication.

Advantages	Disadvantages
Allows participants to read body language and facial expressions Builds trust and understanding between the parties communicating Boosts and enhances productivity by allowing participants to brainstorm and bounce ideas off each other Allows for discussions and conclusions to be reached	Difficult to find an appropriate time for large groups of people Organising meetings in large companies and getting all the relevant parties from various areas to meet in one place might be costly Could be ineffective with large numbers of people attending as they get bored and lose concentration

Table 2.4.7: Advantages and disadvantages of face-to-face communication

Figure 2.4.4: Face-to-face communication between colleagues in an office

Videoconferencing

Videoconferencing is a virtual, online meeting between two or more people where you are able to talk to each other through a video and audio call in real-time (Figure 2.4.5). Videoconferencing's popularity increased a lot during the COVID-19 pandemic, with more people needing to learn and work remotely. Examples of videoconferencing platforms are Skype, Zoom, Google Meet and Teams.

Table 2.4.8 describes the advantages and disadvantages of videoconferencing.

Advantages	Disadvantages
Companies can save on travel costs and travel time. Businesses can avoid problems of travel, such as delays, tiredness and jet lag. It also avoids travel through risky areas where there are security concerns. Companies save on meeting costs such as room hire and overnight accommodation. It allows meetings between people in different countries. Businesses can call meetings at short notice and conduct them live. Access to files or data is readily available if needed. It saves people leaving their offices for lengthy periods, so there is better use of people's time. Contributions to meetings, such as expert opinion, can be called in from anyone at short notice. A recording can be made if required. It can make companies more competitive as they are able to respond more quickly to problems that may arise and can make decisions more quickly. Body language and facial expressions can be seen and used to advantage. For example, if an employer is giving an employee feedback, the employer can see from the employee's body language how this is being received. This will help the employer to navigate the conversation successfully without causing distress or anger. Documents, models or technical drawings can be shown close up on screen.	It can be impersonal, especially if the person you are talking to does not have their camera turned on and you cannot see them. It may not work for every kind of situation and every kind of meeting. Meetings involving more complex discussions and decision-making may be better to have face-to-face. Disciplinary meetings are another example of situations where it may be better to have the meeting in person. It may be difficult to control the conference so that everyone is able to participate fully.

Table 2.4.8: Advantages and disadvantages of videoconferencing

Figure 2.4.5: A staff videoconference

Email

Online communication is the swapping of information (sending and receiving) via the internet. There are various platforms available for online communication, e.g., email, **instant messaging (IM)**, videoconferencing and social networks.

Email (electronic mail) is the exchange of messages or files between two or more people via the internet (Figure 2.4.6).

Figure 2.4.6: The global icon used for email

KEY TERM

instant messaging (IM): text-based communication between two or more people within an internet-based chatroom on smartphones or computers.

Table 2.4.9 describes the advantages and disadvantages of email.

Advantages	Disadvantages
It can be a fast, reliable and inexpensive, and an almost instantaneous means of communication. By clicking on 'Reply', the sender can quickly reply to an email without having to type an email address. It is paperless – can be read and deleted, which saves space. Documents and files can be sent as attachments. Agreements made by email can be legally binding.	Some people may find email messages impersonal, as they have no signatures. When discussion is needed, email may take too long and become disjointed. Some staff may overuse the sending of emails so that users spend a considerable amount of time reading incoming messages that are of no interest. You cannot send an email without an email address.
Priority emails can be pinned to the top of your inbox and highlighted so you can see your most important messages first. Confidentiality can be ensured by users keying in passwords to access messages. People travelling can access emails using a smartphone, laptop or tablet. Messages can be sent to multiple email addresses at the same time. Messages can be forwarded to other email addresses. All types of information can be sent (pictures, photographs or graphics).	There may be delays in replying if the recipient does not check emails regularly. Junk mail (advertising emails) can clutter up the inbox and take up room on the computer's hard drive. Phishing – trying to extract personal information by sending an email pretending to come from a bank or other financial institution – can be a danger. There is a risk of catching a virus from an attachment. Individuals sometimes use emails to harass or bully others. Emails may be deleted by accident. The computer could break down or crash.

Table 2.4.9: Advantages and disadvantages of email

TIP

Do not assume that email is always quick. The message may be quick to send but if the receiver does not check emails, the reply could be delayed.

Web-based chat

Instant messaging is an online platform where people are able to communicate by messaging in real-time (Figure 2.4.7). People are notified when a friend logs into the application and they are then able to chat to each other. Examples of instant messaging platforms are WhatsApp, Telegram, WeChat and Snapchat.

Figure 2.4.7: Web-based chat groups global icon

Table 2.4.10 describes the advantages and disadvantages of instant messaging.

Advantages	Disadvantages
Instant communication – short, to-the-point, informal chats Connects people regardless of where they are situated Group discussions are possible Easy to use Captures the attention of the recipient more than email	Can be an ineffective tool for group communication as too many people are sharing opinions and having their say at once May have security issues such as viruses or identity theft Cannot be controlled by management

Table 2.4.10: Advantages and disadvantages of instant messaging

Social media

Social media refers to websites and apps where users and companies are able to connect with one another, communicate, share information and build relationships. Social media accounts for one of the highest uses of the internet. Examples of social media platforms are Facebook, Instagram, YouTube, TikTok, Pinterest and Tumblr (Figure 2.4.8).

Figure 2.4.8: Icons used for interactions on social media

Table 2.4.11 describes the advantages and disadvantages of social media.

Advantages	Disadvantages
User is easily connected to the world Videos and images can be used, which are useful for marketing and advertising Wide audience to promote to, with the ability to target specific audiences Constant news availability Fast means of communication Business advertising opportunities Increased communication	Social media addiction, causing employees to make personal use of it during work hours Health issues such as depression, anxiety, loneliness and self-harm Concern for privacy, as account may be hacked with loss of confidential information Emotional bond is missing, as it leads to decreased face-to-face communication and enables the use of false identities

Table 2.4.11: Advantages and disadvantages of social media

Posters

A poster is a sheet placed in a public area to promote something, or put on a wall for decoration. It communicates a message through graphical blends. It is eye-catching, informative and visually attractive. It is usually aimed at a specific target market. A poster may contain text as well as graphics or one or the other.

Table 2.4.12 describes the advantages and disadvantages of posters.

Advantages	Disadvantages
It is easy to understand the message.	Preparing posters is time consuming.
Any products or events can be promoted.	Limited information can be given on a poster.
A business can convey information to a large audience as they are placed in strategic places.	A poster may be affected by adverse weather conditions, especially rain.
It can be used by both people who are literate and people who are illiterate.	If not placed strategically, a poster may not reach the target audience.
Using design features, such as bright colours, can help them grasp more audience attention.	It could be destroyed by passers-by and therefore the information will not reach the target market.
The message can last for a longer period of time.	

Table 2.4.12: Advantages and disadvantages of posters

TIP

Method of communication is the means of communication, such as a letter or social media post, whereas the type of communication is the chosen channel for the message between a sender and a receiver, such as oral or electronic.

ACTIVITY 2.4.2

a In groups, find out which methods of communication your school administration department uses to reach out to:

   i learners

   ii parents

   iii teachers.

b Make a list of the pros and cons of each method of communication the school uses for each particular stakeholder.

c Share a presentation with the class on your findings.

d As a class, make a list of suggestions on better communication methods your school could be using and explain why you think your choice should be implemented.

e Hand in a written document of the suggestions to your teacher and see if the school implements any of your suggestions.

2.4.4 Factors that affect communication

As the world becomes a single market, the need for rapid communication becomes increasingly important. Transport services across the world have sped up. Communication when arranging travel needs to be efficient, or the benefits of faster transport will not be achieved.

Companies may wish to check, confirm or establish prices for ordering supplies. Many companies rely on speedy delivery of supplies to carry out production. Without rapid and accurate communication, such as email, videoconferencing, web-based chat and social media, production might be slowed down.

Traders want instant information on the state of a market. Information, such as whether or not there is a shortage or a plentiful supply of a certain commodity, or whether or not the share price of a particular company has gone up or down, can now be found at the touch of a button.

Rapid and accurate transmission of information has made possible the international system of banking and finance. Debt between traders in different countries can be settled electronically without the use of currency. Profits made by multinational companies can be moved from one country to another. **Internet banking** – banking online using a bank's website and an individual security number – has expanded rapidly. Many people no longer visit a bank branch. Instead, they carry out their banking transactions online or by using a mobile app (Figure 2.4.9).

Figure 2.4.9: Mobile apps need an internet-enabled smartphone to download and use

KEY TERM

internet banking: banking online using a bank's website and an individual security number.

Rapid communication has improved services provided to customers. Customers can obtain information about goods and services online and can purchase these either by phone or using the internet. Potential customers are demanding more and more information about the products they are interested in buying.

Email and the mobile apps have made communication easier, giving instant communication to people and businesses all over the world. These rapid forms of communication have enabled business opportunities to be taken up and problems to be resolved as quickly as possible. They have given people the opportunity to 'network' – to make contacts and to share ideas and experiences. They are benefiting from being able to communicate anywhere at any time, and when the costs of doing so are falling. Communication in all its forms is becoming an ever important part of everyone's lives.

Barriers to communication

Communication may not always be successful. **Barriers in communication**, or reasons for failure to communicate, may result in poor communication.

KEY TERM

barriers in communication: reasons why communication fails or is poor.

There are many reasons for poor communication:

- distance between sender and receiver – it is generally easier to communicate over shorter distances as less technology is required and more communication channels are available
- language problems
- the wrong choice of communication method
- message distortion where lines of communication are overly complicated within a business, meaning that a message has to pass through too many people before it reaches its intended recipient. This increases the chance of an error being introduced, or someone forgetting to pass something on.

Poor communication may lead to mistakes, poor performance and falling sales.

When selecting the method of communication, the following factors need to be considered:

- urgency – if information is required urgently, it may be sent electronically. The time available is the main factor to be considered. Higher cost may be justified to ensure the message is sent in time.
- cost – although letter post was regarded as a cheap means of communication, email (once the costs of the computer and network have been paid) is now cheaper. When deciding which method to use, the result obtained for cost should justify the expense.
- security – to make sure a message is received, it may be necessary to send it by registered post. When sending an email, you may ask for an acknowledgement of receipt of the email. Sending a message via courier will also ensure it arrives safely. Privacy should also be considered, e.g. ensuring IT protection systems are in place if sending confidential information electronically.

- distance – if the sender and the receiver are in the same building, the method of communication used may be different from when they are in different countries.
- availability of networks – often the choice of method of communication depends on what is available. The sender and the receiver must have supporting technological communication tools for it to be effective.
- importance of the message – verbal communication may need written confirmation. The main drawback of a phone is that there is no record of the conversation. If proof of a transaction is needed, written evidence, such as a contract, commercial documents or a letter, will be required. The use of informal or formal channels should also be considered, e.g. email versus instant messaging.

REFLECTION

Do you think creating a summary of this chapter would improve your understanding of the content? If not, what other method could you use to help your learning?

ACTIVITY 2.4.3

a Divide into three groups.

b Each group chooses one of the following scenarios:

  i a business trying to negotiate a contract with a foreign supplier

  ii a customer service team dealing with a difficult customer complaint

  iii a marketing team developing a new advertising campaign.

c As a group identify and discuss the main barriers to communication in your chosen scenario. Think about internal and external barriers.

d Each group draws a table with the barriers identified. Explain how you identified these barriers and how you would address or overcome the barriers.

e Share the tables drawn up with each group to get an overview of all three scenarios.

SELF-EVALUATION CHECKLIST

After studying this chapter, complete this table.

You should know about:	Needs more work	Almost there	Ready to move on
the difference between written, oral, electronic and visual communication			
different methods of communication			
factors affecting the choice of communication method			

Knowledge check

1 Which of the following is not a type of written communication?
   a email
   b letter
   c face-to-face meeting
   d memo

2 Which of the following is an advantage of oral communication?
   a permanent record of the communication
   b allows for detailed explanations
   c receiver might not listen
   d provides time to review information

3 Which of the following is a disadvantage of electronic communication?
   a very quick
   b low cost
   c many people can access at the same time
   d security threats

4 Which of the following is an example of visual communication?
   a pie charts
   b email
   c letter
   d memo

5 How is the head office of an international company most likely to make regular contact with its sales office in other countries?
   a airmail letter
   b courier
   c email
   d phone

6 Explain what written communication is and provide three examples of different methods of written communication.

7 Explain the term 'oral communication'. State two advantages and two disadvantages.

8 Provide an explanation of a mobile app.

9 Why may communication not always be successful?

10 Name and provide an explanation of four factors which need to be considered when choosing a method of communication.

Practice questions

1 *An international cricket club uses a variety of communications in its operations. The club is making increased use of air transport to send equipment for matches.
   a Explain **one** example of oral communication that might be used by the cricket club. [2]
   b Explain why letters are used by the club when signing new players. [3]

Cambridge O Level Commerce 7100, Paper 22, Q2a, b, June 2022

2 *Discuss the importance of communications in international trade. [6]

Cambridge O Level Commerce 7100, Paper 23, Question 5c, June 2021

3 Discuss two factors which affect the communication choice. [4]

> Unit 3

Globalisation of trade

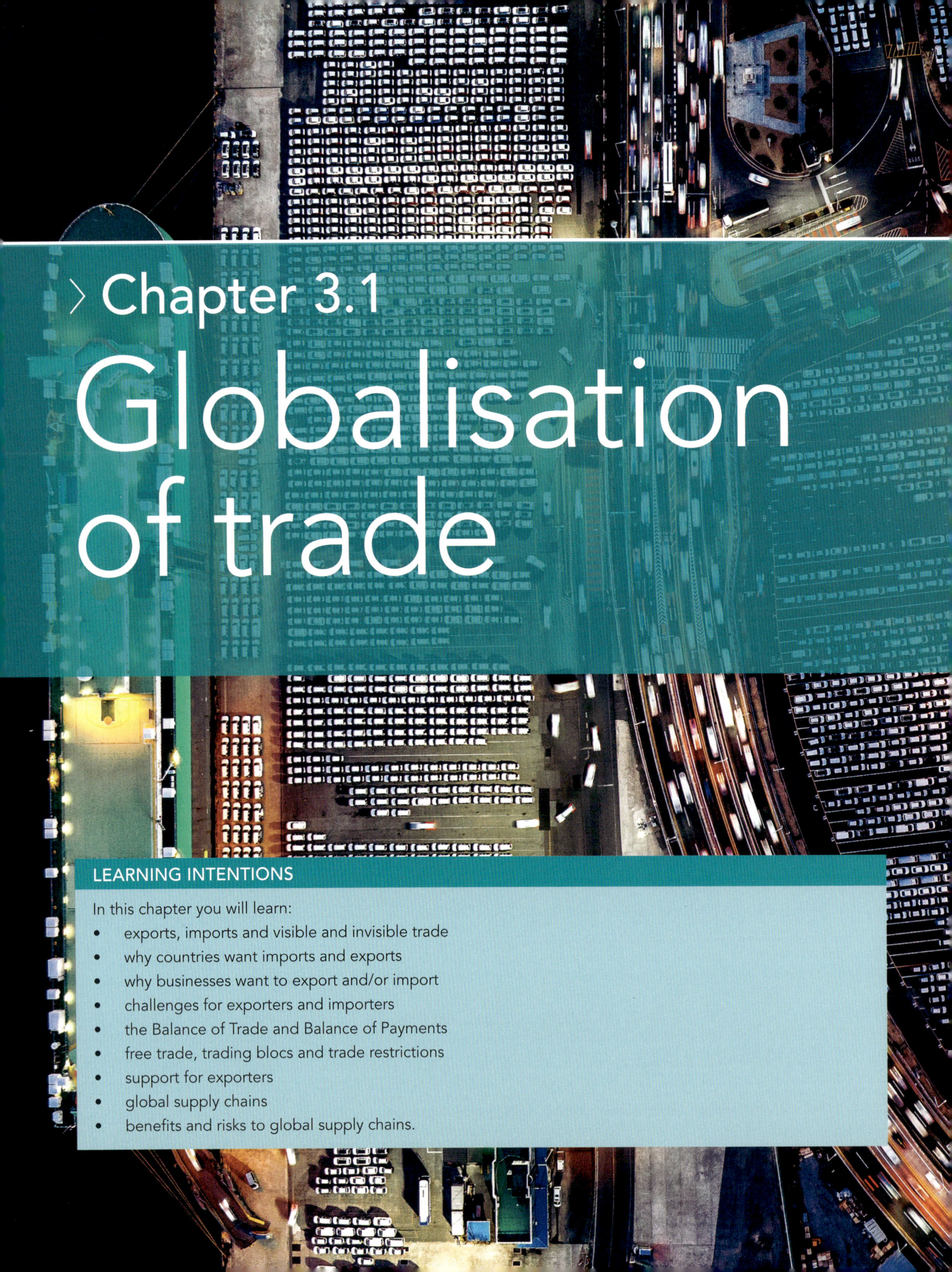

› Chapter 3.1

Globalisation of trade

LEARNING INTENTIONS

In this chapter you will learn:

- exports, imports and visible and invisible trade
- why countries want imports and exports
- why businesses want to export and/or import
- challenges for exporters and importers
- the Balance of Trade and Balance of Payments
- free trade, trading blocs and trade restrictions
- support for exporters
- global supply chains
- benefits and risks to global supply chains.

3.1.1 International trade

Buying and selling goods and services across different countries is called international trade. International trade occurs because each country differs in its demand for goods and services and in its ability to supply them.

International trade enables countries to obtain goods and services that are not available in their home country, are available only in limited quantities or are too expensive or difficult to produce in their own countries.

Over time, countries have become more aware of the benefits of international trade. In general, countries have become wealthier, allowing people's **standard of living** (a measure of how wealthy people are) and expectations to rise. This has led to greater demand for a wider range of goods and services that are available from across the world. Consumers then choose to buy goods and services from other countries to meet their needs and wants. There has been a growth of multinational businesses that operate in multiple countries. For example, Toyota and Coca-Cola both manufacture and sell their products in many different countries.

> **KEY TERM**
>
> **standard of living:** a measure of how wealthy people are and what they can afford to have.

International trade has grown over time. This growth has been supported by developments in technology, such as quicker communication through email and other digital methods. Moving goods from one country to another has also become easier and cheaper as transport and communication have improved.

The world is becoming a global market, which means one large market for goods and services. As the whole economy of the world is becoming more integrated into a single 'global market', globalisation is taking place. Globalisation encourages more connections between businesses and consumers in different countries. The same goods and services can be found in many countries throughout the world. A traveller going round the globe is likely to see many of the same types of cars, mobile phones, fast-food restaurants and soft drinks whatever country they are in. Businesses often focus on what is happening in the global market rather than in the home market. For example, a business might decide to relocate the manufacturing of its products in a country with lower wages.

Each country has its own currency that is used to buy and sell goods and services. For example, USA uses dollars, Japan uses the yen and Pakistan uses rupees. When people visit other countries or businesses trade internationally, they will need to use foreign currencies.

Exports, imports and visible and invisible trade

Exports include goods and services sold to other countries that bring money to the country. For example, Apple Inc. is an American company; however, many Apple products, such as mobile phones, are manufactured in China and exported to countries around the world.

Imports include goods and services from other countries that are paid for by paying money to other countries. Lots of countries need to import raw materials and food that they are not able to produce themselves. For example, tea is a popular drink in the UK. The country's cold climate makes growing tea difficult so the UK imports tea from several countries including Kenya, India and Zimbabwe.

Visible exports are goods sold to other countries whereas **visible imports** are goods bought from other countries.

Invisible exports are services sold to buyers in other countries, e.g., insurance and transport, whereas **invisible imports** are services bought from sellers in other countries, e.g., holidays abroad and films made by foreign companies.

Visible exports and visible imports make up **visible trade** (Figure 3.1.1). Trade in goods is known as visible trade because goods can be seen moving in and out of a country.

> **KEY TERMS**
>
> **visible exports:** goods sold to other countries.
>
> **visible imports:** goods bought from other countries.
>
> **invisible exports:** services sold to other countries.
>
> **invisible imports:** services bought from other countries.
>
> **visible trade:** the import and export of goods.

Invisible exports and invisible imports make up **invisible trade**. The trade in services is known as invisible trade because unlike goods, services offered overseas are not seen.

KEY TERM

invisible trade: the import and export of services.

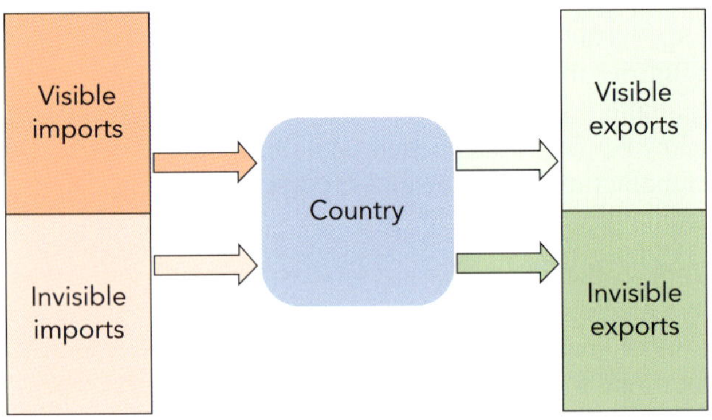

Figure 3.1.1: Visible and invisible trade

TIP

It is easy to mix up imports with exports, and visible trade with invisible trade. It is worth spending time learning the definitions and differences so that you always use the terms correctly.

Why countries need imports and exports

Each country's government decides its own policies and laws to control its international borders. Countries will use their laws to decide which goods, services and people are allowed into the country and which are allowed out of the country.

Most countries allow and encourage international trade because of the many benefits it can bring to a country and its people.

As international trade has increased over time, the global market has become larger with many countries now importing from and exporting to all over the world. According to the World Trade Organization (WTO), the volume of world trade grew by 4% in 2021. The biggest exporting countries are China, the USA, Germany and Japan. China is the world's largest manufacturer, making over a quarter of all manufactured goods produced worldwide, many of which are exported. China's biggest exports include machinery, computers, furniture and plastic goods and vehicles.

There are several benefits that countries can receive from importing and exporting goods and services:

- wider choice of goods
- lower cost of imports
- job creation
- higher standard of living
- greater investment.

Wider choice of goods

Importing gives countries the opportunity to have goods that would otherwise be unavailable, or only available in small quantities or for a high price. The size of a country affects its ability to produce the wide range of goods it needs. Small countries tend to be especially dependent on international trade and appreciate the benefits.

Some raw materials are only found in certain countries. Countries that do not have a particular raw material, or only have small quantities, must import it or go without. For example, Zimbabwe imports oil, Bangladesh imports iron and chemical products and Brunei imports gas.

Countries differ in their climate and amount and types of land. Many countries do not have the right climate or enough land to produce all the food they need for their population (Figure 3.1.2). In these circumstances, it is essential to import the rest of the goods that they need.

Figure 3.1.2: Climate influences where food is grown

1 Climate, including temperature and rainfall, affects the ability to produce all the food a country's population needs. For example, European countries import bananas from countries with tropical climates where bananas grow best.

2 Some countries do not have enough land to produce all the food needed for their population. The Maldives imports food including rice and sugar as it cannot grow all the food its population needs on its small islands. China has the world's largest population and needs to import some food, such as soybeans and corn, from the USA and Brazil.

Different countries' populations have varying levels of education, skills and specialist knowledge. For example, Japan and South Korea have developed a workforce with high levels of technological expertise, and have developed businesses that can produce many electronic products of high quality at low cost. As a result, other countries are keen to import their mobile phones, televisions and robotics. Germany and USA have expertise in the pharmaceutical industry and other countries import their medicines. See Chapter 1.2 for further details of specialisation.

Lower cost of imports

Climate and land differences mean that some countries can produce many primary goods more efficiently and at lower cost than other countries. For example, the UK would need to use expensive greenhouses to produce many of the fruits and flowers that it demands throughout the winter. It is much cheaper for the UK to import fruit and flowers from other countries instead.

Products are more expensive to manufacture in some countries than others. The cost of employing people is a large part of the cost of producing many products. Wages vary a lot between counties. Countries that have higher wage levels are more likely to find that it is cheaper to import some goods than to produce their own. For example, European countries import many manufactured goods from countries like China and India that have lower labour costs and have well-developed manufacturing industries.

Some countries that have high wages can still produce products at lower cost provided they efficiently use skilled labour and invest in the right equipment. For example, wages are high in Germany, but successful businesses in Germany still produce and export high-quality vehicles, machines and chemical products at lower costs than many other countries.

Job creation

A growing export market for a business's products can lead to the business growing and employing more staff. The growth of many businesses in a country due to exports will then lead to a reduction in unemployment and an increase in wages.

Other businesses that provide services to exporters, such as insurance, banking, transport and warehousing, also grow and create more jobs. These export services have expanded over the years as international trade and the global market have increased.

Higher standard of living

Standard of living is a measure of how wealthy people are and what they can afford to have. The higher the standard of living, the wealthier people are. International trade allows countries to specialise in making the goods and services that they are best at producing. If a country concentrates on producing a few goods and services, it is likely to become more efficient at producing those goods and services. However, the country will also become less focused and produce less of other goods. As a result, the country may become less self-sufficient. It will need to export more of the goods it does produce so that it can afford to import other goods that it is less efficient at producing.

By concentrating on producing what it is best at, and exporting these goods and services, a country will have growing businesses, leading to more jobs, increases in wages and a higher standard living for its population. If a country remained self-sufficient, it would be less efficient at providing the wider range of goods it needs for all its population. As a result, the country will have a lower standard of living.

Some countries also use exporting to diversify from the products they have traditionally produced. Expansion into new products and markets can encourage economic growth and reduce risks from producing a small range of products. For example, Dubai is a big exporter of oil. It has also developed other industries and its re-export trade, resulting in a high and growing standard of living. Its airport is now an international hub serving many parts of the world. Dubai has also become a popular destination for tourists.

TIP

Refer back to Chapter 1.2 and remind yourself of the meaning of specialisation and its advantages to a country. An understanding of specialisation will help you to understand why international trade can lead to a wider choice of goods and a higher standard of living.

Greater investment

Businesses that sell in many countries can benefit from bigger markets and more customers. Growing demand for a business's products means that the business can afford to invest more in itself, such as new machinery, technology and staff training, resulting in the efficient production of large amounts of goods. Many of the world's biggest businesses have grown through international trade. For example, Amazon has grown by focusing on ecommerce, Apple Inc. manufactures and sells computers and phones and Volkswagen produces and sells vehicles. All of these companies trade in many countries across the globe.

International trade can also lead to greater investment into a country from foreign investors, who will choose to invest anywhere in the world where they see opportunities for a good return on their investment. For example, Nissan is a large Japanese company that has invested large amounts of money in overseas manufacturing sites including in Mexico and the UK. This investment is beneficial to Mexico and the UK and can lead to more local jobs, higher wages and a higher standard of living.

Why has international trade become easier?

Circumstances that have encouraged the growth in international trade include the following:

- Better electronic communication, such as business websites, email and video calls, have improved marketing and contact between sellers and potential buyers.
- The faster movement of products through improved coordination and the use of quicker methods of transport, such as **air freight**, makes it easier to transport products. This is especially useful for perishable goods, such as fruit and cut flowers.
- Trade agreements between countries have reduced trade protection (see Section 3.1.3).

KEY TERM

air freight: goods carried by air/aircraft that carry goods by air.

TIP

We often focus on the export and import of goods, but remember that services are also exported and imported. High skill levels required by some services, such as engineering, financial and business management, and telecommunications, make these services particularly common for international trade in many countries.

ACTIVITY 3.1.1

Working with a partner or in a small group, choose three countries and research each country's imports and exports.

For each country, include the following:

i What goods and services are its biggest exports?

ii Which countries does it sell most exports to?

iii What goods and services are its biggest imports?

iv Which countries does it import most goods and services from?

a Which of your three researched countries has the most imports and exports? Give reasons for your answer.

b Present your findings to the class.

c After listening to the presentations from others in your class, did you find that some countries imported and exported more than others? Why might the amount of international trade vary between countries? Were there some types of goods that were internationally traded more than others?

Pakistan

Key exports: cotton textiles including clothes, bed sheets and pillow cases, rice and cereals, leather goods

Big export markets: USA, Germany, China, UK and United Arab Emirates

Key imports: machinery, iron and steel, pharmaceuticals and chemicals, food, petroleum, oil

Main suppliers of imports: USA, Saudi Arabia, China, United Arab Emirates and Indonesia

South Africa

Key exports: platinum and iron, gold, coal, cars

Big export markets: China, USA, Germany, Japan and UK

Key imports: petroleum, cars and trucks, phones

Main suppliers of imports: China, Germany, USA and India

Mauritius

Key exports: clothing, sugar, meat and fish, clothes, gems and precious metals

Big export markets: South Africa, France, UK and USA

Key imports: machinery, petroleum products, chemicals, vehicles

Main suppliers of imports: China, United Arab Emirates, India and South Africa

Figure 3.1.3: Exports and imports for Pakistan, South Africa and Mauritius

REFLECTION

Discuss your answers to Activity 3.1.1 part **c** with another student. Did they reach the same conclusions, or did they have different views? If your conclusions differed, why might this have happened?

How would you defend your conclusion? Or can you now criticise your conclusion?

Why businesses decide to export and/or import

Many businesses choose to export or import goods and services rather than only operate in their home market. International trade may be more challenging than home trade for exporters and importers, but there are many potential benefits of trading internationally that make it worthwhile.

Table 3.1.1 describes common reasons why businesses choose to import or export.

Why do businesses export?	Why do businesses import?
To grow by having access to more customers in a bigger market	To make a profit from importing goods or services. For example, a business might be able to import goods that are cheaper than home-produced products or of higher quality
To reduce risk of business failure by diversifying into different goods and services and new markets	To benefit from demand for a product in the home country where the product is not currently available
To increase sales by exporting to countries with better market conditions. For example, exporting to countries with lower taxes, less competition or wealthier customers To extend the life of a product that has declining sales in the home country but has not been sold in other countries	To obtain raw materials or components for use in manufacture that are not available in the home country

Table 3.1.1: Reasons why businesses import and export

TIP

When you are thinking of the reasons to trade internationally, be clear about whether you are considering the benefits from the point of view of a business, consumer or country.

Challenges for exporters and importers

Exporters and importers typically have many more challenges than home businesses, which only buy and sell in one country. Businesses trading internationally must have knowledge of overseas markets and enough understanding to overcome problems of operating in other countries.

Businesses must make decisions about which countries to trade with. The amount of trade that businesses choose to do with a country may be determined by the costs of operating in particular countries, which is influenced by economic factors. Economic factors include the amount of industry in the country, the standard of living, market size and population trends, and the wealth of the country.

There are several main challenges to businesses that come from importing and exporting goods and services:

- distance
- language
- documentation
- transportation
- customs duties
- non-payment
- different currencies and methods of payment
- foreign exchange rates
- competition
- different legal systems.

Distance

Distance can be a huge difficulty for exporters and importers, especially where large or heavy goods need to be moved long distances, e.g., businesses based in Asia buying from and selling to the UK. Distances can cause both transportation and communication problems.

- Goods travelling long distances may be more likely to get damaged, lost or stolen. Longer distances also increase the costs of getting the goods to the customers.
- Distances make it harder for buyers and sellers to meet face-to-face. However, developments in electronic communication, such as online meetings, have reduced these problems.

Language

There are often language barriers in international trade, and interpreters may have to be employed. Labels, instructions, advertisements and any other documents will all have to be produced in each importing country's language. This will add to a business's costs.

Communicating in different languages can also cause misunderstandings through inaccurate use of language by mistake.

Documentation

Commercial documents, such as air waybills and bills of lading and letters of credit, are often required for international trade but are not required for home trade. The country of origin of a product will need to be identified for customs purposes, so certificates of origin are used to prove where the goods originally came from. All these additional requirements add to the complexity and costs of trading internationally.

See Chapter 2.3 for further details on documents of international trade.

TIP

Check your notes and revise Chapter 2.3 on documents of international trade. Revision of this topic will help you understand the additional paperwork required for international trade.

Weights, measures and technical specifications can all vary from country to country. Sorting out these differences can add to a business's costs. For example, some countries use grams and kilograms while others use pounds and ounces. Voltages for electrical appliances may differ and products may need to be modified, such as cars that might need to be right- or left-hand drive depending on the country. Differences are likely to lead to increased paperwork requirements.

Transportation

Road and rail transport is often used for importing and exporting across countries within the same continent, e.g., from France and Germany to other countries in Europe. Sea and air transport is more commonly used for exporting between continents, such as from Africa to Asia (Figure 3.1.4). Transport adds to the costs of the products. Insurance costs will be higher than for home-produced products because there are more risks associated with the movement of goods. Risks include increased chance of damage to the inventory and disruption to transport such as a vehicle breakdown causing delays in getting products to their destination.

Goods that must go long distances often need to be transferred from one type of transport to another as they travel to their destination. Transfers add to the complexity of transporting goods, although this complexity can be helped using **container transport**. Standardised containers are transferred from one form of transport to another without unpacking the goods. The containers are used for bulky goods and can help to reduce the costs of transport.

Deliveries can take much longer than for home-produced products and delivery dates may be less predictable and inaccurate dates may be given to customers. More packaging may be needed to transport goods between countries.

KEY TERM

container transport: use of standardised boxes (or containers) to move goods using more than one mode of transport, such as by sea and rail.

Figure 3.1.4: Transporting containers by sea

Customs duties

Many countries operate some forms of trade restrictions on imports. Trade restrictions may raise money for the government and support home businesses. Customs duties are a type of taxation that the consumer must pay on imported goods that they buy. Customs duties will make imported goods more expensive to consumers. This higher price will make it more difficult for an importer to compete with home businesses.

Risk of non-payment

International trade is usually conducted on credit, and customers do not pay invoices until several weeks after the purchase has been made (see Chapter 2.1 for details of invoices and credit). Whenever goods are sold on credit, there is always a risk that the customer does not pay the money they owe. This risk is even higher when selling overseas because it can be more difficult to find out whether the customer is trustworthy and will pay for the goods.

The risk of non-payment is particularly high if there is political instability in a country, such as riots or an attempt to overthrow the government. Any uncertainties can affect the confidence that a business has about trading internationally and the risk of non-payment for goods that have been sold. See Section 3.1.5 on global supply chain risks for further details of political instability.

Different currencies and methods of payment

When businesses purchase goods from suppliers, they will commonly receive an invoice and then have a few days or weeks before they must pay. Possible methods of payment include cash, cheque, credit card, debit card, electronic transfer and documentary credit. These methods are explained in Chapter 5.2.

Payment problems may happen because it is more complicated to use different countries' banking systems and different currencies (Figure 3.1.5). Imports and exports are often paid for in highly trusted currencies that are used widely for international trade, such as the US dollar or the Japanese yen. The trusted currency is then exchanged into local currencies. Importers and exporters will need to use methods of payment that can manage differences between currencies. These methods of payment, such as electronic transfer or letters of credit, can be more complex than those payment methods used by businesses that only operate in one country.

Figure 3.1.5: Foreign currencies

Foreign exchange rates

An exchange rate is the price of one country's currency expressed in terms of another country's currency. The rate at which one currency is exchanged for another currency is called the rate of exchange, e.g., the price of the US dollar against the Zimbabwean dollar.

In home trade, one currency is used. In international trade, different currencies are usually required. Exchange rates can change at any time, and there are always risks that the rate of exchange will change between the time that the prices were quoted and the time that payment is due. A change in the exchange rate will lead to a change in the value of the import or export. This may lead to unexpected losses for the importer or exporter.

Foreign exchange rates affect the types and quantities of goods and services that are exported and imported. For example, if the Bangladeshi taka becomes stronger than the Singapore dollar, the Singapore importer may not be able to import the same quantity of goods as before, since the Bangladeshi goods will be more expensive. The Singapore trader may therefore look elsewhere for cheaper products.

Competition

The more businesses that trade internationally, the more competition there is likely to be. It can also be especially challenging for a business trading internationally to compete against competition from local businesses that operate in the country where the goods will be sold. The home business will not have incurred some of the costs that an importer has, such as transportation. Advertising and other promotional material must be designed for the customers in the country where the goods and services will be sold. Home businesses may also be able to compete by providing better after-sales service that is available locally.

Different legal systems

Each country has its own laws affecting how businesses operate and the products and services that can be sold. There are laws governing safety standards, saleable quality, protection of consumers and how goods can be advertised. These laws will vary from country to country. For example, children's toys imported into the UK will have to prove that they conform to UK toy safety legislation.

A government may also change its laws on international trade. There may be changes in the **regulations** that affect imports of particular goods, causing problems for the importer. For example, a foreign government may suddenly introduce limits on the use of foreign currency or new trade restrictions (see Section 3.1.3).

Despite the problems and challenges, international trade is often worthwhile as it can help businesses grow and become very profitable.

KEY TERM

regulations: a rule or law that a business must follow. The regulations govern trade activities between businesses based in different countries.

3.1.2 The Balance of Trade and Balance of Payments

The Balance of Trade and the Balance of Payments are both calculations that countries make to assess their international trade.

Balance of Trade

The **Balance of Trade** (balance of visible trade) is the difference between the money received from a country's exported goods (visible exports) and the payments made for a country's imported goods (visible imports) over a period of time.

Goods include:

- primary products, such as crops, oil and fish
- semi-manufactured products, such as steel and chemicals
- finished goods that have been manufactured, such as clothes, vehicles and processed foods like sweets and packets of instant noodles.

The Balance of Trade can be calculated as follows.

FORMULA

Balance of Trade = receipts from visible exports – payments for visible imports

If a country's receipts from the exports of goods are greater than payments for imports of goods in a specific time period, it means that visible exports are greater than visible imports and there is a positive Balance of Trade. This is called a favourable or **surplus Balance of Trade**.

If a country's receipts from the exports of goods are less than payments for imports of goods in a specific time period, it means that visible exports are less than visible imports and there is a negative Balance of Trade. This is called an adverse or **deficit Balance of Trade**.

KEY TERMS

Balance of Trade: the difference in financial value between the total exported goods and the total imported goods.

surplus Balance of Trade: when the value of a country's visible exports is greater than the value of its visible imports.

deficit Balance of Trade: when the value of a country's visible exports is less than the value of its visible imports.

Balance of Payments

A country's **Balance of Payments** is a record of its total foreign trade including both goods and services over a period of time.

KEY TERM

Balance of Payments: the difference in financial value between the total exported goods and services and the total imported goods and services over a period of time.

Table 3.1.2 gives examples of services that are commonly imported or exported.

Invisible exports	Invisible imports
Transport, such as shipping and flights, provided to people in other countries	Payments to overseas businesses for use of their transport, such as shipping and flights
Financial, banking, communications and insurance services provided to other countries	Financial, banking, telecommunications and insurance services received from other countries
Tourists visiting from other countries	People going abroad on holiday
Receipt of aid from other countries	Aid given to other countries

Table 3.1.2: Examples of services that are commonly imported or exported

The Balance of Payments can be calculated as follows.

FORMULA

Balance of Payments = Balance of (visible) Trade + Balance of (invisible) Trade

where

Balance of (invisible) Trade = receipts from invisible exports − payments for invisible imports

As with the Balance of Trade, the Balance of Payments calculation may show a surplus or a deficit.

If a country's receipts from the exports of goods and services are greater than payments for imports of goods and services in a specific time period, there will be a positive Balance of Payments. This is called a surplus or favourable Balance of Payments.

If a country's receipts from the exports of goods and services are less than payments for imports of goods and services in a specific time period, there will be a negative Balance of Payments. This is called a deficit or adverse Balance of Payments.

WORKED EXAMPLE 3.1.1

Calculating Balance of Trade and Balance of Payments

The following information is available for a country.

	2023 ($ million)	2024 ($ million)
Receipts from visible exports	400 000	550 000
Payments for visible imports	500 000	510 000
Receipts from invisible exports	300 000	400 000
Payments for invisible imports	400 000	410 000

Required

a Calculate the Balance of Trade in **i** 2023 and **ii** 2024.

b Calculate the balance of invisibles in **i** 2023 and **ii** 2024.

c Calculate the Balance of Payments in **i** 2023 and **ii** 2024.

Answer

The Balance of Trade and Balance of Payments calculations are shown below.

		2023 ($ million)	2024 ($ million)
	Visible exports	400 000	550 000
	Less visible imports	− 500 000	− 510 000
a	Balance of Trade	**−100 000 (deficit)**	**40 000 (surplus)**
	Plus invisible exports	+ 300 000	+ 400 000
	Less invisible imports	− 400 000	− 410 000
b	Balance of invisibles	**− 100 000 (deficit)**	**− 10 000 (deficit)**
c	Balance of Payments (Balance of Trade + balance of invisibles)	**− 200 000 (deficit)**	**30 000 (surplus)**

In the worked example, the Balance of Trade deficit for 2023 shows that the value of goods that the country imports is greater than the value of goods that it exports. However, the Balance of Trade is in surplus in 2024 because the value of goods that the country imports is less than the value of goods that it exports.

The country's Balance of Payments changes from a deficit in 2023 to a surplus in 2024. The Balance of Payments is also in surplus in 2024 because its surplus in visible trade is bigger than its deficit in invisible trade.

Sometimes a country can have a Balance of Trade deficit and a Balance of Payments surplus at the same time. This combination will occur if the Balance of Trade deficit is smaller than the surplus on invisible items (services).

TIP

It is important to be aware that the Balance of Trade focuses on goods only. The Balance of Trade does not focus on services. However, the Balance of Payments considers *both* goods and services.

The impact of international trade on the Balance of Trade and the Balance of Payments

The more successful a country's businesses are at producing and exporting goods and services the stronger the country's Balance of Trade and Balance of Payments are likely to be. Each country must be able to afford any imports that it needs or wants to buy. Having a Balance of Payments deficit (imports are greater than exports) for several years can lead to problems for a country, as it will find it difficult to afford to buy imports. Therefore, the country's government will need to take action to increase exports and/or decrease imports.

- To increase exports, the government can support and encourage home businesses to produce and export more goods and services.
- To decrease imports, the government can encourage consumers to purchase products made in the home country. The government can also reduce imports by increasing customs duties on imports or introducing other trade restrictions (see Section 3.1.3 for an explanation of trade restrictions).

Some countries regularly have a Balance of Trade surplus. Other countries regularly have a Balance of Trade deficit and find it difficult to alter the situation, especially in the short term.

Pakistan has had a Balance of Trade deficit for many years. This is partly because the value of the country's exported clothing and other goods has not been enough to offset country's demand for significant amounts of imported oil. However, China produces huge quantities of manufactured goods for export, which allows it to import what it wants while keeping a Balance of Trade surplus.

Countries that have a deficit on their Balance of Trade sometimes have a surplus on invisible trade, which helps their overall Balance of Payments. For example, the UK imports many goods but is a big exporter of services, such as finance and insurance.

3.1.3 Free trade, trading blocs and trade restrictions

Figure 3.1.6: Checks made on imports and exports

Many countries have checks and controls on goods that are imported and exported (Figure 3.1.6). Each country will use its own customs authorities to carry out the following functions:

- assess and collect **tariffs** on imports. A tariff is a type of taxation that must be paid whenever an importer brings goods into a country. The tariffs imposed are decided by the government.

- keep records of exports and imports. This information can be used to:
    - calculate the volume and value of imports from each country, and the volume and value of exports to each country where the goods and services are being sent
    - calculate the Balance of Trade and Balance of Payments
    - assess trends in international trade, which the government can use to decide trade policies and calculate tax revenue from import tariffs.
- supervise the movement of goods across a country's borders. This involves the inspection of goods and relevant documentation to prevent smuggling and enforce any bans on goods such as firearms or agricultural products.
- enforce **quotas**. Quotas are limits placed on the amount of goods allowed to be imported into a particular country over a particular time period.

KEY TERMS

tariff: a type of taxation that an importer must pay on goods brought into a country.

quota: a limit on the amount of a product that is allowed to be imported into a country in a year.

TIP

It is easy to mix up customs duties with tariffs. Check the definitions for both terms so that you can use each of them correctly.

Free trade

Free trade means trading between countries without any barriers to trade. Barriers to trade can include import tariffs or other trade regulations aimed at protecting a country's home businesses. Free trade allows the import and export of goods without government interference.

KEY TERM

free trade: trading between countries without any customs duties, tariffs or other trade restrictions.

Free trade encourages more international trade to occur. This leads to a country benefiting to a greater extent from all the advantages of international trade, such as wider choice of goods, higher standard of living and lower unemployment.

In practice, many countries impose some restrictions on goods or services coming into their country. Countries impose restrictions because, while free trade can bring lots of benefits to a country, there are also disadvantages.

Disadvantages of free trade include the following:

- some home businesses are more likely to fail because they find it difficult to compete with goods and services that are produced more cheaply in other countries.
- free trade encourages an uneven distribution of wealth, with some people benefiting from increased trade while others become poorer.
- some products are 'dumped' in a country. These products are very cheap imports, such as clothing. Home businesses cannot keep their prices low enough to be able to compete and as a result the country then becomes reliant on these imported goods.

Figure 3.1.7: Trade between countries

Trading blocs

A **trading bloc** is a group of countries that work together to promote trade between themselves. The countries that are members of the bloc make free trade agreements between each other. The trading bloc also creates a common tariff to countries outside the bloc to discourage imports from countries that are not members of the bloc.

Types of trading bloc

The types of trading bloc are listed below.

- **Free trade areas** are groups of countries that have no obstacles to trade, such as customs duties, between member countries. For example, Australia has several free trade agreements with countries including Singapore and Malaysia.
- **Customs unions** are groups of countries where there is free trade between member countries and an external tariff against goods from outside the customs union. An example is the South African Customs Union. Its members are South Africa, Lesotho, Namibia, Botswana and Eswatini.
- A **common market** or single market is a customs union that also allows free movement of capital and labour, and reduces other difficulties associated with international trade, such as documents and technical standards between member countries.

KEY TERMS

trading bloc: a group of countries that have made a free trade agreement between themselves and have agreed a common external tariff to non-member countries.

free trade area: an area within which there are no restrictions to trade.

customs union: a group of countries where there is free trade between member countries and an external tariff against goods from outside the group.

common market: a customs union that also allows free movement of capital and labour within the member countries.

Table 3.1.3 gives three examples of trading blocs.

	ASEAN (Association of Southeast Asian Nations)	SADC (South African Development Community)	SAARC (South Asian Association for Regional Cooperation)
Year established	1967	1980	1985
Member countries	10 member countries: Singapore, Malaysia, Indonesia, Brunei, Thailand, the Philippines, Vietnam, Cambodia, Laos and Myanmar	16 member countries: Angola, Botswana, Comoros, Eswatini, Lesotho, Malawi, Mozambique, Namibia, Seychelles, Tanzania, Zambia, Zimbabwe, South Africa, the Democratic Republic of the Congo, Madagascar and Mauritius	8 member countries: Afghanistan, Bangladesh, Bhutan, India, the Maldives, Nepal, Pakistan and Sri Lanka
Tariffs	ASEAN uses a common preferential tariff scheme, which only charges low tariffs between member countries (0–5%).	SADC has a free trade agreement between member countries.	SAARC has a free trade agreement between member countries.

Table 3.1.3: Examples of trading blocs

There are both advantages and disadvantages for a country joining a trading bloc, as described in Table 3.1.4.

Advantages of joining a trading bloc	Disadvantages of joining a trading bloc
It encourages more trade between member countries. There is free access to larger markets. The removal of controls such as quotas or import tariffs means more competitive prices. This encourages businesses to compete by becoming more efficient. There is a wider choice of goods for consumers living in the trading bloc. Sales and profits may increase for some businesses in the trading bloc. Businesses have greater access to cheaper land, skilled labour and raw materials in other countries, and can produce wherever it is most cost effective. Trade is easier because member countries may agree factors such as trading laws, measures, weights, documents, equipment and sometimes currency. There are more employment opportunities for the people who live in member countries if they can work and move freely between countries. A trading bloc is in a stronger bargaining position to negotiate good trade deals with other countries or trading blocs.	Tariffs on products from outside the trading bloc make those products more expensive to import. Competition from other businesses in the trading bloc may cause some businesses to fail. Businesses may lose grants and subsidies previously given by their own government. Businesses may have to change their goods or services to suit the preferences of consumers in the trading bloc. The trading bloc may impose extra rules and regulations on each country in terms of how their businesses operate. Each country must contribute to the trading bloc's budget.

Table 3.1.4: Advantages and disadvantages of joining a trading bloc

Free ports

Some countries do not have free trade for the country as a whole but will have **free ports**. Free ports are specific geographical areas inside a country where the production and processing and packaging of goods can occur without the requirement to pay any taxes, including export tariffs on goods.

Free ports are often seaports, but can also be inland areas, such as airports. Examples of free ports are Dubai, Hong Kong, Singapore, Liverpool in the UK and Port Louis in Mauritius.

Free ports are important in international trade because they encourage trade and make trading easier. Trading is cheaper because no customs duties are charged on goods entering or leaving the free port.

Trade restrictions

Trade restrictions occur where a country puts tariffs or other barriers on international trade, particularly imports. Such restrictions on international trade are called **protectionism**. The aim of protectionism is to protect a country and its businesses from foreign competition. The main risk of protectionism is that other countries may retaliate and also impose protectionist policies. Protectionism leads to less trade between countries.

KEY TERMS

free ports: geographical areas inside a country where the production and processing and packaging of goods can occur without the requirement to pay any taxes, including on goods.

protectionism: the placing of restrictions, such as quotas, on international trade to make trade more difficult and to protect industries within a country.

Table 3.1.5 describes the main types of protectionism.

Types of protectionism	Explanation
Tariffs on imports	Tariffs increase the cost of the imported goods and services. This leads to higher import prices, making it more difficult for foreign goods to compete against home-produced goods that do not pay the tariff. This encourages customers to buy home-produced goods rather than more expensive goods from overseas.
Quotas	A quota is a limit on the amount of a product that can be imported or exported. Import quotas lead to less imports of a particular product being available. This encourages home industries to produce and sell more to the home market.
Embargoes	An embargo is a complete ban on the import of a product, the export of a product or any trading with a particular country. Embargoes with a country are usually for political reasons.

Table 3.1.5: Types of protectionism

KEY TERM

embargo: a ban on the import of a product, the export of a product or any trading with a particular country.

The effects of trade restrictions

There are several reasons why countries decide to put trade restrictions in place.

- To protect domestic industry from businesses that operate in other countries that are able to keep costs down by paying workers much lower wages. More developed countries often use this argument to put protectionist policies in place against imports from countries where very low wages are paid. Some international companies refuse to buy goods from businesses that provide their workers with poor working conditions or pay extremely low wages to their employees.
- To protect industries that are of strategic importance to the country. For example, agriculture and fuel are considered essential products. Some countries are not willing to risk a reduction in supply of these products, especially in times of war, by relying on foreign supplies of the products.
- To protect **infant industries**, which are industries that are in the early stages of development. New businesses often have higher costs than established competitors. A country may choose to protect home businesses in a new or growing industry to give them time to develop. For example, if a country has not previously produced computers, it might choose to support new home computing businesses in their first few years by imposing some form of protectionism on computing imports.
- To deter import **dumping**. A product is said to be 'dumped' when it is exported at exceptionally low prices, often below cost. Dumping may occur when a foreign business has excess of its goods. For example, farmers in one country may have excess supplies in a year with a very good harvest. The business chooses to get rid of the excess by selling it cheaply abroad rather than selling it at a lower price in its home market. Dumping may also occur when a foreign business charges very low prices in the short term to try to make its competition fail. Once the competition has had to close down, the foreign business may put its prices back up and make large profits.
- To protect employment. This may occur in countries where there is a significant risk of high unemployment without protectionism.
- To improve the country's Balance of Trade. If the value of imports is greater than the value of exports in the longer term, protection may be used to reduce imports, leading to an improvement in the Balance of Trade.
- To provide the government with more revenue by creating import tariffs.

KEY TERMS

infant industry: an industry that is in the early stages of development within a country.

dumping: occurs when a product is exported at much lower prices than it charges in its home country.

Trade restrictions can also have other impacts on commercial activities.

- Overall trade restrictions lead to less international trade and less output across the world.
- A country will produce a wider range of goods and services itself instead of specialising in industries that it is best at.
- There will be higher prices for goods that rely on imported raw materials that are subject to import tariffs.
- There is likely to be retaliation by other countries that may put their own protectionist policies in place. This may lead to reduced exports along with job losses in export industries that are affected by other countries putting on their own protection policies in retaliation.
- There will be a lower standard of living for the population than if there had been more international trade.

3.1.4 Support for exporters

Exporters must manage many challenges when they export their products and services. However, there are several sources of support that are available too:

- international trade fairs
- insurance guarantees
- cheaper bank loans.

International trade fairs

A **trade fair** is an opportunity for businesses in the same industry to gather and meet each other in one place and promote their goods.

> **KEY TERM**
>
> **trade fair:** an opportunity for businesses in the same industry to gather and meet each other in one place and promote their goods.

Exporters may also use trade fairs to sell their products. A trade fair might take place over a few days. At a trade fair, many businesses in the industry will set up exhibition stands (stalls) with leaflets, posters and other promotional material giving information about their products and services. Trade fairs can be especially useful at raising awareness of new products and services. Employees or representatives of other businesses in the industry will visit many different stalls to find out about potential suppliers or customers as well as competitors. If an exporter is running a stall they will need to ensure that it looks attractive to compete with other stalls and encourage people to visit.

Employees might travel overseas especially for large or specialist international trade fairs. If a trade fair is well attended, exporters can use it as an efficient way to meet and talk with suppliers or customers, promote their products and find out about competitors.

Insurance guarantees

Exporters face many risks. Goods can be damaged while being transported long distances, there can be lower receipts or higher payments due to changes in foreign exchange rates and there can be greater risks from non-payment from foreign customers.

Businesses can buy insurance cover from insurance companies to help protect against many of these losses. For example, insurance that covers losses from overseas customers who do not pay for the goods they have bought is called export credit insurance. Insurance is explained in more detail in Chapter 5.2.

Sometimes risks are high, and exporters are unable to buy insurance. However, exporters may be able to get support from their country's government. Many governments recognise the benefits of international trade to their country and are willing to offer insurance guarantees to support businesses that export. Guarantees are usually organised through a country's export credit agency. They will insure a business against risks such as the failure of a foreign business customer, or the inability to deliver an export because of political issues, including new trade restrictions or political unrest.

Cheaper bank loans

Commercial banks offer a range of advice and support to exporters, including suitable methods of payments and the buying and selling of foreign currency. Banks also offer loans to businesses and will charge **interest** in return. Interest is money received as a reward for savings or money paid as a cost of lending. Bank loans are explained in more detail in Chapter 5.2.

Each bank will decide what interest it will charge on any bank loan. Interest rates depend on several factors, but in general the higher the risk that a business is unable to repay a loan the higher the interest rate.

As with insurance guarantees, exporters may be able to get support from their country's government. Support might be in the form of guarantees to the banks and other direct lending, which reduces the risks to the banks and allows exporters to have cheaper bank loans with a lower rate of interest.

KEY TERMS

commercial bank: a bank that provides a range of banking services to both business and private customers.

interest: money received as a reward for savings or money paid as a cost of lending.

ACTIVITY 3.1.2

Choose one of the following topics of global trade:

i benefits and challenges of imports and exports

ii Balance of Payments

iii trading blocs and trade restrictions.

Review your notes and the textbook information then produce a mind map on your chosen topic.

Explain your mind map to another student.

REFLECTION

When answering Activity 3.1.2, how did you choose which topic to review? Did you pick the topic you knew most or least about?

How useful was it to create a mind map? Did it help you to learn the topic? Do you think there are better ways of learning this topic? If so, why?

3.1.5 Global supply chains

As you learned in Chapter 1.2, a supply chain considers everything involved in getting a product or service, from the initial raw materials through to the final customer receiving the finished item. One supply chain can include several different commercial enterprises. A supply chain involves the physical movement of raw materials and finished products from one enterprise to another, such as from supplier to manufacturer or from wholesaler to retailer. A supply chain also involves the flow of information between the enterprises. Information is important to help coordinate the different activities. Each party needs information about the progress of earlier activities so that they can prepare their operations to efficiently work on their required task.

Local supply chains are used for products that can go through all their stages in one country. Global supply chains involve more than one country, as goods may be moved or information shared internationally.

TIP

Global supply chains build on your earlier knowledge of this topic. Review your notes on local and global supply chains from Chapter 1.2.

Global supply chains can be grouped into two different types:

- simple supply chains
- complex supply chains.

A **simple supply chain** involves three stages: supplier to manufacturer to consumer. The initial supplier(s) will provide the raw materials. These raw materials are transported to the manufacturer who will turn them into finished goods. The finished goods are then delivered to the consumer.

KEY TERM

simple supply chain: a supply chain that involves three stages: supplier to manufacturer to consumer.

For example, a furniture maker may be part of a simple supply chain. The furniture maker will buy its wood, metal and other items from suppliers. The furniture maker can then sell its furniture directly to consumers.

The furniture maker will be part of a global simple supply chain if any of the suppliers or consumers are in other countries.

TIP

Remember that although a simple supply chain only has three stages (supplier to manufacturer to consumer), it can have more than one supplier and more than one customer.

A **complex supply chain** involves more stages than a simple supply chain. There are usually five stages in a complex supply chain: supplier to agent to wholesaler to retailer to consumer.

Having more stages in a supply chain can make it more challenging to communicate and coordinate between the enterprises involved at different stages. This can mean that problems such as delays are more likely to occur. An agent (sometimes known as a supply chain manager) is used to manage and coordinate the activities carried out at each stage and among the different businesses involved in a supply chain.

See Chapter 1.2 for further information on the role of agents, wholesalers and retailers in a supply chain.

The type of supply chain may vary according to the nature of the product and the demand for the product. For example, a coffee wholesaler will be part of a complex supply chain. The wholesaler may use agents to buy coffee from lots of individual farmers. The wholesaler will sell large quantities of coffee to retailers who sells smaller quantities to each consumer. Coffee is part of a global complex supply chain because coffee grows better in some climates than others. Much of the world's coffee is grown is Brazil, Vietnam, Columbia, Indonesia and Ethiopia; however, coffee is consumed worldwide, with huge quantities being consumed in the USA and much of Europe.

Supply chain management

Supply chains can involve many different enterprises and all sectors of production, from primary to manufacturing and construction to services like retailing. Planning and coordinating all these enterprises and different stages can be challenging. The more complex the supply chain the more challenging the process is likely to be. **Supply chain management** describes the organising of all the stages that products or services must go through until they eventually reach the final customers.

The supply chain is divided into two elements, which are referred to as **upstream operations** and **downstream operations** (Figure 3.1.8). Upstream operations focus on getting the materials to the enterprise that is a producer/manufacturer. Downstream activities support the process of distributing the products from the enterprise (producer/manufacturer) to the consumer. The enterprise divides the upstream and downstream operations.

KEY TERMS

complex supply chain: a supply chain that involves more stages than a simple supply chain. There are usually five stages: supplier to agent to wholesaler to retailer to consumer.

supply chain management: the organising of all the stages that products or services must go through until they eventually reach the customers.

upstream operations: activities that support the delivery of the materials and/or other resources to the producer/manufacturer.

downstream operations: activities that support the process of distributing the products from the producer/manufacturer to the consumer.

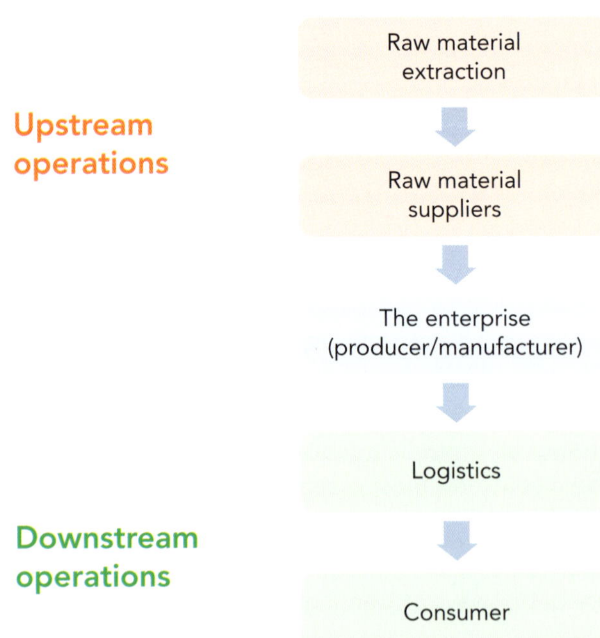

Figure 3.1.8: Upstream and downstream operations

In a global supply chain, the businesses/people providing the upstream and/or downstream operations are based in different countries.

There are additional challenges when operating as part of a global rather than local supply chain, which include:

- delays to the transportation of materials and/or products. Although there can be transportation delays in any supply chain, the risk of disruption increases if the businesses/people are based in different countries, for instance, supply may be delayed due to extreme weather events in one or more countries or port delays/congestion.
- communication. It is important that all businesses/people share information to support the efficient distribution and flow of goods through the global supply chain. This can be more challenging if the supply chain is global due to time differences, for example.

Trade barriers often affect global supply chains. These government restrictions affect the profitability of operations and the efficiency of the movement between the stages. Supply chains where all businesses/people are based in the same country do not face trade barriers.

The importance of suppliers

Choosing suppliers is an important part of managing global supply chains. Having reliable suppliers that provide their products on time and to the correct standard is very important. If the wrong supplier is chosen, products may arrive late or the products may be of poor quality. This means that the supply chain is broken, and there are likely to be negative effects on other businesses in the supply chain. Ultimately the customer may not get the products they wanted.

As an example, many fast-food brands rely on having food that tastes identical whichever restaurant a consumer visits. This relies on having suppliers that can consistently produce ingredients of an agreed standard over time, including colour and taste, etc.

Any issues with suppliers or transportation or storage can lead to a restaurant running out of products for their customers. There have been occasions when well-known brands have had negative publicity because of problems with suppliers, such as McDonald's running out of milkshakes or KFC (Kentucky Fried Chicken) running out of supplies of chicken.

Benefits to global supply chains

Well-managed supply chains can lead to several advantages for businesses.

Lower costs of production

Some countries specialise in particular industries and products. They may have developed a skilled workforce or benefit from the availability of natural resources. Supply chains will often make use of goods and services from countries and businesses that specialise in the production of a particular product, leading to lower costs of production. For example, the furniture industry requires skilled labour and a supply of bulky raw materials. Over time, Vietnam has developed a skilled workforce that can use the local supply of good-quality wood to specialise in producing good-quality furniture at lower costs than many other countries. Bangladesh also effectively uses its climate and land to specialise in growing rice and tea, and can do so much more cheaply than countries that have colder climates.

Lower labour costs

Labour costs depend on the efficiency of workers and on wage rates. The efficiency of workers will depend on the workers' skills and motivation and the equipment that they have available to use.

Wage rates vary from country to country. In general, people in wealthy countries, such as Singapore and Brunei, have a higher standard of living and higher wage rates. People in less wealthy countries, such as Nepal and Malawi, have a lower standard of living and lower wage rates.

Businesses will carefully consider labour costs when deciding where to source goods. Supply chains often include suppliers based in countries with lower labour costs for the production of goods that require a lot of labour. For example, clothing bought in wealthy countries is often manufactured in lower-wage countries, many miles away.

Lower cost of purchasing

Suppliers may be able to offer lower prices because of lower labour and other production costs. Businesses may also be able to negotiate lower purchase prices with their suppliers for other reasons. Being able to buy from anywhere in the world means that there are more suppliers competing for sales. By researching lots of potential suppliers, businesses can find and choose the cheapest. Suppliers may offer lower prices if they know there is lots of competition for their products. Suppliers may also agree to offer a discounted price if a customer purchases a large quantity.

Improvements in logistics

Logistics involves the planning and coordinating of the transportation and storage of goods throughout the supply chain. Global supply chains can be very complicated and challenging to organise. They may involve suppliers in several countries, with different time zones and languages. A problem with any one link in the chain can affect the ability to get goods to their eventual consumer.

Well-organised logistics will result in efficient use of storage space for goods and quicker deliveries with less hold-ups. For example, goods can be tracked as they travel across the world, helping to coordinate different types of transport in different locations.

Good logistics will lead to lower costs and goods that are more likely to arrive at their destination on time and in good condition. The benefits of having good logistics have encouraged businesses to invest in their continuous improvement over time so that further savings can be made. (See Chapter 4.1 for further information on logistics.)

Improvements in communication

Improvements in communication, especially electronic communication, including emails, video calls and websites, are all useful when communicating with other parts of the supply chain. Suppliers can communicate with customers more easily, and having supply chains across several countries is eased by instant electronic communication. Technology can also help to overcome language differences, with electronic tools that translate text or speech into different languages.

As with logistics, the benefits of having good communication have encouraged businesses to invest in their continuous improvement over time so that further benefits can be made.

Risks to global supply chains

All supply chains have risks. The more complex the supply chain the more things can go wrong. Supply chains that work across several countries have additional risks due to the distances and differences between countries (Figure 3.1.9).

Figure 3.1.9: Global supply chain risks

Environmental risks

Environmental risks occur because of the actions people take and the way people and businesses use the environment. There are many different environmental risks, including water and air pollution and deforestation. Deforestation involves cutting down and removing many trees in one area without replacing them. This might occur because the land is needed for other reasons, such as roads or farming.

The environment can affect suppliers' ability to supply their products to businesses and for products to reach consumers. For example, a manufacturer of furniture may find it more difficult to find suppliers who can provide high-quality wood, such as teak wood, because of shortages of supply caused by deforestation. As a result, manufacturers will need to pay high prices, search extensively for suppliers or use alternative types of wood.

Pollution in the sea may cause a decrease in the number of fish available for fishing. This will affect the whole supply chain for getting fish to consumers. Fishing boats will catch less fish, and this will affect the number of fish available for wholesalers, retailers and ultimately consumers, leading to higher costs per fish and higher prices for the fish that is available.

Businesses are increasingly aware of the importance of acting in ways that minimise harm to the environment. Many consumers prefer to buy from businesses that have a reputation for protecting the environment. For example, consumers may choose to buy goods that may have been supplied locally rather than transported across the world. This is further explained in Chapter 6.1 on sustainability in the supply chain.

Natural disasters

While environmental risks can have long-term effects, specific natural disasters, such as hurricanes or floods, can have a big effect on supply chains in the short term.

For example, a manufacturer of packaged food, such as breakfast cereal, will rely on farmers to supply the raw materials that they need to make their goods. Farmers may agree to provide a set amount of raw materials needed. A natural disaster such as a flood or drought will affect the amount of produce that the farmers can grow. This will affect the supply chains as it will affect the ability and reliability of farms to supply produce to food manufacturers and to supply food of the right quality.

As well as the availability of products themselves, natural disasters can disrupt the transportation of goods and their punctual arrival to customers. For example, adverse weather conditions such as a storm or fog may affect sea or air transport and cause delays (Figure 3.1.10). The more complex the supply chain the greater the impact one disruption can have on other parts of the supply chain.

Figure 3.1.10: Flood causing disruption to road transport

Financial risks

All businesses have financial risks. However, these risks are often bigger for businesses that have global supply chains. Financial risks that worry many international businesses often focus on the payment or non-payment of invoices. For example, a business may pay its suppliers when the order is placed; however, the goods may not arrive or they may not arrive in good condition.

Financial risks may also arise from changes in foreign exchange rates, which can result in businesses having to pay more than expected for their supplies.

See Section 3.1.1 on challenges from financial risks for exporters and importers relating to financial risks from non-payment and foreign exchange rates.

Ethical risks

Ethics in business means making decisions about what is the morally right or fair thing to do. Many consumers make ethical decisions about their purchases. Many businesses also aim to make ethical decisions that reflect the values of their stakeholders, including those of their customers.

KEY TERM

ethics: doing the 'right' thing. It is about the moral behaviour of individuals and managers when operating a business and making business decisions. Ethics focuses on exceeding the legal minimum, i.e., the standard required by law in the country.

A business may use ethics when making decisions about its supply chain. While ethical decisions may relate to the environment, ethical decisions might also consider social factors and the impact on people, including workers. For example, a business might be considered to behave ethically by paying suppliers punctually or by only using suppliers that treat their workers fairly, such as those who pay workers sufficient wages to live on, provide good working conditions and do not use child labour.

Ethical decisions may be more expensive. However, making unethical decisions can also risk higher costs along with an effect on the business's reputation and sales. For example, if consumers find out that a well-known brand of clothing uses suppliers that rely on cheap or child labour then there is likely to be critical publicity and sales will fall.

Technological risks

Advances in technology have supported the growth in international trade over time. For example, advances in electronic communication methods such as email and video calls have helped supply chains to improve because information about purchases and sales can be transferred easily and quickly from one country to another.

Customers can access business websites from anywhere in the world and order goods delivered to their home. Businesses that sell goods to key international markets have further developed their websites to direct customers to the part of their website specific to consumers in that country, with their language and prices in the country's currency. Goods can be tracked as they are transported across the world.

Increasingly, reliance on technology to support the supply chains comes with risks. Any problems with the technology can cause a lot of disruption. For example, introducing a new computer system can lead to many unexpected problems, such new software that has errors or staff who are not fully trained. As a result, goods may not be ordered correctly from suppliers, or a transport link is not arranged for the correct time. These problems might lead to a shortage of goods, unhappy customers and higher prices.

Cyberattacks are a particular risk of technology. Cyberattacks are caused by people who illegally try to damage a business's computer system. An attack might cause a business to lose important information about its suppliers or supplies. An affected business may find it difficult to find and correct the attack. For example, a cyberattack on a bank might mean that businesses cannot get access to their money and pay their suppliers.

Political risks

Political factors include stability or instability of the government and the attitude to corruption and to democracy in the country. Instability might be caused by a change of government, or riots or an attempt to overthrow the government. Any uncertainties can affect the confidence that a business has about trading internationally and concerns over possible disruption to supply chains, such as the reliability of supplies and the price of goods supplied. For example, a new government might put an embargo in place or set new tariffs. Significant instability such as a civil war can have a big impact by cutting off transportation routes or power supplies, which might stop the safe movement of supplies altogether.

Risk assessments

Many of these difficulties and risks to global supply chains can be managed and overcome. Large businesses such as multinational companies may overcome many of the difficulties by having specialised staff and departments that focus on purchasing and logistics (see Chapter 4.1). Smaller businesses can still manage risks if they organise supply chains carefully and use computer software to help.

Specific risks can often be overcome or minimised, provided they are identified and assessed.

Businesses may carry out a **risk assessment** of their supply chains. A risk assessment is a careful study that aims to identify things that might go wrong and assess what the impact might be. The business can use the information to decide whether to accept the risk, find solutions to reduce the risk or get rid of the risk altogether. For example, a risk assessment could identify that a cyberattack would cause a lot of problems to a business that relies heavily on its computer systems to manage its supply chains. As a result, the business might decide it is worthwhile to buy a security system to reduce the risks. Another business's risk assessment might identify financial risks from the possible theft of goods while in transit and recommend purchasing insurance to manage this risk (see Chapter 5.2 for further details on insurance).

KEY TERM

risk assessment: a careful study that aims to identify things that might go wrong and judge what the impact might be.

ACTIVITY 3.1.3

Have a class debate to discuss and decide which is the biggest risk to global supply chains.

To prepare for the debate, work in a small team and do the following.

a Research the risks to global supply chains.

b Choose one risk that you can argue is the biggest risk to global supply chains.

c Plan your arguments ready for a classroom debate.

d Choose one member of the team to represent the group and speak in the debate.

The representative of each group should give an introductory argument (2 minutes each). The rest of the class may then join in for questioning and debate.

At the end of the debate, all students should vote to decide which team gave the strongest argument for its chosen risk being the biggest risk to global supply chains.

Note: your teacher may facilitate the debate itself and each team's choice of risk, to ensure that each team chooses a different risk.

SELF-EVALUATION CHECKLIST

After studying this chapter, complete this table.

You should know about:	Needs more work	Almost there	Ready to move on
exports, imports and visible and invisible trade			
why countries want imports and exports			
why businesses want to export and/or import			
challenges for exporters and importers			
the Balance of Trade and Balance of Payments			
free trade, trading blocs and trade restrictions			
support for exporters			
global supply chains			
benefits and risks to global supply chains			

Knowledge check

1 Define an exchange rate.

2 Complete the following sentences:

A surplus Balance of Trade means the value of a country's visible exports is .... than the value of its visible imports.

A deficit Balance of Trade means the value of a country's visible exports is .... than the value of its visible imports.

3 Define a customs duty.

4 Explain two disadvantages of free trade.

5 State two benefits of global supply chain management.

6 What is a disadvantage of joining a trading bloc?
- a All exporters must have insurance guarantees.
- b Joining enables free access to larger markets.
- c More competition from others in the bloc.
- d Joining leads to increase in tariffs.

7 Free trade can be defined as:
- a countries that agree a common external tariff
- b a customs union
- c international trade without trade restrictions
- d products exported without transportation costs.

8 An international trade fair is an example of:
- a a source of support for exporters
- b a trade restriction
- c globalisation
- d supply chain management.

9 International trade can benefit a country through:
- a changing foreign exchange rates
- b different legal systems
- c improvements in communication
- d a wider choice of goods.

10 What is a risk to global supply chains?
- a free trade
- b lower costs of production
- c natural disasters
- d tariff reduction

Practice questions

1 The following information is available for Country X in 2024.

	2024 ($ billion)
Visible exports	47
Invisible exports	59
Visible imports	70
Invisible imports	44

Required:

a i Calculate the Balance of Trade. [1]

ii Calculate the balance of invisibles. [1]

iii Calculate the Balance of Payments. Show your working. [2]

b Analyse why Country X has a Balance of Payments deficit or surplus in 2024. [3]

c State two types of trade restrictions. [2]

d Country X is considering joining a trading bloc with neighbouring countries. Evaluate whether joining a trading bloc is a good idea for Country X. [6]

2 XY Trading Ltd is a medium-sized manufacturer of children's toys. It sells to retailers in its home country. XY Trading Ltd has been growing in recent years and has now decided to begin exporting its products. The business has heard that its country's government encourages businesses to trade abroad.

a Explain three benefits of international trade to a country. [6]

b State two sources of support for exporters. [2]

c Do you think it is a good idea for XY Trading Ltd to begin exporting its goods? Give reasons for your answer. [3]

d Evaluate the challenges to XY Trading Ltd of starting to export their products. [6]

Unit 4

Logistics in commerce

Chapter 4.1

Transportation

LEARNING INTENTIONS

In this chapter you will learn:

- the functions of transport in the supply chain
- transport types and methods
- the benefits and drawbacks of different transport methods
- the factors affecting the choice of transport method
- the aspects of containerisation
- the benefits and drawbacks of containerisation.

4.1.1 The importance of transportation in the supply chain

Transport is one of the most important parts of supply chain logistics. Logistics is the management of the flow of goods from the place of production, either from where the raw materials are obtained or from the factory where they are made, to the marketplace or the consumer. Logistics involves the combination of information, purchasing, stock control, warehousing, packaging and transportation as well as security. Logistics is responsible for the geographical repositioning of raw materials, semi-finished goods, components and finished goods to where they are required. It might be described as having the right product, at the right time, in the right quantity, in the right condition, at the right price and with the right customer.

Raw materials are moved from where they are produced (e.g., mines, farms or plantations) to where they are processed. Transport is also used to move finished goods from factories to warehouses, wholesalers, retailers or directly to consumers. It enables people to obtain a greater variety of goods, thus improving their standard of living. Many people now use imported goods that would not have been available to them before improvements in transport.

Transport has helped to create an interdependent world. It encourages countries and regions to specialise in the production of goods they are best suited for. For example, Japan specialises in car manufacture and the production of electronics. Australia produces dairy products, meat and minerals. Transport moves these products to markets all over the world.

Effective transport leads to the expansion of markets. If transport can deliver goods quickly, producers will try to find markets further away from the place of production. Transport helps trade and businesses to expand and produce more. It has helped the growth of overseas markets and the expansion of the global economy.

Efficient transport ensures that goods are distributed effectively to avoid problems of surpluses, rising prices, falling prices and shortages. If goods are stored and not distributed, there will be surpluses in the warehouses and shortages in shops. Prices may rise because goods are in short supply. Transport evens out supply, which ensures there is stock available in the shops as well as in the warehouse.

4.1.2 The functions of transport in the supply chain

There are three functions of transport in the supply chain.

Time

Customers need to have access to the product when they demand it. Transportation methods ensure deliveries inbound and outbound flow smoothly and arrive at destinations on time. The ease and speed at which a product can be purchased, and used, increase its **time utility**. Services such as same-day delivery and 24/7 availability ensure the product is available at the time it is required.

Consumer demand will vary, due to factors such as everyday needs, the changing season and weather conditions. When demand increases, the company should produce and deliver more of the product to the market.

Place

Customers need to have access to the product where they demand it – this is known as **place utility**. Traditionally, this might have been a physical place or building, such as a shopping mall or retail store. This has changed with the digital age, which has led to many products being immediately available online. Companies are able to maximise place utility through their website.

> **KEY TERMS**
>
> **time utility:** providing the consumer with the desired goods at the time when they are required.
>
> **place utility:** having products available where they are needed by the customers.

Quantity

Customers need to have access to the quantity of product required when and where they demand it. Transportation ensures that this quantity of product is available. Supply chain managers use forecasting (predicting or estimating), scheduling (planning or arranging for an action to take place at a particular time) and inventory (the goods a business has in stock to sell) to achieve **quantity utility**. Having too much stock increases cost. Having too little results in items being out of stock when customers demand them.

> **KEY TERM**
>
> **quantity utility:** ensuring that the right amount of product is available to satisfy the consumer's demand.

Place, time and quantity utilities work together to create value for customers.

Sometimes transportation is the reason for a customer's dissatisfaction if there are late deliveries or products incur damage while in transit. This could lead a customer to buy from a competitor in the future. However, when deliveries are on time and products are undamaged, customers are more likely to be satisfied and loyal to the company in the future.

4.1.3 Types and methods of transport

Road transport

A growing amount of freight is carried by road all around the world. Road transportation companies and couriers provide services to manufacturers, distributors, wholesalers, mail-order and online businesses, local councils and private individuals. Some companies have their own **fleet** of road transport. A fleet is a group of motor vehicles made up of transport vehicles owned by the company.

> **KEY TERM**
>
> **fleet:** a group of vehicles owned by the company.

Trucks

Trucks are vehicles for transporting bulk goods, materials and equipment. Trucks have a cab and an area for cargo, and may be able to tow more than one trailer. Trucks are able to get to places that other forms of transport, such as ship and air transport, are not able to get to, e.g., directly to the warehouse, factory or retail shop.

Trucks carry heavy goods like cotton, vegetables, iron, etc. A few examples of types of trucks are:

- emergency vehicles, e.g., fire engines
- livestock vehicles, which transport hens, pigs, cows, sheep, goats, etc.
- refrigerated trucks, which transport food and drink
- large-load vehicles, e.g., cement mixers and car and bike transporters.

Delivery vans

Delivery vans may be of various sizes. They are used for deliveries straight to the consumer as well as commercial businesses. They carry small quantities of goods. They may be refrigerated to carry food or ice cream. Goods may be transported from the factory or farm to a warehouse or a point of sale, such as a retail store. In many countries, consumer demand has led to supermarkets delivering straight to the consumer's door, as well as fast food deliveries.

Couriers

Couriers use panel-van vehicles (vans with a large body and no side windows or rear seats) for delivering small packages and important documents, which are usually lightweight, to people who live in a nearby location or national and international location. Their services are quick, reliable and door-to-door due to the type of vehicle being used. Couriers deliver goods for commercial and private interests.

Table 4.1.1 describes the advantages and disadvantages of road transport.

Advantages of road transport	Disadvantages of road transport
Road vehicles can be of almost any size.	It is a slow method of transport when over a long distance.
There are specialised trucks for specialised loads, e.g., concrete mixers mix concrete on the move and refrigerated vans carry fish and meat, keeping them fresh.	Overland transport is usually considered unsuitable for bulk loads of heavy products, as trucks have limited load capacity.
Door-to-door delivery is available, taken directly from the supplier to the final destination.	It is not suitable for very large objects, such as boats, generators and earth-moving equipment, which cannot be divided into smaller loads.
It is fast and competitive over short distances and more economical than ship and air transport.	There is a high cost of operating road transport. Oil and diesel are becoming progressively more expensive.
Companies are able to use their own transport for large quantities and reduce the risk of loss by theft or damage.	Vehicles require maintenance, insurance and licencing.
It is suitable for carrying fragile goods.	Labour costs of moving goods by road are high.
Roads are accessible almost everywhere.	Traffic delays cause holdups.
Routes can be altered to avoid traffic problems or poor road conditions.	Trucks and other transport may break down.
It is easy to locate and track goods through global positioning systems (GPS) and fleet management software.	There are dangers of natural disasters affecting the roads, e.g., floods, landslides and poor weather conditions.
Paperwork involved in road transport is simpler compared to sea or air transport.	There is a risk of theft of the truck and its load in isolated areas of countries where security is poor.
There are fewer packaging costs as road transport has a less complicated packaging technique.	Roads may be unsuitable for very large trucks.
Road transport can act as a feeder to other means of transport.	In many countries there are limitations on how long drivers can drive. Long-distance truck drivers have to break their journeys, adding to the journey's length and cost.
	Some roads have restrictions on weight of loads carried.
	The social costs of road transport are an increasing concern. Larger trucks damage roads, bridges and buildings. Taxpayers have to bear these social costs.
	Pollution from vehicles is a major problem.
	Noise of road transport is a perpetual problem for those living near busy main roads.

Table 4.1.1: Advantages and disadvantages of road transport

TIP

Remember that road transport cannot be used for journeys that involve crossing seas or oceans unless trucks and other vehicles are carried on ferries.

Express-road routes are highways or major roads used to link cities and to speed up long-distance road transport. They have helped to make long-distance transport by truck much more economical. They also link cities with airports, such as the Pan Island Expressway in Singapore. These roads are two-, three- and four-lane highways, usually with a central barrier. Express-road routes may be known as freeways, superhighways, autoroutes, autobahns, parkways, expressways or motorways. They may be interstate highways, such as the Hume Highway in Australia or span across a number of countries, such as the Pan-American Highway.

Direct motorway connections between cities have become a major factor in deciding on the location of factories and warehouses. Many business parks, industrial estates, large warehouses and regional distribution centres for large-scale retailers are often sited at motorway junctions.

Many major cities have ring roads. These may be called beltways, loops or orbital motorways. These are roads that join together to form an orbital distributor-style road, such as the Boulevard Périphérique around Paris in France, the Johannesburg ring road in South Africa, the Sydney Orbital Network in Australia and the M25 around London in the UK.

Rail transport

The rail network can be a critical part of the transport system. In countries where raw materials are produced, railways are essential for moving these commodities to power stations and steelworks. In landlocked countries such as Botswana and Austria, routes may be essential for moving large quantities of goods from ports in other countries. Across continents such as Australia and Europe, railways are used, amongst others, by freight trains.

Freight trains carry freight (goods being transported), especially bulk loads. There are many types of rolling stock (railway vehicles), including:

- flatbed wagons (which have a flat, full-length deck) for heavy machinery and containers
- animal wagons (a type of railway vehicle designed to carry livestock)
- coal wagons (an open-top railway goods wagon used to carry coal, iron ore and other mine products)
- car transporters
- tankers (large railway vehicles used to transport large quantities of substance).

In some countries, scheduled long-distance express freight trains operate between industrial centres and ports. They have facilities for rapid loading and unloading.

Table 4.1.2 describes the advantages and disadvantages of rail transport.

Advantages of rail transport	Disadvantages of rail transport
It is suitable for bulk and heavy goods, such as coal, metal ores and oil, especially when carried for long distances.	It often requires transshipment – the need for another method of transport, usually road, to take goods to their final destination.
It often provides direct access from the place of production to ports or processing plants.	The need for transshipment means delays and more risk of damage or theft to goods because of extra handling.
Railway networks are not affected by traffic jams and not so much by weather conditions – although winter snow sometimes halts UK trains.	Rail transport is not suitable for carrying small quantities of goods required urgently.
Rail transport, especially if the track is electrified, causes less air pollution than roads.	Rail transport is unsuitable and uneconomical over short distances.
Rail transport economises the use of labour compared to road transport. Trains may be operated by only a driver with a guard (although there will be other people employed in goods yards and railway stations).	It cannot provide access to places without a rail system, and there are many areas of the world without railway, such as Libya and Cyprus.
	Rail transport may be disrupted by maintenance work on the line.
A goods train operated by two people could carry the same quantity of goods as 60 trucks driven by 60 people.	Rail transport uses large areas of land.
	The set-up and maintenance costs of railways are high.

Continued

KEY TERM

transshipment: the movement of goods from one kind of transport, e.g., ship, to another, e.g., road.

Advantages of rail transport	Disadvantages of rail transport
Rail transport is very energy efficient, and much more environmentally friendly than road transport.	Rolling stock is expensive. Rail transport is regarded as inflexible. Many trains run on a timetable. They will run irrespective of whether they are full or empty and so may operate at a loss. Railways cannot respond to sudden demand, and so the use of trains for speedy delivery of a particular cargo is not very suitable. Many countries use single track-ways so trains have to be carefully timetabled to avoid collisions. This can slow down train movements, as one train has to wait in a siding (a short track at the side of the railway line) for the train coming in the opposite direction to pass.

Table 4.1.2: Advantages and disadvantages of rail transport

The decline of industries that were dependent on railways, such as the coal and steel industries, has led to a decrease in the demand for goods trains in some countries. This has helped to make rail transport uneconomical in those countries – as the demand declines, the running costs increase as the transport is not used as often. Unless governments are willing to subsidise railways, unprofitable lines must be closed. Some countries own national railway systems, with the taxpayer funding the railways. In other countries, the railway system has been privatised, which is where the ownership and the operation of a service or industry passes from the government to a private organisation. In these cases, the railway system is expected to perform profitably.

In some countries, however, railways are being improved in order to compete with transport by road and, to some extent, air transport. Improvements to rail networks include automatic signalling, modernisation of railway vehicles and the electrification of railway lines. Chongqing Rail Transit (Figure 4.1.1) is used to transport commuters from the city centre at a high speed and lower cost.

Figure 4.1.1: Chongqing Rail Transit

Air transport

Air transport has grown in importance over recent years. According to Sheffield School of Aeronautics, air transport is regarded as a safer method of transport than road transport because the air is less congested with aeroplanes than roads are with vehicles (Sheffield School of Aeronautics, 2021). Pilots also undergo far more training and licencing than people who drive a vehicle. Although a major proportion of air travel is passenger traffic, the transport of goods by air has rapidly increased.

Figure 4.1.2: Loading the container in the freight plane

Freight planes are used to carry freight and usually do not take passengers. They have one or more large doors to help with loading and unloading (Figure 4.1.2). Many cargo airlines use older, converted passenger aircraft to carry freight. The glazed windows are replaced with opaque panels for structural strength for the weight of the cargo, the cabin floor is reinforced and a large cargo door is installed.

Airlines may be seen as symbols of pride for the countries from which they operate. They may be state owned (such as Air Mauritius) or privately owned (such as British Airways). They are often named after the country of origin, such as Air France and Royal Brunei Airways. These airlines usually belong to the International Air Transport Association (IATA), which is the trade association for over 300 airlines worldwide. Its main aims are to ensure that aircraft fly around the world safely and securely.

Table 4.1.3 lists examples of goods carried by air transport.

Examples of goods carried by air transport	
Valuable goods	Gold, stamps, currency, jewels, such as diamonds
Perishable goods	Flowers, vegetables, fruit, newspapers and magazines
Fragile goods	Glassware, china, electronics
Urgently required goods	Medicines, human organs, blood, government documents, examination papers, mail
Emergency aid	Food, medical equipment, medicines, vehicles, tents, blankets for victims of floods, famines, earthquakes and wars
Small bulk items	Scientific instruments, computer equipment, toys
Live animals	Racehorses, days-old chicks, tropical fish, zoo animals, pets
Goods able to bear the cost of air freight	Lightweight office equipment, feather goods, sportswear, clothing, spare parts for vehicles or machinery

Table 4.1.3: Examples of goods carried by air transport

Table 4.1.4 describes the advantages and disadvantages of air transport.

Advantages of air transport	Disadvantages of air transport
Air transport is the fastest method of transport between countries and between major cities within a country, provided that the final destination is not too far away from the airport. Air transport takes the shortest straight-line route, as an airliner is not obstructed by hills or mountains. Air transport (often using small planes) is very useful for transporting items to inaccessible areas, such as islands or jungle, forest, desert, arctic or mountainous regions, where even transport by road is difficult. Because of its speed, air transport is very suitable for carrying important, urgent, lightweight and expensive loads. More of these kinds of goods are being demanded. It can transport long distances over both land and sea without having to be unloaded. Items are not likely to be with an airline for too long and so they may be less at risk of theft or damage compared to some other methods of transport.	Travel or transport of goods by air is expensive. Airlines have high capital investments in aircraft and costs such as labour, fuel, insurance, office administration and airport charges when they use an airport. Although air travel is fast, many airports are situated outside cities, so the journey time of the aircraft in flight is offset by several factors. These include time taken in travelling to the airport and delays in reaching the final destination. Aircrafts have limited carrying capacity compared to sea transport. They are becoming larger, but nothing compared to a ship. Transshipment is also needed with air transport. Aircraft are sometimes affected by weather conditions, particularly ice, snow and fog, which cause the closure of airports and delays in flights.

Continued

Advantages of air transport	Disadvantages of air transport
Insurance, packing and storage costs may be less. With the development of low-cost airlines and the expansion of the air freight business, charges made for air transport are becoming cheaper in real terms. Documentation is simpler than for transport by ship. Aircrafts are now faster and regarded as reliable, with good safety features, such as autopilot and navigational aids. If goods arrive more quickly, they are likely to be sold more quickly, so risks of deterioration or going out of fashion are reduced.	With concerns over global warming, many people are worried about pollution caused by the vast number of aircraft flying worldwide, and the increased demand for aviation fuel as more air routes are opened. Many countries are applying taxes to aviation fuel to increase the cost of air transport and thus trying to dampen demand for the use of aircraft. Air transport requires specialised skills and a high level of training for its operation.

Table 4.1.4: Advantages and disadvantages of air transport

Airport authorities usually operate airports. They are responsible for the management of the airport and for the maintenance of airport services.

Airports need to be as near to city centres as possible so that cargo can reach centres of population as quickly as possible. They also need to be situated where dangers can be avoided, such as sites where bird strikes are less likely. There also needs to be a suitable, level runway space as far from buildings and hills as possible.

KEY TERM

airport authority: an organisation that controls an airport, e.g., British Airports Authority or the Civil Aviation Authority of China.

Sea transport

Three-quarters of the earth's surface is water, so transport by sea is critical for linking the continents and islands of the world. Most goods moved overseas are still transported using sea transport (Figure 4.1.3).

Figure 4.1.3: A container vessel sailing near coastline

Ferries

Ferries (roll-on, roll-off ships/RO-RO ships) are ships that carry trucks that drive on and drive off without unloading. They are designed to carry passengers and also to carry cargo loaded in vehicles. They use a shore-based ramp system to load and unload vehicles and cargo.

They are used for relatively short distances, e.g., across sea channels such as the Tasman Sea or the English Channel, across rivers such as the Zambezi between Zambia and Botswana, or to connect several islands such as in the Maldives. In the Maldives they are known as *dhonis*.

Loaded vehicles, such as trucks, vans and cars are driven aboard, parked where required and driven off at the destination in reverse order, without the cargo on the vehicles being unloaded (Figure 4.1.4).

The term 'roll-on, roll-off' (RO-RO) is also often applied to large ocean-going vessels that carry cars long distances from manufacturers to their markets.

Figure 4.1.4: A lorry disembarking a ferry

Tankers

Tankers are ships specially built to carry oil, petroleum, gases or chemicals in bulk. The vessels have a double-hull structure to prevent the liquid from leaking in the case of an accident. They often carry the commodity from the point of extraction to refineries or processing plants, or to storage, ready for use. Many oil tankers are super-tankers that require deep-water offloading. Special facilities, such as those at the Louisiana offshore oil port in the USA, have been developed.

Container ships

Container ships carry most of the world's dry cargo. They are designed to hold three layers of containers below decks and stacks of containers as deck cargo. It is possible to unload container ships ten times quicker than general cargo ships by using automated platforms. They may operate on fixed routes and to a fixed timetable.

Cargo liners

Cargo liners are ships that operate on fixed routes and to a fixed timetable. They may carry passengers, mail and mixed general cargo, and some are equipped with cranes for unloading. They are owned by shipping companies that organise their cargoes. There are many kinds of specialised cargo liners, such as tankers, bulk carriers and container ships.

TIP

When learning examples of sea transport, make sure that you know and can name the specific types, such as ferries, container ships and cargo liners.

Table 4.1.5 describes the advantages and disadvantages of sea transport.

Advantages of sea transport	Disadvantages of sea transport
Sea transport is a relatively cheap way of carrying heavy, low-value goods in bulk over long distances as well as short ones.	Sea transport is a slow method of transport, so it is not suitable for goods that are urgently needed.
If large ships are used for bulk cargoes, the unit cost per tonne is very low.	Transshipment is needed to and from docks to inland destinations.
Ships have access to many parts of the world. They can travel from port to port, loading and offloading cargo.	Damp and salty conditions over a long time period mean that goods can deteriorate easily.
With the development of containerisation, the transport of goods by sea has sped up. Containerisation is an integrated transport system using standard-sized containers that can be moved from one method of transport to another.	The costs of insurance, packing, storage and port charges can be expensive, adding to the charges made for carrying goods by sea.
	Several complex documents, such as the bill of lading, the insurance policy and various port documents have to be completed when sending goods by sea.

Continued

KEY TERM

containerisation: an integrated transport system using standard-sized containers that can be moved from one method of transport to another.

Advantages of sea transport	Disadvantages of sea transport
The risks of damage and theft, always associated with moving goods by ship, have also been reduced. Specialised ships are available for specialised cargoes. For example, tankers carry oil while refrigeration in ships enables them to carry perishables, such as meat, fruit and dairy products. Roll-on, roll-off ferries carry cars and other vehicles, which is quicker as the vehicle itself can be driven on and off at each port. Although ships, harbours and ports have to be maintained, there are no maintenance costs for looking after the seas and oceans unless large-scale oil pollution takes place.	Weather conditions may delay the arrival of the ships or result in losses of containers, among other things, at sea. Some ships sink or run aground. These disasters may result in oil spillages, which require very expensive clean-up operations and cause the loss of sea life. Not every country has a shoreline. Some countries are landlocked and are dependent on other countries' ports and transport systems, especially for supplies of imported raw materials or oil that they cannot produce. Tracking the goods is difficult.

Table 4.1.5: Advantages and disadvantages of sea transport

ACTIVITY 4.1.1

a In groups or individually, choose a method of transport: road, rail, air or sea.

b Research information on how your method of transport is used within your country and the types of products transported via this method.

c Summarise your transportation method of choice used within your country and ways it can be improved. Write a report on your findings.

Pipelines

Pipelines consist of a long pipe that may go overland, be buried underground or be put under water. They are used for carrying liquids, such as oil and water, gases and sometimes solids, such as grains, sand and sugar, using specialised machinery.

This section will look at three main categories of pipeline. The main type of pipeline is a transportation pipeline used to move liquids and gases between cities, countries and even continents. These pipelines may stretch from oil fields to refineries, such as the Trans-Alaska Pipeline. They connect ports with inland depots or refineries, such as the pipeline from Beira in Mozambique to Mutare in Zimbabwe. They may be pipelines carrying water from reservoirs to towns and cities.

A second type of pipeline is a gathering pipeline. This is a group of small interconnected and welded-together pipelines that bring crude oil or natural gas a short distance from wells to a treatment plant, which is an area where contaminated substances are purified, or from deep-water production on oil or gas platforms.

The third type of pipeline takes products to the final consumer. These are feeder lines that take water or gas to homes and businesses or pipelines at terminals to distribute products to storage facilities or road tankers.

Table 4.1.6 discusses the advantages and disadvantages of pipelines.

Advantages of pipelines	Disadvantages of pipelines
Pipelines are cheap to operate and usually take a direct route. A continuous flow is guaranteed as long as the machinery is working. Pipelines have a high capacity. They are not affected by weather. There is less pollution of the atmosphere compared to using many road tankers.	Pipelines are expensive to construct and repair. There must be a guaranteed long-term supply to justify the construction of a pipeline. They may be susceptible to sabotage and terrorist or military attack. If one part of the pipeline is damaged, the whole pipeline may be out of action.

Continued

Advantages of pipelines	Disadvantages of pipelines
They are a safe means of transporting flammable commodities, such as petrol and gas.	Pipelines are usable only for a limited range of commodities – mainly liquids.

Table 4.1.6: Advantages and disadvantages of pipelines

ACTIVITY 4.1.2

a In groups or as an individual, choose from these different types of goods: perishable goods, hazardous materials or oversized goods.

b Research the most appropriate method of transport for your chosen type of goods. Brainstorm other factors that might influence the choice of transport method, such as cost, speed, reliability and environmental impact.

c Choose a country and research the methods and its types of transportation and the products transported via these methods. Describe why these are the most relevant methods and types of transportation for these products in that country.

d Make a poster to be displayed in the class of the types of transportation used in your chosen country and the products transported via these methods.

REFLECTION

In choosing a country, products and transportation method, how did you evaluate the factors that led you to your conclusion? Did you consider several factors with regard to the transportation method or just focus on one factor?

Discuss your conclusion with another group member or another student. Did they reach a different conclusion? How would you defend your own conclusion, or can you now criticise it?

4.1.4 Factors affecting the choice of method of transport

Choosing the best transport system means considering a number of important questions:

- How can costs be minimised?
- How do you make sure that goods arrive safely and on time?
- What are the best routes?
- Should you use your own transport or hire someone else's transport?

The following factors should be taken into account before choosing a particular method of transport.

The nature of the goods

The nature of the goods to be carried needs to be considered. Do the goods need special handling? Do they need a specialised container? Are the goods bulky, expensive, fragile, low-value, durable, heavy, lightweight or perishable? Answering these questions will help you determine which method of transport is the most efficient to use for your products.

Urgency

If goods are required urgently, the quickest method of transport is likely to be used. Machinery spares may be sent by courier if a production line in a factory is halted. Medical supplies may be needed in a military situation and so a helicopter may be used.

Cost

The cost of transporting the goods is an important consideration, as transport costs form part of the price at which goods will be finally sold. Transport charges tend to decrease with distance. Air freight is usually more expensive than any other method of transport. The most economic method of transport is likely to be chosen unless other factors, such as urgency, are more important.

Security

The security needed for the goods is another consideration. Expensive goods may be transported by road or by air. The journey time is shorter than using rail or ship, and there is likely to be more supervision of the cargo.

Distance

The distance of transportation required should be taken into account. Road is often used for short distances. Sea transport is cheaper for the long-distance carriage of goods in bulk.

Reliability

Consider the reliability of the transport services offered. This would be an important factor if a carrier was hired or chartered to move goods on a regular basis. Raw materials supplied to a manufacturer operating a just-in-time (JIT) form of stock control must arrive when they are required on the production line. If they are delivered late, production is disrupted. Therefore, it is essential that goods arrive on time and in good condition.

TIP

Make sure that you can explain why a factor affects the choice of transportation method. For example, when considering distance, sea transport can cover long distances across oceans, which would not be possible for modes of land transport.

4.1.5 Containerisation

Containerisation is a system of integrating freight transport using standard-sized containers that can be loaded intact from road to rail, ship or aircraft, or ship to road or rail, in a very short time (Figure 4.1.5). Containers are large boxes made of steel and plywood floors and come in standardised sizes.

Figure 4.1.5: Refrigerated container being loaded on a container ship

Main features of containerisation

Containerisation has overcome the problems of packing odd-shaped goods, the need for frequent loading and unloading, customs inspections at points of entry, damage because of careless handling and the under-use of dock workers and equipment. It has sped up the transport of goods, particularly by sea.

Containerisation has had a huge influence on transport. It has directed the kinds of ships being built. It has influenced how goods are produced and packed so that they can be easily put into containers. It has influenced the construction of trucks, with the bodies of container trucks now being made in standard sizes. It has also meant the worldwide use of freight pallets (wooden, plastic or metal platform used to stack boxes or cargo). There has been a development of large container companies, such as COSCO Shipping Development and A. P. Møller – Mærsk and Hapag-Lloyd. Containerisation has led to the building of massive container ships, called the triple E class, which are over 400 metres long, and capable of carrying 19000 containers at any one time. Containerisation has also meant the development of container terminals, special trains to carry just containers, trucks specially designed to carry containers and the invention of equipment designed specifically to handle containers.

Giant overhead cranes are used to load and unload containers. They are not usually manned. Computers are programmed to give the precise order in which containers are moved and stacked. The aim is that a container's journey from one method of transport to another should be as short as possible. In some container ports, such as Rotterdam, in the Netherlands, the vehicles that move containers from the stacks to the cranes are driverless. They pilot themselves using infrared technology.

Containers

As mentioned, containers used are of standard sizes (usually expressed in imperial measurements). They are 8 ft wide and 8.5 ft high and come in two lengths, 20 ft and 40 ft. The 20 ft container is the most common size of container worldwide, but the 40 ft container is becoming more popular. This is partly because road trailers are becoming longer and partly because it is more economical to carry larger containers.

There are various types of container for different uses:

- general-purpose containers for cartons, cases, boxes, bales and drums
- temperature-controlled containers for perishable goods
- tank containers for bulk liquids and dangerous goods
- ventilated containers for organic products, such as food
- platform containers for crates, drums and machinery.

Containers are designed to be permanent and capable of repeated use. They are fitted with devices for easy handling and can be filled (stuffed) and emptied (stripped) easily.

In summary, containers have the following main features:

- their lengths can vary
- they have a standard height and width
- they are made of metal
- they are fitted with handling devices or lifted by cranes
- they are fitted with locks and can be locked
- they can be carried on different forms of transport
- they can be refrigerated
- they are individually numbered for identification purposes.

Specially designed 'igloo' containers are used for aircraft. The igloo shape fits the internal wall contours of a narrow-body aeroplane. Standard size containers would not fit onto an aeroplane.

Transport International Routier (TIR) is an international customs transit system used to move goods across the borders of countries without unloading. This has sped up the transport of goods because it reduces holdups at borders. Customs officials inspect the contents, issue a certificate of the contents and seal the container, which is labelled.

KEY TERM

Transport International Routier (TIR): an international customs transit system to move goods in sealed vehicles across the borders of countries without unloading.

Advantages and disadvantages of containerisation

Table 4.1.7 explains the advantages and disadvantages of containerisation.

Advantages of containerisation	Disadvantages of containerisation
Containerisation has sped up the transport of goods. Mechanisation (the introduction of machines) and special handling equipment have simplified the processing of goods. Containers are unloaded without unpacking the contents. Goods can be transshipped from road to docks to ship to rail without being unpacked.	Containerisation has led to job losses, as workers are not needed to load and unload containers from ships. High costs are incurred in training the workforce needed to operate the sophisticated equipment for loading and unloading containers. Careful loading at piers is necessary to avoid container ships capsizing. Containers that are loaded/unloaded at only one end of the ship are likely to make the vessel unstable.

Continued

Advantages of containerisation	Disadvantages of containerisation
Standard sizes of containers mean they are easy to pack together efficiently.	Container ports are often deserted places with few people working there, so ports become cluttered and unsightly areas.
Transshipment reduces handling costs and transport costs between factory and port and port and destination. Transshipment may take longer but ensures minimum transport costs for freight forwarders due to less handling time and labour costs and packing costs.	Security in container ports is essential. However, many people are worried about the potential threats posed by terrorists and smuggling, particularly of weapons and nuclear material. It is thought that only about 5% of all the containers shipped into US ports each year are inspected by US coastguards (customs officials).
Transport of containerised goods is more reliable than traditional methods as there is less chance of theft or damage because goods are packed and locked in strong metal containers.	Although goods packed in containers are considered safe, it should be remembered that many containers are lost overboard – between 2000 and 10 000 each year.
Often, unclaimed containers are used for other purposes, such as storage, offices and even housing. They are recycled.	Because of the imbalance between imported goods and exported goods in some countries, container ships may leave a port empty. It costs money to transport empty containers, for which you are not receiving money for as you are not transporting goods.
Containers do not need to be warehoused. The container acts as the warehouse, so goods are packed into a container at the source, namely the factory or warehouse, in the country of departure. This saves time and money.	Many containers are abandoned, so ports can become cluttered with unclaimed containers.
Containers can also be stacked in container parks, saving dock and airport space.	The size of a container ship is limited by the routes it uses. The Straits of Malacca linking the Indian Ocean and the Pacific Ocean is one of the busiest shipping lanes in the world, and there are limits on the size of ships using it.

Table 4.1.7: Advantages and disadvantages of containerisation

ACTIVITY 4.1.3

a In pairs, research one of the five busiest shipping routes in the world.

b Research the main products transported via this route and the types of containers that will be needed for these products.

c Present a slideshow presentation to the class using a world map and showing your chosen route. Explain the main products transported via this route and the types of containers required for these products.

Figure 4.1.6: Containers fitted with locks. It is important to check that these are secure before moving them

REFLECTION

Once other groups have presented their oral presentations from Activity 4.1.3, give feedback to each other. Look at another group's findings and think about:

1. How much evidence was given in their presentation?
2. How clearly did they communicate their evidence?
3. Have they made good use of their research. Did they make use of the map and the routes as part of their findings?
4. Provide feedback to the teams, describing:
   a. two things that you liked
   b. one thing which could have been improved
   c. one thing that you did not know before.

SELF-EVALUATION CHECKLIST

After studying this chapter, complete this table.

You should know about:	Needs more work	Almost there	Ready to move on
the functions of transport in the supply chain			
transport types and methods			
the benefits and drawbacks of different transport methods			
the factors affecting the choice of transport method			
aspects of containerisation			
the benefits and drawbacks of containerisation			

Knowledge check

1. Define the term 'logistics'.
2. State and provide an explanation of the three functions of transportation in the supply chain.
3. State the advantages of sending goods by road rather than rail.
4. Which factor would be most important when choosing a method of transport to move gold bars from South Africa to New York, USA?
5. Explain the benefits of using ferries to transport freight across sea channels.
6. Explain two advantages of using containers for transporting goods.
7. Study the pie chart. Which percentage of goods would **not** be delivered to customers' homes?

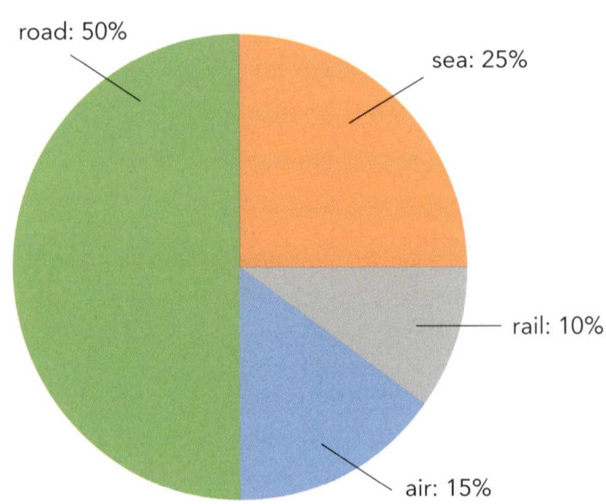

a 12%
b 25%
c 50%
d 10%

8 Why should an exporter of high-value goods use Transport International Routier (TIR)?
   a Warehouse facilities are provided at ports at no charge (free).
   b Shipment can be made in sealed vehicles across borders.
   c Temperature controlled containers are not required.
   d The goods require sophisticated loading equipment.

9 For which consignment would delivery by air transport be suitable?
   a daily delivery of perishable goods to supermarkets
   b large quantities of iron ore from Australia to Taiwan
   c medical supplies delivered to Cape Town from London
   d sand delivered in bulk from the Middle East to Australia

10 State an advantage of transporting goods in containers.
   a Containers may remain in ports and airports for months.
   b The damage to goods and theft of goods is reduced.
   c Goods unpacked before transferred to other transport.
   d Packaging and insurance costs increase with container use.

Practice questions

1 *Over 50% of all the world's visible trade is transported by sea in shipping containers.

Firms need to consider several factors, such as security, when deciding to use sea transport to move their goods.

Evaluate **two other** factors a company should consider before using sea transport. Which one is more important? Give reasons for your answer. [8]

Cambridge O Level Commerce 7100, Paper 21, Question 3d, November 2022

2 *Discuss how important air transport is in the chain of distribution. Give reasons for your answer. [6]

Cambridge O Level Commerce 7100, Paper 21, Question 1e, November 2019

3 *Many imported and exported goods are transported using containers. Identify **two** features of a container used to transport goods. [2]

Cambridge O Level Commerce 7100, Paper 21, Question 3c i, November 2018

4 State three methods of transport used to carry containers. [3]

5 Explain why grain is not usually transported in container ships. [2]

Chapter 4.2

Warehousing

LEARNING INTENTIONS

In this chapter you will learn:

- warehouse functions in the supply chain
- warehouse types
- warehouse automation and its uses
- warehouse automation benefits.

4.2.1 Storage and warehousing

Warehouses are shed-like buildings arranged with an open-plan layout and used to store goods. They have minimal fixtures and fittings. The ordered goods are assembled using trolleys, pallets, forklift trucks or automated systems. There is usually a large space for loading, unloading and moving vans and trucks. Warehouses may have loading bays through which trucks are loaded.

They are likely to be located in industrial areas where land is relatively cheap, and they can occupy sites with sufficient room for a large building and for trucks to move around. Warehouses belonging to manufacturers will usually be sited on the factory site. Warehouses operated by wholesalers will have to be near the customers to save on transport costs. They will also have to be convenient for suppliers, with good road connections. Regional distribution centres (RDCs), the warehouses of large-scale retailers, are central to the branches they supply, with good road connections close to main highways.

4.2.2 Functions of a warehouse

Warehousing is essential for any business that deals with physical goods. In simple terms, a warehouse is a building for storing goods. A warehouse is an important part of the operations of a business and can help a business generate more profit if used efficiently. The functions of a warehouse are as follows.

- To provide storage for:
  - raw materials before manufacture
  - components to be used in the manufacturing process – e.g., lights, batteries for cars, machines and tools
  - semi-processed products that may be assembled in another factory
  - finished goods awaiting transport, sale or export.
- To protect goods from theft, deterioration, weather and damage. Warehouses may not be able to prevent deterioration but may help to extend the life of a product, especially if cold storage is used, e.g., for fruits. Warehouses may not stop theft, but goods have a lesser chance of being stolen if they are locked in a warehouse than if they are left in the open air.
- To help in stockpiling (where a large amount of stock is accumulated). Warehouses act as reservoirs for production ahead of demand. They assist in balancing out the supply of goods with the demand for them. This helps to prevent goods flooding on to the market as well as shortages of goods.
- To provide a place for any packaging, grading, **sorting** (arranging items systematically into specific groups) and labelling to take place before goods are offered for sale. Some goods may be broken up into smaller quantities or put into attractive packaging. Some goods improve in quality with time. Products such as wine, spirits and cheese are often warehoused for some time to mature. Warehousing is important in the re-export trade. This is where goods that a country has previously imported are then exported again. For example, machinery may be sent to a country for testing and then exported elsewhere after testing is complete. During this time, goods may be stored and packaged in a warehouse.
- To even out the supply so that prices are kept reasonably stable.
- To provide a place for product collection and distribution. Some warehouses, such as RDCs belonging to large-scale retailers, function as collection points for the variety of products required in the branches of a chain of supermarkets. Goods are distributed from these warehouses to the branches of the supermarket in the area serviced by the RDC.
- To break bulk quantities into smaller quantities.
- To provide places where prospective buyers can inspect goods, such as cash-and-carry warehouses, where retailers serve themselves and load the goods they want on to trolleys.
- To enable production to be ahead of demand. Manufacturers usually make goods ahead of demand. They need warehouses, either their own, wholesalers' or retailers', to store these goods until there is demand.

KEY TERM

sorting: arranging items systematically into specific groups.

- To meet unexpected demand. If the rainy season is unexpectedly long, the demand for umbrellas and raincoats may increase. Unless there is surplus stock in a warehouse, this demand cannot be satisfied. In very hot weather, large quantities of bottled water, cold drinks and ice cream will be consumed. Retailers may run out of these goods; unless they can obtain emergency supplies from a warehouse, they will miss valuable sales.

Keeping a warehouse organised

Organisation is an important aspect to becoming or sustaining a successful business. The warehouse is the foundation of a business and should therefore be organised. Below is a list of ways in which businesses can keep their warehouses organised:

- Keep the warehouse clean.
- Only retain inventory that is really needed.
- Reduce clutter in the warehouse.
- Assess the space and shelving utilisation to maximise the available space.
- Eliminate traffic barriers – no barriers in the warehouse should stop the 'easy flow'.
- Make use of a warehouse management system.
- Have accurate stock control to avoid a mess.
- Use a labelling system.
- Invest in warehouse automation.
- Plan the receiving area – make sure there is enough space for all the stock when it arrives.
- Make use of clear warehouse signage so that it is easier and quicker to navigate the warehouse and to search for particular items.

Seasonal production

Some products are produced only at certain times of the year, such as potatoes, apples and rice. This is known as **seasonal production**. The products can be stored in warehouses and then released when required. This enables everyone to have a supply of these basic commodities throughout the year. It also helps to stabilise prices. If all the potatoes came on to the market as soon as they were harvested, much of the product would be wasted. The price would also be very low. For the rest of the year, there would be no or few potatoes available and the price would be very high. There would also be shortages and hardships for the many consumers who are dependent on potatoes as a major part of their diet, but who cannot afford very high prices.

Seasonal production should not be confused with goods for which there is only **seasonal demand**, e.g., summer clothing, garden furniture and greeting cards for festivals. Products of seasonal demand may be produced all year round so that continuous production can be maintained. These products are then stored in warehouses awaiting demand.

KEY TERMS

seasonal production: goods produced at certain times of year, e.g., fruit.

seasonal demand: goods produced all the year round for which there is demand only at certain times of the year, e.g., greetings cards for Chinese New Year.

TIP

Make sure you know the difference between seasonal demand and seasonal production. Seasonal demand means demand at certain times of the year. Seasonal production means that production happens at particular times of the year, so these products, usually basic foodstuffs, need to be stored.

Demand

The main function of a warehouse is to provide storage between the time goods are produced and the time they are either traded in the home market or exported.

Many goods are produced in very large quantities ahead of demand. They are transported in bulk to wholesalers, directly to retailers and to other traders.

Delivery times have become an increasingly important factor for many businesses wishing to remain competitive. Manufacturers may operate 'just-in-time' (an inventory system where goods are received from suppliers only as they are needed) deliveries of raw materials to economise on storage and to avoid tying up working capital in unused materials. They require supplies when they want to use them. Retailers wishing to economise on storage space require regular deliveries on time to prevent shortages.

Consumers do not want to wait for goods. Shorter delivery times are used as a method of attracting consumers to buy goods. A company that can deliver the next day is going to gain trade over one whose products arrive a week after the order has been placed. Goods need to be stored so that delivery times can be shortened. Warehousing and the logistics of getting goods to the consumer, using systems that make them quickly available, are becoming increasingly important in trade.

Although many companies operate a just-in-time approach to their supplies so that raw materials and components are delivered as they are needed in the factory, there is still a need for some storage for supplies. Mass or batch production is a method where a group of identical items are produced at the same time rather than individually. Companies using mass or batch production methods to produce goods in large quantities need adequate storage for finished products until they are sold.

It is, however, possible that artificial shortages can be created. Dealers hold on to stocks to increase prices. If shortages become noticeable to consumers, many of them will buy even if they do not need the product at the time. As demand increases, supplies become limited and prices will rise.

For example, when lockdown was announced due to the COVID-19 pandemic, many people panic-bought toilet paper across the world. Due to the demand increasing, a shortage arose and the price increased. Many shops were left with empty shelves in the toilet paper aisle.

Protecting supply and price stability

Accuracy and accountability keep the supply chain stable. By ensuring supply of stock is available in warehouses, a company is able to ensure that satisfaction is delivered to clients. Warehouses play an important part of the distribution of products to suppliers and fulfilling orders on time. The efficiency of a supply chain can be increased by ensuring supplies are available.

Warehouses assist in controlling price fluctuations. Warehouses store goods when supply is more than demand. The goods are taken out when the demand increases again. Warehouses ensure that supply is always available when the demand for the goods rises, which is essential for price stability. When demand for goods decreases, having too much stock in store may mean the price decreases to get rid of the stock. This could lead to losses on the product. Having a warehouse to store the goods until demand increases again will help to ensure losses are not made on the product.

A raw material warehouse stores materials that will be used to manufacture products. The materials are unprocessed and will be used to make products. By storing these materials in warehouses, close to the manufacturing plant, it ensures the materials are available for processing when the demand for the products increases, which is essential for price stability.

Warehousing also helps to reduce transport and distribution costs. Bulk deliveries are made to warehouses such as RDCs or wholesalers' warehouses, which may be close to markets, e.g., shops. When orders are received, trucks or vans can take full loads to supply these shops. Many retailers own their own road transport to move goods from their warehouses to their shops. Without strategically placed warehouses across a country, these transport fleets would not function effectively and would not be worthwhile.

Logistics postponement

Logistics postponement means keeping stock that is not yet complete in storage and postponing the final product assembly until the actual customer demand is known. By doing this, companies can react more quickly to the demand when it arises and offer better customisation options.

The goods used as part of logistics postponement are kept in warehouses at one or a few strategic locations to allow easy flow of goods to the designated area when the product demand arises.

An example of logistics postponement is a company supplying T-shirts. The company may not be aware of what the in-season colour will be for next year's summer season. They make and store many white T-shirts well

KEY TERM

logistics postponement: when part of the process of producing a product is delayed until the customer demand is realised.

ahead of the summer season. Closer to the summer season, when they are aware of the in-season colour, they can dye the T-shirts the relevant colour and meet demand as early as possible, instead of only starting the production process when they become aware of the in-season colour.

ACTIVITY 4.2.1

a Work in groups and research a specific function of a warehouse (e.g., storage of raw materials, protection from theft and damage, stockpiling, offering a place for packaging, sorting and labelling etc.). Prepare a short presentation.

b Present your findings to the class, including examples of how your assigned function is performed in real-world warehouses.

c After each presentation, discuss the importance of each function and how it contributes to the overall success of a warehouse operation.

4.2.3 Types of warehouses

Warehousing plays an important part in both home trade and international trade. As a result, different types of warehouses have been developed to make trade flow as smoothly as possible. Each warehouse serves the specific needs of manufacturers, wholesalers, retailers, importers and exporters.

Bonded warehouses

Bonded warehouses may be situated anywhere, but they are found mainly at ports, airports and border crossings. They are used for storing taxable goods on which duty has not yet been paid.

KEY TERM

bonded warehouse: a warehouse where dutiable goods are stored before payment of duty.

These warehouses are usually privately owned. Their owners give a bond to the customs authorities that goods will not be removed until the necessary duties are paid. A bond provides financial security or protection for businesses or individuals storing goods in a storage facility. Customs officials supervise the goods, preventing importers from evading customs duties and disobeying import regulations.

Goods taken into bond include:

- tea and coffee
- wines, beers and spirits
- perfumes
- electronic goods and televisions
- cigarettes and tobacco.

While in bond, goods can be processed – e.g., graded, blended, bottled and packaged – but not manufactured.

Once the goods are in the bonded warehouse, they cannot be removed until duty has been paid. When the duty is paid, a customs warrant is completed, certified by the warehouse keeper and presented to customs officials so that goods can be released.

Goods may also be moved from one bonded warehouse to another bonded warehouse.

An importer may have goods in bond in Cape Town in South Africa, for example. They may transfer them to a bonded warehouse in Johannesburg if they realise that the demand for their goods is greater in Johannesburg than in Cape Town.

Bonded warehouses are important because:

- they are used by importers of dutiable goods on which duty has not been paid. The importer may wish to postpone payment of duty. They may be looking for buyers. They may remove a sample of the goods, paying duty on only that sample, in order to show it to potential buyers. They may sell the goods in bond and it will be the buyer who pays the duty. This enables the importer to economise on working capital because they do not have money tied up in import duty paid on unsold goods. If an importer has imported a very large quantity of goods, the goods can be withdrawn in separate batches. This again helps to spread the payment of duty.

- they may be used by people who are involved in the re-export trade: the **entrepôt trade**. They import the goods, may make them more saleable in the bonded warehouse and then export them again. For example, India imports rubber from Thailand, processes the rubber and then exports the processed items to Japan. By storing them in the bonded warehouse, the importer does not have to pay duty. This is particularly important in the tea trade. Teas may be imported from Sri Lanka and India and then are blended in London before being packaged and exported to Canada.
- bonded warehouses located in cities and towns are important to producers of dutiable goods such as beer, which is brewed for sale in the home market. While in the bonded warehouse, the brewer will not have to pay any duty. Only when the beer is to be used will the duty be payable. Scotch whisky is a major export for Scotland. It is subject to duty if it is consumed in the UK. If it is exported, no duty has to be paid. A bonded warehouse is important to the distiller of Scotch whisky because it can be left to mature without any payment of duty and then sold for export.

KEY TERM

entrepôt trade: the re-export trade, when a country exports goods that it previously imported without changing them.

Advantages and disadvantages of bonded warehouses

There are a number of important benefits to the users of bonded warehouses, but despite the advantages there are a number of disadvantages as well. These are listed in Table 4.2.1.

TIP

Bonded warehouses store goods on which duty has not been paid. They do not store goods on which duty has been paid.

Advantages	Disadvantages
They can enable the postponement of payment of duties and taxes.	Goods may only be stored for a maximum of two years.
They can store goods for a long time.	The clearing process is time consuming.
They have the ability to provide customers with a better service by providing the goods as demanded.	Licences are required in order to establish bonded warehouses.
They maintain the quality of the goods.	The importer may fail to pay customs duties. The customs authorities then must auction the bonded goods to recover the duty costs.
They provide the security and safety of the goods.	
They are located close to ports and airports, therefore reducing transport costs, time and the possibility of damages.	

Table 4.2.1: Advantages and disadvantages of bonded warehouses

Cold storage warehouses

Cold storage warehouses are temperature-controlled warehouses that help to preserve perishable foods for long periods (Figure 4.2.1). Produce such as apples may be kept cool in special compartments. Some products, such as butter, may be refrigerated to store it. Other products, such as meat and fish, may be frozen. Cold storage warehouses may be owned by specialist companies. They may also be part of a food processor's factory complex. They may be part of the warehousing facilities offered by general wholesalers.

KEY TERM

cold storage warehouse: a temperature-controlled warehouse used to preserve perishable goods, such as fruit.

Cold storage warehouses are important because:

- produce that is produced at particular times of the year – i.e. through seasonal production – can be stored so that it is available in good condition to meet demand throughout the year.
- it allows countries to develop their export businesses. For example, countries such as Australia, New Zealand, South Africa and Spain have been able to develop their export businesses in dairy products, meat, fruit and vegetables. The Maldives, which is heavily dependent on exporting fish and fish products, has also benefitted from the development of cold storage warehouses as well as refrigerated containers on ships. Zambian, Zimbabwean and South African fruit and vegetables can be taken long distances to other markets in Botswana, Mozambique and Namibia using refrigerated trucks. A lot of fresh fruit and vegetable produce comes from Spain and is exported to other European countries in large trucks equipped with refrigeration.
- general wholesalers and cash-and-carry warehouses are able to extend the range of products they offer for sale by having a freezer section and refrigerated units. They can store ice cream, meat, fish, cakes and readymade meals.

Figure 4.2.1: A cold storage warehouse

Advantages and disadvantages of cold storage warehouses

There are both advantages and disadvantages to using cold storage warehouses for preserving perishable goods. They are listed in Table 4.2.2.

Advantages	Disadvantages
The low temperature helps to lower the deterioration rate of the perishable goods. The risk of food poisoning is avoided. There is cost efficiency by avoiding rotting products. There is energy efficiency as electricity usage is less than fridges and freezers. Hiring a cold storage warehouse for products and ingredients could free up space for preparation and cooking at a restaurant. Cold storage facilities will have back-up batteries in the case of a power outage. Due to the airtight seals, and if the batteries fail, it will maintain the cold temperature for a long period of time.	There are additional costs for equipment and maintenance of the equipment. There are extra staffing costs for the warehouse – for example, protective and warm clothing to work in the cold temperatures. Frequent inspections are required to ensure safety regulations are being met.

Table 4.2.2: Advantages and disadvantages of cold storage warehouses

Cash-and-carry warehouses

Cash-and-carry warehouses are important because they serve retailers, mainly small-scale retailers, within their local areas, helping them to survive the competition from supermarkets, hypermarkets and multiple chain stores. Cash-and-carry warehouses offer self-service wholesaling – they are wholesale supermarkets. No credit is given to buyers. There are no deliveries of goods to buyers. There is no help with loading, there are no sales representatives and there is no invoicing. By reducing expenses such as staffing costs, the wholesaler can offer competitive prices.

KEY TERM

cash-and-carry warehouse: a warehouse that offers self-service wholesaling with no credit and no delivery services.

The retailer can make as many visits as they like, thus using the cash-and-carry warehouse as the retailer's warehouse for storage. The retailer is also offered other wholesaling functions in the cash-and-carry warehouse – breaking bulk, preparing goods for sale, display of items in the warehouse and special offers.

Cash-and-carry warehouses sell a wide variety of goods. Many of their products are foods and drinks, but they may also sell textiles, clothing, pet supplies, gardening supplies, hardware and general household goods. Most of the products are ranges that sell quickly. There is minimal display, with goods stacked in small boxes or packs on pallets, on the floor or on shelves.

Cash-and-carry warehouses usually have long opening hours to help their customers – weekends, early mornings, and/or late into the evenings. They usually have restricted access – people are admitted on production of a membership or identity card.

Advantages and disadvantages of cash-and-carry warehouses to the wholesaler

Cash-and-carry warehouses have advantages and disadvantages to the wholesaler, listed in Table 4.2.3.

Advantages	Disadvantages
More trade from more small-scale retailers	Long working hours
Can attract other businesses as customers, such as restaurants, canteens and caterers	Capital cost of checkouts and other equipment
May also sell to other consumers who qualify for membership cards	Often large amounts of cash on the premises – danger of theft
No bad debts from buyers as they pay cash, which helps the wholesaler to pay when purchasing from manufacturers	

Table 4.2.3: Advantages and disadvantages of cash-and-carry warehouses to the wholesaler

Advantages and disadvantages to the small-scale retailer of buying from the cash-and-carry warehouse

Cash-and-carry warehouses also have advantages and disadvantages to the small-scale retailer, listed in Table 4.2.4.

Advantages	Disadvantages
Prices are cheaper than buying from a general wholesaler because the cash-and-carry warehouse's expenses are lower.	There is no delivery available. The retailer needs transport for collecting the goods, which adds to the retailer's costs.
The retailer has immediate access to the warehouse at their convenience and does not have to wait for deliveries.	It may not be convenient to visit the cash-and-carry warehouse when the retailer is short of stock. Shortages imply increased demand, meaning more customers. The retailer may find it difficult to leave the shop in order to restock.
The retailer can obtain goods to meet sudden demand, e.g., for ice cream.	No credit is available, so the retailer must have the funds to be able to pay immediately for the goods purchased.
The retailer saves on storage space in their shop premises.	
The retailer does not waste time on administrative work relating to placing orders, checking deliveries and settling monthly accounts.	
The warehouse is open at times convenient to the retailer.	

Table 4.2.4: Advantages and disadvantages to the small-scale retailer of buying from the cash-and-carry warehouse

Regional distribution centres (RDCs)

Regional distribution centres are used by large-scale retailers such as supermarkets, hypermarkets and multiple chain stores in many parts of the world to supply both the branches of their business and also their online businesses (Figure 4.2.2 and Table 4.2.5). They are very large warehouses, usually situated at busy road junctions, often where major highways meet.

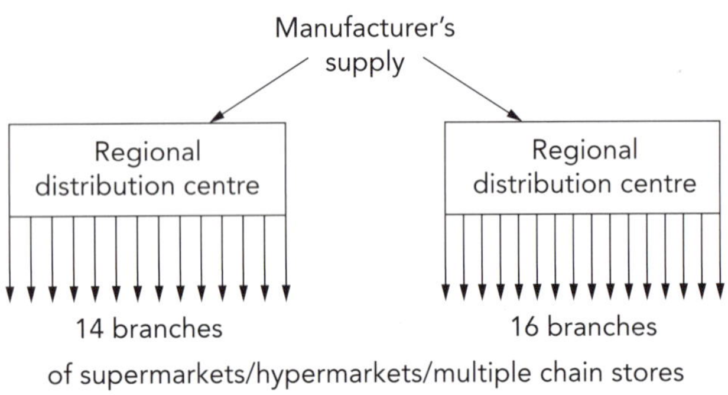

Figure 4.2.2: An illustration of who supplies regional distribution centres and who they supply the goods to

RDCs are important because:

- they provide easy access for the manufacturers who supply them.
- they are close to the branches they supply, ensuring constant supplies.
- they help to reduce the retailer's costs.
  - The business usually owns its own transport; so it saves on transport costs.
  - It saves renting someone else's warehouse.

Store	Location
Amazon	USA and elsewhere
Pick n Pay	South Africa
Coles Supermarkets	Australia
Tesco	UK
Walmart	USA and elsewhere
SPAR South Africa	South Africa
Cold Storage	Singapore
Sea Limited	Southeast Asia

Table 4.2.5: Examples of large-scale retailers that use RDCs

TIP

Make sure that you can specifically describe the different kinds of warehouses and their features, rather than just warehouses in general.

ACTIVITY 4.2.2

a Brainstorm different types of products that need to be stored in a warehouse. Work in groups or individually.

b Research about the different types of warehouses, focusing on the types of warehouses required for the relevant products brainstormed in part **a**.

c Present your findings to the class. Your presentation should include information about the type of warehouse, its purpose and examples of products that can be stored in it.

d As a class, discuss the different types of warehouse presented and their importance in the supply chain management system.

REFLECTION

Once other groups have presented their project findings for Activity 4.2.2, give feedback. Look at their presentations and think about:

1 How much information was given?

2 How clearly did they communicate that information?

3 Provide feedback to the teams, describing:

  a two things that you liked

  b one thing that could have been improved

  c one thing that you did not know before.

4.2.4 Automation in warehousing

Warehouse work involves lifting and carrying heavy objects. This type of work takes a toll on human workers as they can injure themselves with repetitive strain or accidents. Automation makes equipment or a system operate automatically on its own. The aim of warehouse automation is to automate repetitive and tedious manual tasks in warehousing operations. Automation makes manual work less labour-intensive to reduce labour costs, increase productivity and accuracy, and improve safety. Automation saves time by eliminating the time spent going from one spot to another by the machine bringing the product to the worker.

Digital automation is the process of using digital technology to create, automate and improve business operations. A warehouse management system is made up of software and processes that allow businesses to control and administer warehouse operations. This takes place from when the products or materials arrive at the warehouse until they leave the warehouse.

Smart digital automation is the use of smartphones and tablets in supply chain and logistics operations. There are many warehouse and inventory management apps available. Warehouse managers and their workers are able to use the same devices, which allows them to run reports and access information to make quick decisions.

Digital automation relies on software and electronics to reduce or remove manual processes. Physical automation includes the various forms of mechanically automated machines, which are physically in the warehouse, such as robotics or smart shelving. Smart shelving makes use of technology and networking with retail shelves that detect when an item is purchased and removed from a shelf. This makes it easier to keep track of the inventory and restock the shelves when necessary.

The main objective of warehouse automation is to remove time-consuming and labour-intensive tasks. Employees are therefore able to concentrate better on important jobs like quality control.

Robotics

A warehouse robot is an independent machine designed to take the place or work side-by-side with human workers in a warehouse.

Warehouse robotic technology is advancing at a rapid pace. Robots are now able to sense if there is an object in their path and successfully move themselves around the object. Robots can pack, pick, palletise and transport items.

Unlike humans, robots do not get tired. Robots require recharging when their battery is low or flat and can be replaced when needed. Lifting and carrying heavy objects does not cause physical strain to robots as it does to humans. Robots can replace and work alongside humans in warehouse work, thereby removing humans from stressful positions and potential injuries, and preventing fatigue and burnout.

Types of warehouse robotics

There are several kinds of robots specialising in different tasks.

Automated guided vehicles (AGV) and autonomous mobile robots (AMR)

These types of robots help to transport materials, supplies and inventory around the warehouse. Some follow established routes marked on the floor. Other are more advanced and use cameras or infrared to navigate and avoid obstacles and collisions.

Aerial drones, unmanned aerial vehicles (UAV) and automated guided carts (AGC)

Flying drones are small and can get to places humans cannot. They move at high speeds and work well for inventory scanning. They can estimate the amount of stock inside and update the inventory system automatically. UAVs are controlled by human operators whereas an aerial drone has independent navigation. An AGC is similar to an AGV; however, an AGC is able to carry smaller loads.

Automated storage and retrieval systems (AS/RS)

Automated storage and retrieval systems help to automate inventory management and can help with speedy retrieval and placement of products. They move on fixed tracks and use cranes or lifters to pick up products.

Collaborative robots (cobots)

Some cobots are programmed to work independently and others are programmed to follow humans. They move around warehouses picking various orders. They can also follow human pickers around the warehouse floor and act as mobile storage bins for picked orders. Others direct workflows through the warehouse, leading associates and transporting loads.

Articulated robotic arms

These robots are just arms, sometimes attached to a base with wheels for transport. They are used to pick products, pack them, assemble parts, unload containers or set up pallets (Figure 4.2.3).

Goods-to-person (G2P)

Pickers stay in the same place and the G2P vehicle delivers items from the shelves to the person. Pickers can be human or robotic.

Figure 4.2.3: Articulated robotic arms working in a warehouse

Automated sorting systems

Sorting is the process of identifying items and redirecting them to a specific destination within an operation – in this context, this refers to physical items rather than digital items. Manual sortation depends on human workers identifying products and redirecting them as necessary. Automated sortation uses a variety of technologies to achieve this job. Technologies such as sensors, barcode scanners and conveyor belt systems are used in automated sorting. The technologies can be tailored to suit the needs of the specific operation in which they are being used.

Types of automated sorting systems

There are two types of automated sorting systems, namely:

- case sorters – these receive inputs in any order and sort them by separating into channels and then transporting whole cases of orders.
- unit sorters – these are used when sorting individual items during the production process.

Unit refers to a single item, whereas case refers to boxes of multiple units.

There are different types of case sorters:

- pop-up wheel sorters
- pusher sorters.

Different types of unit sorters include:

- tilt-tray sorters
- crossbelt sorters
- push tray sorters
- bombay sorters, also known as flat sorters.

The following can be used as a case or unit sorter depending on the operation needs:

- sliding shoe sorters
- narrow belt sorters.

Figure 4.2.4: Rubber tyre on a conveyor belt

Advantages and disadvantages of automated sorting systems

Automated sorting systems have many benefits. However, they also have drawbacks. Some of each are listed in Table 4.2.6.

Advantages	Disadvantages
Automatic sorting systems reduce labour costs. The sorting system can store useful data while it is working. Sorting systems ensure the goods are sorted correctly and safely. It offers highly effective sorting. They are able to process a large volume of products in a short space of time. They are accurate, have a high capacity and are fast paced.	There is a high initial investment. Maintenance of the equipment is necessary, which may lead to equipment downtime. Employees will require technical skill and training. They are not suitable for operations with a wide variety of products changing from week to week or month to month. The equipment works according to pre-set systems, so it likes regular, predictable and repetitive tasks.

Table 4.2.6: Advantages and disadvantages of automated sorting systems

Voice picking systems

Voice picking systems use language to communicate information from supply chain systems to warehouse workers. Voice picking is a hands-free and eyes-free system that uses an intelligent voice agent and speech recognition software to direct associates through their tasks. Pickers wear headsets with a microphone that connects to a mobile device that runs a voice application (Figure 4.2.5). The voice application tells warehouse workers where to go and what to pick. Pickers say a reference and the system tells them the picking location and product. This frees up the pickers' hands from carrying papers around and allows them to pick up heavy items.

KEY TERM

voice picking system: a hands-free, paperless system that uses voice prompts to direct workers to specific locations in a warehouse.

Figure 4.2.5: Warehouse picker using a voice picking system

4.2.5 Benefits of warehouse automation

Warehouse automation has many benefits for a business and can have a positive impact on a business in the long run. The benefits include:

- less human error – decreasing the number of decisions that humans need to make improves accuracy and reduces errors when picking and packing items. Automated systems can quickly identify and correct errors when they do arise.
- fewer safety risks for human workers – warehouse automation systems bring the products to the workers, eliminating the workers from picking up the products. This results in less traffic of people and equipment in the warehouse, which improves safety.
- increased warehouse productivity – the speed and accuracy of robots is high when compared to humans. However, humans have a cognitive ability that robots do not have. Humans and robots can therefore work well together to achieve an effective combination.
- less processing time – automation speeds up the process and reduces the handling time. Humans are not capable of working at the speed of robots.
- optimised storage space – machines do not need as much space as humans to operate. Narrowly spaced high-rise shelves can be used to optimise the space in an automated warehouse.
- lower operation/labour costs – automation reduces staff administration and training costs, storage costs and product handling, mishandling risks and product losses.

- improved customer service – the time required for preparing orders and shipping is reduced with automation. If a customer is not satisfied with their product, the returns process is also automated. All of this reduces the time taken to get the product or speeds up the refund process for the customer.

ACTIVITY 4.2.3

a Look at the benefits of warehouse automation and decide which type of automation each one applies to. Include things such as how much human involvement is required for each task and to what extent it can be automated. Are there any safety concerns with implementing automation? Consider the long-term maintenance costs of an automated system.

b Present your findings in an article to be handed in to your teacher.

REFLECTION

How easy or difficult did you find deciding on the type of automation? Did you struggle to choose between a few automation options for a benefit or did you struggle to identify one type of automation relating to the benefit? If you struggled to identify a type of automation, how did you overcome this? Did you do more research, or ask your teacher or friend for help?

SELF-EVALUATION CHECKLIST

After studying this chapter, complete this table.

You should know about:	Needs more work	Almost there	Ready to move on
warehouse functions in the supply chain			
warehouse types			
warehouse automation and its uses			
warehouse automation benefits			

Knowledge check

1 State the primary function of a warehouse.

2 Identify five ways in which to keep a warehouse organised.

3 Define the term 'logistics postponement'.

4 Identify which kind of warehouse is used by large-scale retailers such as supermarkets.

5 Explain the main purpose of using automation in warehousing.

6 How can automation help improve workplace safety in warehousing?

7 What is the effect of storing goods required seasonally?

a It balances supply and demand of these goods.

b It causes prices to fluctuate.

c It enables retailers to be supplied in bulk.

d It prevents theft and damage to goods.

8 What is an advantage to a producer of warehousing?

a It allows the producer to manufacture large quantities of goods ahead of demand.

b It allows the producer to offer trade credit to reliable customers.

c It enables the producer to make customers aware of its products.

d It enables the producer to operate a cash-and-carry service for customers.

9 A bonded warehouse is a place where:

a customs officials store confiscated and smuggled goods

b dutiable goods are stored until duty has been paid on them

c goods are manufactured in the warehouse and ready for sale

d merchants store all their goods awaiting export.

10 The figure shows the function of a regional distribution centre (RDC) that belongs to ABC Stores.

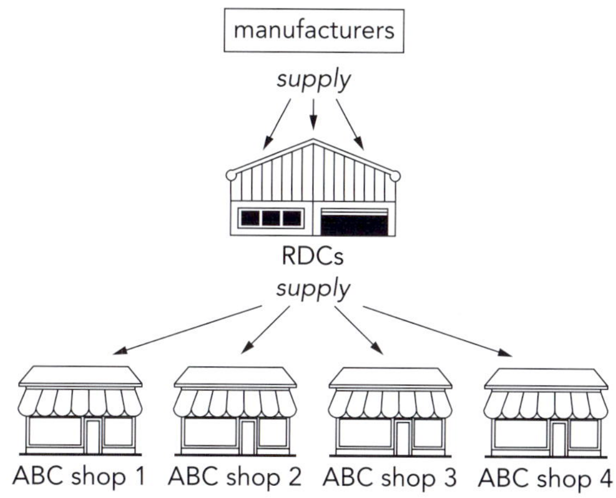

Which business is likely to own a regional distribution centre?

a chain of supermarkets

b large-scale farmer

c an oil company

d a toy manufacturer

Practice questions

1 Explain what type of items are contained in a bonded warehouse at an airport. [2]

2 *CC Foods is a private limited company that needs finance and insurance for a new cold storage warehouse.

State **two** features of a cold storage warehouse. [2]

Cambridge O Level Commerce 7100, Paper 21, Q4a, November 2021

3 *There are many types of warehouses used in home and international trade.

Explain how warehousing is used for

i seasonal production [2]

ii price stability [2]

Cambridge O Level Commerce 7100, Paper 22, Question 4b, June 2018

Unit 5

Aids to trade that support commerce

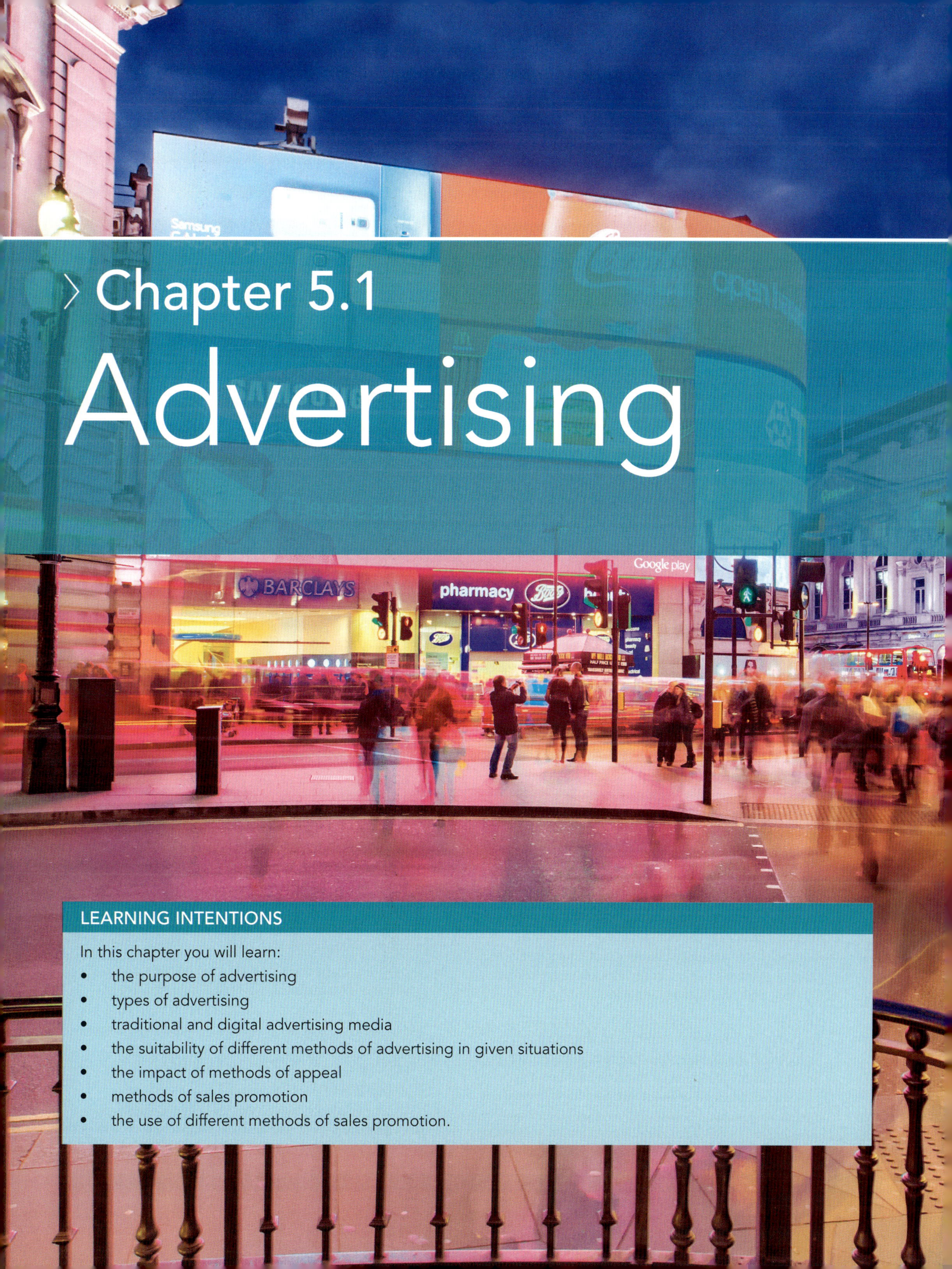

Chapter 5.1

Advertising

LEARNING INTENTIONS

In this chapter you will learn:

- the purpose of advertising
- types of advertising
- traditional and digital advertising media
- the suitability of different methods of advertising in given situations
- the impact of methods of appeal
- methods of sales promotion
- the use of different methods of sales promotion.

5.1.1 Types of advertising

Advertising is a source of communication with consumers that aims to inform and persuade them to buy a particular product, service or brand. Advertising is used in most countries. It has an impact on everyone, whether they are at work, in the street, at home or at other venues.

The purpose of advertising

The overall purpose of advertising is to promote a product, service or brand and encourage people to buy from the business. If more people buy a business's products or services, then there is increase in the business's sales revenue and profit.

Advertising can have a number of specific purposes depending on the business circumstances, including:

- to launch a new product. Consumers will not usually know that a new product exists until it is advertised. Advertising is used to gain people's attention and attract customers. Businesses use advertising with the aim of encouraging sales of their new product or service by informing people of its existence and persuading them to buy.
- to inform the public about changes. Changes, such as the relocation of a business or alterations to a product's size, materials used or packaging, can be done through advertising.
- to build a brand. A brand is the name that a business uses for its products or services that is specific to a business, such as Coca-Cola, Toyota and Samsung. Advertising can be used to build awareness of a brand name and to develop brand loyalty, so that customers will repeatedly buy products with the same brand.
- to remind consumers of existing products or services. A business advertises to keep the attention of consumers, so the consumers do not buy a competitor's brand instead. Advertising can also help consumers to remember a particular product so they make repeated purchases.
- to make people more aware of a business and improve the business's reputation. Businesses sometimes choose to advertise themselves instead of individual products or services because it is more cost effective than advertising each individual brand or product. For example, large banks such as HSBC often advertise the company rather than each of its banking services individually.
- some businesses advertise even if they do not have any direct competition. They may advertise to provide themselves with a good reputation and to keep the brand in the consumer's mind.

Advertising types

There are several different types of advertising:

- informative
- persuasive
- collective
- competitive.

Informative advertising

Informative advertising provides facts to consumers, usually about a product or service, rather than directly trying to persuade consumers to make a purchase.

> **KEY TERM**
>
> **informative advertising:** advertising that provides facts to consumers, e.g., health risks.

Informative advertising is often used in the following circumstances:

- to tell consumers about a product's availability. Adverts may focus on giving facts, such as the business name, a product's price, where it can be purchased and how the product works.
- by local and national government to inform the public about issues such as health risks, new or changing government services, or election information.
- by travel companies to display information, such as the arrival and departure information of buses, trains and aircraft.
- by small businesses that provide a trade or service. The business may place advertisements in local newspapers or shop windows offering services to local people, such as window cleaning, phone repairs, sports classes and painting. The advertisements usually give basic information together with contact details.
- to let people know about local events, such as charity walks, fetes or concerts. These

advertisements may inform people about the event, its location, time and cost. Individuals also place informative advertisements, perhaps to advertise the birth, marriage or death of a family member.

- to tell people about job vacancies. These may be advertised in local newspapers, trade magazines or on the internet. They inform potential applicants about the job, along with when and how individuals can apply.

Persuasive advertising

Many advertisements combine information with **persuasive advertising** because a business might want to tell people about a product but will also want to encourage people to buy the product or service.

Persuasive advertising tries to influence people and persuade them to take action and buy particular goods or use particular services. Most advertising is persuasive. Persuasive advertising may try to link a product or service with emotions, celebrities, ambition and social acceptance (see Section 5.1.3). Methods used to persuade people might include the use of vague information or promises.

Persuasive advertising can be very effective at attracting customers. However, it only emphasises the positive features of a product or service. Persuasive advertising can be considered wasteful and repetitive.

Depending on the product, persuasive advertising tries to influence the consumer in one of the following three ways.

- The advertiser will try to encourage consumers to make impulsive decisions to buy the advertised product. For example, consumers might buy relatively inexpensive products, such as sweets, books or magazines, without having planned to.
- The advertiser will try to encourage consumers to make a conscious choice by comparing similar goods and services, to encourage the consumer to make a decision in terms of price, quality and availability. This approach is often suited to expensive goods, such as houses and cars.
- Some consumers buy a certain brand or product because they always have, and they think that other brands are not as good. The advertiser of a different brand will aim to make consumers interested in trying a new brand, while the advertiser of the existing brand will emphasise the benefits of continuing to rely on their brand.

Collective advertising

Collective (generic) advertising is when a group of businesses in the same trade or industry, such as milk or wool, cooperate and advertise a product or service together instead of competing with each other. Individually, each business may not be able to afford a big **advertising campaign** with lots of individual advertisements. However, together they can be more effective.

Collective advertising aims to promote the product and to increase general demand for the product. The advertising may be arranged by a marketing board (for agricultural produce), by a tourist board or by a trade association. A trade association is an organisation that represents the interests of all the firms in a particular industry, supplies information and promotes that industry. The costs of collective advertising are shared by the group of producers or paid for by the trade association. For example, holiday businesses or representatives of the tourism industry might work collectively to advertise a particular location.

Competitive advertising

Competitive advertising is the term used for advertising carried out by individual businesses that are in competition with other businesses which sell similar products. Businesses use competitive advertising with the aim of increasing sales of their own products or services. For example, Toyota or Honda will both use competitive advertising to promote their cars.

KEY TERMS

persuasive advertising: advertising that aims to persuade people to buy a particular good or service.

collective (generic) advertising: a group of organisations in the same industry or trade that join together to advertise the product.

advertising campaign: a coordinated group of advertisements that communicate the same message.

competitive advertising: advertising by individual businesses to increase sales of their own products or services.

A business may use advertising to suggest that its products or services are better than competitors' products. For example, an advert may suggest that a particular product is more reliable, higher quality or lower price.

Advantages and disadvantages of each type of advertising

Table 5.1.1 describes the advantages and disadvantages of different types of advertising.

Type of advertising	Advantages	Disadvantages
Informative	Attracts new customers, especially for small businesses such as window cleaners Gives consumers useful facts Improves consumers' knowledge of a business, brand or product	Can be expensive May be less appealing than persuasive advertising Does not directly increase sales
Persuasive	Effective at attracting customers Improves the reputation of a business, brand or product Encourages quick decisions from consumers that increase sales	Can give misleading information to consumers Gives biased information that only emphasises the positive features of a product or service Can be wasteful and repetitive Encourages impulsive buying of products that customers may not really want and cannot afford Expensive
Collective	Cheaper for each individual business More effective and seen by a larger number of consumers than competitive advertising Encourages cooperation between businesses Improves the image of a trade or industry	Each business has less control of the advertising Individual businesses may disagree on advertising decisions or how to fairly share advertising costs Advertising is generic and does not focus on an individual business's products or services
Competitive	Can focus on a product's key features Encourages consumers to choose an individual business's goods instead of the competitor's goods Increases consumers awareness of an individual business, brand or product Competition can encourage businesses to improve their products and/or lower prices	Can give misleading information to consumers Can be expensive

Table 5.1.1: Advantages and disadvantages of different types of advertising

TIP

Remember that both collective and competitive advertising can be either informative, persuasive or both.

5.1.2 Advertising media

Advertising media is the channel used to advertise and can be grouped into two main types:

- traditional advertising media
- digital advertising media.

Traditional advertising media

Advertising has been used for many years. Over time, many different types of advertising media have developed. **Traditional advertising media** are use channels that have been in existence for many years, such as print and broadcasting media. **Digital advertising media** have become available in more recent years and involve using digital methods, such as the internet, to advertise products.

There are several methods of traditional advertising media including those shown in Figure 5.1.1.

KEY TERMS

traditional advertising media: types of media that use channels that have been in existence for many years, such as print and broadcasting media.

digital advertising media: types of media that use digital methods to advertise products, services, brand or business to customers.

1. Television
2. Radio
3. Cinema
4. Newspapers
5. Magazines and trade journals
6. Leaflets/flyers
7. Packaging
8. Direct mail
9. Sponsorship
10. Catalogues and brochures
11. Posters and signboards
12. Transport vehicles
13. Window and point of sale displays
14. Word-of-mouth

Figure 5.1.1: Methods of traditional advertising media

1 Television

Television uses sound, pictures and animation to attract the attention of viewers. Television advertising can reach big national audiences. It is often used by national manufacturers and retailers. Advertisements are placed between television shows or at intervals during the shows. Television advertising can be very expensive. The costs vary depending on the expected size of the audience, which is affected by the time of the day and the programme being watched. For example, 'peak time' is usually between 6.00 p.m. and 10.00 p.m., when more people watch television, so an advertisement will be more widely viewed. Advertisers decide when to advertise based on who is likely to be watching. For example, a toy manufacturer may advertise during children's programmes.

Table 5.1.2 lists the advantages and disadvantages of using television for advertising campaigns.

Advantages of television advertising	Disadvantages of television advertising
Can reach a large number of consumers Suitable for people who cannot read but have a television Can target specific groups of consumers by choosing the time of day and the television programme Can attract attention by using **methods of appeal**, such as music and humour. A method of appeal is an advertising technique designed to associate a product or service with something to which a consumer can relate Suitable for advertising a wide range of consumer products, such as food, toys, cars, electronic goods and cleaning materials Product can be shown and demonstrated visually	Expensive Not suitable for small, local businesses with a small number of customers, as it will advertise to consumers who will never buy the product Increased availability of programme recording and catch-up television, rather than watching of live television, means that people can avoid watching advertisements Advertisements are short (usually 10 or 30 seconds), so consumers may not remember them

Table 5.1.2: Advantages and disadvantages of television advertising

KEY TERM

method of appeal: advertising technique designed to associate a product or service with something to which a consumer can relate, such as the use of humour or music in advertisements.

TIP

Be aware that television advertising can reach a lot of consumers but is not likely to be an appropriate media for small businesses because of the high cost. Small businesses usually have small advertising budgets and are more likely to choose cheaper media, such as leaflets and local newspapers.

2 Radio

A radio advertisement may be a short verbal announcement that includes the main points of a product. A radio advertisement may be repeated several times. Radio advertisements are found on independent or commercial radio stations. Some radio stations are national. Others are regional or local to a city or a group of small towns. The size of the audience may vary a lot, depending on the radio station, time of day and the country in which it operates.

Table 5.1.3 lists the advantages and disadvantages of using radio for advertising campaigns.

Advantages of radio advertising	Disadvantages of radio advertising
It is cheaper than television. Advertisements can be easy to produce because they do not have video or pictures. It can reach many consumers on national radio stations. It can be targeted at specific groups of consumers by broadcasting during a special interest programme. It can be appealing if the advertisements make good use of music and humour.	Advertisements are short (usually 10 or 30 seconds) and can be easily missed. Unlike newspapers and leaflets, there is no written record that consumers can look at more than once. Lots of consumers have a radio on in the background and do not listen carefully.

Table 5.1.3: Advantages and disadvantages of radio advertising

3 Cinema

Going to the cinema is popular in many countries. Cinema is often used for advertising, especially during social activities, e.g., local restaurants and shops that can be visited after the cinema.

The type of audience may vary with the specific film being shown and therefore the response to the advertising will also vary. Advertisements are usually shown just before the main film begins.

Table 5.1.4 lists the advantages and disadvantages of using cinema for advertising campaigns.

Advantages of cinema advertising	Disadvantages of cinema advertising
Consumers are more likely to concentrate on advertisements here than on those on television or radio. It is suitable for local businesses with a small number of local customers such as independent shops as it will advertise to consumers who are more likely to be interested in the product. Good quality sound and pictures can make consumers more likely to remember the advertisement.	Most consumers go to the cinema less often than they watch television or listen to the radio, so the advertisement is usually seen only once by consumers. Dependent on the size of cinema audience, the advertisement may only be seen by a few people.

Table 5.1.4: Advantages and disadvantages of cinema advertising

4 Newspapers

How many consumers read a newspaper and will see an advertisement will often depend on whether the newspaper is a local or national newspaper. Newspapers are usually printed, and many newspapers can now also be read online.

National newspapers serve a whole country. Most countries have national daily or weekly newspapers, such as *The Daily Prothom Alo* in Bangladesh and *The Herald* in Zimbabwe. Manufacturers, large retailers and national services, such as car hire companies and airlines, often use national newspapers for advertising.

Figure 5.1.2: Checking the classified advertisements

Local newspapers are those that may serve a region, city or town rather than a whole country. Local newspapers usually focus on local news and events. Some local newspapers are funded by the advertisers and are free for consumers. Small businesses that sell to consumers, such as restaurants and garages, are more likely to choose to advertise in local than national newspapers.

Different newspapers have different types of readers with different tastes. Businesses may choose which newspaper to advertise in based on whether the people who read the newspaper are likely to be future consumers of the product or service being advertised. Retailers of expensive items such as new cars are more likely to advertise in newspapers where readers have higher incomes.

The costs of advertising in a newspaper vary depending how many people receive the newspaper, the size of the advert and where the advert will appear in the newspaper. For example, a small advert on page 1 of a newspaper may cost much more than a whole-page advert on page 10 because an advert on page 1 is more likely to be noticed.

Most newspaper advertising contains text and images.

Newspapers also contain classified advertisements (Figure 5.1.2). Classified advertisements are usually text only and are all placed together in a specific part of a newspaper. Individuals or small businesses may place classified advertisements to sell products and services, promote job vacancies and make public announcements.

In most countries, there has been a decline in the number of people buying printed national newspapers, as more people get their news from television and the internet. However, there are still many people who regularly read printed newspapers. With a large potential readership all over the world, newspaper advertising continues to be important to advertisers.

Table 5.1.5 lists the advantages and disadvantages of using newspapers for advertising campaigns.

	Advantages of newspaper advertising	Disadvantages of newspaper advertising
Local	It is cheaper than national advertising. It can give detailed information. A printed advertisement can be seen repeatedly, especially in weekly newspapers that consumers may keep for reference. Newspapers have a wide circulation in an area, especially if they are delivered free to all homes in an area, so advertising gets wide local coverage. It is suitable for personal advertisements, such as births, marriages and deaths.	Local newspaper advertising will not be seen by people who cannot read and do not buy newspapers. It is less attractive to consumers than television or radio as there is no movement or sound, and the advertisement is less likely to be in colour. Free newspapers are more likely to be thrown away unread as they may have more advertisements than news articles. An advertisement may not be noticed if it is small or on a later page.
National	It can reach a large number of consumers. It is cheaper than television advertising. It can give detailed information. Unlike magazines, newspaper advertisements can usually be added, cancelled or changed at short notice. An advertisement can be repeated using different sizes in the same issue or in later issues of the newspaper. It can be placed within the newspaper to target particular audiences, e.g., a holiday advertisement in the travel section. Any printed media can be kept for reference.	It is more expensive than local newspaper advertising. It is less attractive to consumers than television or radio as there is no movement or sound, and the advertisement is less likely to be in colour. Advertisements do not always stand out from the rest of the large number of advertisements that may be placed in one newspaper. National newspaper advertising will not be seen by people who cannot read and do not buy newspapers. An advertisement may not be noticed if it is small or on a later page.

Table 5.1.5: Advantages and disadvantages of newspaper advertising

5 Magazines and trade journals

Magazines are generally published weekly or monthly. They are usually in colour and more expensive to buy than newspapers. They may have wide circulation, e.g., many fashion magazines, especially those targeting women. Others are more specialised and appeal only to a small audience, e.g., *The Cricketer* in Pakistan. Manufacturers of cosmetics, clothing and articles for the home all advertise in women's magazines. Retailers also publish magazines to advertise products and recipes for their products.

Trade journals are specialist magazines used for selling within specialist trades, e.g., the *Pakistan Textile Journal*. They are often read by businesspeople within a particular trade with knowledge of the trade.

> **KEY TERM**
>
> **trade journals:** specialist magazines used for selling within specialist trades.

Table 5.1.6 lists the advantages and disadvantages of magazine and trade journal for advertising.

Advantages of magazine and trade journal advertising	Disadvantages of magazine and trade journal advertising
Magazines and trade journals are usually kept by consumers for longer than newspapers, so advertisements may be reread. It can give detailed information and is useful for advertising messages that are long or need to be read carefully. It may target people with special interests, such as a particular sport, photography or fashion. Unlike most newspapers, magazine advertising can use colour, which may make advertisements more noticeable and appealing. Magazines may be passed on to other consumers, which increases the number of consumers that will see advertisements.	It can be expensive. Advertisements usually have to be placed well before the publication date. It is less likely to attract attention than some other forms of advertising, as there is no music or sound. The advertisement may not be noticed among other advertisements in the magazine/trade journal.

Table 5.1.6: Advantages and disadvantages of magazine and trade journal advertising

6 Leaflets/flyers

Printed leaflets and flyers are often used to give detailed information about a product or service, e.g., a new washing machine or a type of insurance. They are often used by small businesses to advertise locally and may be hand delivered or sent by post.

Table 5.1.7 lists the advantages and disadvantages of using leaflets and flyers for advertising campaigns.

Advantages of leaflets and flyers	Disadvantages of leaflets and flyers
They can be kept for future reference. They can be targeted at a particular group of consumers. They can include detailed information and are useful for advertising messages that are long or need to be read carefully. Unlike most newspapers, leaflets can use colour, which may make advertisements more noticeable and appealing.	People often throw them away without reading them.

Table 5.1.7: Advantages and disadvantages of leaflets and flyers

7 Packaging

Packaging on products usually has the manufacturer's or retailer's name or logo printed on it to advertise the product. Some businesses will modify the packaging from country to country to coordinate with the brand image they are emphasising in a particular country. Packaging may also show other information, such as the brand name, ingredients and directions for use.

Table 5.1.8 lists the advantages and disadvantages of advertising on packaging.

Advantages of advertising on packaging	Disadvantages of advertising on packaging
The packaging exists anyway, as it is for the protection of the products. Therefore it is an efficient use of packaging. It is a cheap form of advertising.	The packaging may be thrown away without being read.

Table 5.1.8: Advantages and disadvantages of advertising on packaging

8 Direct mail

Figure 5.1.3: Receiving direct mail

Direct mail refers to advertising addressed to individuals, including catalogues and leaflets, that is sent by post (Figure 5.1.3). Direct mail may use **sales promotions**, such as free gifts, prize draws or competitions, to encourage consumers to take notice of the advertising (see Section 5.1.4).

> **KEY TERM**
>
> **sales promotion:** the use of short-term sales techniques to bring products to the attention of consumers to increase demand for a product or service.

Table 5.1.9 lists the advantages and disadvantages of using direct mail for advertising campaigns.

Advantages of direct mail	Disadvantages of direct mail
It is cost effective as the business can reach a specific target group of consumers. Postal services may offer special prices for posting large volumes of direct mail, which can reduce the cost further. Consumers can keep the advertisement for future reference. The advertisement can include detailed information. Direct mail is useful for advertising messages that are long or need to be read carefully. Unlike most newspapers, direct mail can use colour, which may make advertisements more noticeable and appealing.	Direct mail is often regarded as junk mail and so may be thrown away without being read. Mailing lists with the names and addresses of consumers can go out of date.

Table 5.1.9: Advantages and disadvantages of advertising by direct mail

9 Sponsorship

Businesses may pay towards the cost of activities, such as staging concerts, sporting and charity events, or supporting groups or individuals. This is called sponsorship. Television and radio programmes may also be sponsored, with the advertiser paying towards the cost of the programme being made. Businesses can use **sponsorship** to display their name or logo on literature, programmes, posters, uniforms, sports equipment and clothing to gain consumer attention.

> **KEY TERM**
>
> **sponsorship:** businesses making payments or offering other support for an event or team, such as entertainment, sporting, community and charity events.

Table 5.1.10 lists the advantages and disadvantages of sponsorship.

Advantages of sponsorship	Disadvantages of sponsorship
It can help to improve the public image of the business. It may enable the product to be used at the event to gain consumer awareness and confidence.	It is expensive to the business that may provide money, staff time and free products. There may be little opportunity to give detailed information about a product or service.

Table 5.1.10: Advantages and disadvantages of sponsorship

10 Catalogues and brochures

Catalogues and brochures are commonly used by shops, travel companies and mail order companies. They give detailed information about the goods offered and their prices.

Table 5.1.11 lists the advantages and disadvantages of catalogues and brochures.

Advantages of catalogues and brochures	Disadvantages of catalogues and brochures
Provide detailed information Often make products look attractive Can be used over a period of time Can be referred to repeatedly	Products may differ from the pictures in the catalogue Expensive to produce May be seen by few people May be thrown away unread

Table 5.1.11: Advantages and disadvantages of catalogues and brochures

11 Posters and signboards

Posters and **signboards** are both types of advertising that involve displaying images, text or logos. Posters are smaller than signboards and are likely to be found on bulletin boards or in shop windows to advertise events, goods for sale, **special offers** or sales. Signboards are larger display boards, such as signs in a shop, train station or school, showing important messages such as opening hours and directions. Special offers are price discounts or cost-effective opportunities for customers.

KEY TERMS

signboards: large display boards, such as signs in a shop, train station or school.

special offers: price discounts or cost-effective opportunities for customers, such as 'buy one, get one free' (often known as BOGOF) promotions.

Table 5.1.12 lists the advantages and disadvantages of using posters and signboards for advertising campaigns.

Advantages of posters and signboards	Disadvantages of posters and signboards
Cheap Available at lots of different locations Stay in a place for a long time Consumers may see them repeatedly Can be seen by lots of consumers if they are put in a popular location, such as in busy shopping centres	Can be damaged by bad weather or vandalism if located outdoors in a public place Difficult to target particular groups of consumers Not suitable for information that takes a long time to be read Difficult to measure how effective the advertisement has been

Table 5.1.12: Advantages and disadvantages of advertising through posters and signboards

12 Transport vehicles

Advertising is often seen on the sides of taxis, buses, trucks, trains and other forms of transport. A business may advertise itself on its own transport. Table 5.1.13 describes the advantages and disadvantages of using transport vehicles for advertising campaigns.

Advantages of advertising on transport vehicles	Disadvantages of advertising on transport vehicles
It is a cheap form of advertising. It can provide a regular reminder when the vehicle is travelling or when parked.	There may be little opportunity to give detailed information about a product or service. It is difficult to target particular groups of consumers.

Table 5.1.13: Advantages and disadvantages of advertising on transport vehicles

13 Window displays and point of sale displays

Displays of goods are often used in shops and in shop windows (Figure 5.1.4). Sometimes manufacturers supply display materials and signs to make the display very noticeable and appealing to consumers. This is known as merchandising. Individual window displays in departmental stores may focus on a range of goods, such as luggage or sportswear. Special themed window displays to celebrate national holidays may be particularly appealing to consumers. Other goods, particularly small items such as sweets, may have a **point of sale display** at the checkout, to attract attention and encourage purchases on impulse.

Figure 5.1.4: Consumers looking at a shop window display

KEY TERM

point of sale display: a display of products located where customers make the payment for purchases to attract attention and encouraging additional purchases.

Table 5.1.14 lists advantages and disadvantages of using displays for advertising campaigns.

Advantages of displays	Disadvantages of displays
They encourage consumers to buy products they had not planned to purchase. They help to make shops look attractive. They can be changed quickly.	Point of sale displays can slow down service at the checkout or cash till. There may be little opportunity to give detailed information about a product or service.

Table 5.1.14: Advantages and disadvantages of advertising through displays

14 Word-of mouth

Word-of-mouth advertising occurs when people who have already bought a product or service from a particular business give a personal recommendation to consumers. Personal recommendations are usually from people who have nothing to gain financially from advertising. As a result, other consumers are likely to trust their recommendation and purchase the item. Word-of-mouth advertising is not chosen or controlled by the seller. As a result, there are no advertising costs for the business to pay.

KEY TERM

word-of-mouth advertising: personal recommendations from people who have already bought a product or service or from a particular business.

Table 5.1.15 lists the advantages and disadvantages of word-of-mouth advertising.

Advantages of word-of-mouth advertising	Disadvantages of word-of-mouth advertising
There are no costs directly involved. It is trusted by the consumers receiving the message. It can increase sales.	The business has no control over what consumers are saying. It is difficult to measure the impact on consumers.

Table 5.1.15: Advantages and disadvantages of word-of-mouth advertising

TIP

There are many methods of traditional advertising media. For each method, you must understand its features and its advantages and disadvantages.

Digital advertising media

Digital advertising involves using digital methods to advertise products, services, brands or businesses to customers. There are several different methods of digital advertising, including those shown in Figure 5.1.5.

1. Internet advertising
2. Social media advertising
3. Social media influencers
4. Display and video adverting
5. Email marketing
6. Digital billboards

Figure 5.1.5: Methods of digital advertising media

1 Internet advertising

Advertising on the internet has expanded in recent years as consumers' use of the internet has grown. Many businesses have websites. These often consist of a home page (the first page) followed by more detailed pages. Business websites may give information about the business and its products or services. Business websites may also allow customers to communicate with the business through chat boxes that pop up on the screen on the website.

Ecommerce businesses use websites to sell directly to customers by enabling people to place an order and pay for products online. The products will then typically be delivered to the customer's home or other place of choosing. The internet allows businesses to reach consumers in different countries without the cost of running shops in each country. Some businesses only sell online, while others have both retail outlets and online shopping websites (see Chapter 1.1).

Business websites that are used for interacting with consumers are carefully designed with the aim of making the customer so satisfied that they will return again (Figure 5.1.6). A successful website will be easy to use and attractive to look at.

Figure 5.1.6: Customer interacting with business website

Search engines, such as Google, Bing and Yahoo, are computer programs that help people to find information online or specific websites. The user puts in a few key words to indicate what they are looking for. The search engine will then quickly check the internet to find the information. The search engine will present the results to the user. These results are usually given to the user in the form of a list of web pages in order of relevance. The list can be very long. Most users will look at very few of these web pages and typically only click on those at or near the top of the list.

A successful website is easy to find using search engines and will come near the top of a list provided by an internet search. Businesses use search engine optimisation to make it more likely that their website appears at, or near, the top of a search engine' list of results. There are various actions that businesses can take to achieve search engine optimisation, such as regularly updating the website content and using common keywords on the website that search engines will pick up on. Some businesses employ specialists to help them with these activities, and sometimes businesses pay search engines to help them appear at the top of a web search list.

Search engine optimisation can lead to more consumers visiting a particular website. For example, if a consumer is looking to buy a pair of shoes, they may put 'buy shoes' as keywords in a search engine. There will be a long list of results. If the website of a business that sells shoes is at the top of the list, the user is more likely to click on the link provided on the results page, visit the business's website and buy shoes from that business (Figure 5.1.7).

Figure 5.1.7: Searching for online sellers

When someone does an internet search, advertisements are also displayed at the top or bottom of a page of search engine results. These advertisements may include a short piece of text (the headline), an image or other text, and a link that typically leads to the advertiser's website.

Mobile advertising is the term used for paid advertising that appears when using webpages or apps on mobile devices such as smartphones and tables (Figure 5.1.8). Mobile advertising is becoming an increasingly important part of internet advertising because mobile phones are used by so many people worldwide. For example, more people now own mobile phones than televisions, and more people now view the internet using mobile devices rather than other devices such as laptops or desktop computers.

KEY TERM

mobile advertising: paid advertising that appears on mobile devices such as smartphones and tablets.

Table 5.1.16 lists advantages and disadvantages of using the internet for advertising campaigns.

Advantages of advertising on the internet	Disadvantages of advertising on the internet
It is less expensive than most traditional advertising. A business can reach many consumers in different countries. It can target specific individuals or groups. It provides businesses with useful data, such as how many people click onto a website. Businesses can analyse this data to inform future advertising decisions. Advertisements can use a range of appealing styles, including text, images and video.	There can be lots of competing advertisements on the internet, and creating advertisements that attract consumers' attention can be difficult and time consuming. Some groups of consumers do not have access to the internet or choose not to use the internet. Not all businesses can appear at or near the top of an internet search results list. It is often small businesses that do not have the expertise to achieve a high position. People can use adblocker software to avoid seeing online adverts on their devices.

Table 5.1.16: Advantages and disadvantages of advertising on the internet

Figure 5.1.8: Mobile advertising

Use of social media

Social media are communication channels that let people create and share information and ideas online in the form of text, pictures and videos. Social media enables people to carry on conversations and build up relationships online with a few or many people worldwide. Users can be individuals, businesses or other organisations.

Different types of social media exist, including:

- social and business networks, where individuals and businesses can connect, such as Facebook and LinkedIn
- blogging and microblogging, where people can create and share content
- forums, where people have discussions by posting questions and messages, such as Reddit
- picture sharing, video sharing and live streaming, such as Instagram, TikTok and YouTube.

Social media may reach no one or may reach millions of people. Many people regularly use social media, especially on mobile devices, and the number of users continues to grow. Social media are used by all age groups and are a part of everyday life for many people.

Social networks, such as Facebook, Instagram and TikTok, allow individuals to build relationships, and businesses that use these networks can interact directly with consumers. Comments about products can be posted or reposted. Social network sites also provide a large amount of information about products.

2 Social media advertising

Businesses may use social media channels to promote a product or brand to consumers. This is called social media advertising. Businesses can advertise by creating content that aims to attract people's attention and encourages them to share content across their social networks. This means the message about a product, a brand or a company is spread from consumer to consumer. The content might be regular information about the products, or persuasive advertisements, and might include text, images or videos.

Businesses sometimes use **pay-per-click advertising (PPC)** as a form of both social media advertising and internet advertising. With pay-per-click advertising, the advertisement includes a link from social media or a webpage to the business's website. The business only pays a fee when a person sees the advert and clicks on the link. Pay-per-click advertising encourages more people to visit a business's website.

> **KEY TERM**
>
> **pay-per-click advertising (PPC):** online advertisements that include a link to a business's website. The business only pays a fee when a person sees the advert and clicks on the link.

Many different types of business, both large and small, invest in pay-per-click advertising, as it can be a cost-effective method of advertising because a business only pays when people engage with the advert and click on to the website. People who click on an advert are more likely to go on to buy something from the website.

As well as using social media to promote products to large numbers of consumers, businesses can also use social media for advertisements to specific consumers at specific times. For example, a company that sells holidays may advertise widely but also send specific adverts or social media posts to individual consumers who have been viewing travel websites. Being able to advertise to consumers who are more likely to be interested in a business's products can lead to an increase in sales.

Businesses may use social media to gain useful market information. For example, customers may choose to review their experience of a product or business, both good and bad, such as adding Instagram or Facebook posts and photos from an enjoyable (or disappointing) visit to a restaurant or a great (or terrible) hair cut from a local salon. Businesses can see and use consumers' social media posts and comments to analyse consumer opinions and views on products, services and competitors. This is a cheap method of market research and provides current information about consumers. It also allows the business to react quickly to positive or negative feedback.

A business can use digital information available from social media advertising to find out whether a social media advertisement was worthwhile by using **data analytics**.

KEY TERM

data analytics: the collection, organisation and interpretation of data to find useful information, such as patterns or trends in the data, from which conclusions can be drawn and informed decisions can be made.

Data analytics is the collection and interpretation of data to find useful information, such as patterns or trends (Figure 5.1.9). For example, if a business runs a set of pay-per-click Facebook advertisements, it can use data analytics to find out how many times people clicked from the advert to the business website and what the consumers did once they reached the business website, including which products they looked at and what (if any) goods they bought. This information can then help the business to decide whether to run more pay-per-click Facebook adverts in future or to try a different type of advertising.

Figure 5.1.9: Presenting and interpreting marketing data

The use of social networks by businesses has risen a lot in recent years. Social networks can reach more people than more traditional advertising media. Use of social media is much less expensive than traditional advertising, although there are costs of employing people to manage social media interaction and to maintain consumer trust in the product or service.

Social media advertising is a form of internet advertising and has the same advantages and disadvantages as internet advertising. However, some groups of consumers are less likely to use social media. For example, many teenagers and young adults use social media whereas people over 65 are much less likely to use social media (Figure 5.1.10).

Table 5.1.17 lists advantages and disadvantages of using social media for advertising campaigns.

Advantages of advertising using social media	Disadvantages of advertising using social media
Comments can be shared and reposted, leading to high numbers of consumers seeing the advertisements. Businesses can use comments to engage directly with individual consumers. Advertisements can use a range of appealing styles, including text, images and video.	Negative comments made on social media by consumers can be posted and reposted. Creating social media content and responding to consumer comments can be time consuming. Some groups of consumers do not have access to the internet or choose not to use the internet.

Table 5.1.17: Advantages and disadvantages of advertising using social media

Figure 5.1.10: Many young people use social media frequently

3 Social medial influencers

Some people participate in social media conversation hoping to influence others. **Social media influencers** is a term used to describe people that use social media to create content that affects others, perhaps encouraging them to think a certain way or buy a particular product. Some businesses use social media influencers such as popular bloggers or vloggers (video blogger) to promote their products and services to consumers. For example, an influencer might discuss or review a product or brand and share their views with their followers. Often influencers are paid by the business or given free products to encourage them to use their influence to promote a product with consumers.

> **KEY TERM**
>
> **social media influencers:** people that use social media to create content that affects others, perhaps encouraging them to think a certain way or buy a particular product.

Table 5.1.18 lists advantages and disadvantages of using social media influencers for advertising campaigns.

Advantages of advertising through social media influencers	Disadvantages of advertising through social media influencers
Consumers trust the advertisement because it comes from someone the consumer trusts. Businesses can target specific individuals or groups that follow an influencer.	It is reliant on the personal image of the influencer. Any negative views of the influencer can affect the reputation of whatever is being advertised. Some groups of consumers do not have access to the internet or choose not to use the internet.

Table 5.1.18: Advantages and disadvantages of advertising through social media influencers

4 Display and video advertisements

Businesses may use a variety of ways to display advertisements on the internet, including the following:

- **pop-up advertisements** appear in their own window as the user is browsing a website. They typically appear in front of another website that the user is looking at and can be annoying because they hide the original web page.
- **banner advertisements** are usually placed horizontally at the top of a web page that has interesting and relevant content, such as a newspaper article. The user may click on to the banner to move to the advertising business's website.
- **sidebar advertisements** are placed vertically at the side of a web page to attract the attention of the user of the web page. They are often larger than banner advertisements.

Display advertisements typically use images or text but may also use video content. **Video advertisements** are advertisements that use video content. Video advertisements often try to get people's attention by being visually attractive. For example, if a consumer clicks on a popular YouTube video, the first thing that appears may be a short (e.g., 5 seconds) advert. The requested YouTube video can only be watched after the advert has finished.

Display and video advertising are both forms of internet advertising and have the same advantages and disadvantages as other internet advertising (Table 5.1.16).

> **KEY TERMS**
>
> **pop-up advertisements:** advertisements that appear in their own window as the user is browsing a website.
>
> **banner advertisements:** advertisements embedded into a web page. The banner is usually placed horizontally at the top of a web page.
>
> **sidebar advertisements:** advertisements placed vertically at the side of a web page to attract the attention of the user.
>
> **video advertisements:** advertisements that use video rather than images or text.

5 Email marketing

Emails are used widely in business and by individuals. In **email marketing**, businesses use email to give customers up-to-date information about new products and services, and to promote their goods and services.

Businesses will try to build up a list of email addresses from individuals that are willing to receive emails from the business. These individuals are called **subscribers**. Businesses may try to get names and email addresses in several different ways, such as collecting the information when customers buy goods, having a form on the business website or advertising on social media encouraging consumers to subscribe. Businesses sometimes encourage people to subscribe by providing subscribers with special offers, discounts and other promotions.

The content included in emails that businesses send to consumers will usually be informational, persuasive or both. The content can include pictures as well as text, and emails can have documents attached, such as company newsletters.

KEY TERMS

email marketing: when businesses send emails to consumers to promote their products or services.

subscribers: individuals who have agreed to receive emails from a business and have provided the business with their email address.

Table 5.1.19 lists advantages and disadvantages of using email marketing for advertising campaigns.

Advantages of advertising using email marketing	Disadvantages of advertising using email marketing
Low cost. It can be cheaper to use email marketing rather than sending messages by more traditional methods, such as letters or phone calls. Staffing costs can also be much lower and there are no costs of printing or postage.	Businesses cannot send an email without an email address. Businesses often have to work hard to gain and keep subscribers. It is also easy to make a mistake when writing an email address.
Easy to use. Most people know how to send and receive emails so employees do not need to have training before emails can be sent to consumers.	Consumers can unsubscribe from receiving email marketing whenever they choose to.
Different types of content can be sent. For example, pictures, photographs and graphics can be sent. Documents can be attached to emails.	Two-way discussion is difficult. There may be delays in replying if the recipient does not check emails regularly.
Emails can target specific groups of subscribers. A business can choose to send an email to all its subscribers, a group of subscribers or an individual. Choosing to send the email to a group allows the business to target a particular group of people with similar characteristics.	Use of junk mail folders and clutter filters can mean that emails do not always reach the audience.
Messages are sent quickly, anywhere in the world.	
It is better for the environment as emails are paperless and do not need to be transported.	

Table 5.1.19: Advantages and disadvantages of advertising using email marketing

6 Digital billboards

Digital billboards are large screens that digitally display advertisements such as images or videos. They can change more frequently than traditional billboards or signboards. Digital billboards are often placed on the sides or fronts of buildings. They are often used in areas where there are lots of people, such as city centres and railway stations.

Digital billboards are more expensive than non-digital billboards but can provide much more engaging and up-to-date information that draws the attention of consumers.

Table 5.1.20 describes the advantages and disadvantages of digital billboards for advertising campaigns.

Advantages of digital billboards	Disadvantages of digital billboards
Can use sound, colour and video to appeal to consumers and attract attention	More expensive than traditional signboards
Can stay in a place for a long time	Can stop working if there is disruption to the power source
May be seen by consumers repeatedly	Difficult to target particular groups of consumers
Can be effective at being noticed by consumers if they are put in a popular location	Not suitable for information that takes a long time to be read
	Difficult to measure how effective the advertisement has been

Table 5.1.20: Advantages and disadvantages of digital billboards

KEY TERM

digital billboard: an advertising screen that can digitally display images and/or videos.

TIP

It is easy to mix up posters, signboards and digital billboards. Learn the differences between these three different methods of advertising media.

Growth in digital advertising

Digital advertising has grown rapidly in recent years, as more businesses choose digital methods of advertising over more traditional methods that do not use the internet. There are several reasons for this growth.

- There have been significant changes in technology. Technology that enables digital advertising has developed over time and become more available for both businesses and consumers, such as improved internet connections and smartphones.
- More consumers are using the internet. People are spending more time online. People are browsing the internet and using social media. Digital advertising lets businesses reach more consumers with their advertisements.
- Digital advertising offers businesses the ability to target specific consumers. Some types of digital advertising let businesses target specific groups of consumers more easily. Information about people's browsing history and social media profile can be used to personalise advertisements. Being able to target consumers who are more likely to be interested in a business's products can lead to an increase in sales.
- Digital methods are often more cost effective than traditional methods. Advertising can be expensive. Digital advertising is often (but not always) cheaper than other forms of advertising, such as television and newspapers. Businesses want to ensure that they gain sales revenue as a result of the advertising in order to make the advertising cost effective. Digital marketing is usually better at targeting the right consumers leading to more sales. Therefore, digital advertising is often more cost effective.
- Digital advertising offers businesses the ability to monitor and measure the results using data analytics. It is possible to track people's internet use and collect useful data that can be used by the business to make decisions on future advertising.

Choosing a method of advertising

There are many different methods of advertising available. Choosing the best method(s) for a particular business and its products depends on some or all of the following factors:

- audience
- cost

- cultural and legal considerations
- flexibility to change
- local and international market coverage
- multi-channel advertising
- timing
- type of product.

Audience

The number of potential customers that might see an advert and the type of people that the business wishes to target, such as their gender, income and leisure activities, will affect the type of advertisement that a business chooses to use. For example, businesses are more likely to advertise toys using early evening television, when many children are more likely to be watching. Young people's fashion might be best advertised using social media advertising or influencers, while perfumes and expensive beauty products are often found in women's magazines.

Cost

Advertising can be very expensive. A business must decide how much it is prepared to spend on an advertisement, which will be affected by how much the business can afford. A business will also need to consider the expected cost-effectiveness of an advertisement, that is, are the likely benefits from running an advert sufficient to justify the cost? If an advertisement is cost effective, it is likely to be noticed by consumers and encourage enough of them to buy the business's products to justify the cost of the advertisement. For example, a small market stall trader is unlikely to use television. However, McDonald's can afford charges for peak television time to advertise its food.

Cultural and legal considerations

Cultural issues can be a very important consideration, especially if a business is selling in other countries. For example, newspapers, magazines and direct mail would not be suitable in countries where the literacy level is low. Internet and social media advertising would not be suitable where few people own a computer or mobile phone.

Laws and regulations governing what can be advertised will also affect the choice of advertising in many situations. Each country will decide what legal restrictions are put on advertisements. For example, in many countries, advertising alcohol and cigarettes is carefully regulated or banned.

Flexibility to change

Some forms of advertising can be changed much more easily and quickly than others. When choosing a form of advertisement, a business may want to consider whether it can be changed or cancelled at short notice, particularly if a business wants to make quick decisions or changes its mind. Magazine advertising can be inflexible, as the advertising space needs to be booked well in advance of publication, while newspaper advertising can be changed more easily. For example, a small food retailer might find that it has a large amount of perishable goods that must be sold in the next two days or they will need to be thrown away. In this case, it might be most appropriate for the retailer to do a quick point of sale display or social media message to promote the products.

Local and international market coverage

Businesses will consider where its customers are based when choosing a method of advertising. Businesses that produce large volumes of products may advertise nationally or internationally, while those producing a small number of products are more likely to choose local advertising or word-of-mouth. Some of the world's largest companies, such as Coca-Cola, McDonald's and Apple, advertise to ensure that they can effectively sell their products worldwide.

Multi-channel advertising

Multi-channel advertising means using more than one advertising medium. Businesses often use several media to reinforce their message and ensure that it reaches many consumers. Each method of advertising media should complement the others. For example, a digital billboard at an athletics stadium advertising sportswear could be reinforced by advertising on the radio or social media. More information is then available on the business's website where the sportwear can be purchased online.

KEY TERM

multi-channel advertising: the use of more than one advertising medium, such as combining television with newspaper advertising, to advertise the same product, service or brand.

Timing

Timing can be especially important for seasonal products. Businesses that produce or sell seasonal products will typically concentrate their advertising just before the season starts. For example, beachwear and ice-cream producers will increase their advertising towards the summer.

A business must also decide how long it wants to use the same advertisement and whether an advertisement should be repeated. For example, information in leaflets may become dated and have to be reprinted. Adverts in monthly magazines have a longer life span than daily newspapers, as the magazine can be reread or kept for future reference.

Type of product

A product or service that is widely used by many consumers will be widely advertised and is more likely to use more than one advertising media. For example, a brand of washing-up liquid might be advertised nationally on television, in newspapers and on digital billboards. However, specialist equipment used in a particular industry will be advertised in trade journals, specialised magazines or email marketing.

How new a product is and how long the product is likely to be on the market can also affect the advertising medium used. For example, a new book by a famous author may use window and point of sale displays, social media advertising and the author's website. Once the book has been available for some time, the book is likely to be advertised less and the focus may move towards word-of-mouth recommendations.

ACTIVITY 5.1.1

Working with a partner or in a small group, research two advertisements: one traditional and one digital.

a For each advertisement, answer the following:

- **i** What is being advertised? Is it a product, service, brand or business?
- **ii** What advertising media is being used?
- **iii** Is that choice of media the most appropriate? Give reasons for your answer.

CONTINUED

- **iv** How could the advertisement be improved?

b Present your findings to the class.

REFLECTION

When answering Activity 5.1.1, how did you find the advertisements to research? Was it easier to find information for traditional or digital advertising? Why?

Discuss with another student what you think you learned from this activity. Did the requirement to present your findings help to consolidate your understanding? Why?

5.1.3 Methods of appeal

Methods of appeal consider how an advertisement is presented. Methods of appeal aim to link a product or service with something that the consumer can relate to and to make an impact on the consumer. They may be concerned with the content of the advertisement, the tone of the advertisement or the sound used in presenting the advertisement.

Many advertisements try to appeal to people's emotions and fears to attract the consumer's attention and encourage consumers to make purchases.

Types of appeal methods used in advertising

There are many different types of methods of appeal used in advertising including those outlined below.

Emotion

Advertisers often try to gain an emotional reaction from consumers. They play on people's hopes and fears or try to gain sympathy from the consumer. They may use humour or music to make an advertisement memorable.

Emotional methods of appeal include:

- fear – people have many different fears that advertisers may consider, such as the fear of accidents or being ill. For example, advertisers of smoke alarms might use pictures or descriptions of what might happen if there was a fire in someone's home and how a smoke alarm might save people and property.
- social acceptance – people want to be accepted by friends and work colleagues. For example, advertisements suggesting that customers can join particular social groups if they buy a particular product are popular with manufacturers of some styles of clothing. These advertisements play on people's fear of being alone and not being part of a social group.
- ambition – advertisers may appeal to people's desire to succeed in their work or an aspect of their personal lives. For example, an advertisement might show a successful or beautiful person using the product. Consumers may then feel that if they use the product, they will also be successful or beautiful.
- romance – this is a widely used advertising device, especially when aimed at younger adults. Products such as perfume, alcoholic drinks and cosmetics are often advertised in a romantic way, where they are associated with young adults, relationships and being attractive.
- adventure – some advertisements appeal to consumers' sense of adventure, wish for excitement or curiosity about new things. For example, an advertisement for a holiday might focus on exploring new places, doing something different and having an adventure.

Humour

People like to smile and laugh. Advertisers often introduce humour into the situations shown in advertisements. They may make use of jokes, cartoons or funny situations. Some of the most successful advertisements and most remembered are those that make people laugh.

Rational

Consumers like to think of themselves as logical and rational. Advertisements use logic or reasoning by providing facts about a product or its advantages over its competitors. For example, an advertisement for a type of food may focus on how healthy, easy to cook or inexpensive it is.

Music

Music is used widely in television, cinema and radio advertisements to make them more emotional, entertaining and memorable. For example, pop music with a quick tempo may make an advertisement exciting. Classical music may be interpreted as relaxing.

Endorsement by celebrities

Celebrity endorsement involves using someone who is well known, such as an actor, singer or footballer, to advertise a product or service. The celebrity is paid and/or may be given the product for free.

Use of celebrities in advertisements can encourage consumers to make purchases of a particular product by appealing to their wish to copy someone that they may admire. It can also appeal to their wish to be part of a group of people that own or use the same product or service. Celebrity endorsement is used to advertise many different products and services, including clothes and sports equipment. Businesses should try to match the celebrity with the product, e.g., it may be better to use an athlete to promote sports equipment rather than an actor.

KEY TERM

celebrity endorsement: the use of someone who is well known, such as an actor, singer or footballer, to recommend a product or service to consumers.

Social media influencers

As you learned in Section 5.1.2, social media influencers are people who have many followers on social media platforms such as Instagram, TikTok and Facebook. Social media influencers have often become popular by creating and sharing interesting content, reviews and recommendations. They may focus on a specific topic, such as beauty, fitness, music or travel.

Social media influencers can be useful in advertising because they are often trusted by their followers and can influence their followers' opinions and encourage them to buy a product.

Use of social media influencers in advertising has become popular in recent years as the use of social media among consumers has grown. As with celebrity endorsement, it is more effective when businesses choose an appropriate influencer for their product or service so that the product matches the followers' interests.

TIP

Check that you are clear that you understand the difference between celebrities and social media influencers.

Choosing methods of appeal to use in advertising

When choosing methods of appeal to use in an advertisement, it is important to consider:

- the nature of the product or service to be advertised
- the consumers to which the campaign is directed.

The business should be clear about who the consumers are that it wants to attract with the advertisement and what characteristics they share: for example, their age, gender, income and lifestyle. Once the advertiser is clear on the product and the consumers, it can choose a method or methods of appeal that are most likely to gain consumers' attention and support the message that the business wants to give them about the product.

Advertisements need to be liked. If people like them, they will remember them. The most successful advertisements are often those that people remember. They will talk about them to friends and family, and even switch from another brand to buy the advertised brand. It is about both the choice of media and also the method of appeal used.

ACTIVITY 5.1.2

a Think of an advertisement that you remember from your childhood. Explain to a partner:

   i what the advertisement was and what media was used

   ii why the advertisement was memorable

   iii whether or not the advertisement encouraged you or your family to make any purchases, and why.

b In pairs, outline a design for a new advertisement for a product of your choosing that uses at least two methods of appeal.

c Join up with another pair of students in your class. Share your design ideas and give feedback on how effective each advertisement might be.

5.1.4 Sales promotion

Sales promotion involves using techniques to bring products to the attention of consumers to increase demand for a product or service, leading to more sales. A sales promotion is often short term and will have a particular focus, such as to stop sales from falling, to launch a new product or to sell old inventory before new inventory arrives. It may be for a limited time, such as a particular month. It may be for a special occasion, such as a big sports event. Advertising and sales promotion often work together to encourage more sales than either method might achieve on its own.

Methods of sales promotion

There are several methods that can be used for sales promotion as outlined in Table 5.1.21.

Methods of sales promotion	Explanation
Point of sale	Point of sale is where customers make the payment for the goods they are buying, such as a checkout or cash till in a shop or the online checkout on a web page. Point of sale sales promotion involves trying to encourage further purchases at this point. For example, additional products are often displayed beside checkouts to attract the attention of customers while they are waiting to pay, and the customer may be tempted to buy them. The goods might be small and cheap, such as sweets and magazines. When buying online, customers might be shown some extra goods linked to the purchases they are making. For example, when going to an online checkout to buy flowers or food, the customer might be offered a larger size for a small additional charge, or when purchasing an electronics item, the customer might be asked if they also want to buy batteries.
Special offers	Special offers are price discounts or cost-effective opportunities for customers, such as 'buy one, get one free' (often known as BOGOF) and 'two for the price of one' promotions that encourage customers to buy more of a product or brand.
Sponsorship	Businesses may sponsor an event, team or individual by paying towards the costs involved, such as entertainment, sporting, community and charity events (see Section 5.1.2).
Displays	Displays often occur in retailers and consist of a way of promoting products by making them look interesting or appealing. Retailers might have displays in their shop windows, at the shop's entrance and at the end of an isle of shelving, where consumers are most likely to notice products. A display of a particular product or brand of products might be accompanied by eye-catching posters, signboards or free samples. Free samples are small quantities of products given to consumers without charge.
Competitions	Customers may be invited to take part in competitions or free draws for a cash prize, or other rewards such as a holiday or a car, if they buy a particular product or service. Competitions often aim to increase awareness of a product or brand and gain new customers.
Coupons	Coupons may be given to the customer when a sale is made. The coupon can then be used in part-payment of a future purchase of the product. They aim to encourage customer loyalty and repeat purchases.
Sales period	A sales period is a specific time period, such as a few days or weeks, when a business reduces its prices or provides other special offers for customers. Sales periods are often designed to occur during holidays or changes in the season, such as January sales or summer sales. The prices are reduced so that remaining inventory can be sold before the new season's inventory arrives. Sales periods can also be very useful for products that become dated, such as fashionable clothes, or that might deteriorate, such as the dessert Halwa, which is most popular during festivals. Selling inventory at a lower price might increase demand for the product so the business can sell a bigger quantity of products. It also provides the business with cash to pay for new inventory.
Loss leaders	Loss leaders are products sold at a lower price than the cost of making or buying them with the aim of attracting customers into a shop. While in the shop, it is hoped that the customer will buy other goods, so that the shop still earns a profit for all the products sold.

Continued

Methods of sales promotion	Explanation
Free gifts	Free gifts may be given when a customer purchases a more expensive item. For example, a customer buying a coffee maker may be given a free packet of coffee. Free gifts are sometimes offered if a customer spends a certain amount of money on a product, e.g., 'Spend $100 and you will receive this free gift valued at $30'. Sometimes free gifts will have the brand or business's name on it, which is another way of advertising.
Free samples	Small samples may be given to consumers without charge. Free samples encourage consumers to try a product and encourage them to purchase a larger amount in future. Free samples are often used for new products, such as a new perfume or a new flavour of soft drink. Free samples might be provided in shops, or sometimes they are available in magazines, e.g., sachets of a new shampoo or skincare product.

Table 5.1.21: Methods of sales promotion

KEY TERMS

free samples: small quantities of products given to consumers without charge.

sales period: a specific time period, such as a few days or weeks, when a business reduces its prices or provides other special offers for customers.

loss leaders: products sold at a lower price than the cost of making or buying them, with the aim of attracting customers into a shop where they will make other purchases.

Factors affecting choice of sales promotion methods

Businesses that want to use sales promotion will need to choose between the different methods of sales promotion available. Some businesses will choose more than one method but are unlikely to choose all of them. Which methods of sales promotion to choose depends on several factors.

Business type

The kind of business promoting the goods or services affects what sales promotion is used. Whether the business is a manufacturer, departmental store or online retailer will all affect the sales promotions decisions made. For example, a manufacturer might use sponsorship, introductory offers or packaging to promote its products. A departmental store might use window displays, point of sale promotions, special offers and sales periods. An online retailer might give special offers, such free delivery if a minimum value of products is purchased.

Competitors

The activities of competitors will also help to decide what sales promotion to use. For example, there is often close competition between supermarkets. If one supermarket chooses to make use of loss leaders, its competitors are more likely to compete by also offering loss leaders, or by using other price discounts, such as special offers or coupons.

Cost

Sales promotions will cost a business money to set up and operate. Some sales promotions are more expensive than others. The business will decide how much can be spent on sales promotion. Special offers may be expensive, whereas displays at point of sale may be cheap to stage.

Nature of the product

The nature of the product itself is important. If a product is a luxury or expensive item, then expensive sales promotion may be used, such as money-off coupons, free credit terms for a period of time and after-sales service. If a product is seasonal, that then a sales period will be helpful, so that old inventory is not left unsold in a warehouse or on the shelves of a retailer.

New/old product

If a product is new, the business will need to make consumers aware of the product. As a result, the business may do a lot of advertising and sales promotion, such as an introductory offer. However, if the product has been on the market for a number of years, consumers are already likely to be aware of the product, but may be encouraged to make purchases through a special offer, such as buy one get one free.

Timing

Timing is very important when choosing a sales method. For example, discounting seasonal clothing is most effective if it is done towards the end of the season. Coupons usually have a short end date by which the coupon must be used, or it will cease to be valid. This helps a business to plan and allows it to calculate how much the sales promotion has cost as soon as the end date has passed.

ACTIVITY 5.1.3

Visit a physical shop or online retailer such as a supermarket. At your chosen venue, look carefully and see what sales promotions are being used.

Make a list of all the sales promotions that you find.

For each promotion, state the product or service, the method being used and briefly explain why it is appropriate. If possible, include photos or images of any promotions.

When you are back in the classroom, discuss your findings with another student in the class.

SELF-EVALUATION CHECKLIST

After studying this chapter, complete this table.

You should know about:	Needs more work	Almost there	Ready to move on
the purpose of advertising			
types of advertising			
traditional and digital advertising media			
appropriate methods of advertising			
the impact of methods of appeal			
methods of sales promotion			
the use of different methods of sales promotion			

Knowledge check

1 Complete the following sentences.
   a Posters and signboards are methods of .... advertising media.
   b Social media advertising and internet advertising are methods of .... advertising media.

2 Give two advantages of advertising on transport vehicles.

3 Give two disadvantages of using direct mail to advertise.

4 Define the term 'search engines'.

5 Facebook is a social media platform. Identify two other examples of social media platforms.

6 Window displays and signboards are examples of:
   a collective advertising
   b digital media
   c sales promotion
   d traditional advertising media.

7 What is the name of small quantities of products given to consumers without charge?
   a free gift
   b free sample
   c special offer
   d sponsorship

8 A builders' trade association advertises the industry on behalf of all businesses in the building trade.
   What type of advertising is the trade association using?
   a appealing
   b collective
   c informative
   d persuasive

9 What method of sales promotion prices products below the unit cost with the aim of attracting customers into a shop where they will make other purchases?
   a coupons
   b free samples
   c loss leaders
   d sales period

10 Why is music often used in radio advertising?
   a Music is a method of appeal.
   b Music is a method of promotion.
   c Music is inexpensive.
   d People like different types of music

Practice questions

1 Shona owns a small business that sells jewellery. Shona wants to try digital advertising but only has a small budget.
   What is an appropriate method of digital advertising media that Shona can use? [1]
   a email marketing
   b multi-channel
   c television
   d word-of-mouth

2 A café is planning some persuasive advertising.
   What is an example of a method of appeal that they can use? [1]
   a cinema
   b humour
   c informative
   d websites.

3 Hasan designs and makes hats and headdresses for special occasions such as weddings. Hasan sells them in his own independent shop in the middle of a small city.
   Hasan always ensures that he has attractive displays in the window and inside his shop. He has never used any other form of advertising media.
   a Define traditional advertising media. [1]
   b Apart from window and point of sale display, explain two other methods of traditional advertising media. [4]
   c State two advantages to a business of having an attractive window display. [2]
   d Hasan is considering some form of digital advertising media to encourage more visitors to visit his shop. A friend has suggested social media advertising or email marketing.
   Discuss each of these two options. Justify which one of these two options Hasan should choose. [8]

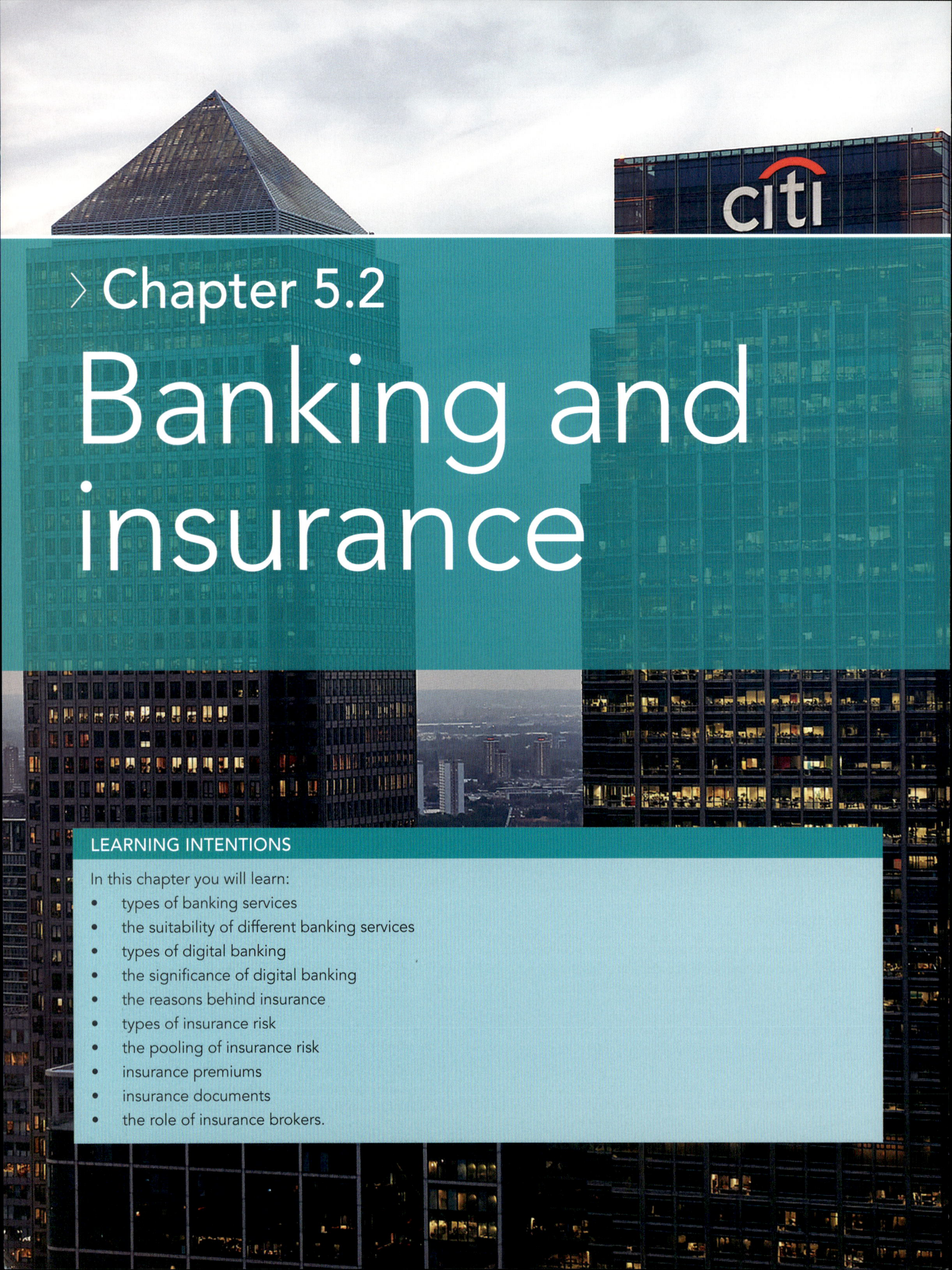

Chapter 5.2

Banking and insurance

LEARNING INTENTIONS

In this chapter you will learn:

- types of banking services
- the suitability of different banking services
- types of digital banking
- the significance of digital banking
- the reasons behind insurance
- types of insurance risk
- the pooling of insurance risk
- insurance premiums
- insurance documents
- the role of insurance brokers.

5.2.1 Banking services

Banks exist because individuals and businesses require bank accounts to keep their money safe and allow them to make payments. Banks also offer lending and savings facilities.

There are two main types of bank:

- a country's central bank, such as the Bank of England and the State Bank of Pakistan
- commercial banks, such as Standard Chartered, Barclays Bank and Sonali Bank PLC. Commercial banks are usually large multinational companies with many branches.

Central banks provide banking services to the government and to commercial banks while commercial banks provide banking services to businesses and individuals.

Commercial banks are usually public limited companies. Commercial banks receive money from customers. Some of the money received is kept available for withdrawals and the rest is offered as personal loans, mortgages for house purchase or for businesses to start up or expand. Commercial banks also lend to governments, make investments, buy and sell foreign currencies and provide financing for projects.

Banks' income comes from the interest charged on lending, charges for services provided to customers, and commission on foreign currency dealings.

Commercial banks provide banking services to their customers, including bank accounts and payment and lending services. Financial advice and information are available on the range of products that a bank offers, such as loans, mortgages, savings and investments. Help might be available online, in leaflets or by visiting a bank branch to talk to an adviser.

Bank accounts

Commercial banks offer many different bank accounts, which can be grouped into two main types:

- **savings accounts** – bank accounts that allow the account holder to deposit money for a period of time and earn interest
- **current accounts** – bank accounts that provide the account holder with a variety of services, including methods of payment, deposit services and possibly an **overdraft** facility. An overdraft is a form of flexible borrowing up to an agreed limit.

KEY TERMS

savings account: a bank account that allows the account holder to deposit money for a period of time and earn interest.

current account: a type of bank account that provides the account holder with a variety of services including methods of payment, deposit services and possibly an overdraft facility.

overdraft: a form of flexible borrowing up to an agreed limit using a bank current account.

Savings accounts

A savings account (also known as a deposit account) is a safe place to keep money. Commercial banks offer a wide range of savings/deposit accounts. Some savings accounts provide the customer with instant access to their money any time, while other savings accounts are for a fixed period, such as two years. Some savings accounts are for people to deposit a lump sum of money while others encourage people to save regularly, perhaps with a monthly deposit from the person's current account. Some accounts may be online only while others can be accessed via bank branches.

Interest is received on the amount of money held in the savings account monthly or annually. The interest rates for savings accounts are usually higher than the interest rates for current accounts. The longer you agree to keep the money in the account and the greater the amount saved, the higher the rate of interest that the bank is likely to offer.

Current accounts

A current account is a suitable account to keep money where money is unlikely to be stolen. The account also provides the customer with various banking services including payment, withdrawal and deposit facilities. The current account holder will typically be given a debit card, which can be used to make payments and to retrieve cash. Access to a current account can be made online, by telephone or by visiting a branch of the bank.

With the bank's permission, a current account holder can withdraw more money than they have in their account. This is called an overdraft. Fees and interest are usually charged to the customer for overdrafts.

Interest is sometimes received on any money held in the account, but the rate of interest is usually low. Surplus money will earn more interest if it is transferred to a savings account. Banks may also charge customers (especially businesses) for using their current accounts. Some banks only make charges if the account becomes overdrawn.

Both current and savings accounts make use of two key documents:

- **paying-in slips** – documents that are completed by the account holder to accompany money being put into a current account using a bank branch
- **bank statements** – documents available to the customer to show details of the customer's bank account.

KEY TERMS

paying-in slip: a document that is completed by the account holder to accompany money being put into a current account using a bank branch.

bank statement: a document available to the customer to show details of the customer's bank account.

Paying-in slips

When a customer uses a branch to put money into their current account, they must also complete a paying-in slip. The paying-in slip gives details of the amount, the date, the person paying in the money, the account number and the branch's individual identity number (sort code). Paying-in slips are used to ensure that money paid into the bank is put into the correct bank account.

Bank statements

A bank statement provides a detailed record of every transaction on an account, including any interest and charges. There is a running balance after each transaction of each day. The bank statement may show a credit balance (where more money has been paid in than withdrawn) or a debit balance (where more money has been withdrawn than paid in, i.e. 'overdrawn').

Banks send bank statements to customers at regular intervals, such as every month. Bank statements may be viewed online and/or received through the post. Upon receipt, a customer should check their latest bank statement to know their financial position. If the customer believes that there has been an error or fraud, they should contact the bank immediately so that it can be investigated.

Choosing bank accounts

Current accounts are the most widely used type of bank account by individuals and businesses. Current accounts include a range of banking services and allow customers to go overdrawn with the bank's agreement. Many people have their salaries paid directly into their current account and use it to pay their regular bills.

Savings accounts are less versatile than current accounts. Customers cannot go overdrawn, so they must always make sure that they have enough money in their account to cover any payments. If they try to spend money that is not available in their savings account, then the payment will be refused. Savings accounts pay customers higher interest than current accounts, so are suitable for people who have cash available with no immediate plans to spend it.

Many people will have both savings and current accounts.

Customer services

Commercial banks offer a range of customer services, including automated teller machines (ATMs), cash deposit machines (CDMs) **night safes** (chutes in the walls of banks that enable people to deposit money after banking hours), foreign currency, financial advice and telephone banking.

KEY TERM

night safe: a chute in the wall of a bank that enables people to deposit money after banking hours.

ATMs

By using a debit card or credit card and a PIN (personal identification number), customers can use ATMs at any time instead of going into a branch during the bank's open hours. ATMs are often found outside bank branches, at airports or in shopping centres (Figure 5.2.1). Some ATMs can now be used without debit and credit cards through bio-metrics.

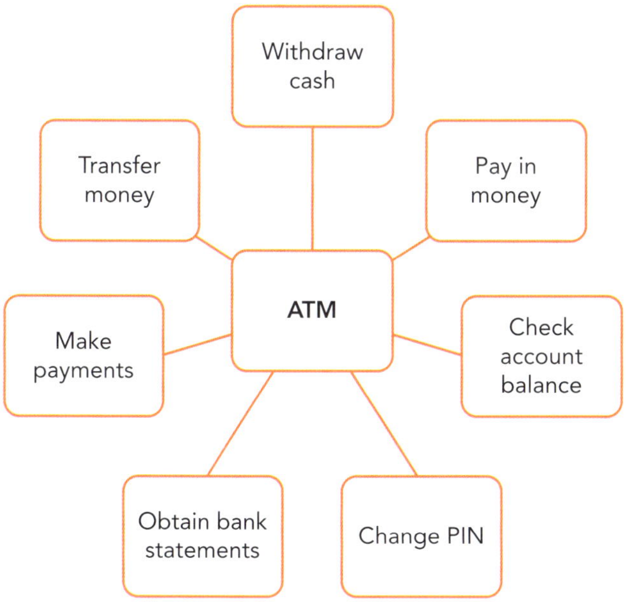

Figure 5.2.1: Common functions of ATMs

Many ATMs are provided by banks and are free for customers to use. However, some ATMs are installed by independent cash-machine operators who charge fees for their use. Independent ATMs are more likely to be found in motorway service stations, petrol stations and shops.

ATMs can be very convenient to customers and are widely used. However, there are some disadvantages of using ATMs, including the risk of forgetting your PIN, the risk that a machine may break down or run out of cash, and the possibility of having the cash stolen from you at an ATM.

Night safe

A night safe (Figure 5.2.2) is used by some businesses, such as restaurants, that want to deposit money outside normal banking hours. The night safe is usually built into the outside of the bank. Businesses put the money to be deposited into secure bags provided by the bank and then put the bags into the night safe. The night safe consists of a chute that sends the bags straight into the bank vault. The account holder is provided with a key for the night safe. The bank may open the bag the next day or wait until the account holder visits the bank with the paying-in slip.

Using a night safe reduces the risk of cash theft from business premises overnight, although it can also be risky to take money from the business premises to a night safe. When a business deals with large amounts of cash, it may use a security company to take the money to the bank.

Figure 5.2.2: A night safe

Foreign currency

Each country has its own currency that is used to buy and sell goods and services. When people visit other countries or businesses trade internationally, they will need to use foreign currencies. The cost of buying a foreign currency depends on the exchange rate (see Chapter 3.1).

One of the services that banks offer to customers is to buy and sell foreign currency. Each bank will decide what exchange rate to charge customers. This will depend on the demand and supply of a currency, so the exchange rate offered by one bank may be slightly different to the exchange rate offered by another bank. Exchange rates change regularly, usually at least once per day. Banks will advertise their exchange rates, typically online or on a signboard in each bank branch. Banks may also charge commission to cover the administrative costs of buying and selling currency.

TIP

Reading and revising currencies from Chapter 3.1 will help you understand the foreign currency banking services.

Financial advice

Both individuals and businesses can be confused with the many different banking services available and which one to choose in any particular situation. Customers may also want broader support with organising their money and making decisions about savings, investments, pensions and insurance. Banks will offer advice to help customers understand what is available from their bank and what might be suitable in different circumstances. Advice can be in the form of leaflets, online information and phone calls or meetings with banking staff.

Most banks also employ specialist business advisers to help business customers. Bank business advisers will assist existing businesses, and people wishing to start businesses, with their financial needs, offering services such as:

- setting up business bank accounts with regular statements, a debit card, chequebook and credit card
- payment services
- creating business plans
- establishing direct debit systems for collecting debts from customers
- financial forecasting
- arranging lending.

Telephone banking

Traditionally, customers would visit a bank branch whenever they wanted to use their bank accounts or access one of the bank's customer services. From the 1980s onwards, developments in technology meant that banks have been able to offer customers the ability to securely access their accounts and services via telephone rather than requiring a visit to a branch. Security is essential in telephone banking. Banks have procedures in place, such as use of unique passwords and codes, to minimise the chance of fraud.

Most bank services can be accessed via the telephone, including checking how much money is available in your bank account, making payments, ordering foreign currency and getting financial advice. The main services that are not available are those that involve the immediate and physical use of cash, such as use of ATMs and night safes.

Many customers preferred the convenience that telephone banking gave them. Telephone banking increased in popularity until further developments in technology allowed for the move towards internet and mobile banking in the 2000s.

ACTIVITY 5.2.1

Visit a bank branch. At your chosen venue, look carefully and see what banking services are available. There may be leaflets, posters or a member of staff that can help you. If there is no bank branch nearby, this activity can be completed using a bank's website instead.

Make a list of all the services that you find.

Choose any three services and briefly explain the features of each service. If possible, include photos or copies of leaflets that you find.

When you are back in the classroom, discuss your findings with another student in the class.

Means of payment

There are several ways that bank customers can make payments. The most appropriate means of payment will depend on the situation. Means of payment include those shown in Figure 5.2.3.

1. Cash
2. Cheque
3. Credit card
4. Debit card
5. Store card
6. Standing order
7. Direct debit
8. Electronic transfer
9. Documentary credit

Figure 5.2.3: Examples of how bank customers can make payments

1 Cash

Cash is widely trusted and is legally required to be accepted as a means of payment in many areas. Notes and coins are usually convenient to carry and use, except in very large volumes. Cash is commonly used to pay for small-value purchases. People generally avoid using cash for high-value purchases due to the risk of theft. If cash is stolen, it can be difficult to retrieve.

2 Cheque

A cheque is a written order to pay the person who has been named on it. It is signed by the person making the payment (the drawer). The person receiving the cheque will pay it into their bank account and the bank will arrange the money to be transferred from the drawer's account.

Cheques used to be a popular alternative to cash. However, in recent years, cheques have been used less and less as improvements in technology have led to the growth of newer methods of payment (such as electronic transfers).

Table 5.2.1 lists the advantages and disadvantages of using cheques.

Advantages of using cheques	Disadvantages of using cheques
They can be cancelled if lost or stolen. This makes cheques less risky than carrying large amounts of cash. They are easier and safer than cash to send by post.	They are not always accepted as a means of payment. It can take several days for the money to arrive in the recipient's bank account. It can be inconvenient to the recipient as they must physically take the cheque to a bank to be paid in. There is a risk of forgery and fraud. Other methods of payments such as debit cards are now considered more efficient and less risky alternatives to cheques. Cash or debit cards are considered more suitable for small sums of money.

Table 5.2.1: Advantages and disadvantages of using cheques

3 Credit cards

Buying on credit means 'buy now, pay later'. Credit relies on the seller trusting the buyer to pay later.

Credit cards, such as Visa and Mastercard, are used worldwide to make payments for goods and services. They provide credit so the user can postpone payment. Credit cards can be especially useful for online purchases. They are also useful to customers travelling overseas because they avoid the need to carry local currency.

> **KEY TERM**
>
> **buying on credit:** buying now, paying later.

4 Debit cards

A debit card is a plastic card (Figure 5.2.4) that allows the customer to make instant payments for the purchase of goods or services. The card is either inserted into a card reader and the PIN is typed into the card reader, or the card is tapped on the machine where contactless payment is accepted. The amount is automatically deducted from the person's bank account and credited to the seller's account. This transaction may occur on the same day, or may take a few days.

Debit cards are very popular as a means of payment online or in shops because the seller receives the money almost instantly (unlike a credit card payment). If there is no money in the account of the customer, the debit card will be rejected at the time of the purchase. Therefore, the seller can be confident that they will receive the money for the sale.

Debit cards do not offer credit. This makes debit cards popular in countries where buying on credit is considered unacceptable. There is no annual charge and usually no transaction charge. There is no limit to the value of the transaction, provided there is sufficient money in the current account of the customer.

Figure 5.2.4: Paying by plastic card

5 Store card

Store cards are plastic cards provided for customers by large-scale retailers such as departmental stores and multiple chain stores. To the cardholder, store cards function in a similar way to credit cards but can only be used at a specified retailer.

Credit cards are generally more widely used than store cards. However, there are often incentives offered to encourage store card use, such as free gifts, discounts or free delivery on purchases.

> **KEY TERM**
>
> **store card:** a plastic card provided to customers by a large-scale retailer, through which credit is given (often on a monthly basis).

Table 5.2.2 describes the advantages and disadvantages of store cards to the cardholder.

Advantages of store cards to the customer	Disadvantages of store cards to the customer
They enable the shopper to use the store without needing to carry cash or other plastic cards. They provide interest-free credit if paid off each month. The cardholder may receive incentives from the retailer. The card can be used in every branch of a particular store.	The cardholder may have to pay interest if debts are not paid off monthly. Cardholders may spend more than they can afford.

Table 5.2.2: Advantages and disadvantages of store cards to the cardholder

Table 5.2.3 describes the advantages and disadvantages of store cards to the retailer.

Advantages of store cards to the retailer	Disadvantages of store cards to the retailer
Store cards encourage shoppers to use the retailer, which can lead to customer loyalty and increased sales.	It costs the retailer to organise the cards and ensure customers pay any money they owe. There may be problems of non-payment and recovery of debts.

Table 5.2.3: Advantages and disadvantages of store cards to the retailer

6 Standing order

A **standing order** is an instruction by the bank account holder to a bank to pay regular amounts at regular intervals, e.g., rental payments. The account holder completes a bank form stating the amount, when to make the payments and who to make the payment to.

> **KEY TERM**
>
> **standing order:** a bank service that allows the user to pay regular bills at regular intervals after authorisation. It saves remembering payments, such as rent and subscriptions.

Table 5.2.4 discusses the advantages and disadvantages of using standing orders.

Advantages of using standing orders	Disadvantages of using standing orders
A safe way of making payments. They are convenient for regular payments, ensuring that they are never forgotten. It is cheaper and easier than writing and sending cheques.	It is easy to forget that the payment is to be made, and the current account might go overdrawn without realising. They are not suitable when the amount varies.

Table 5.2.4: Advantages and disadvantages of using standing orders

7 Direct debit

Direct debits are similar to standing orders, but direct debits can also be used to pay varying amounts on varying dates. This makes them useful for some bills, e.g., telephone and electricity.

Direct debit payments are authorised by the account holder, but payments are only made when the business that is owed the money requests them. This ensures that the company who is owed the payment receives it on the due date.

Table 5.2.5 summarises the advantages and disadvantages of using direct debits.

Advantages of using direct debits	Disadvantages of direct debits
It is safe and easy to make variable payments. Payments are made on time and never forgotten. It is cheaper and easier than writing and sending cheques.	It is easy to forget that the payment is to be made, and the current account might go overdrawn without realising. Errors can lead to the wrong amount being taken from the bank account.

Table 5.2.5: Advantages and disadvantages of using direct debits

8 Electronic transfer

An electronic transfer is any movement of funds that is done electronically without the completion of any paper documents or physically visiting a bank. For example, paying the balance on a credit card online from a current account. A **credit transfer** (also known as a 'bank transfer' or 'bank giro') is a specific type of electronic transfer. A credit transfer occurs where a customer instructs their bank to pay directly from their current account into someone else's bank account.

Credit transfers can be for single payments, or for paying multiple bills at the same time. The customer can choose to make the payment immediately, or they can choose a different payment date. Standing orders and direct debits are examples of credit transfers.

Credit transfers are quicker than cheques and safer than cash. Credit transfers are a very efficient and secure way for an employer to pay wages and salaries directly into employees' bank accounts. The business provides the bank with a list of its employees, their bank account details and the amounts to be paid to each employee. The bank debits the business's account for the total amount and transfers the money into the employees' bank accounts.

KEY TERM

credit transfer: method of payment allowing the direct transfer of money from one bank account to another using electronic means.

9 Documentary credit (letter of credit)

Documentary credit (letter of credit) is a letter issued by an importer's bank and sent by the importer to the exporter to guarantee the payment for goods. It is explained in more detail in Chapter 2.3.

The advantages of documentary credit include the following.

- Documentary credit is issued by a bank so it is likely to be more trustworthy than if it was issued by an individual importer.
- The exporter has a guarantee of payment before the documents are handed over to the importer's bank.
- The importer has ownership of the goods by possessing the documents before the payment is made.

TIP

When you are thinking of any advantages or disadvantages of any payment method, it is important to be clear whether you are considering:

- the advantages/disadvantages to the buyer making the payment

  or

- the advantages/disadvantages to the seller receiving the payment.

Sources of finance from banks

Businesses need money to operate. Money is needed to buy expensive items, such as equipment and premises, and also to pay for day-to day expenditure, such as rent, wages and lighting. Sometimes a business will not have enough cash to pay for what it needs and instead it must borrow the money. Banks are a very common source of funds to businesses that need to borrow money.

Commercial banks offer different sources of finance:

- loans
- overdrafts
- mortgages
- **hire purchase** (often known as HP).

This section explains the main sources of finance available from banks. Further sources of finance are explained in Chapter 5.3.

KEY TERM

hire purchase: a business makes a deposit and pays regular instalments to a finance company for the purchase of an asset. During the payment period, the business is renting or hiring the asset. When all the payments have been made, the business becomes the owner of the asset.

Loan

Loans are a way of borrowing a set amount of money to be paid back to the lender in an agreed amount of time. Loans are usually for large amounts of money and interest must be paid on most forms of loan. Banks are a common source of loan for businesses. Repayments are made by regular instalments. Loans are usually for a set purpose, such as buying a vehicle or other business asset such as machinery. Loans may typically be arranged for any period from 2 years to 20 years.

Banks may require assets to have **security** when lending very large sums of money. These secured loans work in the same way as mortgages (see the section on mortgages) because if the company fails to meet the loan payments or stops trading, the lender becomes the owner of the asset.

KEY TERM

security: an asset that is used to secure a loan, where the lender may take the security in payment if the borrower is unable to repay the loan.

Overdraft

An overdraft is a form of borrowing where a bank current account holder takes out more money than they have in their account. A fixed overdraft limit is usually agreed with the bank. The business can then withdraw or repay funds when it likes, within that limit. A fixed time for repayment is given. For example, a bank agrees that a business can have a maximum $10 000 overdraft for 12 months.

Interest is charged on the daily amount overdrawn. If the account is not overdrawn, no interest is charged. If the current account holder exceeds the agreed limit, they must pay extra charges to the bank.

Businesses use overdrafts to enable them to pay bills when there is insufficient income to pay them. They should not be used for long-term expenditure as they are classed as current liabilities on the business (see Chapter 5.3 for more information on current liabilities).

Mortgage

Mortgages are a form of secured loan that are usually paid back in monthly instalments over a long period, such as 20 to 25 years. They are used to buy houses or business land/premises. The property or land is used as security. This means that, if the company fails to meet the mortgage payments or stops trading, the lender becomes the owner of the property. Mortgages are offered by banks or building societies and usually involve large sums of money.

Hire purchase

Hire purchase (often known as HP) involves an agreement with a **finance company**. The customer makes a deposit and pays regular instalments for a set period of time for the purchase of an asset. During the payment period, the business is renting or hiring the asset. When all the payments have been made, the business becomes the owner of the asset. Businesses often buy assets such as equipment and company cars using hire purchase.

KEY TERM

finance company: a financial organisation that offers hire purchase agreements and collects the payments.

Choosing a source of finance

The most appropriate source of finance will depend on the situation. Each source of finance has different advantages and disadvantages that makes it suitable in different situations, as can be seen in Table 5.2.6.

Source of finance	Advantages to the business	Disadvantages to the business
Loans	They are quicker to arrange than selling shares. This speed avoids delays when buying assets and is especially useful if there is an urgent need for money such as buying new machinery to replace a broken machine.	Interest is paid at a fixed rate. Any interest charged adds to a business's costs. A fixed interest rate means that a business does not benefit from any fall in the bank's interest rate. Security may be required, which the business may not have, especially a small new enterprise that does not own premises or other valuable assets.
Overdrafts	They are simple to arrange, which is really useful for a busy sole trader or new entrepreneur. They are flexible, as the business can withdraw or repay funds when it likes within an agreed limit. This can be helpful for businesses that have seasonal changes in sales and costs such as farming and tourism. No interest is charged on days when the account is not overdrawn. Overdrafts are often cheaper than loans because of the variable interest payments.	Interest is charged. If the current account holder exceeds the limit set, the bank charges higher interest and extra charges. Banks can reduce the overdraft limit or call in the overdraft for repayment at a day's notice. The interest rate is higher than a loan.
Mortgages	They are available for large sums of money, making them especially useful for a growing business that wants to purchase expensive assets such as buying instead of renting premises. They have a lower rate of interest than many other forms of borrowing.	If the company fails to meet the mortgage payments or stops trading, the lender becomes the owner of the property. Interest must be paid.

Continued

Source of finance	Advantages to the business	Disadvantages to the business
Hire purchase	The business has the use of the asset straight away. The buyer may be able to purchase better-quality goods than they could otherwise afford. For example, a manufacturer may use hire purchase to buy specialised equipment or a transportation business may use hire purchase to gain access to a fleet of new trucks or delivery vehicles.	Interest rates can be high, and the total payments will be more than the cash price of the asset. The business does not own the asset until the last payment has been made. The asset can be repossessed if all payments are not made. The amount of paperwork means that the transaction may take some time to arrange.

Table 5.2.6: Advantages and disadvantages of sources of finance from a bank

5.2.2 Digital technology in banking

Commercial banks use technology extensively to provide their services. Many bank operations are computerised. An increasing number of customers benefit from the convenience of online services that can be accessed from anywhere from their smartphones and other mobile devices.

Internet banking

Mobile and internet banking are growing in popularity across the world. A bank account that includes internet banking is very convenient and allows the account holder to access it from anywhere at any time, without having to go into the bank branch (Figure 5.2.5). It also provides detailed information on bank services.

Mobile banking

Mobile banking refers to banking services that are accessed through a smartphone or tablet, often using a dedicated banking app. Mobile banking can be used anywhere with an internet connection. Mobile banking is now extensively used across the world. Mobile banking is particularly useful for those living in remote or rural areas where there are likely to be fewer local bank branches available to customers.

Customers can log into the banking app using personal security details, such as passwords and PINs. Customers can then see their account balances and have access to online banking services. Multiple security details are required to reduce the risk of fraud, attempting to ensure that no unauthorised users can access a customer's accounts.

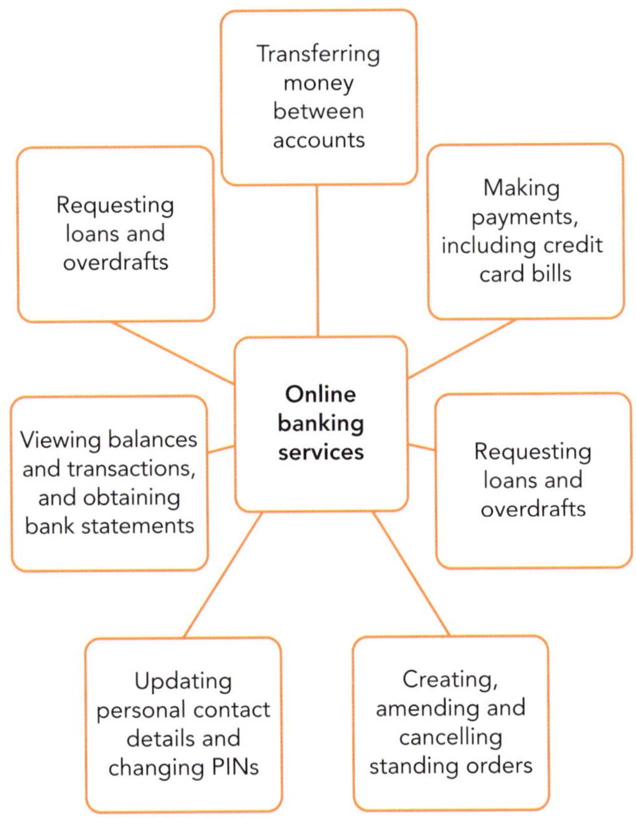

Figure 5.2.5: Typical online banking services

The mobile wallet

Debit and credit card details can be put on a smartphone to allow customers to use their phone to make payments, instead of using plastic credit or debit cards (Figure 5.2.6). A digital container, running on the phone, keeps together an electronic version of debit and credit cards, tickets, loyalty cards, etc., which are all items that might previously be found in a physical wallet. This is called a **mobile wallet**.

Figure 5.2.6: Making a payment using a mobile phone

KEY TERM

mobile wallet: a digital container on a smartphone or other mobile device designed to keep together and use digital versions of payment cards, vouchers, tickets, receipts and loyalty cards.

The introduction of systems such as Google Pay and Apple Pay allow users of mobile phones and other similar devices to make payments from their digital or mobile wallets on their phone. Making payments in this way means that users can be confident that their payment information is always kept private from retailers. Some users also appreciate being able to make payments without touching any surfaces.

The advantages and disadvantages of digital banking

Digital banking has advantages and disadvantages for customers and banks, as described in Table 5.2.7.

Advantages of digital banking	Disadvantages of digital banking
Banking services to customers are convenient and are available anywhere and at any time.	Some customers do not have the computers or mobile phones needed to access digital banking.
New banking services become available, such as alerts on customers' mobile phones if they go overdrawn and the ability to temporarily stop missing debit and credit cards from working.	Errors in a bank's main computers can cause problems for large numbers of customers, such as a temporary inability to make any payments.
There can be lower operating costs for banks, such as fewer staff and premises.	Security risks can arise. For example, if a customer's password is guessed, their account might be accessed by criminals and money taken illegally.
There are likely to be fewer errors than if bank staff manually organise receipts and payments.	

Table 5.2.7: Advantages of using digital banking for customers and banks

The impact of digital banking

The expansion of internet and mobile banking has implications for banks and their customers.

Implications for banks

The implications of digital banking for banks include the following:

- There may be lower costs of providing banking services, e.g., the closure of bank branches, fewer staff and less equipment.
- More digital-only banks may be set up, or existing banks may close all of their branches and become digital-only.
- Banks must put in place and maintain systems and procedures to minimise security risks, including passwords, security codes and telephone hotlines to call if the customer thinks they have been a victim of fraud.

- If most banking activities can be carried out using the internet, banks may decide that most of their branches can be smaller branches, and only offer limited services such as cash withdrawals and cash deposits. These mini-branches may be situated in shops or post offices that many people visit for other reasons.
- There is increased competition for banks because customers can switch banks more easily. There is also more competition from other organisations offering competing financial services without the need to establish an expensive network of branches.

Implications for customers

The implications of digital banking for customers include the following.

- Banking can be quicker and more convenient with fewer visits to bank branches and the ability to undertake digital banking anywhere and at any time.
- Switching banks is easier, so customers are less loyal to one bank and have a greater choice of banks and services.
- Online transactions are processed more quickly and so payments and deposits appear in a recipient's bank account more quickly.
- Closure of bank branches, especially small branches, leading to an overall reduction in the number of branches available, can cause problems for customers. Some customers do not have online bank accounts. Other customers may prefer to talk to bank staff about their accounts or to get advice in person. Business customers may need to pay in their cash takings regularly.
- There is the concern that online banking has a risk of fraud, such as phishing and identity theft. Phishing scams are usually emails that appear to come from the person's bank but do not. People try to obtain a customer's personal banking details. Identity theft involves the theft of personal information, e.g., name and banking details, in order to illegally obtain money, goods or information.

Cashless society

The use of cash as a means of payment has been declining for years, but cash has not been completely eliminated. The move towards a cashless society, where electronic payment systems replace cash, has sped up substantially following the pandemic in 2020. Table 5.2.8 describes arguments for and against a cashless society.

Arguments for a cashless society	Arguments against a cashless society
Online transactions are safer for both customers and businesses than carrying cash.	There are risks of crimes associated with electronic means of payment.
Retailers will save time and resources counting cash and keeping cash safely on their premises.	People may spend more. This may be because online spending is easy to forget about, while people will notice if they are spending lots of cash.
Transactions at checkouts are faster and more accurate.	New technology may have unexpected faults that cause problems for consumers. For example, a user might not be able to make a payment when they expect to.
Cash cannot be used online.	Some groups of consumers may be marginalised, such as the very young and old.
The cost of manufacturing cash would be saved.	

Table 5.2.8: Arguments for and against a cashless society

ACTIVITY 5.2.2

You and a business partner own a small market stall that sells fruit. Currently you only accept payments using cash.

A local bank adviser has suggested that you consider accepting other means of payments from your customers.

To help you decide whether to accept any other means of payment, write a short report for your partner. Include answers to the following questions in your report:

a What other payment types might be available?

b What are the benefits of accepting other means of payment?

c What are the drawbacks of accepting other means of payment?

d Will you accept other means of payment from your customers? If so, what means of payment will you accept?

5.2.3 Insurance

Insurance is a way of reducing financial risk by sharing potential losses among a large number of organisations or people who all contribute to a common fund (pool). For example, a business may want to insure its property against damage. A person may want to insure their car in case it is stolen.

A customer who buys insurance cover is called **the insured**. Customers can be individuals, businesses, governments or other organisations. The business that provides the insurance is called the **insurer**.

The payment(s) that a customer makes to the insurer to purchase the insurance cover is called an insurance premium. In return, the insurer provides **financial protection** by agreeing to pay **compensation** if the customer needs to make a claim for a loss.

KEY TERMS

the insured: a customer who buys insurance cover.

insurer: a business that provides insurance cover.

financial protection: keeping the insured safe from financial losses.

compensation: the payment(s) made by an insurer to the insured for a loss incurred from an insured risk.

The purposes of insurance

There are several reasons why businesses and individuals choose to take out insurance cover.

Risk reduction

Risk considers the chance of an event or a loss happening. For example, there is a risk that a person's home might be flooded, or that a person might have an accident (Figure 5.2.7). We do not know whether either of these events will definitely occur, but some events are more likely than others. Risk of flooding is higher if you live near a river. Risk of an accident is higher if you participate in sports such as rock climbing or diving.

Insurance is a way to manage and reduce financial risk by shifting the risk from the insured to the insurer.

Figure 5.2.7: A flooded home can cause lots of damage

Compensation

Insurance provides financial compensation if losses occur. The compensation is usually paid directly to the insured. However, sometimes compensation may be paid to other people who have suffered losses because of the insured's actions. For example, if someone's car is stolen then the insurer will pay the insured. However, if the insured is responsible for a car accident that leads to another person's car being damaged then it is the owner of the other car who receives the compensation.

Financial protection

Insurance can provide financial protection to the insured against many different types of risk. Insurance does not stop the event from happening, but it reduces financial losses. For example, without insurance, people might be homeless if their houses burned down, or employees might lose their jobs if their workplaces were flooded.

Business confidence

Insurance helps to give confidence to a business because the owners know that the business will receive compensation if a loss occurs. Insurance can be taken out for many common business risks, such as damaged or stolen inventory or an accident on business premises affecting employees or customers. Claims for compensation can be made for loss of revenue and profits.

Some compensation payments are for very large amounts. Without insurance, a business would be worried that it might fail in the event of a large loss, or it must keep a lot of money in reserve in case it needs to pay for any large loss.

Investment

A lot of money is paid to insurance companies each year as insurance premiums. Instead of keeping lots of cash in the business and waiting for claims to be made, the insurer will invest the cash in other businesses or lend it to the government. The insurer will earn interest or dividends on their investments, which can later contribute towards profits for the insurer and paying compensation.

Some types of insurance can be used by the customer as a type of investment. For example, some insurance policies involve customers paying regular premiums. Then, at the end of an agreed fixed term, the insured will receive a lump sum from the insurer.

Types of insurance risk

Individuals and businesses both face risks. Some risks only affect individuals, some risks only affect businesses and some risks affect both. Businesses can buy different types of insurance to cover different types of risk. Insurance needs will vary depending on the business's size, its products or services and the type of work that it does.

Some insurance policies cover specific individual risks, but other policies cover several risks. For example, risks from fire, theft and accident may all be covered in one policy, such as premises insurance or motor insurance.

Premises insurance

Premises insurance covers losses from damage to buildings. Damage might come from many risks, such as floods, falling trees, lightening or vandalism and theft. Premises insurance can be just for a building, including its permanent fixtures and fittings, such as lighting and heating systems. However, premises insurance usually also includes the contents of a building, such as damage to inventory and equipment as well as burglary and theft.

Premises insurance is especially important for businesses that keep valuable inventory and equipment on site, and risks are higher if the premises does not have employees on site at night.

The premium charged will depend on the risks involved. The higher the risk the higher the premium is likely to be. For example, risks may be higher in an area where vandalism is common but can be lower for a business that has a security device in place, such as alarms or CCTV.

Individuals often take out premises insurance on their homes. This is often referred to as home or household insurance rather than premises insurance. As with premises insurance for a business, home insurance may cover the buildings and/or its contents, such as furniture and computers.

Motor insurance

Many people and businesses own vehicles. It is a legal requirement to have insurance cover for any car being driven on public roads in most countries. Once the customer has paid the premium, they will receive a certificate of insurance from the insurer to prove that the owner has insurance.

There are three common types of motor insurance:

- **Third-party motor insurance** only covers claims made by other people (third parties). If the insured has a car accident and it is their fault, then other people affected by the car accident can make a claim if they have been injured or if there is damage to their vehicle or other property.
  - The third party is likely to be a passenger in the car driven by the insured, the driver or passengers in another vehicle or someone walking nearby.
  - Third-party insurance is usually the cheapest form of motor insurance because it does not provide any payment for damage to the insured vehicle. Third-party insurance is often used by owners of old vehicles that are not worth very much.
  - The minimum requirement by law in most countries is third-party insurance.
- **Third-party, fire and theft insurance** cover provides third-party motor insurance plus it will pay the insured if the vehicle gets damaged by fire or theft.
- **Comprehensive insurance** includes third-party, fire and theft plus it will pay for accidental damage to the insured's vehicle, and pay compensation if the driver has any injuries in an accident or if items are stolen from the vehicle (Figure 5.2.8). Most motorists have comprehensive insurance.

Businesses owning vehicles must also have third-party insurance as a minimum. Businesses may also have fleet insurance to cover all the vehicles owned by the business.

Figure 5.2.8: Motor insurance is important in case of accidents

Fire insurance

An accidental fire can have huge and devastating consequences. Fire insurance is most commonly used to cover buildings and the contents kept inside buildings. It can also be taken out for other items of value, such as cars and boats.

Fire insurance may be purchased by individuals and by businesses. Individuals might take out fire insurance for their car or their home and its contents. Businesses might take out fire insurance for vehicles and premises, including all its equipment and inventory stored inside. Fire insurance is often part of a broader **insurance policy** (an insurance policy being the contract of insurance setting out the terms of the policy). For example, premises insurance usually covers the risk of fire to the premises and motor insurance usually covers the risk of fire to the vehicle.

Consequential loss insurance

Businesses usually buy insurance policies that cover several risks together, such as theft of inventory, fire and other risks, such as lightening, floods and vandalism. These insurance policies will make payments so that damage can be repaired. However, a business may also suffer other consequences. For example, if a shop has to close for three months because of a fire, it will also lose the revenue that it would expect to earn from selling goods during those three months.

Consequential loss (business interruption) insurance covers losses that happen as a 'consequence' of another type of risk, by providing financial protection to a business where its normal trading is disrupted or stopped.

A consequential loss insurance policy will usually cover:

- loss of revenue because the business is not able to operate as normal
- hiring of temporary premises
- interest on existing business loans
- wages and salaries to staff who must be kept on until the business restarts
- other business expenses, such as advertising.

Theft

Many different things may be stolen, including cash, credit cards, inventory and equipment. There are different types of insurance policy to cover differ types of theft. Some theft is covered by premises or motor insurance while other more specialist types of insurance are used for particular types of theft.

Fidelity insurance covers a business against losses resulting from theft by an employee, e.g., if a member of staff steals cash from the checkout or takes money from the business bank account.

Cash in transit insurance covers the theft of money, bank notes, cheques and credit cards that are being carried by employees. Cash in transit insurance is especially useful for businesses that have to regularly move money to or from a bank, such as restaurants and market traders.

KEY TERMS

insurance policy: the contract of insurance setting out the terms of the policy.

consequential loss (business interruption) insurance: insurance that covers losses that happen as a 'consequence' of another type of risk, such as fire, by providing financial protection to a business where its normal trading is disrupted or stopped.

fidelity insurance: insurance that covers a business against losses resulting from theft by an employee.

cash in transit insurance: insurance that covers the theft of money, bank notes, cheques and credit cards that are being carried by employees.

Goods in transit insurance covers the loss or damage of goods while they are being transported. Goods in transit insurance is useful for businesses that send or receive goods, such as manufacturers, wholesalers and retailers.

> **KEY TERM**
>
> **goods in transit insurance:** insurance that covers the loss or damage of goods while they are being transported.

Liability insurance

Every business has legal responsibilities to ensure that its products are safe for the customers that purchase the products, and any business activities or business premises are safe for employees and the public. A business is at risk of being legally responsible (liable) for injury or damage to other people or organisations. This risk may occur if a business or its employees has been **negligent**. Being negligent means not taking enough care to prevent an injury or damage from happening.

A business can buy liability insurance to cover legal claims against the business because it is responsible for the injury or damage of others. It is important that businesses take out liability insurance because a claim by another person can be very expensive if large amounts of compensation are legally awarded for injuries.

There are two main types of liability insurance:

- **Employer's liability insurance** protects a business against claims resulting from an accident or injury to an employee while at work. If the employer is negligent, the employee will be awarded damages depending on the severity of the injury.
- Public liability insurance protects the business against claims made by members of the public. If a business were negligent, the insurer would pay the compensation to the person that suffered injury or damage. For example, cafés and shops may use public liability insurance to protect themselves against claims from customers who have accidents while on their premises, such as hurting themselves by slipping on a wet floor.

> **KEY TERMS**
>
> **negligent:** not taking enough care to stop an injury or damage from happening.
>
> **employer's liability insurance:** insurance that protects a business against claims resulting from accidents or injuries to employees at work.

> **TIP**
>
> Be aware that some types of insurance, such as motor insurance, are suitable for both individuals and businesses, while other types of insurance, such as employee liability, are appropriate for businesses but not for individuals.

> **ACTIVITY 5.2.3**
>
> Choose two of the types of insurance risk.
>
> Review your notes and the information in this chapter, then produce a set of revision questions and answers on your chosen types of insurance risk. Make sure that you have at least six questions.
>
> Working with another student in your class, take it in turns to test each other's knowledge using the revision questions you have both written.

> **REFLECTION**
>
> When answering Activity 5.2.3, how did you choose which types of insurance risk to use? Did you pick types you knew most or least about? Why?
>
> How useful was it to ask and answer questions with a partner? Did it help you to learn the topic? Do you think you have a better understanding of the types of insurance risk that you revised or the ones your partner asked you questions on? Why?

Using insurance

When a business buys insurance or makes a claim, it must ensure that it knows what action is needed, what forms to fill in and how their insurance premiums are calculated.

Pooling of insurance risk

Insurance uses the idea of sharing or pooling risk. **Pooling of insurance risk** means that risk is shared between a group of people or businesses that are all insured (Figure 5.2.9).

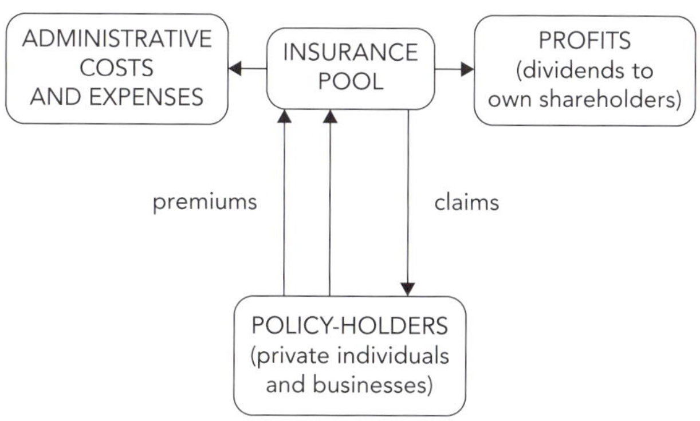

Figure 5.2.9: Pooling of risk showing how funds are paid into and out of an insurance pool.

Individuals and businesses that purchase insurance cover pay premiums to the insurer. These premiums are collected into a common fund or pool. Those who make claims are paid out of this pool of money. Therefore, the insurance premiums from the insured who do not have to make claims for compensation are helping to pay for the compensation to the insured who do make claims.

The pool is also used to pay for all other costs of running the insurance company, such as salaries and telephone expenses, and for the insurance company to make a profit.

KEY TERM

pooling of insurance risk: risk is shared between a group of people or businesses that are all insured.

Insurance premiums

The price that someone must pay for insurance can vary a lot. The insurance premium for each customer is decided by the insurer. It is important that the insurer carefully calculates the insurance premiums that it charges customers for its insurance. Insurers must make sure that they have enough money to pay claims for losses by insured people. If premiums are too low, the insurance company will not be able to cover the claims made. If premiums are too high, customers may buy insurance from other, cheaper insurers instead.

The price of insurance premiums depends on two main factors: the pooling of risk and levels of risk.

The pooling of risk

As explained in the 'Pooling of insurance risk' section, many people pay premiums into a pool of funds, from which those who make claims are compensated. There is a different pool for each risk. The insurer manages the pool and must ensure that there is sufficient money in the pool to cover the cost of the claims and also the expenses of operating the pool. To ensure that the funds in the pool are sufficient, premiums will therefore be affected by the number of people and organisations that contribute to the pool. If few people are in the pool, then the premium may be higher to ensure that there is sufficient money to pay claims and expenses. However, if many people are in the pool, premiums may be lower.

Levels of risk

Some risks involve higher amounts being paid out for each claim, and some risks are more likely to occur than others. Premiums are affected by the amount of risk involved. The higher the risk, the higher the premium. For example, the risk of vandalism occurring is higher in some locations than at others. An insurer will want to know the location of the premises. If the building is in a location at higher risk, the insurer will then charge a higher premium for premises insurance. As another example, the risk of employees having an accident while working in a factory is usually higher than the risk to those working in offices. An insurer will want to know about the activities carried out by employees and any safety procedures put in place. It will then decide the premium to charge for employer's liability insurance based on the risk.

Some insurance policies include a condition that means that the **policyholder** has to contribute to reducing the risk. For example, a business may be required to put in security alarms if it wants to take out premises insurance on a building that is left empty overnight (see section on insurance documents later in this chapter).

> **KEY TERM**
>
> **policyholder:** term used to describe an insured individual or organisation that has taken out insurance cover.

Other factors affecting insurance premiums

Insurance premiums must also be high enough to pay the insurer's expenses, such as wages and rent, and allow the insurer to make a profit.

Insurance premiums are based on general factors that relate to all customers and specific factors that may vary depending on the customer's individual circumstances.

The insurance premium charged to an individual customer will be affected by:

- any additional or specific risks. For example, some businesses have to use potentially dangerous equipment.
- the period of time covered. For example, one year's insurance will be more expensive than one month's insurance.
- the amount of insurance cover required. For example, insuring premises worth \$800 000 will be more expensive than insuring premises worth \$200 000.
- the amount of **excess** (the part of the claim not paid by the insurer) that the insured accepts. For example, the insurer may set an excess of the first \$300 of any claim has to be paid by the insured instead of the insurer. Setting an excess stops claims for small amounts of money.
- precautions taken by the insured to reduce the risk. For example, the risk of a widespread fire in a building may be reduced by fitting smoke alarms, a sprinkler system or fire doors.
- the past record of the customer. For example, if a customer has made lots of claims in the past, the insurer will charge them a higher premium.
- the insurer's circumstances and priorities. Some insurers will charge higher premiums than others to cover its costs and make a profit.

> **TIP**
>
> When discussing insurance, the word 'policyholder' can be used in place of the term 'the insured'.

Sometimes an insurer will refuse to provide insurance cover to a customer. Common reasons for refusing insurance cover are:

- there is a high chance that the loss insured against will happen. For example, it may be difficult to insure premises located near a river that often floods.
- there is not enough information available to assess the risk and decide a suitable premium.
- the insurance cover required is very high. The insurance company may not want to take the risk. Sometimes the insurer may be prepared to offer insurance jointly with other insurance companies. For example, insuring a large and expensive ship.
- the customer does not meet requirements that the insurance company wants. For example, a customer may be refused premises insurance if it has not fitted sufficiently strong locks on its premises.

Calculating insurance premiums

Insurers keep information on the value of claims that have occurred in the past. This information comes from the insurer's own claims and also from official or government sources. An insurer analyses the statistics to estimate the chance of future claims for different risks. These estimates of claims are then used by **underwriters** to calculate insurance premiums.

> **KEY TERMS**
>
> **excess:** part of a claim for loss that is funded by the insured and not paid by the insurer.
>
> **underwriters:** people who review a customer's application for insurance cover to determine the risks to the insurer. They then decide whether or not the insurer should accept the insurance application and calculate the premium to be charged.

An underwriter is a person who reviews a customer's application for insurance cover to determine the risks to the insurer. The underwriter will then decide whether or not the insurer should accept the insurance application, calculate the premium to be charged (Figure 5.2.10) and decide other terms and exclusions to be applied to the insurance cover. Most underwriters work for insurance companies, although some underwriters may work independently.

Figure 5.2.10: Insurance calculations are important for making sure the insurer covers its own risks

If an insurer is looking to cover both its costs and all the claims made by its customers, the insurance premium it charges a typical customer can be calculated as follows:

FORMULA

Average insurance premium per customer = (total value of claims + insurer's costs) ÷ number of customers insured

Insurance premium calculations can be illustrated in an example.

WORKED EXAMPLE 5.2.1

Calculating insurance premiums

An insurer offers fire insurance to businesses for their premises.

The insurer has the following information available:

- 8000 customers
- 2% of businesses are damaged by fire each year
- average compensation paid is $250 000
- expenses of operating the pool are $600 000 each year.

CONTINUED

Required

a Calculate the estimated number of claims next year.

b Calculate the total amount that the insurer will expect to pay out in compensation next year.

c Calculate the insurance premium the insurer should charge each customer next year to meet all expected claims and cover the expenses.

d Calculate the insurance premium the insurer should charge each customer next year to achieve a profit of $400 000.

Answer

a Based on past records, the estimated number of claims next year is:

$(8000 \times 2) \div 100 = 160$ claims

b On average, each claim will be for $250 000, so the total amount that the insurance company will expect to pay out in compensation will be:

$\$250\,000 \times 160 \text{ claims} = \$40\,000\,000$

c If the company is to have the money in its pool, it will need a premium from each customer of $(\$40\,000\,000 + \$600\,000) \div 8000 = \$5075$ per year.

d To cover costs and make a $400 000 profit, the insurer will need a premium from each customer of $(\$40\,000\,000 + \$600\,000 + \$400\,000) \div 8000 = \$5125$ per year.

In practice, not all customers in the Worked example will pay exactly $5125. The insurance premium charged to an individual customer will be affected by their individual circumstances. For example, a customer that has smoke alarms and other extra precautions against fire, or has not made any claims in previous years, is likely to pay a lower premium. However, a business that must use lots of chemicals or ovens that might increase the risk of fire, or has made several claims in the past, is likely to pay a higher premium.

TIP

When calculating insurance premiums, remember that the time period must be consistent.
For example, to calculate an insurance premium for *one year*, use the total claims for *one year* and expenses for *one year*.

The value of claims is not the same each year. For some types of risks, in some years there may be few claims; while in other years there are many. For example, there may be an unusually big flood in one year, resulting in many claims. Most insurers will build up a pool of money from premiums so that they can pay out for claims in bad years.

Premiums are often based on the value of the items insured. For example, a business may wish to insure its inventory against theft. The insurer may offer to cover the inventory based on the value of the inventory. For example, an insurer might offer businesses theft insurance each at a premium of \$1 per \$5000 of inventory. If a business has inventory valued at \$100 000, then the insurance premium is (\$100 000 ÷ \$5000) = \$20. However, if a business has inventory valued at \$500 000, then the insurance premium is (\$500 000 ÷ \$5000) = \$100.

TIPS

Make sure you practise calculations of insurance premiums.

It is common to calculate premiums for a year. However, premiums can be calculated for other periods of time, such as monthly.

Arranging insurance cover

Customers that want to purchase insurance can find the process time consuming and complicated.

Customers will usually start the process of purchasing insurance by getting information about insurance cover by telephoning insurance companies or by visiting their websites. Insurance companies also spend a lot of money on promoting their insurance services, such as by producing leaflets, using email marketing and other types of advertising.

The process of arranging insurance can be especially challenging if a customer wants to get insurance premiums quotes from several insurers before choosing which insurance cover to buy. **Insurance quotations** (quotes) give people who are looking for insurance cover details of the premium they must pay and possible cover they can receive from an insurance policy. Insurance quotes will vary for different levels of cover and between different insurance companies.

Often the premiums vary between different insurers because the level of cover offered varies. If several quotations are obtained, the customers should consider the following factors before deciding which insurance policy is best for them:

- the premiums to be paid
- the insurance cover offered
- any exclusion clauses (statements that clarify what cannot be claimed for)
- the amount of the excess when a claim is made.

KEY TERM

insurance quotation: a document that tells an applicant for insurance details of the insurance cover and the cost of insuring.

Some insurance companies specialise in particular types of insurance, while other insurance companies offer a full range of insurance cover.

Procedures for taking out insurance cover

1 The customer must decide the type of insurance required, such as public liability, consequential loss, etc., and the value of the cover needed.

2 The customer will then contact an insurance company, either directly or through an **insurance broker**. An insurance broker is an insurance expert who can advise people that want to buy insurance and put them in contact with insurers. The customer may be given a prospectus, such as a leaflet or online document, which gives details of the insurance cover that the insurance company offers. The prospectus may show what cover is provided, the premium, and the compensation that may be paid in the event of a claim.

KEY TERM

insurance broker: insurance expert who can advise people that want to buy insurance and put them in contact with insurers.

3 The customer completes a **proposal form** and sends it to the insurer. The proposal form is the application form for insurance.

4 The insurer will use the information on the proposal form to assess the risk and make sure that insurance principles are met, including:

   a that the customer has an insurable interest in what is to be insured.

   b that the insured is not over-insuring and is not trying to make a profit from a loss (indemnity).

5 The insurer calculates the premium that the customer must pay for the insurance cover. Premiums may be stated as either:

   a a set amount for a time period, e.g., \$200 for one year

   b a percentage of the value of the item or as a charge on each \$100 of value, e.g., 3% of the value of inventory. Therefore if the inventory is valued at \$100 000 then the premium will be $(3 \div 100) \times \$100\,000 = \$3000$.

6 The customer pays the insurance premiums.

7 The insurer produces the insurance policy and sends it to the customer, who is now insured. The insurance policy can take time to produce, so for some types of insurance, such as motor insurance, the insurer may issue a **cover note** that proves the customer has immediate insurance cover.

8 The insured should check the policy when they receive it to ensure that they are clear on what has been covered and whether there are any unexpected conditions or exclusion clauses.

   For example, a motor insurance policy may set conditions such as the vehicle must be kept in a roadworthy condition. A motor insurance policy may exclude claims for electrical failure or unexpected events such as war or riots.

9 The insured should then keep the policy securely in case they ever need to make a claim.

KEY TERM

proposal form: the application form for insurance completed by the customer.

cover note: a document, produced more quickly than the more detailed insurance policy, that is evidence that a customer is insured.

Insurance cover is usually for an agreed period of time, such as a year. When an insurance policy is about to come to an end, the insurer will usually send the insured a renewal notice. The renewal notice gives information about the premium for the next period of time plus any changes to the conditions of the policy. The renewal notice invites the insured to renew the policy.

Insurance documents

The main documents relating to insurance are the:

1 proposal form
2 cover note
3 policy.

Figure 5.2.11: An insurance proposal form

1 Proposal form

The proposal form is the application form for insurance (Figure 5.2.11). Each customer must complete the proposal form to give the insurer all the information that they need to know about the risk to be insured. The insurer can then use the information in the proposal form to assess the risk, decide whether to accept the risk, calculate the premium to be charged and produce the contract of insurance.

Information that the insurer will ask for in the proposal form will depend on the type of insurance cover that the customer wants to buy. Typically, the proposal form will include the following:

- details of the customer applying for insurance, such as name and contact details
- the type of insurance required and details about the item(s) to be insured, such as type of vehicle or value of premises

- details that will affect risk, such as any previous claims and security information, e.g., the use of smoke alarms for fire insurance and burglar alarms for premises insurance
- the customer's signature and date of the request, confirming that proposal form has been completed accurately and includes all relevant facts.

2 Cover note

A cover note is a document that is evidence that a customer is insured. It can be produced much more quickly than the main insurance policy document. The purpose of a cover note is to make it clear that temporary insurance cover is in place as soon as the first premium has been paid but before the more detailed insurance policy is available.

A cover note will include the following information:

- details of the insurer
- a cover note reference number and insurance policy number
- customer details and the item(s) insured
- the time period of the insurance
- any conditions or exclusions from the insurance cover
- the insurer's signature.

3 Insurance policy

An insurance policy is a contract for insurance cover. It is written evidence of the contract between the insurer and the insured. The policy will state what is insured, the period of time covered and the insurance premium. The policy will also state any conditions or exclusions and the amount of cover provided. Information from the policy is used by the insured if they need to make a claim to the insurer.

An insurance policy will include the following information:

- details of the insurer and the insured, such has names and contact details
- the insurance policy number
- what is insured and the value of the insurance
- the insurance premium
- the time period of the insurance
- any conditions or exclusions from the insurance cover
- how to make a claim
- the insurer's signature.

TIP

Businesses use lots of different documents. Make sure you learn which ones relate to insurance.

The role of an insurance broker

Businesses and individuals can arrange insurance directly with an insurer. However some choose to use an insurance broker instead. Insurance brokers are intermediaries that help customers to find a suitable insurer and insurance cover. Insurance brokers should have expert knowledge about the insurance market. Insurance brokers are not insurance companies but instead will advise customers and organise insurance cover for customers with insurers.

Insurance brokers may see customers face-to-face or may be online or telephone-based businesses.

The main functions of insurance brokers are:

- to give advice on insurance matters to those looking for insurance
- to obtain quotations from several insurers
- to help customers to choose the most suitable insurance policy considering price of the premium and the level of insurance cover
- to arrange the insurance with insurance companies
- to collect insurance premiums on behalf of the insurer
- to arrange the documentation of insurance and pass it on to clients
- to help the insured with making claims.

Insurance brokers' income comes from receiving commission. Commission is a percentage of the insurance cover. It is usually paid by the insurance company rather than the person who buys the insurance.

The benefits to the customers of using insurance brokers are:

- saves time and effort in finding insurers and then comparing what cover they offer
- clearer and specific information to help customers make a decision about which insurance cover to choose
- may be able to find or negotiate lower premiums.

Insurance brokers can be especially helpful to customers that have multiple or complex insurance needs. Insurance brokers can use several insurers for different parts of an insurance package. For example, the broker may organise insurance cover against theft from one insurer, fire insurance from a second insurer and personal liability from a third insurer and then present the total insurance package to the customer.

SELF-EVALUATION CHECKLIST

After studying this chapter, complete this table.

You should know about:	Needs more work	Almost there	Ready to move on
types of banking services			
the suitability of different banking services			
types of digital banking			
the significance of digital banking			
the reasons behind insurance			
types of insurance risk			
the pooling of insurance risk			
insurance premiums			
insurance documents			
the role of insurance brokers			

Knowledge check

1 Why is a mortgage a suitable source of finance for the purchase of property?

2 Explain two advantages of digital banking.

3 State five types of insurance risk.

4 Define the term 'pooling of risk'.

5 Describe the information that must be provided on an insurance proposal form.

6 Which of the following is not a type of bank account?

- a current
- b deposit
- c overdraft
- d savings

7 A business wants to be able to withdraw cash from its local bank branch at any time of day or night. Which type of banking service should it use?

- a ATM
- b credit transfer
- c night safe
- d telephone banking

8 Which method of payment is also known as a letter of credit?

- a cheque
- b credit transfer
- c documentary credit
- d standing order

9 Which of the following is an insurance document?

a bill of lading

b certificate of origin

c cover note

d statement of account

10 A business wants to purchase insurance that will provide financial protection if its normal trading is disrupted or stopped.

Which type of insurance does the business need?

a consequential loss

b employer's liability

c investment

d public liability

Practice questions

1 Mia owns an online business buying sandals and selling them in her online shop. Her online shop only allows customers pay by debit card or credit card.

a Describe two types of bank account that Mia may use. [4]

b Explain why Mia is unlikely to use a night safe. [2]

c Do you think it is a good idea for Mia to require customers to pay by debit card or credit card? Give reasons for your answer. [3]

d Mia is looking to expand her business. She currently uses an old laptop and would like to buy a new computer system to support the expansion. Mia does not have the money available so she is considering a loan or hire purchase. Discuss each of these two options. Justify which one of these two options Mia should choose. [8]

2 An insurer offers insurance to businesses to cover against damages or loss of their assets.

The insurer has the following information available.

Number of customers	10 000
Proportion of businesses claiming for damages	3% per year
Average compensation paid	$40 000
Expenses of operating the pool	$1 000 000 per year

Required:

a State two purposes of insurance. [2]

b Explain two types of insurance risk. [4]

c Calculate the insurance premium the insurer should charge each customer next year to meet all expected claims and cover the expenses. [4]

d Calculate the insurance premium the insurer should charge each customer next year to achieve a profit of $2 million. [2]

e Do you think it is a good idea for a new business to purchase insurance? Give reasons for your answer. [3]

Chapter 5.3

Sources of finance and commercial performance

LEARNING INTENTIONS

In this chapter, you will learn:

- why enterprises need finance
- sources of short-term and long-term finance
- the advantages and disadvantages of different sources of finance
- the suitability of different sources of finance
- trade discounts and cash discounts
- calculations that help to assess business performance
- how the financial performance of a business can be improved.

5.3.1 Sources of finance

All businesses need money to operate. The money may be used to buy assets, such as machinery, vehicles and equipment. Money can also be used to pay for day-to-day expenditure, such as rent, wages, heating and lighting.

Finance is the money put into a business so that it can function. Finance may come from borrowing or the capital from the owners of the business.

Capital is the name given for money invested in a business by its owner(s). Capital is used to acquire assets that the business needs so that it can trade.

The need to raise finance is important to both entrepreneurs setting up new businesses and more established businesses (sometimes known as enterprises). **Entrepreneurship** involves the setting up of a new business. Entrepreneurship has lots of challenges, as the entrepreneur tries to develop their products or services, organise the running of the enterprise and attract customers. Finding sources of finance is one of these challenges. Entrepreneurs need to spend money before they begin trading. However, many entrepreneurs do not have lots of personal savings that they can use as capital for the business.

KEY TERM

entrepreneurship: setting up a new business.

The need for finance

Reasons why a business may need finance include:

- to generate start-up costs, such as the cost of buying machinery and equipment, before it can begin trading. A new business will also need cash to pay for purchases of inventory to sell.
- to meet daily (day-to-day) costs. Goods must be bought or made before they are sold. Therefore money is needed to buy raw materials, pay suppliers, wages, salaries and other expenses before money is received from selling goods or services.
- to expand/grow the business, e.g., buy more capital items, such as bigger premises, more equipment, a new computer system, develop new products.

Just as businesses may have different reasons for needing finance, there are many different types of finance available to meet those needs. Types of finance can be split into **short-term finance** and **long-term finance**.

Short-term finance is money available for a short period of time, typically up to one year, and must be repaid within that time. Short-term finance is often used for day-to-day spending, such as paying suppliers and to cover any shortfall in cash because income is less than expenditure.

Long-term finance is money available for a longer period, such as five or ten years. Some types of long-term finance are never paid back. Long-term finance is used to pay for long-term projects, such as expansion, and to buy assets that will be kept for a long time, such as buildings and equipment.

Table 5.3.1 lists some sources of finance.

Short-term finance	Long-term finance
• Overdraft • Trade credit • Debt factoring • Leasing • Sale and leaseback • Hire purchase • Selling assets • Owner's savings • Retained profit	• Shares • Loans • Debentures • Venture capital • Crowdfunding

Table 5.3.1: Sources of short-term and long-term finance

KEY TERMS

short-term finance: money available for a short period, such as up to one year.

long-term finance: money available for more than one year.

Sources of short-term finance

There are many different sources of short-term finance. These can be split into those that come from external sources (outside the business) and those that come from internal sources (inside the business). As all external sources come from another organisation such as a bank, the business must apply to the organisation for the finance (Figure 5.3.1).

Figure 5.3.1: Applying for finance

External sources of short-term finance

Overdraft

An overdraft is a form of borrowing where a bank current account holder takes out more money than they have in their account. Overdrafts are the most common form of short-term source of finance from banks and are explained in full, including its advantages and disadvantages, in Chapter 5.2.

Trade credit

Trade credit occurs when a business buys goods from a supplier but pays for them later. For example, a business buys inventory for $1000 on 1 January and is given one month's credit. This means that the goods must be paid for by 1 February.

Trade credit is a very common form of short-term finance for a business. There is no interest to pay; so it is cheaper and more attractive to businesses than using an overdraft.

Suppliers may encourage early payment by offering cash discounts for payment within a certain period (see Section 5.3.2 for further information on cash discounts).

Debt factoring

Debt factoring is used by businesses that have customers who buy on credit.

An organisation called a debt factor, often a bank, takes over the debts owed to the business by customers. The debt factor quickly pays the business most of the total debt (at least 80%) and is then responsible for collecting the debts from the customers. After collecting the debts, the debt factor pays the remainder of the debt to the business, less the fee charged for the service (as much as 5% of the total debt).

Leasing

Leasing involves making regular payments, which allows the business to use or rent an asset without the need to buy it. Leasing is often used for vehicles and equipment, such as photocopiers. It is also often used where technology changes rapidly and products may become out of date quickly and need regular replacement, such as computers.

A service or maintenance contract is usually included in the contract. This can be expensive, but it reduces the risk of sudden large expenditure if the leased product breaks down.

Sale and leaseback

Sale and leaseback involves selling an asset that a business owns, to raise money, then leasing the same asset from the organisation that it sold the asset to. The business will sign an agreement to lease back the asset for several years and will pay rent. Sale and leaseback can be a suitable source of finance for established businesses that already own valuable assets, such as land and buildings, and want to continue to make use of the asset but also want to raise finance for other business purposes.

KEY TERMS

debt factoring: selling the debts owed to a business to another organisation. This other organisation will provide a lump sum based on the total of the invoices sold, and will then collect the debts.

sale and leaseback: a way of raising finance by selling an asset and then renting back the same asset.

Hire purchase

Hire purchase and its advantages and disadvantages are explained in Chapter 5.2.

Hire purchase (often known as HP) is used by both businesses and consumers. It is often used by businesses to buy assets such as equipment and company cars. Hire purchase is often used by consumers when buying expensive household items, such as televisions, kitchen appliances and furniture (Figure 5.3.2). The products bought all have a second-hand value and can be repossessed by the hire purchase finance company if payments are not kept up.

Hire purchase is strictly controlled by legislation. When goods are bought on hire purchase, a written agreement is signed by both the seller and the buyer. If an agreement is signed away from the seller's premises, the buyer has the right to withdraw from the agreement within the next few days. This is known as a cooling-off period.

Figure 5.3.2: Televisions can be obtained using hire purchase

Hire purchase agreements may include the following details.

- The buyer may have the right to end the contract once 50% of the payments have been made. The goods must be returned to the seller, and any damage to the goods must be paid for.
- Goods may not be sold until the payments are completed. Legally, the goods are the property of the seller until the last payment is made. If the hirer wishes to sell the goods, the outstanding debt must be paid before the sale.
- If less than one-third of the purchase price has been paid and the hirer falls behind with payments, the seller can repossess the goods.
- If more than one-third of the purchase price has been paid, the seller needs an order from a court to take back the goods.
- If over two-thirds of the purchase price is paid, the goods cannot be retrieved from the buyer. Instead, the buyer may be taken to court for non-payment.
- The buyer can terminate the agreement at any time in writing but needs to bring the repayments up to 50%.

A retailer may either finance hire purchase transactions itself, or act as an agent for a finance company, which will pay the retailer the full price of the goods. Payments are then made by the customer either through the retailer to the finance company or directly to the finance company using direct debit.

TIP

It is important to remember that goods can be repossessed when buying on hire purchase. However, hire purchase agreements usually state that once the buyer has paid more than an agreed proportion of the money owed, the goods can no longer be repossessed.

Advantages and disadvantages of external short-term sources of finance

Each external short-term source of finance has advantages and disadvantages for the business. The advantages and disadvantages of overdrafts and hire purchase are listed in Chapter 5.2. The advantages and disadvantages of other external sources of short-term finance are listed in Table 5.3.2.

Source of finance	Advantages to the business	Disadvantages to the business
Trade credit	There is no interest to pay. It eases cashflow in a business because it makes it possible for the business to wait until its customers pay their bills before it pays its suppliers.	It may not be available, especially to a new small business that has not yet built up strong relationships with its suppliers.
Debt factoring	It avoids the time and cost of collecting debts. The debt factor provides immediate cash for the business instead of waiting for customers to pay.	Business will only receive a proportion of the total money that the customers owe.
Leasing	It avoids a large initial outlay to buy the item. It is useful for equipment that may become out of date quickly and will need replacement at regular intervals. Service contracts cover repairs and maintenance and can reduce risk of breakdown costs. It helps cashflow as it avoids the need to pay out a lump sum to buy an asset.	There is a high overall cost with expensive service contracts. As the equipment is not owned, it cannot be sold. The asset may be repossessed if the business does not keep up the regular payments.
Sale and leaseback	It is a way of raising money without borrowing. It allows a business to keep the use of an asset that has been sold.	Rental payments must be made. A business may lose the use of the asset after the lease period.

Table 5.3.2: Advantages and disadvantages of sources of external short-term finance

Internal sources of short-term finance

The sources of finance explained in the previous section all come from external sources, that is, they come from outside the business. Sometimes, businesses can finance themselves using **self-financing** or internal finance. This means that the finance comes from within the enterprise.

Methods of self-financing include:

- selling assets
- owner's savings
- retained profit.

KEY TERM

self-financing: finance provided from within the business.

Selling assets

An existing business can raise finance by selling off some of its assets, such as part of its business, some of its buildings or unused land (Figure 5.3.3).

Figure 5.3.3: Businesses may sell unused assets such as land

The advantages of selling assets are that the business avoids the need to borrow money, pay interest and make repayments. However, the assets may take a long time to sell and may have to be sold for a low price.

It is important that a business only sells assets that it no longer needs; otherwise, future sales and profits will be adversely affected.

Owner's savings

Personal savings are often used by entrepreneurs starting new small businesses. These savings may have been built up over time or come from redundancy payments if the entrepreneur has lost their job with a previous employer.

The main advantage of using savings to finance a new business is that it reduces the amount that must be borrowed. It does, however, mean that the owner's savings are tied up and cannot easily be taken out of the business for the owner's personal use.

Capital from savings is at risk if the business fails. It is important that the entrepreneur also considers the likely return a new business may give using these savings, compared with the interest that could otherwise be earned if the savings were invested elsewhere.

Retained profit

Retained profit are the profits made by a business that are kept within the organisation for future business use rather than given to the owners/shareholders.

By retaining some of its profit, there is less need for a business to raise finance from external sources. Retained profit has advantages over borrowing because it does not need to be repaid and there is no interest. However, a business does not always have large amounts of retained profit available, especially if it's a new business or one that has made little or no profit. A business may also want to keep some of its retained profit in reserve in case of unexpected business costs in the following year.

Sources of long-term finance

Shares

Capital is always needed to start up a business. Additional capital may also be used to grow a business. The capital for a sole trader comes from the owner and the capital for a partnership comes from the partners. However, the capital for a limited company comes from selling shares (Figure 5.3.4).

Figure 5.3.4: Company shares for sale

Shares are bought by shareholders who become the owners of the company. This applies to both private and public companies. (See Chapter 2.1 for further information on companies.)

There are two main kinds of shares available:

- **ordinary shares** – capital for a limited company where the shareholders are part-owners of the company
- **preference shares** – a type of share that pays fixed dividends and is less risky than ordinary shares.

Ordinary shares are the most common types of share. Owning shares is risky. If the company earns a profit, shareholders receive a share of the profits, which is called a dividend. The amount of dividend will vary depending on the amount of profit, and if a company makes a loss, then the ordinary shareholders will not receive any dividends.

Unlike the owners of soles traders and partnerships, shareholders have limited liability if the business fails. Personal possessions are not at risk and a shareholder's liability for losses is limited to the actual amount invested. Shareholders may also earn profits from selling their shares for more than they paid for them.

KEY TERMS

ordinary shares: capital for a limited company where the shareholders are part-owners of the company.

preference shares: a type of share that pays fixed dividends and is less risky than ordinary shares.

Ordinary shareholders have a say in how the company is run by using their voting rights. Ordinary shareholders have one vote per share owned. These voting rights can be used at the annual general meeting of the company to vote on the general policies of the company and to choose the directors to run the company.

Preference shares are an alternative way for a shareholder to invest in a business. Preference shares are much less risky to the shareholder than ordinary shares because the shareholders receive fixed dividends regardless of the level of profit. Preference shareholders do not have voting rights.

TIPS

- Revise forms of business organisation from Chapter 2.1. This will help you understand the differences between capital from sole traders/partnerships and shares from company shareholders.
- Remember, sole traders and partnerships cannot issue shares. Only limited companies issue shares.
- Because ordinary shares are the most common form of shares, the word 'shares' is often used in place of the term 'ordinary shares'.

Loans

Loans are a way of borrowing a set amount of money to be paid back to the lender in an agreed amount of time. Loans may come from many sources, including family and friends and from banks. As bank loans are the most common form of long-term source of finance from banks, they are explained in full in Chapter 5.2.

TIP

Remember, some loans are secured while other loans do not have any security. Banks and other lenders are more likely to require security on loans for very large amounts of money that are to be paid back over a very long period of time.

Debentures

A **debenture** is a fixed interest, long-term loan to a private or public limited company, repayable at a set date. Debentures are paid after a set period, e.g., 20 years. Some debentures have security. Such debentures are secured against the company's assets, which the lenders (debenture holders) would take if the company failed to meet the interest payments. This makes them very low risk to the debenture holder.

Venture capital

New businesses often find it difficult to raise finance because they are considered more risky than established businesses and more likely to fail. **Venture capital** is a type of long-term finance given to a new enterprise from a venture capitalist that specialises in lending to new, high-risk businesses. The finance is used to help enterprises survive and grow in their early years.

In return for the finance, the venture capitalist will receive a share of the enterprise and a share of the business's profits.

KEY TERMS

debenture: a fixed interest long-term loan to a company repayable at a set date.

venture capital: finance to a new enterprise from a venture capitalist that specialises in lending to new, high-risk businesses in return for a share of the business.

Crowdfunding

Crowdfunding is a source of finance where the funds come from lots of individuals called sponsors, who each provide a small amount of money. Crowdfunding has grown in popularity in recent years and is increasingly used by entrepreneurs looking to raise money for new projects and unusual business ideas that may be unproven and risky (Figure 5.3.5).

KEY TERM

crowdfunding: funds for a new business venture come from lots of individuals called sponsors who each provide a small amount of the money.

Banks and other established lenders usually try to avoid lending to enterprises that might be at high risk of failure and therefore non-payment of the debt. Crowdfunding can offer entrepreneurs finance that is not easily available from more established lenders, such as banks.

Sponsors may choose to fund the project because they are interested and want to support an entrepreneur in a new or innovative business venture. Sponsors might invest and become a part-owner of the business or expect to be repaid with interest. Alternatively, sponsors for some crowdfunding projects can be offered unusual rewards rather than a share in the business or repayment. For example, a business designing a new game may offer an advance copy of a game being developed.

Sponsors may hear about a particular business venture from social media or online advertising, and invest via a crowdfunding website such as Kickstarter or GoFundMe. On some crowdfunding websites, the business must set a target amount that it aims to raise. If it fails to reach the target, then it receives nothing.

Advantages and disadvantages of long-term sources of finance

Each long-term source of finance has advantages and disadvantages for the business, as listed in Table 5.3.3.

TIP

Be aware that a long-term source of finance becomes a short-term source of finance when it gets near to the final repayment date. For example, a five-year loan is considered long-term finance for the first four years but becomes a short-term form of borrowing in its final year.

Figure 5.3.5: Crowdfunding can fund new ideas and projects

Source of finance	Advantages to the business	Disadvantages to the business
Ordinary shares	There is no interest to pay. Dividend payments do not have to be paid if the business has made a loss. The capital is not repaid.	There is less control for existing shareholders. Arranging a new sale of shares (or 'share issue') is expensive and time-consuming.
Preference shares	There is no interest to pay. The capital is not repaid.	Dividend payments must be made even if the business has made a loss.
Loans	They are quicker to arrange than selling shares.	Interest is paid at a fixed rate. Security may be required.
Debentures	There is no loss of control unlike the sale of shares. They are available for large sums of money.	Interest must be paid. Unlike shares, which are permanent finance for a company, debentures must be repaid. If the company fails to meet the repayments or stops trading, the debenture holders become the owners of the assets held as security.
Venture capital	It is likely to be available for new, risky businesses. There is no interest to pay.	The venture capitalist owns a share of the enterprise and is entitled to a share of its profits.
Crowdfunding	It may be the only available way of raising money for a risky business idea. It helps the entrepreneur find out how much interest there is in the business idea among consumers. It encourages potential customers to interact with the enterprise and develop an interest and involvement in the business.	Depending on the agreement, rewards or a share of profits must be paid to sponsors. With some forms of crowd funding, if the business does not raise the full amount it is aiming for, then the business will receive nothing.

Table 5.3.3: Advantages and disadvantages of different sources of long-term finance

Choosing a source of finance in given situations

Deciding which sources of finance are best to choose will depend on the circumstances. There are a number of factors to consider. The main factors can be seen Figure 5.3.6.

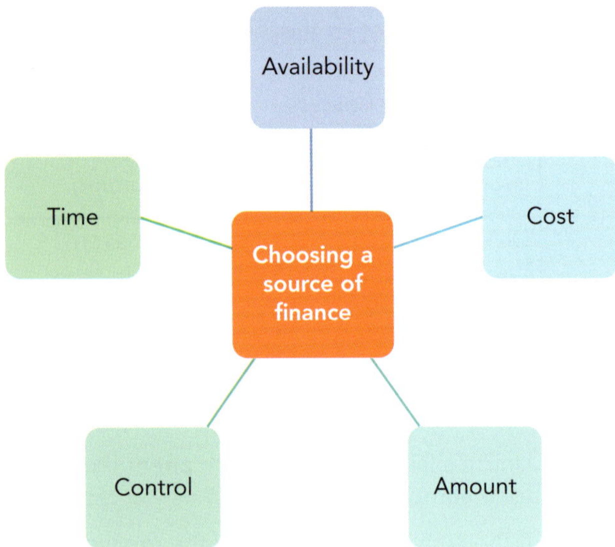

Figure 5.3.6: Choosing a source of finance

Availability

Some sources of finance are only available to certain types of business. Sole traders and partnerships may be able to raise money from the owners or partners, or by inviting extra partners to join their business, but only limited companies can raise finance by selling shares and debentures.

The larger the size of the business and the more profit it earns, the greater the choice of sources of finance and, often, the better the terms offered by lenders. This is because larger and more profitable businesses are seen as less risky than smaller ones.

Sometimes a lender will refuse to lend to a business if it is considered risky and the lender is concerned that the business may not be able to pay back the debt. A lender may consider lending to be high risk if the business already has a lot of borrowing compared to its size, or if the business is not making a profit.

Some lenders will give money only for certain purposes. Some projects are riskier than others. Other projects can show a return more quickly than others.

Sale of assets and retained profits will only be available to an established business that owns valuable assets or has made profits in the previous years. If a company aims to achieve steady growth, that growth may be financed internally by retained earnings. If the company wishes to make large profits quickly, it may need to borrow. However, if an established business is making big losses and is finding it difficult to borrow money, then it may be forced to sell assets to pay its suppliers and other debts.

If a business needs to raise money quickly, such as if its suppliers need to be paid very soon, then it will need to receive funds as soon as possible, even if it is at a high rate of interest. Some sources of finance are quick to arrange, such as an overdraft, while others such as crowdfunding take much longer to arrange.

Cost

Finance is not free. A business wishing to borrow may find it useful to compare lending institutions to find out what their interest rates are and what are the additional charges they impose.

Some sources of finance such as debentures and share issues will have additional costs involved, such as the costs of arranging the finance. Arranging a share issue is very expensive.

Time

A business may need to raise finance to meet its short-term or long-term needs. Several sources of finance are designed to be used for a short period of time, while others are designed to be long-term. Businesses will often use a short-term source of finance for a short-term need and a longer-term source of finance for a longer-term need. This means they aim to match the length of the debt/finance to the life of the asset.

Short-term sources of finance, such as overdrafts, are useful to meet short-term needs. This may occur when goods have to be bought or made before they are sold, and therefore money is needed to buy raw materials and pay suppliers, wages, salaries and other expenses before money is received from selling the goods.

Long-term sources of finance are useful for longer-term needs, such as buying machinery and premises. The longer the finance is required, the more permanent the finance is likely to be, e.g., shares.

Some sources of finance can be used for different time periods. For example, a three-year loan might be suitable to buy a new computer that a business might expect to replace in about three years, while a ten-year loan may be more suitable to buy an expensive piece of machinery that the business expects to keep for many years.

TIP

Remember that businesses should aim to match the length of the debt to the expected life of the asset.

Amount

There are limits to the amount a business can borrow using some forms of finance. Where large amounts of money are involved, lenders may only be willing to provide finance if security is available against property or other business assets. This means that debentures or secured loans may be the only form of borrowing a business has available to choose from.

Lenders may require security because it reduces their risk of financial loss if a business fails to make the repayments. If a business is unable to offer any security, these sources of finance will not be available. A business may then need to consider other forms of finance, such as venture capital or crowdfunding.

Control

Some sources of finance affect who owns and controls a business. Therefore, the views of existing owners are important when deciding whether to choose one of these sources.

One option for a sole trader might be to raise funds by taking a partner. The partner would invest capital in the business. In return, the partner would become part-owner of the business and will therefore share any profits and have a say in business decisions.

If an existing company sells more shares, this will also result in having more shareholders who need to receive dividends and who have voting rights.

When raising very large amounts of money, such as for business expansion, companies will have to make a choice between widening the ownership of the company – by selling shares – or borrowing, perhaps in the form of debentures or a secured loan. In practice, most companies use a mixture of borrowing and share ownership.

ACTIVITY 5.3.1

Working with a partner or in a small group, choose a commercial bank and research the sources of finance that the bank offers to businesses.

Include the following:

a What types of lending does the bank offer businesses?

b What interest rate(s) does it charge?

c Apart from interest, what other bank charges might a business have to pay?

d What information does the bank require for it to decide whether to lend or how much to lend?

Produce a poster on A2 paper to illustrate your findings.

REFLECTION

When answering Activity 5.3.1, how much information and advice did you find that the banks provided on their websites or in leaflets and other literature? What research methods worked best to find out the information you were seeking? How did you use the information in your activity?

Discuss your thoughts on the information available from banks with another student. Did they use different research methods or reach different conclusions about the amount of information available? If so, why?

5.3.2 Cash and trade discounts

Businesses that buy and sell products commonly make use of two common types of discount:

- trade discounts
- cash discounts.

Figure 5.3.7: Business customers often receive trade discounts

Trade discount

A trade discount is a reduction in the catalogue or list price of a product given to businesses within the same trade (Figure 5.3.7). For example, a manufacturer may give a trade discount to a wholesaler or a retailer, or a wholesaler may give a trade discount to a retailer.

The discount allowed will vary in different trades and at different times. It may be only 1–2% or can be as much as 40%. The trade discount may vary because the costs of manufacture may vary, or the seller may wish to encourage a particular buyer to purchase more goods. Often the larger the quantity bought, the greater the discount given. The rate of trade discount may vary according to the nature of the trade. It is common to find a low rate of trade discount with branded goods such as chocolate, sweets and soft drinks, whereas furniture and electronic goods may attract a higher trade discount. Trade discount applies whether or not the payment is made quickly.

Trade discount is calculated as a percentage of the normal (list) price of goods. The price after the trade discount has been applied is called the net price.

TIP

Always show your workings when doing calculations. It can help make your answer clearer even if the final figure is wrong.

WORKED EXAMPLE 5.3.1

Calculating trade discount

The price for 500 exercise books is $500, and the seller offers a 30% trade discount.

Required

a Calculate the trade discount.

b Calculate the net price charged by the seller after trade discount.

Answer

a trade discount = $500 × (30/100) = $150

b net price charged by the seller = $500 − $150 = $350

Advantages to the seller

The advantages of trade discount to the seller are as follows.

- Although giving trade discount may mean less profit, the seller can increase sales if the trade discount is attractive enough.
- The seller avoids the costs of reprinting price lists when prices change. The seller can adjust the trade discount instead.

Advantages to the buyer

The advantages of trade discount to the buyer are as follows.

- The buyer can obtain goods at a very cheap price, thus making a profit on the goods by selling at an increased price.
- The buyer may obtain higher rates of trade discount by buying in bulk from one supplier.

Cash discount

A cash discount is a deduction from the price of goods shown on the invoice that is bought on credit. Cash discounts are given to customers to encourage them to pay promptly. The payment is required within a specified period of time. The rate of discount is usually low, typically between 2% and 5%. The rate may depend on the period of credit allowed, e.g., 5% for 7 days, 2% for 30 days.

Cash discount can be calculated as shown in Worked example 5.3.2.

WORKED EXAMPLE 5.3.2

Calculating cash discounts

A business received an invoice from a supplier totalling \$200. The supplier offers a cash discount of 5% for payment received within 30 days of the invoice date.

Required

a Calculate the cash discount.

b Calculate the amount payable if payment is made within the 30 days.

Answer

a cash discount = \$200 × 0.05 = \$10

b amount payable with cash discount = \$200 − \$10 = \$190

Advantages to the seller

Advantages of cash discount to the seller include:

- offering cash discount helps the seller to reduce bad debts.
- prompter payments provide the seller with cash that can then be used to buy more inventory or to pay bills to improve cashflow.
- giving cash discount may encourage the customers to buy again from the same seller in the future rather than go to another supplier.
- although giving cash discount means a smaller profit for the trader, it may be cheaper to give the discount rather than to allow debts to accumulate.
- the number of debtors (people who owe money) will decrease, and the amount of administrative work in chasing debts will be reduced.
- income will be coming in steadily.
- the cash received may help the seller to take advantage of cash discounts offered by its own suppliers.

Advantages to the buyer

Advantages of cash discount to the buyer include the following.

- The cost of goods is reduced, which gives the buyer a larger margin of profit when the buyer sells the goods.
- The discount received is likely to be greater than any bank interest earned.

If the buyer does not pay within the time period allowed, the buyer will forfeit the cash discount. The buyer may decide to do this because there is a shortage of money to pay bills, there may be more urgent bills to pay, or the money could be used more advantageously elsewhere.

Cash discount is sometimes given if a buyer pays in cash. By offering cash, the buyer is saving the seller the costs of bank transactions. The seller may be willing to offer a small discount in these circumstances, but this type of discount should not be confused with cash discount offered to encourage prompt payment.

If a customer is allowed both a trade and cash discount, the trade discount is always applied before the cash discount is calculated.

Worked example 5.3.3 demonstrates the calculation of trade and cash discount.

WORKED EXAMPLE 5.3.3

Calculating trade and cash discounts

A trader is offered 25% trade discount and terms of 5%, 14 days' or 2%, 28 days' cash discount on an invoice totalling \$1000. The trader receives the invoice on 1 March.

Required

a Calculate the trade discount.

b Calculate the net price charged by the seller after trade discount.

c The trader pays the invoice on 20 March. Calculate the cash discount.

d Calculate the amount that the trader must pay on 20 March.

Answer

a trade discount = \$1000 × 0.25 = \$250

b net price after trade discount = \$1000 − \$250 = \$750

c cash discount = \$750 × 0.02 = \$15

d The trader is entitled to the trade discount plus the 2% cash discount for payment within 28 days. Therefore, the amount paid with cash discount = \$750−\$15 = \$735.

TIPS

Be clear about the distinction between trade and cash discount.

The cash discount is deducted from the trade price after the trade discount has been deducted.

Remember that cash discount is a deduction to encourage prompt payment. It is not a deduction for paying with cash.

ACTIVITY 5.3.2

a Design a set of cards, each card approximately 6 cm × 6 cm. You will need at least 30 cards.

b Using half of the set of cards, write 'cash discount' on one card, 'trade discount' on another card and the name of a source of finance on each of the remaining cards.

c On the remaining cards, write a definition of each source of finance, 'cash discount' and 'trade discount'.

d Shuffle all the cards together.

e Use as a revision tool by matching each card with its definition.

5.3.3 Commercial performance

Businesses want to measure how successful they currently are and what changes must be made to improve their commercial performance in the future. A range of commercial calculations can be used to help businesses assess their current performance. This information can then be used to help owners and managers make decisions designed to improve commercial performance in the future.

Sales, costs and profit

Businesses take risks by buying or making goods or offering services with the aim of selling goods or services in order to gain profits.

Sales is the term commonly used to refer to the amount of goods or services sold. The value of the sales is called revenue (or turnover). Many businesses try to grow their revenue because higher revenue usually leads to more profit. Profit is important to a business because it is the reward to its owners for investing in the business, and retained profit can be a useful source of finance for business growth.

A business will have costs that it must pay if it is to make sales. Sales revenue and costs are used to calculate its profit. If a business's sales revenue is bigger than its costs, then it will make a profit.

Sales turnover (revenue) and profit can be calculated using the following formula.

FORMULAE

Revenue (sales or turnover) = selling price per unit × number of units sold

Profit = revenue − costs

TIP

In practice the terms sales, revenue, turnover, sales revenue and sales turnover are all used interchangeably to mean the value (in $ or other currency) of the units sold. However, only the word 'sales' is also used to mean the number of units sold. However, only the term 'sales' also means the number of units sold.

Costs can be grouped into two main types:

1. **Cost of sales** are the costs of buying or producing the goods/services, such as raw materials, or the cost of purchasing the goods (or inventory) for resale.
2. Expenses are the day-to-day costs of running the business, e.g., rent, insurance, wages and salaries, heating and lighting, telephone, marketing and general office expenses.

KEY TERM

cost of sales: cost of producing the goods/services, such as raw materials, or the cost of buying the goods from outside the business for resale.

There are also different types of profit.

- **Gross profit** is revenue minus cost of sales. This is the profit made before the expenses of the business are subtracted.
- **Profit for the year (net profit)** is gross profit minus expenses. This is the actual profit made by the business.

Profit for the year (net profit) is important because it is the financial reward that businesses aim to receive for taking the risk of operating. The more net profit a business earns, the more successful it is. The business owner can compare the profit gained with what they hoped for or compare the business with another business. It also helps them to plan for the future. Some profit for the year (net profit) may be retained to help finance the future plans of the business.

KEY TERMS

gross profit: the profit that is left after cost of sales has been deducted from sales revenue.

profit for the year (net profit): the actual profit made by a business. It is calculated by subtracting expenses from gross profit.

If a net profit for the year calculation gives a negative figure, then it is described as a 'net loss for the year'.

FORMULAE

Gross profit = revenue − cost of sales

Net profit/net loss for the year = gross profit − expenses

WORKED EXAMPLE 5.3.4

Calculating profit

For the year ending 31 December 2024, a business has revenue of $200 000, cost of sales of $130 000 and expenses of $60 000.

Required

a Calculate the gross profit.

b Calculate the net profit for the year.

CONTINUED

Answer

The gross and net profit for the year calculations are shown in the table.

		$
	Sales turnover	200 000
	Less cost of sales	130 000
a	Gross profit	**70 000**
	Less expenses	60 000
b	Net profit for the year	**10 000**

TIP

When calculating profit, make sure the revenue and costs are for the same period of time. For example, revenue and costs for the year ending 31 December 2024 are used to calculate profit for the year ending 31 December 2024.

It is common to calculate profit for a year. However, profit can be calculated for other periods of time, such as weekly or monthly.

Gross profit margin and mark-up

Gross profit margin is a calculation that is used to show how effectively revenue is turned into gross profit. Gross profit margin is calculated as a percentage.

FORMULA

$$\text{Gross profit margin (\%)} = \frac{\text{gross profit}}{\text{revenue}} \times 100$$

KEY TERM

gross profit margin: a calculation used to show how effectively revenue is turned into gross profit.

Gross profit margin will depend on the cost of sales. Businesses prefer a high or increasing gross profit margin because it means that the business is more likely to be able to cover its expenses and make a profit.

Changes over time to a business's gross profit can be due to a change in the number of units sold. However, changes to gross profit margin are caused by changes in the unit cost or selling price. An increase in cost of sales without a corresponding increase in revenue will lead to a fall in gross profit margin. A decrease in cost of sales without a corresponding decrease in revenue will lead to a rise in gross profit margin.

Businesses aim to make profits, so a business will almost always sell a product for a higher price than the cost of purchasing or making the product. **Mark-up** is the difference between the cost of each product and its selling price.

The cost of buying or making each product is called its unit cost. Mark-up is calculated as a percentage.

FORMULA

$$\text{Mark-up (\%)} = \frac{\text{selling price} - \text{unit cost}}{\text{unit cost}} \times 100$$

For example, if a business purchases a product for \$8 and chooses a selling price of \$10, the mark-up is:

$$\text{Mark-up (\%)} = \frac{\$10 - \$8}{\$8} \times 100 = 25\%$$

This means that the selling price is 25% higher than the cost of purchasing or making the product.

Mark-up can also be calculated using revenue and cost of sales figures rather than prices and costs per unit. For example, if the business in the previous calculation buys and sells 10 000 units then the cost of sales is \$80 000 (\$8 × 10 000), the revenue is \$100 000 (\$10 × 10 000) and the mark-up can be calculated as follows:

$$\text{Mark-up (\%)} = \frac{\$100\,000 - \$80\,000}{\$80\,000} \times 100 = 25\%$$

KEY TERM

mark-up: the difference between the unit cost of a product and its selling price.

WORKED EXAMPLE 5.3.5

Calculating gross profit margin and mark-up

Required

Using the information from Worked example 5.3.4:

a Calculate the gross profit margin.

b Calculate the mark-up.

Answer

a $\text{Gross profit margin (\%)} = \frac{70\,000}{200\,000} \times 100 = 35\%$

b $\text{Mark-up (\%)} = \frac{\$200\,000 - \$130\,000}{\$130\,000} \times 100 = 54\%$

TIP

Mark-up is calculated as a percentage, so it will be the same: whether it is calculated for all the inventory or for each unit.

It is a common mistake to mix up gross profit margin and mark-up. When calculating gross profit margin, remember that the denominator is revenue while the denominator for mark-up is unit cost or cost of sales.

Assets and liabilities

Assets are items that a business owns that have value. Assets can be grouped into two types:

- **non-current (fixed) assets** – assets that a business keeps for more than a year. For example, land, machinery and equipment.
- **current assets** – assets that a business keeps for less than a year, including inventory, **trade receivables** (money owed to the business by its customers), money in the bank and cash.

KEY TERMS

non-current (fixed) assets: assets that a business owns for more than a year.

current assets: assets that a business owns for less than a year.

trade receivables: money owed to a business from its customers who have bought on credit.

Liabilities are debts that a business owes to others. Liabilities can also be grouped into two types:

- **long-term liabilities** – debts that a business has for more than a year. For example, loans and debentures.
- **current liabilities** – debts that a business has that must be repaid in less than a year, including **trade payables** (money owed to suppliers) and any overdrafts.

KEY TERMS

long-term liabilities: debts that a business has for more than a year.

current liabilities: debts that a business has for less than a year.

trade payables: money owed to suppliers for goods bought on credit.

Capital and working capital

The capital of a business is the money invested in the business by its owners. In a limited company, this is the value of the shares (see Section 5.3.1).

Working capital is the money available for the day-to-day running of a business. It is used to pay expenses and to buy inventory.

Working capital is calculated using the following formula:

FORMULA

Working capital = current assets – current liabilities

WORKED EXAMPLE 5.3.6

Calculating working capital

On 31 December 2024, a business has the following financial information:

	$
Inventory	310
Trade receivables	150
Trade payables	200
Cash	20
Overdraft	170

CONTINUED

Required

a Calculate:

  i current assets

  ii current liabilities.

b Calculate the working capital.

Answer

a i Current assets = inventory + trade receivables + cash

= $310 000 + $150 000 + $20 000 = **$480 000**

ii Current liabilities = trade payables + overdraft

= $200 000 + $170 000 = **$370 000**

b Working capital = $480 000 – $370 000 = **$110 000**

TIP

If you are given a table of figures, check whether the figures are given in $, $000 or $m (million).

Working capital is very important to a business because the amount of working capital indicates whether a business has enough money readily available to pay its bills. It needs to be able to do this to maintain the flow of cash through the business and to maintain its reputation and its ability to obtain credit.

Working capital may be required to meet unforeseen expenses, e.g., a repair to a machine. If it does not have enough working capital, it will not be able to carry out these transactions.

5.3.4 Improving commercial performance

When looking to make improvements, businesses focus on four aspects of commercial performance:

- sales turnover
- profit
- mark-up
- working capital.

Methods to improve sales turnover

There are many ways of improving revenue (sales turnover). It will depend on the kind of business, the size of business and how successful the business is at the time.

As revenue = selling price × number of units sold, revenue can be increased by either of the following:

- increasing the selling price (without reducing the quantity sold)
- increasing the quantity sold.

Increasing prices

Some businesses can increase prices and consumers will continue buying their goods. This approach works best where a business has a unique product or service that is in high demand. However, if other businesses are selling similar products, increasing prices will encourage customers to buy from competitors instead. This can lead to an overall fall in sales revenue.

A business will often set a target mark-up and use this to decide the selling prices of its products.

FORMULA

$$\text{Current selling price} = \textit{unit cost} + \frac{\text{unit cost} \times \text{mark-up (\%)}}{100}$$

A business may increase its mark-up in order to decide how much to increase prices by. This is illustrated in Worked example 5.3.7.

WORKED EXAMPLE 5.3.7

Increasing mark-up to increase selling price

A business buys inventory for \$10 per unit and uses a mark-up of 30% to set prices.

The business wants to increase its target mark-up to 35%.

Required

a Calculate the current selling price.

b Calculate the new selling price required to meet the new target mark-up of 35%.

c Calculate the increase in selling price.

CONTINUED

Answer

a
$$\text{Current selling price} = \text{cost per unit} + \frac{\text{unit cost} \times \text{mark-up (\%)}}{100}$$
$$= \$10 + \frac{\$10 \times 30}{100}$$
$$= \mathbf{\$13}$$

b
$$\text{New selling price} = \text{cost per unit} + \frac{\text{unit cost} \times \text{new mark-up (\%)}}{100}$$
$$= \$10 + \frac{\$10 \times 35}{100}$$
$$= \mathbf{\$13.50}$$

c Increase in selling price = \$13.50 − \$13 = **\$0.50**

Increasing quantity sold

There are different ways a business can try to increase the quantity sold.

Improving advertising

Actions to improve advertising to increase the quantity sold might include:

- contacting existing customers or previous customers, such as with email marketing, reminding them of what goods are on offer
- trying different advertising media or spending more on advertising
- using sales promotions, such as 'buy one, get one free', or special events to encourage people to come to the business's premises and buy goods or services
- finding new ways of selling goods or services, such as also selling online.

Businesses should be aware that any action to increase the amount sold through advertising may also involve additional costs. If extra costs are higher than any extra sales revenue, then it will result in lower profits.

Introducing new products

A business may introduce new products or services or improve the ones that it currently offers so that customers want to buy them. For example, a clothes retailers may decide to introduce financial or travel services into existing stores, or a post office may decide to also sell birthday cards, wrapping paper and gifts.

Large companies often spend a lot of money on research and development to produce new products or update existing products. For products that rely on fashion or technology, many consumers want to buy the latest style or model, so businesses must provide these to remain competitive.

Reducing prices

Customers may buy more of a good or service if the price is lowered. Reducing prices will only lead to increased turnover if the increased demand outweighs the reduction in prices.

A business may decide to lower the mark-up between the cost price and selling price, and so hope to sell more. If products have a high mark-up already, e.g., some consumer durables such as cookers and washing machines, there may be an opportunity to lower the percentage made on each item in the hope of selling more.

Extending credit

Extended credit (also known as credit sales) is the sale of goods or services using credit. The buyer becomes the owner as soon as the transaction is made. Extended credit is often offered by retailers to their customers. The customer usually makes an initial payment, such as 20% of the total price, and pays the outstanding amount through instalments.

The retailer may offer credit interest-free for a period of time to encourage sales. Many people prefer to buy goods on credit, especially expensive goods. Allowing credit may persuade some people to make the purchase. There are, of course, drawbacks to this. The business will have to wait for payment. However, it is likely to increase turnover, especially if competitors are not offering interest-free credit.

KEY TERM

extended credit: the sale of goods or services using credit. The buyer becomes the owner as soon as the transaction is made.

Methods to improve profit

Profit = sales revenue – costs, therefore profit will increase if any of the following occur:

- increased sales turnover
- reduced cost of sales;
- reduced expenses.

Increasing sales turnover

Methods of improving sales turnover are explained earlier in this chapter. However, it is important to be aware that some ways of improving turnover also increase costs. If an increase in sales turnover is bigger than an increase in costs, then profits will rise. However, if costs rise by more than sales turnover, then net profit will fall.

Reducing the cost of sales

Reducing the cost of sales may be achieved by buying inventory in greater bulk so that a higher discount is received. However, a business will need to take care that they do not tie up too much working capital in inventory. There is also the risk that the inventory might not sell.

Another way of reducing the cost of sales is to change suppliers to those that charge lower prices. However, sometimes a supplier may be cheaper because the quality of the products is lower. This might result in customer complaints and a fall in return business from customers.

Manufacturing companies may look for more efficient methods of making their goods. They may make greater use of technology and use mass production methods. This would help to reduce the cost of the goods they produce and possibly increase output.

While businesses may try to reduce the cost of sales, it will sometimes rise instead. For example, if inventory is damaged or stolen, this will lead to higher cost of sales and lower gross profit. Having too many staff employed directly to produce the goods can also lead to higher cost of sales and lower gross profit.

Reducing expenses

One of the primary expenses of most businesses is its wages and salaries. Some businesses find that if they invest more in machinery or other technology then they need less workers, and can reduce the amount they spend on wages. For example, many retailers increasingly use self-service methods rather than offering personal service.

Businesses have other expenses that they can try to reduce. These may vary depending on the nature of the business and the level of service they offer. Examples might include:

- cutting after-sales service, or providing after-sales services, such as delivery or servicing, but instead of it being free of charge, customers now have to pay for these services

- moving premises to an area where rents are lower
- using overseas call centres to reduce office expenses
- encouraging employees to save on heating and air conditioning to lower these expenses.

Methods to improve mark-up

Mark-up can be increased if either of the following occur:

- increased selling price
- reduced unit cost.

For a retailer, the unit cost is decided by suppliers. However, the retailer may be able to negotiate lower unit costs or find new suppliers that charge lower prices. For a manufacturer, it may be possible to reduce unit costs if they can find ways to produce products more efficiently and cheaply, such as by outsourcing its manufacturing (see Chapter 2.1).

The seller, often a retailer, will consider a number of things when choosing what mark-up percentage to use.

- What is the overall profit that the retailer wishes to make and what expenses have to be covered? A retailer located in an expensive area with high rents and other charges is likely to have a higher mark-up on goods than a retailer located in a less expensive area.
- If the retailer aims to sell large quantities of goods, there will be a low mark-up. This is especially true for perishable goods, such as newspapers, bread and fruit. In this way, the retailer achieves a small profit on each item but quick sales.
- If a retailer sells goods with a seasonal demand, the mark-up may vary. For example, at the beginning of the summer holiday season, products associated with holidays, such as luggage or beachwear, will have a high mark-up. Towards the end of the holiday season, the mark-up will be smaller as retailers try to dispose of holiday products to save storage costs.
- A retailer selling consumer durables, such as cookers, freezers and microwaves, may have a high mark-up on many of the goods. Some of the goods sold (such as kettles and irons) may have a low mark-up to attract customers in the hope that they will buy more expensive goods. The retailer is interested in the overall profit made, not necessarily the profit made on individual items.

Methods to improve working capital

It is important that a business has enough working capital available. A successful business usually has more current assets than it has current liabilities, although this will vary from business to business. If a business is short of working capital, it may not be able to pay its short-term debts as they arise.

There are several ways in which a business might be able to increase its level of working capital.

- By reducing the time between the payment of cash out of the business and receiving cash into the business. This can be done by negotiating better credit terms with suppliers so that goods are sold before payment is due. A business may also offer customers cash discount to encourage them to pay their bills more quickly.
- By monitoring the amount of inventory that the business holds and reducing the amount of inventory held where possible. Too much inventory means that working capital is tied up in unsold goods and raw materials. High levels of inventory also increase the risk that the inventory will deteriorate, go out of fashion or be replaced by new models. Reducing inventory also means that storage costs and wastage are reduced. It is, however, important that enough inventory is held to meet future customer orders.
- By introducing strict credit control for customers and only allowing customers, particularly those with poor records of payment, shorter periods of credit. This could, however, have an adverse effect on a business, as customers may take their business elsewhere where they can obtain longer periods of credit.
- By avoiding buying non-current assets until there is sufficient cash to pay for them, and selling off any unwanted assets quickly.
- By selling the debts owed to the business to a debt factoring company.

While it is essential that a business has enough working capital, it does not want to have too much either. If a business has a lot of working capital, it is not using its assets in the most efficient way. It may have too much cash that it could use for other purposes, or it may be holding too much inventory that it cannot sell.

ACTIVITY 5.3.3

Review all of the calculations and worked examples in this chapter.

Write three calculation questions that test any of the content listed here:

a trade and cash discounts

b revenue and costs

c gross and net profit

d gross profit margin

e mark-up.

Write answers for each of your questions.

Working with a partner, use your questions to test each other's ability to carry out calculations correctly.

SELF-EVALUATION CHECKLIST

After studying this chapter, complete this table.

You should know about:	Needs more work	Almost there	Ready to move on
enterprises' need for finance			
sources of short-term and long-term finance			
the advantages and disadvantages of different sources of finance			
the suitability of different sources of finance			
trade discounts and cash discounts			
calculations that help to assess business performance			
ways the financial performance of a business can be improved			

Knowledge check

1 Explain two advantages to a business of debt factoring.

2 State three sources of long-term finance.

3 Define the term 'trade credit'.

4 Define the term 'working capital'.

5 Explain the difference between gross and net profit.

6 What is the name given to a reduction in the list price of a product given to a business customer within the same trade?

a cash discount

b factoring

c mark-up

d trade discount

7 Which of the following is *not* a method to improve sales revenue?

a extending credit to customers

b improving advertising

c increasing the amount sold

d reducing expenses

8 Abdul owns a business that makes tops. There were 6000 tops sold in 2024. The table shows financial information about the tops.

	$
Selling price	14
Unit cost	4.2
Business expenses for the year	20 000

What is the gross profit margin (%)?

a 30
b 43
c 46
d 70

9 Fatima's business is offered 20% trade discount and terms of 3%, 28 days' cash discount on the list price for goods priced at $1600.

What is the value of the cash discount?

a $32
b $38.40
c $48
d $320

10 How can a business's mark-up be improved?

a increase the selling price
b introduce new products
c reduce expenses
d take out a loan

Practice questions

1 Kazi owns a business that designs video games. The business was set up two years ago and has grown rapidly. Kazi has a good relationship with suppliers who regularly offer him discounts on purchases.

Required:

a Define trade discount. [1]

b Kazi received a supplier invoice for $450. The supplier offers a cash discount of 3% for payment received within 14 days of the invoice date.

  i Calculate the cash discount. [1]

  ii Calculate the amount payable if payment is made within the 14 days. [1]

c Analyse why Kazi's suppliers are willing to offer cash discounts. [3]

d State three sources of short-term finance. [3]

e Kazi is keen to continue to grow the business. He needs to raise finance to support further growth. Kazi does not have the money available so he is considering crowdfunding or taking a loan. Discuss each of these two options. Justify which one of these two options Kazi should choose. [8]

2 Shivvers is a trading business that buys and sells blankets. Shivvers has the following information available for the year ended December 2024.

Cost of purchasing blankets from suppliers	$20 per supplier
Mark-up	60%
Quantity sold	14 000
Expenses	$108 000

Required:

a Calculate the following:

  i sales revenue [2]

  ii gross profit [1]

  iii profit for the year [1]

  iv gross profit margin. [2]

b Explain two differences between mark-up and gross profit margin. [4]

c Evaluate whether reducing expenses or spending more on advertising will help Shivvers to improve net profit for the year. [6]

> Unit 6

Sustainability and ethics

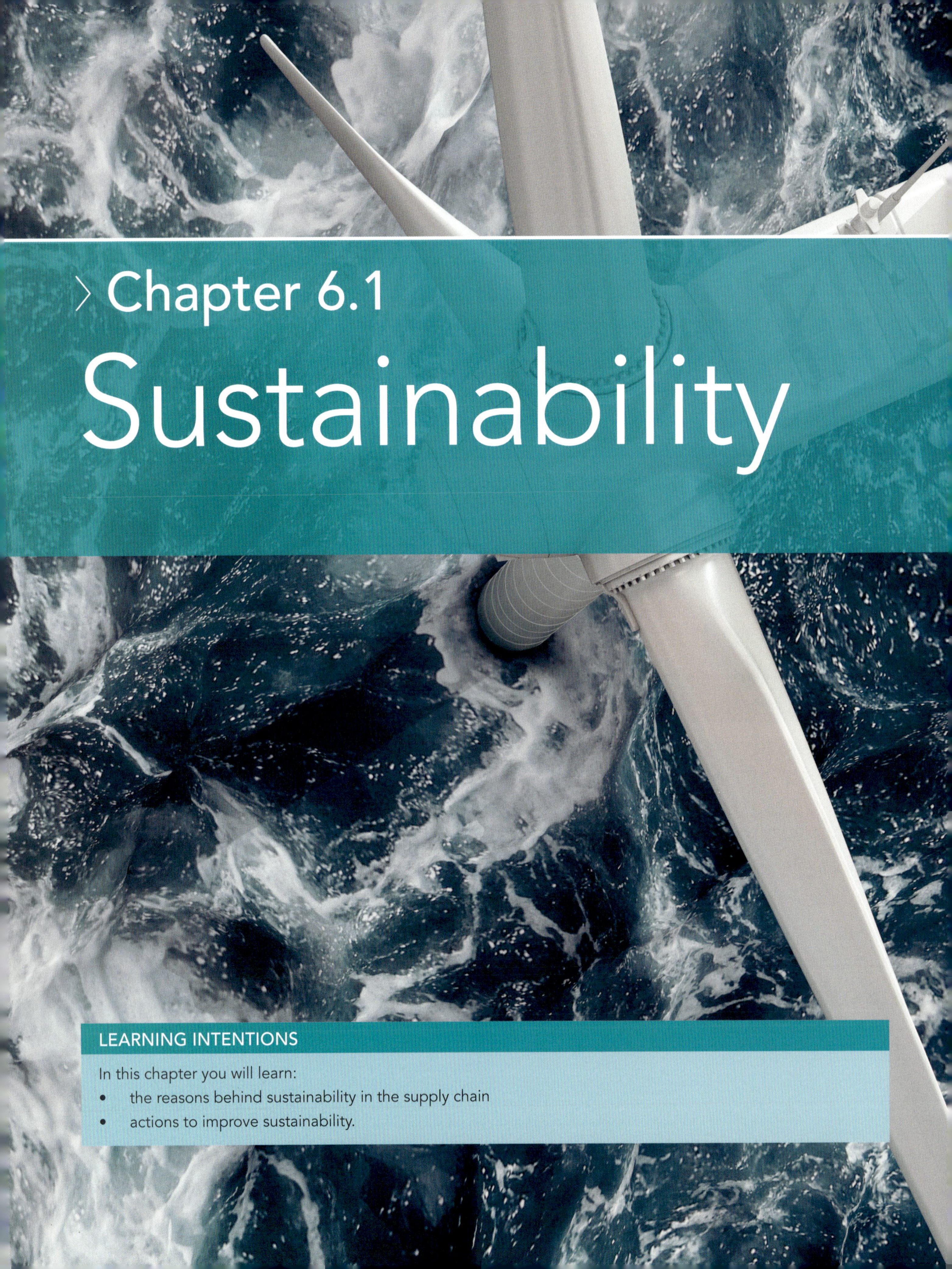

Chapter 6.1

Sustainability

LEARNING INTENTIONS

In this chapter you will learn:

- the reasons behind sustainability in the supply chain
- actions to improve sustainability.

6.1.1 What does sustainability mean?

The environment in which commercial activities take place is very important. The environment provides natural resources, such as crops, fish and minerals, and land, where people can live. It offers pleasure and entertainment, as people enjoy the fresh air and scenery and going for walks, swimming, fishing and climbing. However, the environment is also where waste is dumped, pollution takes place and where factories and commercial activities are located. For these reasons, the environment needs to be protected.

Sustainability in business is the concept of fulfilling the needs of the current generations without compromising the needs of future generations. There needs to be a balance between making use of resources now and replacing them for the future, rather than depleting the resources.

A business is seen as sustainable if it continues to do business without negatively affecting the environment, community or society in general. If a business is able to contribute to the economic growth of the country and make a profit while being environmentally friendly, following ethical standards and abiding by the laws of the country, it is said to be sustainable.

6.1.2 The purpose of sustainability in the supply chain

There are several ways in which businesses attempt to deal with the environmental impact of their actions. Environmental impact is the effect human activity has on the environment. This includes the adverse effects caused by increased commercial activity and industrialisation, and by the release of substances into the atmosphere, such as depletion of natural resources, climate change and pollution.

Businesses and consumers are becoming more environmentally aware and educated. Businesses are making their commercial processes more eco-friendly by:

- causing minimal damage to the environment and using **renewable resources** (that is, resources that can be used more than once) where possible – in this way, they are operating in a sustainable manner
- considering where their supplies are coming from and where they are made – by choosing environmentally responsible suppliers and making use of local materials, businesses will reduce their **carbon footprint**. A carbon footprint is the total amount of greenhouse gases caused by human actions.
- considering the effect their products and services have on the environment
- limiting unnecessary packaging and managing stock production to reduce waste.

A business's reputation – and therefore its potential to sell products, provide services and attract staff – may all be affected by the environmental policies and procedures that it has in place.

Commercial businesses are constantly looking for ways of achieving **sustainable growth**. This means to grow by meeting the needs of the present without risking the ability of future generations to meet their own needs.

Companies need to act in a sustainable way, both in the short term and in the long term. They should use renewable resources as much as possible in order to preserve the capability of the environment to support human life in the future. Examples of renewable resources are solar and wind power, and bioenergy (where organic matter is burned as fuel).

There are certain advantages to doing this:

- it may save energy costs.
- it may attract consumers and investors who want to support these kinds of businesses.
- it may also lead to improved profits.

KEY TERMS

renewable resources: resources that can be used more than once, e.g., wind and solar power.

carbon footprint: the total amount of greenhouse gases caused by human actions.

sustainable growth: to grow by meeting the needs of the present without affecting the ability of future generations to meet their own needs

Businesses will want to present an image to the public of being environmentally sustainable and socially responsible, that is, they are acting in the best interests of their environment and society.

Being environmentally sustainable means behaving in a way that ensures future generations have the natural resources available to live the same way of life, if not better, as the way of life the current generation lives (Figure 6.1.1). Conserving natural resources and protecting global ecosystems are the core focuses of environmental sustainability. Many decisions that impact the environment are not felt immediately, and therefore environmental sustainability focuses on looking forward.

Ways for a business to be environmentally conservative, i.e. not harmful to the environment include:

- avoiding wasting water in manufacturing
- reducing global warming by implementing strategies such as using renewable energy, e.g., solar energy, and **reducing** energy usage in manufacturing
- avoiding the use of plastic bags to keep the oceans clean and using sustainable stationery, products and packaging
- planting trees to help protect the environment
- **recycling** items such as paper, plastic, glass and aluminium
- using environmentally friendly forms of transportation, providing employees the chance to work remotely so they do not have to travel, or offering employees benefits for using public transport.

Figure 6.1.1: It is the responsibility of humans to look after the world we live in for future generations

KEY TERMS

reducing: using less and/or avoiding the use of natural resources where possible.

recycling: reusing resources to produce something else.

ACTIVITY 6.1.1

a In groups, brainstorm ways in which sustainability in the supply chain can benefit a business. Write the ideas on sticky notes.

b Present your ideas to the class. Stick the notes with the ideas on a board.

c As a class, create a list of the main benefits and purposes of sustainability in the supply chain based on the ideas presented.

REFLECTION

Did you find working as a group helped to spark ideas in your own mind in terms of the benefits of sustainability?

6.1.3 Actions to improve sustainability

Sustainability is a concept that businesses of all sizes can implement to make a positive impact on the environment. This section discusses some actions a business can take to improve sustainability.

Using sustainable materials in the production process

Sustainable materials are sourced from renewable resources, or resources with a low environmental impact, and have a longer life cycle. Manufacturing or using these types of materials leaves a smaller carbon footprint. These types of materials are also easier to break down at the end of their life.

KEY TERM

sustainable materials: materials that have a limited negative impact on natural resources and people to avoid depleting the environment.

Examples of sustainable materials are:

- wood: a natural, renewable resource that is plentiful. It can be used for making furniture, paper products and in construction.
- bamboo: a woody, fast-growing grass with a hollow stem. It is strong and durable and can be used for flooring, making furniture and textiles.
- recycled plastic: plastic made from previously used plastic to avoid wastage. It can be used for packaging, printing and making products such as bags, car components, building materials and paint pots.
- recycled paper: this can be used for items like packaging, cardboard, newsprint, labels and gift cards.
- cotton: a natural fibre. It is biodegradable, meaning that it can be broken down naturally by the organisms in an ecosystem. Cotton is easily available and can be used for products such as clothing, insulation, mop heads and rags.
- wool: a natural, biodegradable fibre. Wool is also easily available and can be used for insulation, mattress padding and making textiles.
- hemp: a fast-growing plant that is strong and durable. It can be used for construction materials, plastic, making textiles and paper products.
- recycled metal. This can be used for packaging, construction, making furniture and automobiles.

Implementing sustainable logistics

Sustainable logistics refers to the methods and operations aimed at improving the sustainability of supply chain activities. These extend from the supply of raw materials to the distribution and management of the life cycle of products.

Some practices that companies can use to increase sustainability in logistics include:

- using local suppliers to source their resources or materials
- using recycled materials in their products or processes
- using renewable energy or technologies, where possible
- reducing their waste by removing unnecessary packaging, and **reusing** and recycling packaging
- moving from paper to digital, where possible
- making sure containers are full to avoid wasting energy by transporting partly full loads or empty loads
- using lower-carbon fuels and replacing old trucks used for transportation with eco-friendly vehicles. (Lower-carbon fuels are produced sustainably from municipal or organic waste, biomass, renewables and circular carbon dioxide. They emit no or very little additional carbon dioxide during their production and use.) They could also use the most environmentally friendly freight modes (refer back to Chapter 4.1).

KEY TERMS

sustainable logistics: practices and processes aimed at improving the environmental impact of all logistical operations.

reusing: finding new uses for materials in their original form rather than disposing after use.

Reducing packaging

There is a growing resistance in many countries to the excessive and unnecessary use of packaging. Consumers are concerned about the excessive use of plastic bags that are not biodegradable and that cause a huge litter problem. They are also concerned about the use of single-use plastic for the packaging of products. Many retailers are making use of smaller boxes or bags to combat this.

Some retailers now encourage the use of recyclable bags, and some supermarkets, in countries such as South Africa and Australia, do not provide plastic bags for carrying away goods. Instead, they sell stronger, reusable bags made from recycled material. Many businesses are now using lightweight, responsibly sourced, recyclable packaging, hoping that this may mean lower costs to them as well as helping the environment.

Sustainable packaging strategies

Along with reducing packaging, companies can use other strategies for sustainable packaging, such as:

- sharing ideas with customers on how best to dispose of or recycle a product packaging material
- making use of recycled packaging materials
- using plant-based or edible packaging, or packaging that you are able to plant.
- using **compostable packaging** or **biodegradable packaging** from plastic substitutes (Figure 6.1.2)

The short-term costs may be more expensive to a company; however, the long-term benefits to the environment and to the costs is more. Additionally, consumers might be willing to pay a little extra for a product if the product is either made from recycled material or a sustainable packaging strategy has been applied. Consumers will support businesses who have 'green strategies', as by using these strategies the business is making a positive impact. In this way, sustainable packaging strategies can be a useful marketing tool as well.

Figure 6.1.2: Disposable eco-friendly crockery and cutlery made from bamboo wood and paper

Compostable packaging breaks down in a compost pile and forms decayed organic substances that can be used as a fertiliser and that will benefit the soil. Biodegradable packaging also breaks down over time and will completely return to nature in a relatively short amount of time. However, it does not benefit the soil like compostable packaging does. The following are examples of biodegradable materials:

- paper, cardboard and brown wrapping paper
- corn, sugar starch, seaweed, rice husk and mushrooms, which can be used to make packaging from plant-based materials
- some 'bio-plastics' made from corn or sugar starch
- grass paper boxes and papers containing sundried grass.

Upcycled packaging is another option for eco-friendly packaging. Upcycling takes waste and creates something new from it in its current state. This is different to recycling, which involves the destruction of waste in order to create something new. Upcycling reduces the extraction of natural resources, reduces **landfill** waste and involves less manufacturing, which leads to less carbon emissions. Examples of upcycling include using materials from plastic bottles to make new shoes or using reclaimed wood to make furniture.

KEY TERMS

compostable packaging: packaging that breaks down and forms organic substances that benefit the soil.

biodegradable packaging: packaging that breaks down and returns to nature without benefits to the soil.

landfill: a site where waste is disposed of by burying it in the ground.

ACTIVITY 6.1.2

a Choose a packaging material from the following:

  i plastic

  ii biodegradable

  iii sustainable materials.

b Research the pros and cons of this packaging material. Consider the life cycle of the material, from production to disposal. Consider the cost of the materials, short term and long term. Consider the marketing potential of the material.

c Make a list of your pros and cons and compare it to the work of another student who chose a different material.

TIP

The difference between compostable packaging and biodegradable packaging is that compostable materials benefit the soil and biodegradable materials do not benefit the soil.

Selling eco-friendly products

Eco-friendly products have a lower impact on the environment throughout their life cycle. They often contain materials that have been recycled or are easy to recycle, or have been extracted from a natural resource like bamboo or cotton, for example. Eco-friendly products should, ideally, be made in a building that uses renewable energy, such as a solar-powered factory. They should also use the least amount of water possible.

In addition to reducing environmental impact, the benefits to a business of selling eco-friendly products include:

- attracting new, environmentally conscious customers
- portraying a business as socially responsible, which will improve brand recognition and customer loyalty
- reducing waste, which may save money
- new service offerings becoming available, such as resale, repair or refurbishment, which can lead to more ways of generating income.

KEY TERM

eco-friendly products: products made using natural or recycled materials and that have a lower environmental impact throughout their life cycle.

Recycling and reducing waste

Recycling is the reuse of resources to produce something else (Figure 6.1.3). Less energy is used to reuse and recycle material than to produce the material from scratch. This means businesses and consumers are reducing greenhouse gases and reducing global warming. By recycling, less waste ends up at the landfill, which leads to less pollution.

Figure 6.1.3: The universal recycling symbol

Many products can be recycled, such as paper, cardboard, glass, aluminium cans, some plastics, clothing, builders' rubble, metal, textiles, electronics and garden waste.

One of the main problems of recycling is the separation of recyclable waste from unrecyclable waste, and the costs involved in doing this. Consumers do some of this by separating recyclable items into separate rubbish bins (Figure 6.1.4).

For recycling to be economically viable, there needs to be a steady supply of waste, a system to extract the recyclables, a nearby factory to process it and potential demand for the recycled products. Recycling is a steadily growing industry in many economically developed countries.

Recycling can reduce the carbon footprint of a business. It can also benefit a business by reducing their raw material costs, which leads to increasing profitability. In addition, employees are often more motivated to work for a business that recycles. To work for a business that shows interest in preserving the environment makes employees feel like they are part of the solution and making a positive impact.

Waste disposal is the proper disposal of discarded or discharged material according to local rules and national guidelines. It can be disposed of by incineration, landfill, recycling or composting.

Waste needs to be collected, transported and treated. Sometimes materials can be extracted from waste and can be recycled, but any remaining waste needs to be disposed of. Household waste goes to local household-waste recycling centres where different materials are placed in different containers, and sometimes useful items are resold to the general public. Other waste is sorted in special treatment plants, which use conveyor belts, automated machinery and even magnets to extract metals.

Businesses can take the following steps to reduce waste:

- Measure waste. Businesses can check all the bins that are used for waste just before they are emptied and taken to the landfill. They can calculate the amount of waste leaving the business site on a weekly basis and use this to analyse where less waste could be created.
- Reduce waste going to the landfill. A business can identify which waste materials can be reused or recycled, even this means another local business can make use of it. The business can then change the way it operates to avoid or reduce waste, such as making a change to their manufacturing process.
- Identify local businesses that collect recyclable materials.
- Set up material collection systems at business premises. If businesses have bins available for the different types of recyclable materials, this helps them to separate them from each other for collection.

Figure 6.1.4: Recycling bins labelled for different products

Reducing the need for returns and exchanges

'Returns' refers to the process by which a consumer returns an item, which can be for a number of reasons, e.g., a change of mind, a faulty product or slow shipping. Once the item has been returned, depending on the product and the condition, the seller must decide whether to recycle the item and save useful parts, repair or refurbish it, sell it again or destroy it.

The seller must also decide what type of action to take with the customer, such as offering a refund or exchange, store credit or a product repair.

Returns and exchanges are inevitable: customers will always want to send things back. However, they can be reduced by:

- ensuring the quality of products is up to the standard
- representing products correctly, with a clear description for ecommerce products
- representing sizing correctly on ecommerce sites
- encouraging customer reviews and feedback
- ensuring damage is not caused due to poor packaging
- clearly displaying delivery times
- offering live chat and real-time support for ecommerce
- analysing and improving products, wherever possible.

Returns cost businesses large amounts of money, and in some cases these returns could have been avoided. Reducing the number of returns saves money on replacement products and shipping. It also reduces the carbon footprint of transport emissions and energy usage, as well as materials needed for replacement products. It avoids waste of materials if products are discarded. Finally, it creates a better customer experience and helps to build trust between a business and potential customers.

Offering digital resale marketplaces

A digital marketplace is an ecommerce site that offers different products from different sellers. Examples of well-known online marketplaces are Amazon and eBay.

Reselling used products gives them a second life. A second or third owner may benefit from the product after the previous owner has grown tired of it. Alternatively, used products can be recycled and created into something new.

Resale marketplaces allow consumers to buy second-hand products (Figure 6.1.5). Businesses can encourage consumers to resell their own or purchase others' unwanted products by offering opportunities for them to do so through their website.

KEY TERM

resale marketplace: a digital marketplace where consumers can buy and sell unwanted products that have been previously purchased.

Second-hand products have a positive environmental impact. They reduce carbon emissions and save resources, water and energy. They keep the items from landfills and incinerators and replace the need for new items.

Figure 6.1.5: Digital marketplaces can be used for reselling products

Offering free repair services

If businesses offer free repair services, customers can be more likely to purchase the product from them as it gives the customer ease of mind knowing that, should the product break, it will not cost them more money for the repairs. Repairing the product is also more environmentally friendly than replacing the product, as repairs will use less materials, energy and water than manufacturing a new product. Repairing also leads to less wastage.

Inevitably, a customer will be disappointed if a product breaks. However, if they have a good experience with the repair process, they may stay loyal to the business for future sales and it will have a positive reflection on the brand.

After-sales service is important as it adds to customer satisfaction with the product and brand. It builds trust between the customer and business, and inspires loyalty for further sales. Customer satisfaction leads to good reviews and a positive social media visibility, which all strengthen the brand.

Water stewardship

Companies all over the world recognise the water challenges that present significant risks to communities, ecosystems and their own operations. The term water challenges refers to issues such as the over-extraction of ground water, water pollution and lack of proper water management. Companies are now aware they have a role to play to ensure water security by managing their water use and wastewater discharge. Water security refers to good quality, well-managed water resources and well-managed water supply services.

Water stewardship is the responsible management of water resources to meet the needs of today's and those of future generations.

Companies can do the following to conserve water:

- carry out a water audit to gauge water inefficiencies
- put together a water conservation plan
- use water-efficient equipment and products
- use air-cooled equipment in place of water-cooled equipment
- use non-toxic products and less contaminative processes that will not harm the existing water supply
- conduct routine maintenance checks to prevent and fix leaks
- use brooms to sweep instead of hoses
- use drip-irrigation (where water is slowly dripped on to the soil through a system of plastic pipes) and drought-resistant plants for landscaping
- reuse wastewater from people's houses through a collection and reuse system
- train employees on best practice for water conservation
- install low-flow toilets and faucets, which are designed to use less water
- post notices near sinks for people to be mindful of their water usage.

Water stewardship helps to conserve local water supplies and support the people and wildlife that depend on them (Figure 6.1.6). Water stewardship can boost a company's reputation. Consumers will recognise the business's effort to conserve, and support the business as a result.

KEY TERM

water stewardship: using water in such a manner that is environmentally sustainable and economically beneficial for future generations.

Figure 6.1.6: Conserving water is a priority to ensure water supply for future generations

ACTIVITY 6.1.3

a In groups, choose three brands or businesses that you have bought from before or that you like to follow.

b Research any sustainable business practices they have put in place to improve their environmental impact.

c Present your findings on a poster.

REFLECTION

Did you find any businesses or brands whose sustainability practices excited or appealed to you? Do you think that you would be more likely to purchase from them than from other brands?

SELF-EVALUATION CHECKLIST

After studying this chapter, complete this table.

You should know about:	Needs more work	Almost there	Ready to move on
the reasons behind sustainability in the supply chain			
actions to improve sustainability			

Knowledge check

1 Which of the following is a renewable resource?

- a coal
- b gas
- c oil
- d solar power.

2 Which of the following is not a benefit of sustainable supply chain management?

- a reduced costs
- b increased revenue
- c increased brand value
- d increased waste and pollution.

3 Which of the following is an action a business can take to improve sustainability?

- a Increase energy consumption.
- b Use single-use plastics.
- c Implement a recycling programme.
- d Dispose of hazardous waste improperly.

4 Which of the following is an action a business can take to conserve water?

- a Use water-intensive landscaping.
- b Install low-flow toilets and faucets.
- c Increase water usage for cleaning purposes.
- d Implement a leaky faucet policy.

5 Define the term 'sustainability' and explain its purpose.

6 State four types of sustainable materials and one type of product which can be made from each.

7 Explain the difference between compostable packaging and biodegradable packaging. Explain the benefits to the business of using these types of packaging.

8 Identify five ways to try reduce returns from customers.

9 Define the term 'resale marketplace' and explain how it is a form of sustainability.

10 Define the term 'water stewardship' and explain how companies can conserve water as a form of sustainability.

Practice questions

1 Describe sustainability in the supply chain. [2]

2 a What are some actions a business can take to reduce its carbon footprint? [3]

b How can a business promote waste reduction and recycling? [3]

c What are some actions a business can take to promote sustainable practice amongst employees? [3]

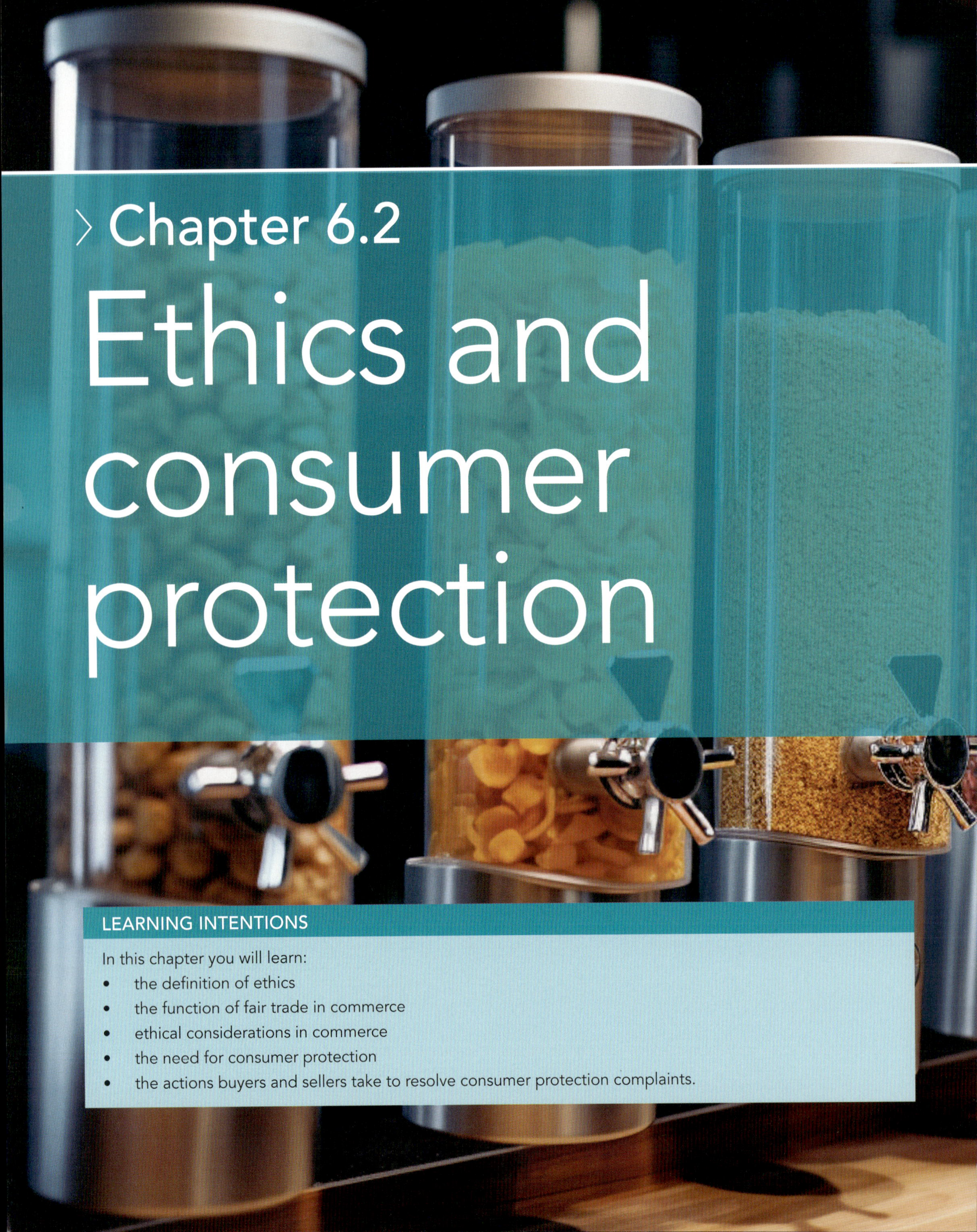

Chapter 6.2

Ethics and consumer protection

LEARNING INTENTIONS

In this chapter you will learn:

- the definition of ethics
- the function of fair trade in commerce
- ethical considerations in commerce
- the need for consumer protection
- the actions buyers and sellers take to resolve consumer protection complaints.

6.2.1 Ethics

All organisations operate to achieve specific aims. These aims are decided by the organisation itself. A private sector business, such as a sole trader, operates to make a profit for its owners. A public sector organisation, such as a hospital, must deliver services to benefit the general population.

Some businesses make poor operational decisions. The managers are so focused on their business aims that they may hurt others, such as customers or employees. Some businesses make mistakes. Some people may act selfishly. All of these may lead to issues connected to ethics.

Ethics are an important part of operations. Ethics focus on doing the 'right' thing. It is about the **moral behaviour** of individuals and managers when operating a business. All businesses must operate in line with the country's legal requirements. However, ethical businesses go over and above the minimum legal requirements. For instance, an ethical business may offer employees more days' holiday than the minimum number of days required by law.

It can be difficult to do the 'right' thing all of the time. It can also be hard to do the 'right' thing for all stakeholders, as the 'right' thing for one stakeholder may be the 'wrong' thing for another. For instance, a business manager may increase employees' pay by 10% as they feel this is the 'right' thing to do for its employees. However, the shareholders of the business may be unhappy with this decision as it will reduce the profit available for them. This decision will therefore be the 'wrong' thing for shareholders.

Ethics can also change over time as people's views develop. Two hundred years ago, many people thought it was acceptable to trade in enslaved people, taking people from Africa and selling them in America. Today, we know this is wrong.

Ethical standards also vary from country to country. Often environmental protection regulations and **employment laws** are stricter in developed countries, like the US or Brunei, than in developing countries, such as Peru or Ghana. Child labour rules are often more rigidly controlled in developed countries.

All businesses use resources to achieve their aims, e.g., financial resources and/or employees. Operating ethically can make achieving business aims more challenging. Ethical business decisions are often more expensive, which can make it harder for the business to achieve its financial aims. For instance, an ethical business will pay its suppliers a fair price for raw materials and will pay on time. Paying on time is the 'right' thing to do as it prevents the supplier experiencing cashflow problems and so it is able to continue to pay its expenses to operate. Unethical businesses may pay suppliers late so that they can keep the cash in their business for longer. This will make their accounts look better, which could be used to attract investors and/or support loan applications. Keeping the cash in the business rather than paying suppliers can make it look like the business is performing better financially.

KEY TERMS

moral behaviour: to act according to one's personal values, beliefs and standards.

employment laws: laws that affect the treatment of employees in the workplace. The laws may affect the terms of employment.

Figure 6.2.1 presents the key ethical issues for businesses.

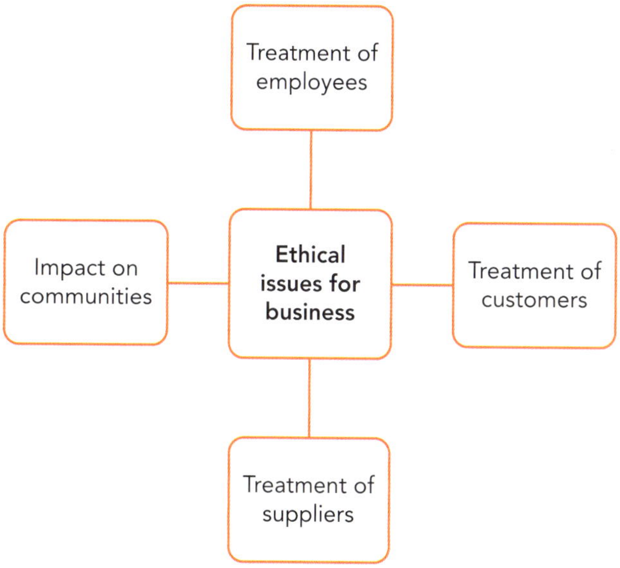

Figure 6.2.1: Ethical issues for business

Treatment of employees

Employees are one of the most important resources for many businesses. Employees are the human resources of the business and supply the labour needed to produce goods and services.

There are many employment laws that affect how employees are treated. Ethical businesses treat their employees better than the legal minimum. For instance, if the legal minimum wage rate in a country is $10 per hour, an ethical employer will pay the employee at least $11 per hour.

Labour costs–costs associated with the employees within the business–can be one of the highest of all expenses to run a business. Sometimes other stakeholders are affected by decisions to treat employees ethically. For instance, providing specialist safety footwear for employees can be expensive and reduces the profits made by a business, leading to lower shareholder dividends. However, in the long term, the employees are likely to be more loyal to an employer who treats them well. Long-serving employees reduce recruitment costs for the business, which can then boost long-term profitability.

Examples of ethical treatment of employees include:

- not using child labour
- paying employees fair wages
- not forcing employees to work very long hours
- providing employees with safe working conditions and giving them the correct equipment for safety
- not discriminating against employees on grounds such as gender, ethnicity or disability
- treating all employees with dignity and respect.

Treatment of suppliers

All businesses rely on a good relationship with their suppliers to produce goods and services. Ethical businesses often have a better relationship with their suppliers, who prefer to work with businesses who treat them fairly. Unethical businesses may try to maximise profits by paying suppliers an unfairly low price for raw materials. This action disadvantages the supplier as they may struggle to cover their costs and could experience cashflow problems. The supplier will have expenses to pay, e.g., employee wages and utilities used to produce the raw materials supplied. Sometimes the supplier may be smaller in size than the unethical business, which can cause issues with power. Cashflow problems can mean that the supplier is unable to pay its own expenses and is forced into liquidation. Ethical businesses respect suppliers and understand that they need to make a fair income from goods and services supplied to be able to afford to continue to trade. If a supplier is forced into liquidation, it will disadvantage the business as it will need to find a new supplier who may offer worse-quality goods and services and/or a poorer working relationship.

Some businesses carefully choose their suppliers as they are aware that the orders that they make can support the supplier to operate a profitable business. Some ethical businesses choose suppliers in developing countries, as it can help the supplier and their employees to make a living and therefore enjoy a better standard of living. Other businesses may choose to work with local suppliers to bring greater economic prosperity to the area that they are based.

Examples of ethical treatment of suppliers include:

- paying suppliers on time
- paying a fair price for supplies.

Treatment of customers

Many customers prefer to purchase goods and services from ethical businesses. The customer may be the end-user of the good or service, or sometimes it may be the wholesaler or retailer (the next organisation in the supply chain).

Unethical businesses can make sales and increase their sales revenue by treating customers unfairly and not marketing honestly. However, customers are unlikely to buy from the business again if they have been treated unfairly and misled. Modern technology enables customers to quickly share reviews and bad experiences, which can impact on a business's reputation. Customers may decide to write a negative review if unhappy about how an unethical business has treated them, which may put other customers off from purchasing from the business. In the long term, ethical businesses have more loyal customers.

During the COVID-19 pandemic, specific products were in high demand globally, such as soap, hand gel and face masks, as people sought to protect themselves from the virus. Suppliers and manufacturers of these products recognised this and some unethical suppliers charged high and excessive prices for these items to profit from people's fears (Figure 6.2.2). There were examples of bottles of hand soap being sold for five times the normal price.

Figure 6.2.2: Unethical suppliers charged excessive prices for hand soap during the COVID-19 pandemic

Some businesses quickly pass price rises on to customers when the price of supplies increases. However, they may be slower to pass on price reductions when the price of supplies falls, and the businesses therefore profit from the lower cost. For example, the price of fuel, such as petrol and diesel, changes rapidly due to supply and demand, but many garages are slow to pass on price reductions, or only partially pass them on, to customers.

Examples of ethical treatment of customers include:

- charging a fair price for products and services
- replacing, repairing or refunding faulty products
- not pressuring a customer to buy a product
- giving honest and accurate product information
- not misleading customers in any way.

Impact on communities

All businesses operate within a community. The community can vary, from the geographic area that it operates within to a stakeholder group. The operations of the business can have an impact on the community. Most production processes involve the generation of waste, e.g., the waste of raw materials or damaged products in the production process. The operation of the business may also affect the amount of traffic in an area, e.g., employees may drive to work and/or supplies of raw materials may need to be delivered to the business by lorry. This traffic may lead to congestion on the local roads and various types of pollution. Ethical businesses are aware of the impact that these issues have on their communities and take action to reduce any negative impacts. For example, an ethical business might encourage employees to car share and/or use public transport to reduce the amount of cars travelling to the site, or only operate on weekdays to minimise the impact of operations on local residents.

Ethical businesses often invest in the local community to make the area more pleasant by contributing to new services. For example, some businesses may offer capital to enable new public services, such as the construction of a new school or sports facility. These actions help the local community accept the business that operates in the area. Some businesses allow their employees to work for one or two days per year on community projects. The employees are paid their normal salary/wage for the day but instead of performing their normal work tasks, they can use the time to work on a community project, such as litter picking in a park or tidying the community garden at a hospital so the area is more pleasant for patients to enjoy. This initiative helps the business to develop positive relationships with the local community, but many employees enjoy being able to give something back to the local community. It can also help teambuilding within the business as employees work together on a project unrelated to the workplace.

ACTIVITY 6.2.1

Tick true or false in the box next to each of the statements in the following table to identify whether or not they are generally considered to be examples of ethical practices.

Statement	True	False
It is ethical to employ young children as long as they are given training, as it will help them learn skills to gain employment when they are adults.		
It is ethical to buy goods from developing countries as it helps businesses in the country to develop.		
It is ethical to miss the deadline to pay a supplier to avoid cashflow problems in the business. This delay will help the business to save the jobs of the employees.		

CONTINUED

Statement	True	False
It is ethical to mislead customers within advertising as they will never know if the claims are true or false.		
It is ethical to make less profit for shareholders so the business can buy new protective clothing for employees.		
It is ethical to offer a bribe to a supplier.		
It is ethical to give an employee generous holiday entitlement.		

REFLECTION

Think about your answers to Activity 6.2.1. Did any of the reasons given by the business to justify each decision make an unethical decision sound acceptable? Why might someone from a different country give different answers to you?

The benefits of operating ethically

Being ethical can bring benefits to businesses as summarised in Table 6.2.1.

Benefit	Outline of benefit
Attracting and retaining employees	Employees trust businesses with ethical employment practices. Most employees prefer working for an ethical business. Many individuals think about how the business treats its employees before applying to work there, so being ethical can help the business to recruit the best employees. Employing highly skilled and experienced employees can then help the business produce high-quality goods and services. Employees are likely to be more motivated if they work for an ethical business as they will be treated fairly. This will increase their productivity and loyalty to the business. Increased productivity will reduce the costs of production per unit. The business will retain employees better, as motivated employees are less likely to leave the business for another job. This will save the business the expense of having to recruit and train new employees.
Customer satisfaction	Many customers prefer to purchase goods and services from ethical businesses. Many people like to support businesses that do the right thing and treat others fairly. They may be prepared to pay more for goods and services if they know that others have been treated fairly during production. Retailers prefer supply of goods and services from ethical businesses. This is because their business reputation may be harmed if they are associated with an unethical business. If customers find out that they sell goods produced by an unethical business they may lose sales. Some retailers have experienced problems if they have bought stock from unethical businesses. Unethical businesses can make sales and increase their sales revenue by treating customers unfairly and not marketing honestly. However, customers are unlikely to buy from the business again if they have been treated unfairly and misled. In the long term, ethical businesses have more loyal customers.

Continued

Benefit	Outline of benefit
Good reputation	Ethical businesses generally have a good reputation. This reputation can help the business to perform better financially and be more profitable. Businesses need to be aware of the risk of gaining negative publicity if any part of their operations could be deemed to be unethical. The business can also use its ethical operations in its promotion to help attract more customers to buy from it.
Higher returns for investors	Ethical businesses often perform better and have a higher chance of survival. This benefits investors as they will have a higher return on their investment. Many investors choose to support ethical businesses only. Businesses that do the right thing may find it easier to raise additional finance when needed. Investing in ethical businesses can make the investor feel and look good. Often grants and subsidies are only available to businesses that meet certain requirements. Sometimes these conditions relate to how ethical the business's operations are. Therefore ethical businesses can often benefit from grants and subsidies.

Table 6.2.1: Benefits to businesses of being ethical

Drawbacks of operating ethically

Operating ethically can be costly. Doing the right thing and treating others fairly is often more expensive than if the business exploited others. For instance, it will cost the business more to pay its employees high wages than the minimum wage. The increased cost can potentially reduce profitability.

However, many of the benefits from operating ethically can help the business generate more revenue. Its improved reputation can attract more customers, who are often willing to pay a higher price for goods and services. The increased revenue can often exceed the increase in business costs, which means that the ethical business earns more profit.

Many businesses claim to be ethical in promotions to enhance their reputation. However, after making these claims, the business needs to be very careful that all operations are ethical. The smoothie brand, Innocent Drinks, was originally founded on ethical values. Its logo symbolises innocence and has always used natural ingredients. The brand is now owned by Coca-Cola and has received criticism from the media and other stakeholders regarding its ethical stance. Stakeholders will be particularly critical of brands that claim to be ethical and quick to criticise if this is not the case. This can put additional pressure on the business and also quickly damage its reputation.

6.2.2 The role of fair trade in commerce

Fair trade is an agreement between businesses in developed countries who trade with producers in developing countries. Fair trade ensures that producers and farmers are treated fairly. For instance, they are paid fair prices for their product, operate in fair working conditions, and use sustainable practices. Fair trade is part of business ethics because it involves doing the 'right' thing for the producers and farmers. Many fruit products can only be grown in specific countries that have the correct climate. Bananas grow in hot, tropical climates, such as South and Central America, India, China and Africa. Businesses in other countries, such as the UK or France, may purchase bananas from producers in Africa. Fair trade ensures that the business pays a fair price to those producers, so the producers can earn a secure income and have an incentive to continue to grow fruit and sell more.

KEY TERM

fair trade: an agreement that relates to trade between producers in developing countries and businesses in developed countries to ensure that fair prices are paid to the producers.

Fair trade also ensures that the terms of trade are fair and that workers have decent working conditions. Without fair trade, producers could be exploited, as the terms of trade could benefit the business and disadvantage the producer. For instance, the producer could be forced to work 7 days per week, for 20 hours per day, which is not fair on them.

Fair trade enables producers to plan, improve their businesses, develop skills and, increasingly, adapt to climate change. The producer has more financial stability as they know that their business is making enough money to operate in the longer term. This enables them to feel confident to plan future improvements and invest in training and development (which they can also afford due to receiving a fair payment). The producer will also have time to reflect and make plans, as they will not be working an exhausting number of hours, seven days per week. The business will therefore be run more efficiently.

The origins of the modern fair trade system date back to the 1940s. An early example was in the United States, where Ten Thousand Villages (formerly Self Help Crafts) started purchasing needlework from Puerto Rico in 1946.

Products supplied as part of the fair trade agreement carry the fair trade mark. This helps customers make choices to purchase fair trade products instead of less ethical alternatives. Many customers actively look for fair trade products, so the logo can differentiate products. Many retailers will only sell fair trade products as part of their ethical commitment to consumers. The fair trade system as of 2023 worked with over 1.9 million farmers and workers globally (Fairtrade.net, 2023).

The fair trade agreement covers the trade of a range of products (Table 6.2.2).

Type of product	Examples
Fruit	Bananas, pineapples, oranges, grapes, mango, dates
Vegetables	Carrots, potatoes, tomatoes, green beans
Drinks	Coffee, tea, fruit juice, wine
Basic ingredients	Sugar, herbs and spices, honey, rice
Textiles	Cotton, wool, yarns, fabric
Beauty and wellness	Hair care, skin care, cosmetics
Flowers	Cut flowers
Chocolate	Chocolate bars, assorted chocolate selections, cake, desserts, drinking chocolate
Gold	Jewellery and gifts

Table 6.2.2: Examples of products covered by the fair trade agreement

Fair trade has helped farmers become more income secure and less vulnerable to poverty. This is important as they can operate financially sustainable businesses. Fair trade has also empowered communities to organise into cooperatives and negotiate a higher price for their products than the conventional market price. Fair trade initiatives have also helped farmers to invest in resources to improve crops and yields, and can provide access to finance and support to tackle climate change.

Some people have criticised the fair trade idea. Many people in China and India have managed to increase their earnings by producing the right goods at the right prices, despite not being protected by fair trade. Some claim that the prices that producers are paid are not much more than they would normally be.

6.2.3 Ethical issues in commerce

There are many different ethical issues that businesses have to consider relating to commerce. Businesses must ensure that they make appropriate decisions to treat all stakeholders fairly.

Misleading advertising

Advertising aims to attract and encourage people to buy products. Advertising is usually designed by the business that sells the product with the aim of selling as many products as possible. Some unethical businesses use **misleading advertising** messages to increase the desirability of their products using false claims. This is unethical because customers are misled into buying products that they may otherwise choose not to buy.

For more about advertising, see Chapter 5.1.

KEY TERM

misleading advertising: publishing or communicating advertising messages that include a false claim or statement to encourage the sale of a product.

Despite laws to encourage accurate advertising messages and the existence of bodies such as the Advertising Standards Authority, which regulates/monitors advertising in the UK, there are regular examples of adverts that mislead. Sometimes the misleading claims are made intentionally to deceive customers, whereas others are unintentional. The business may have been given misleading information about the product that they intend to sell, used test equipment that they did not know was faulty or not used enough care to check that the data is accurate.

Broadband providers have been criticised for their advertising messages. Many customers compare broadband speeds when looking for providers and rely on the information provided by suppliers. However, there are examples of customers receiving slower than expected internet speeds after contracting for the service. The broadband providers claim that the speeds quoted in the advertising are accurate for some areas, but homes in other locations may not benefit from broadband speeds of the level advertised. The speeds quoted in the advertising mislead the customers into buying the service.

The car manufacturer Volkswagen was involved in a large scandal in 2015. It was discovered that Volkswagen manipulated tests carried out on its cars. The manufacturer claimed that its cars caused less pollution than they actually did. These claims had been made in its advertising over a long period of time. Millions of cars sold in different countries were affected by this scandal, and Volkswagen has had to pay out very large sums of money in compensation.

There are many smaller sellers that mislead customers. Unscrupulous people may use online marketplace sites to sell 'fake' designer products or dangerous products. The text in the adverts may include false information to persuade people to buy. These products are scams, as they are sold with the intention of misleading the customer.

Greenwashing

Greenwashing is where a business uses misleading messages in its marketing to make people think that its operations are more environmentally sustainable than they really are. The message may also make people think that its products are more beneficial for the environment than they are. Many customers want to make more sustainable purchasing decisions to prevent further harm to the environment. Businesses are aware of this and use greenwashing to try to attract customers to purchase from them instead of going to a competitor. They use greenwashing to help them generate more sales and increase market share. Greenwashing is unethical as it involves misleading the customer.

The misleading information could be:

- language used, such as use of vague comments to mislead others, e.g., 'natural' or 'eco-friendly'
- images/video, e.g., editing photos or video footage to imply that the business's operations are more environmentally sustainable, or using logos or symbols that may be associated with sustainability
- data, e.g., use of exaggerated data or statistics
- materials, e.g., claims about organic ingredients or materials used to produce the product that may not be true
- colours, e.g., the use of the colour green in an advert to imply that the product is environmentally friendly.

ACTIVITY 6.2.2

Look at advert shown in Figure 6.2.3. The advert was created by a business selling single-use plastic bags. Can you identify any examples of greenwashing?

Figure 6.2.3: Example of greenwashing

REFLECTION

Would this advert change your opinion of this business? Would you buy other products from this business if they were cheaper than others on the market? Were you surprised that ethics may affect your purchasing decisions? How did completing this activity support your understanding of greenwashing?

Many large businesses have been accused of greenwashing in the past, which can harm a business's reputation. For instance, in 2019 the airline Ryanair stated that it was Europe's 'lowest emissions airline'. However, the claim was unsubstantiated and the Advertising Standards Authority quickly banned the adverts.

Harmful disposal of products

Waste disposal is a large issue for many businesses. Most businesses generate waste when producing products. This waste could take many forms, including:

- hazardous materials, such as asbestos, pesticides and clinical waste
- surplus raw material
- damaged products and/or raw materials
- **by-products** from production processes. By-products are secondary products made as a result of making another product. The by-product is not the main product produced but may have a value and/or use.

Disposing of waste is more of a problem for businesses than it was in the past. Historically, businesses disposed of most waste in landfill sites (Figure 6.2.4) or incinerated waste. However, this was unsustainable due to the pollution created from the gases and chemicals released, fire risk and the lack of land, especially in highly populated countries like the UK. Landfill sites take up large areas of land. There is not enough land available to cope with the growing amount of waste from more manufacturing. Landfill sites can spoil landscapes as they can look unsightly.

Waste in the land often produces methane gas and poisons that can cause environmental problems.

Many businesses reduce waste in three ways:

- reducing
- reusing/renewing
- recycling.

Figure 6.2.4: Waste collected in a landfill site

KEY TERMS

by-product: a secondary product made as a result of making another product. The by-product is not the main product produced but may have a value and/or use.

disposing: getting rid of something that is no longer needed by throwing it away.

Reduce

A business can try to overcome the issue of having to dispose of waste by reducing the amount of waste that it produces. If less waste is produced, there will be less waste to have to dispose of. Reducing waste can also reduce the cost of production as less resources are put into the production process. Many businesses have introduced innovative methods of reducing waste, but are always keen to do more. Waste reduction is often part of a business's continuous improvement efforts. Car manufacturer Toyota reduced, reused and recycled its way to a 96% decrease in total non-regulated waste production (non-regulated waste is waste that is not considered hazardous or subject to specific rules or regulations). The 96% waste reduction saved the equivalent of approximately 900 million pounds going to landfill (Rubicon, 2023). Using accurate forecasts to plan production and/or likely customer demand can help a business to reduce waste. If a business accurately matches supply and demand, there is less likely to be unwanted products at the end of the day that may need to be disposed of, especially if the product is perishable and cannot be stored for future use. Computer applications can help managers forecast demand more accurately than was possible in the past, which can support this process.

Many businesses try to reduce packaging. Unnecessary packaging can increase the cost of producing the product and create more waste to dispose of. Only the minimum amount of packaging needed to protect the product should be used.

Reducing transportation can also lead to fewer emissions.

Reuse/renew

Often, waste products can be reused. Sometimes the item can be reused in a different part of the production process. McDonald's collects used cooking oil from its kitchens and turns it into biodiesel. The biodiesel generated is enough to fuel more than half of their delivery fleet. Reusing the cooking oil in this way means that McDonald's does not have to dispose of the oil.

Items can also be reused in the business or sold to another business. For instance, new office desks and chairs may be purchased, but the old desks and chairs could be used by a different department in the business. Alternatively, the business may be able to sell the second-hand furniture to another business. Selling the items will generate money for the business and also avoid the need to dispose of the furniture.

Instead of throwing away an item that is broken, the business can arrange for it to be repaired to reduce the amount of waste. More products today are designed to be repaired, which extends their working life. Repairing items is often cheaper than buying new replacement items and so saves the business money.

Recycle

Most manufactures recycle waste products where possible, such as paper and ink cartridges used in offices. Surplus and damaged raw material can often be recycled or reused. For instance, a manufacturer of plastic drinks bottles may identify a fault in one batch of bottles. Instead of disposing of the bottles, the manufacturer may recycle the plastic into pellets that can then be used to make new plastic bottles that are fit for use. A restaurant could also recycle food waste into compost for the garden. Coral Eyewear produce glasses from a material called ECONYL, which is created from waste found at sea and in landfills. All of Coral Eyewear's glasses can be recycled. When a customer needs a new pair, they can send their frames back to the business for recycling. To encourage customers to recycle, they offer them 10% off their next frame.

Encouraging others to reduce waste

Businesses can take action to influence the amount of waste created from operations. However, ethical businesses can also introduce initiatives to support other stakeholders to reduce waste from the purchase/use of products that they sell.

Trade-in offers

Many retailers offer customers money off of the purchase price of a new product if they trade in an old model. For example, some manufacturers offer customers a £300 discount on a selected mobile phone model if they trade in an old model. This helps customers to dispose of unwanted products responsibly. Businesses can either upgrade or repair the product traded in and resell to another customer, or recycle the parts to manufacture new products. Trade-in offers can help the business to attract new sales, as the customer benefits from the reduced price. It also encourages customer loyalty, as often the retailer will only accept old models of its own brand products.

Helping customers resell and reuse

New businesses have been created to help customers dispose of unwanted products. CeX is a second-hand electronics and entertainment retailer. Customers can buy, sell and exchange mobile phones, consoles, laptops, tablets, computers and games. CeX offers cash for unwanted items, which gives the customer an incentive to sell. CeX has over 600 stores across 10 countries, including the UK, India, Italy, Australia, Mexico and Spain. All products are fully serviced and reconditioned as needed, and the business offers a 24-month warranty on all second-hand products sold online and in store. CeX claims to have prevented over 300 million tech products going to landfill over the past 30 years.

Fast fashion is a sector that has been criticised for having a negative impact on the environment. Clothing retailers like H&M and Zara make low-priced and fashionable clothing to replicate the latest catwalk styles. However, many customers only wear the item on a few occasions. Sometimes customers buy clothing that they never wear.

> **KEY TERM**
>
> **fast fashion:** the production and sale of high-fashion clothing that is cheap to produce and low priced. Fashion-conscious customers buy the clothing to copy the latest catwalk styles, which change rapidly. Due to the low price, customers can afford to wear the item on a few occasions and then buy a new item to replicate the new catwalk style.

The clothing items are then disposed of by the customer to make room in their wardrobe for new styles (Figure 6.2.5). Fashion clothing production contributes significantly to global carbon emissions. It dries up water sources and pollutes rivers and streams. For example, it takes 2000 gallons of water to produce a pair of jeans. Many chemicals are used to produce clothing, such as dyes. It is estimated that 85% of all textiles go to landfill annually (Easy Eco Tips, 2019). Synthetic fibres like nylon, acrylic and polyester take hundreds of years to biodegrade. Clothing brands, such as H&M, are responding by using more organic and recycled materials to produce clothing. Retailers such as Zara are encouraging customers to return used clothing, footwear and accessories that they no longer need to stores. Zara then works with organisations that can recycle or reuse them.

Figure 6.2.5: Fast fashion has a negative impact on the environment

Vinted is an online marketplace where customers can sell unwanted clothing, shoes and cosmetics through its website or app. Vinted was founded in Lithuania and now delivers worldwide. Services of this nature can also reduce textile waste.

Many businesses also offer customers the opportunity to rent products that they are only likely to need once, such as special occasion clothing for a wedding or school prom. Customers save money, as renting is often cheaper than buying the product. Many products that are only needed once may be disposed of in time, so renting reduces the waste going to landfill.

Innovation

Lots of new products are designed to reduce waste. Traditionally, ink cartridges were required to support home printers. However, many leading manufacturers, such as Epson and Hewlett Packard (HP), create models with a lifelong tank. This reduces waste as users no longer have to dispose of ink cartridges (Figure 6.2.6). It is also more convenient for customers as they do not have to purchase ink cartridges and spend time changing them.

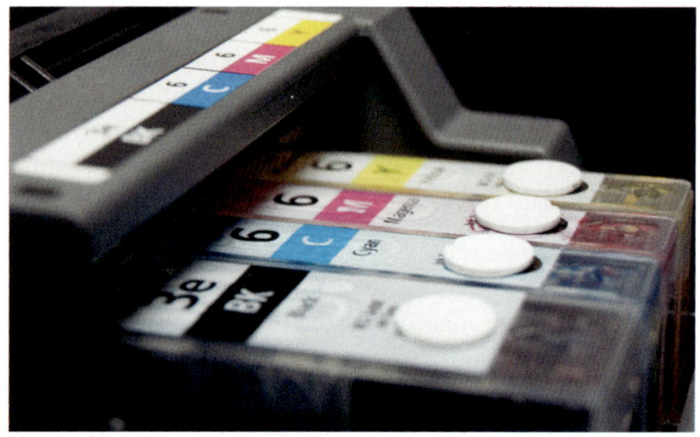

Figure 6.2.6: New models of printers now have lifelong ink tanks, reducing the waste of replacing ink cartridges

Packaging

Many businesses have reduced product packaging. In 2021, Amazon reduced the average plastic packaging weight per shipment by over 7%, which saved 97,222 metric tons of single-use plastic across its global operations network to ship orders to customers (About Amazon, 2022). Ninety per cent of Coca-Cola's packaging is recyclable, which the business aims to increase to 100% by 2025. By 2030, the business aims that all material used for packaging Coca-Cola's products will be recycled and 25% of all drinks will be either in refillable/returnable glass or plastic bottles or in fountain dispensers with reusable packaging (The Coca-Cola Company, 2023).

Digital technology

Digital technology has also supported waste reduction. Banking is an industry that has been revolutionised by digital technologies. Worldwide, over two-thirds of adults make or receive digital payments, with the share of adults making or receiving digital payments in developing economies growing from 35% in 2014 to 57% in 2021 (The World Bank, 2021). Digital platforms enable customers to view banking information in a paperless format. Many banks encourage customers to switch from printed statements and correspondence to digital versions to reduce paper. These options are more secure for the customer and reduce printing costs for the banks.

Helping customers recycle

Ethical businesses are educating their customers to help reduce waste. They are offering information on packaging to help them dispose of waste sustainably by telling them what elements can be recycled. Businesses are also offering customers guidance to empower them to make environmentally friendly choices.

Many retailers offer customers ways to dispose of waste responsibly, such as recycling facilities in store car parks and dedicated bins for recycling packaging/waste of certain materials in stores, e.g., ink cartridges and batteries. Many supermarkets now offer customers the facilities to recycle soft plastics, which are less likely to be included within household recycling collection services. Helping customers dispose of waste is not a legal obligation for retailers, but it is an example of an ethical action to support waste reduction.

The move from a linear to a circular economy

The economies in many countries are moving from a **linear economy** to a **circular economy**. A liner economy is a system where resources are extracted to make products that eventually end up as waste and are thrown away. In contrast, waste does not exist in a circular economy, as products are raw materials that are reused over and over again. Waste is the new raw material. Many government policies are supporting the move to a circular economy by using legislation to stop businesses from disposing of waste in a harmful way. There may also be large fees for the disposal of waste products, which encourages businesses to find ways of reducing, reusing or recycling the waste. Many governments also offer grants and subsidies to help businesses invest in new ways to manage waste.

KEY TERMS

linear economy: a system where resources are extracted to make products that eventually end up as waste and are thrown away.

circular economy: a system that prevents waste from being generated. Raw materials and products are reused over and over again.

Pollution

The operations of a business can result in pollution, which is the release of harmful materials into the environment. Pollution can take many forms, including:

- noise
- air
- land
- water.

Unethical companies may dispose of waste such as chemicals used to manufacture products inappropriately, which leads to pollution. Chemicals and waste water could be poured into lakes and rivers, which can kill fish and marine plants.

Emissions of toxic gases from factories, power plants and offices pollute the air. This can cause health problems such as asthma.

Ethical businesses are fully aware of the pollution that may be created by their operations and take action to minimise it and avoid negatively affecting others. These actions may be costly but the business is keen to do the right thing by others. For instance, they may correctly process any waste created to make it less harmful. Waste may be processed using chemical treatments to alter the composition of waste, and/or biological treatments that use organisms to decompose waste components into simpler organic matter and biomass. Treating waste in these ways before it leaves the factory reduces the quantity and toxicity of waste product before disposal, which reduces potential pollution and therefore lowers the harmful impact on others and the environment.

6.2.4 What is consumer protection?

Consumer protection is any means of safeguarding consumers so that they can obtain a fair deal.

KEY TERM

consumer protection: any means of safeguarding consumers so that they are treated fairly.

Consumers have the right to accurate and unbiased information about the products and services they purchase. Having this information allows them to make informed decisions and prevents them from being misled by businesses. Businesses can be held accountable for the information they provide through consumer protection laws, policies and regulations.

Businesses who abide by consumer protection laws, policies and regulations gain a good reputation among consumers. Examples of agencies who hold businesses accountable include the EU Consumer Protection Cooperation Network (CPC), which is the group of national authorities from the European Union (EU), Iceland and Norway who are responsible for the enforcement of consumer protection laws in their countries. Another example is the Ibero-American Forum of Governmental Consumer Protection Agencies (FIAGC), which was formed by the governmental agencies of Latin America, Spain and Portugal. Consumers become loyal to businesses that abide by customer protection practices, as they trust their products and feel safe buying from the business in the future. This increases the profitability of the business as well as its competitiveness. These factors lead to economic growth in the future.

6.2.5 Reasons for consumer protection

More goods are being imported from abroad. Consumers need protection against the different standards that operate in countries. Consumers may be purchasing online from sellers who are based in many different countries. This could make them subject to fraud when paying for goods from insecure websites, as they are at greater risk of identity theft, or falling victim to fake online stores or reviews.

Consumers have certain rights and should be able to defend:

- their right to be informed – to know details of products so that they can make an informed choice. Consumers often lack knowledge, particularly of technical products, such as computers and cars. Consumers may be exploited through unfair marketing techniques, such as misleading advertising, sales gimmicks and high-pressure sales techniques. They may be sent unsolicited goods– goods they did not order and do not know what to do with. Door-to-door salespersons may persuade them to make contracts that they later regret. They may be subject to persuasive telephone marketing, or repeated emails or letters offering free gifts or chances to win substantial prizes if they buy goods.
- their right to a healthy environment and safe products. Consumers may be ignorant of the dangers to their health, e.g., processed food may contain additives that are harmful to some people. Scientific advances have meant that a variety of materials, medicines, chemicals and additives are now available. Genetically modified products have developed because of experiments in food production. Consumers need to be protected against any harmful effects that result.
- their right to consumer education. The seller should provide information on the ingredients, contents of products or instructions for their use. Protection is also needed from goods sold in incorrect sizes or weights, or articles that are wrongly described on their packaging. There is a particular problem when packaging is not transparent, making it difficult to see whether or not the container is full. Some businesses may offer credit terms that do not give accurate information with regard to the true cost of the goods bought.
- their right to be heard, to be represented and to receive compensation for poor-quality goods or unsatisfactory services. This may sometimes be difficult when an individual consumer is dealing with a powerful multinational organisation. Consumers are often in an unfair bargaining position. They are individuals. Manufacturers and retailers could be small businesses, but they could also be powerful multinational companies who are difficult to deal with. Consumers may have been sold faulty goods that are not fit for the purpose for which they were intended. They may buy products that are so poorly made that they are dangerous to use. For example, sometimes car manufacturers recall batches of cars because a fault has been detected in several cars in that particular batch. Some unscrupulous traders fail to deliver goods or perform services after the goods have been paid for.
- their right to choose. There should be a wide range of products or services from a large number of suppliers rather than a **monopoly** situation, which is when a seller has no competition. In this situation, one company is in control of supply for all the customers and therefore of prices. If there is competition, consumers should be able to obtain

products at competitive prices. In some instances, a group of companies making the same product may have come together to fix the price for the product, so that the price charged is artificially high for the consumer. These cartels are illegal, and the consumer can be severely disadvantaged.

- their right to products that satisfy basic needs such as food, shelter and clothing.
- their right to representation in government policy. Dishonest traders may cheat consumers who are ignorant of their rights. Some consumers may not know, e.g., that they are entitled to parts and free repairs if an electrical appliance is under **guarantee**. A guarantee contains details of how far a seller will go to back up a product or service. The seller may cover parts and repairs to goods for a certain time period, for instance.
- their right to a clean, healthy and sustainable environment that is not threatening to human well-being.

KEY TERMS

monopoly: the seller has no competition. They are the sole seller of the product.

guarantee: details of how far a seller will go to back up a product or service. The seller may cover parts and repairs to goods for a certain time period.

If consumers know and advocate for their rights, retailers are more likely to improve their service, and manufacturers may have an incentive to produce goods of a better standard that consumers will wish to buy.

Retailers and manufacturers and service companies often have customer service departments to deal with customer enquiries and complaints. These help businesses to deal with problems as soon as they arise. All this can work to the manufacturer's or the retailer's advantage. A manufacturer or retailer who is known to produce quality products and provides value for money is more likely to have a good reputation with consumers and to succeed in the competitive commercial environment.

6.2.6 Actions that buyers and sellers take to resolve consumer protection complaints

Actions taken by a buyer

If a consumer has bought a product that has proved to be faulty, the consumer can:

- return the product to the seller together with the receipt, packaging and any guarantee that relates to the product
- request a refund, repair or replacement (some retailers have a returns policy, e.g., refund if returned within 28 days)
- accept a credit note rather than a refund.

If a consumer has bought a product that is found to be of poor quality, the consumer can:

- return the product to the seller together with the receipt and packaging
- point out why the product is of poor quality
- request a refund or a replacement of better quality.

If the complaint is about a food product, the consumer may ask the retailer to check other stock. There is also the option of doing nothing or just eating the food.

If a retailer receives a complaint, the retailer may examine the goods and, in the case of food, check the sell-by date. If the complaint is upheld, the retailer should apologise, may have to contact the manufacturer and may in some instances offer compensation. If the complaint is not upheld, the retailer should explain to the consumer the reasons why.

Some retailers are more receptive to consumer complaints than others, and responses to consumer complaints may vary. Some retailers will not refund money, but will instead offer an exchange or store credit to the value of the returned goods. Some retailers are very willing to listen to complaints, as it builds customer goodwill and encourages return custom. It is not usual for a consumer to have to go to a consumer organisation to obtain support in dealing with a retailer that is unreceptive to their complaint. A consumer organisation is a membership based, non-governmental, non-profit organisation created to promote the interests of consumers of goods and services. In extreme cases, where the consumer gets no satisfaction from the seller, they may sue the seller or contact the police, depending on the country's laws.

Complaints process

Unless people complain, manufacturers and retailers are not aware that there are problems.

People often do not complain. They would rather go to another manufacturer or retailer. Unless the seller is made aware of the problems, there will be no opportunity to correct matters. In many circumstances, sellers will take value from customer complaints and will do their best to improve a product or service to make sure that the problem does not happen again. If a business deals with a complaint satisfactorily, it will mean that the customer is pleased, may come back again and may tell others about the service received.

When making a complaint, buyers:

- should act promptly and not continue to use faulty goods
- should be clear about what they want the seller to do in order to put things right
- may complain in person if the business has a physical presence, via telephone, in writing or via digital communication such as email or social media. Emails or letters can be planned and they provide a record. Social media plays a large role in customer complaints nowadays, and public complaints may have an impact on a business's reputation if not resolved satisfactorily
- should be able to provide any necessary evidence, such as receipts as proof of purchase
- should keep a copy of relevant documents or communications. If buyers are sending a letter, they could keep a copy, use a recorded delivery service or obtain proof of posting from the post office
- may take their complaint to the top officials of a company if they achieve nothing from an assistant
- may need to obtain evidence to support their claim, e.g., a technical report on a car.

When buying goods, buyers are not entitled to a refund if they:

- do not like the goods
- caused damage to the goods themselves
- were told about any faults before they purchased the goods
- could easily see the fault themselves when they bought the goods.

Many retailers will still give a refund, an alternative or a credit note in these circumstances as a gesture of goodwill. The product should be returned as soon as possible so that the retailer has the opportunity of selling it.

When buying services, buyers are entitled to work of an acceptable standard – the work must be completed within a reasonable time, carried out for a reasonable price and done with reasonable skill and care.

TIP

The customer has a right to return an item that is faulty or poor quality. However, it is at the seller's discretion as to whether they refund an item that the customer does not want any more or damaged themselves.

Actions taken by a seller

When the seller receives complaints, they should follow these steps:

- collect the feedback and look for similarities in the complaints.
- share the information with their customer service team.
- determine the main cause of the problem.
- put together a plan to resolve the customer complaints.

The seller should make sure their customer service team is always accessible to the customer. The individual receiving the complaint should:

- listen carefully, engage with the customer and make sure they have a thorough understanding of the complaint
- acknowledge the customer's frustration and encourage the validity of their feelings, as this makes them feel heard and appreciated
- repeat the complaint for clarity purposes and try to resolve the issue within the first call.

Making customers wait only frustrates a customer even more. If the seller is unable to resolve the problem on the first call, they should provide the customer with a plan of action to resolve the problem so the customer feels comfortable knowing they have been heard and a plan is in place.

ACTIVITY 6.2.3

a In groups, research different types of consumer fraud or scams, such as fake online reviews, phishing scams or fake charities.

b Present your findings on how to recognise and avoid that type of fraud or scam in a brief report.

REFLECTION

Do you think creating a summary of this chapter would improve your understanding of the content? If not, what other method could you use to help your learning?

SELF-EVALUATION CHECKLIST

After studying this chapter, complete this table.

You should know about:	Needs more work	Almost there	Ready to move on
the definition of ethics			
the function of fair trade in commerce			
ethical considerations in commerce			
the need for consumer protection			
the actions buyers and sellers take to resolve consumer protection complaints			

Knowledge check

1 Explain two advantages to a business of operating ethically.

2 Give three problems with disposing of waste in landfill sites.

3 Explain two ways that a business can reduce the waste created from producing its products.

4 Greenwashing is an example of:

- a disposing of waste products in an environmentally friendly manner
- b explaining the environmental benefits of a product to consumers
- c exaggerating the environmental benefits of a product to mislead consumers
- d a business which sells green, environmentally friendly products.

5 Which of the following is not a benefit of operating ethically?

- a better able to attract investors
- b customer loyalty
- c higher prices
- d improved reputation

6 Give four consumer rights.

7 Describe four actions a consumer should take if they have bought a poor quality product.

8 Sophie bought an oven that became faulty after ten days. The company refused to give her a replacement or a refund.

Which consumer right has been broken?

a information
b service
c education
d redress

9 Which action should be taken to claim for a faulty product?

a not checking the warranty for the product
b contacting the local press to complain to them
c contacting the retailer to ask for a refund
d using the faulty product

10 Ginny bought a dress at a shop. She decides later that she does not like the dress and takes it back to the shop.

What is the shopkeeper legally obliged to do, according to consumer law?

a replace the dress with another item
b nothing
c offer a gift voucher for the cost of the dress
d provide a credit note

Practice questions

1 a Define the term 'ethics'. [2]
b State two ways in which a business can treat its employees ethically. [2]
c ABC Supermarket has been approached by two manufacturers for a new range of chocolate bars. Chocolate A is fair trade but more expensive. Chocolate B is cheaper but produced by a manufacturer that is known for treating supplier poorly. Which chocolate bar should the supermarket choose? Give reasons for your opinion. [6]
d State four actions a manufacturer could take to reduce waste. [4]

2 a Define consumer protection. [2]
b State two ways in which a consumer can be exploited. [2]
c Mr Jones bought a microwave oven from a large-scale retailer. After two weeks' use, the microwave oven did not work properly. Should the retailer replace the microwave oven? Give reasons for your opinion. [6]
d State four actions a seller should take when receiving complaints. [4]

Commercial calculations: formulae

Balance of Trade = receipts from visible exports − payments for visible imports

Balance of Payments = Balance of (visible) Trade + Balance of (invisible) Trade

where

Balance of (invisible) Trade = receipts from invisible exports − payments for invisible imports

Average insurance premium per customer = (total value of claims + insurer's costs) ÷ number of customers insured

Revenue (sales or turnover) = selling price per unit × number of units sold

Profit = revenue − costs

Gross profit = revenue − cost of sales

Net profit/net loss for the year = gross profit − expenses

Gross profit margin (%) = $\frac{\text{gross profit}}{\text{revenue}} \times 100$

Mark-up (%) = $\frac{\text{average selling price} - \text{unit cost}}{\text{unit cost}} \times 100$

Working capital = current assets − current liabilities

Current selling price = *unit cost* + [unit cost × $\frac{\text{mark-up (\%)}}{100}$]

Glossary

24/7: 24 hours a day, 7 days a week.

advertising: a type of promotion to consumers informing or persuading them to buy a particular product, service or brand.

advertising campaign: a coordinated group of advertisements that communicate the same message.

agent: a person who provides a link between two parties (buyer and seller). They earn commission by acting on behalf of one of the parties.

aids to trade: commercial services that support trade.

air freight: goods carried by air/aircraft that carry goods by air.

air waybill: a document used when goods are transported by air.

airport authority: an organisation that controls an airport, e.g., British Airports Authority or the Civil Aviation Authority of China.

artificial intelligence (AI): the programming of computers to perform tasks that require the intelligence of humans. AI is becoming increasingly sophisticated and applications include visual perception, speech, decision-making, and translation between languages.

assets: Items that a business owns that have monetary value.

automated teller machine (ATM): a machine that can be used to access some banking services such as withdrawing cash, using a bank card and changing a PIN (personal identification number).

Balance of Payments: the difference in financial value between the total exported goods and services and the total imported goods and services over a period of time.

Balance of Trade: the difference in financial value between the total exported goods and the total imported goods.

bank statement: a document available to the customer to show details of the customer's bank account.

banner advertisements: advertisements embedded into a web page. The banner is usually placed horizontally at the top of a webpage.

barriers in communication: reasons why communication fails or is poor.

bartering: the exchange of goods and services without money.

bill of lading: a document used when goods are transported by ship that gives details of the type, quantity and destination of the goods being transported.

biodegradable packaging: packaging that breaks down and returns to nature without benefits to the soil.

board of directors: a group of people who are appointed by the shareholders/members to set strategy and run the business on their behalf. They represent the shareholder's or member's interests.

bonded warehouse: a warehouse where dutiable goods are stored before payment of duty.

brand: the name of a business's products or services that is used for marketing purposes, such as Coca-Cola or Toyota.

break even: reach a point where the business is not making a profit or a loss. The total costs are equal to the total revenue generated.

breaking bulk: taking a large quantity of goods and dividing them into smaller quantities.

bulk-gaining manufacturer: a business that manufactures a product that becomes heavier and/or larger as it is made. The final product is heavier and/or larger than the materials/components used to make it.

business location: a place or structure occupied by an enterprise to run its operations. This includes any building or site used in the operation of the business.

buying on credit: buying now, paying later.

by-product: a secondary product made as a result of making another product. The by-product is not the main product produced but may have a value and/or use.

capital intensive: where production relies mainly on capital, i.e., technology, machinery, robots.

capital: Money invested in a business by its owner(s).

carbon footprint: the total amount of greenhouse gases caused by human actions.

cash discount: a deduction from the price of goods shown on an invoice to encourage customers who bought goods on credit to pay promptly. For example, offering a 5% discount on an invoice due in 30 days if the buyer pays within the first ten days of receiving the invoice.

cash in transit insurance: insurance that covers the theft of money, bank notes, cheques and credit cards that are being carried by employees.

cash-and-carry warehouse: a warehouse that offers self-service wholesaling with no credit and no delivery services.

cash-and-carry wholesalers: these wholesalers accept cash payments and often do not offer delivery services.

celebrity endorsement: the use of someone who is well known, such as an actor, singer or footballer, to recommend a product or service to consumers.

certificate of origin: a document certifying that goods in the shipment are from a particular country.

cheque: a written order by a bank account holder instructing their bank to make a payment.

circular economy: a system that prevents waste from being generated. Raw materials and products are reused over and over again.

cold storage warehouse: a temperature-controlled warehouse used to preserve perishable goods, such as fruit.

collective (generic) advertising: a group of organisations in the same industry or trade that join together to advertise the product.

commerce: supporting the exchange of goods and services and providing services to make the process of exchange more efficient.

commercial bank: a bank that provides a range of banking services to both business and private customers.

commission: a percentage share of the value of the goods sold.

common market: a customs union that also allows free movement of capital and labour within the member countries.

comparative advantage: when a country specialises in producing specific goods and services, they become most efficient at producing them or can do so at a lower opportunity cost than other countries. The country is likely to create a surplus of the type of good or service and will export the surplus quantity to other countries.

compensation: the payment(s) made by an insurer to the insured for a loss incurred from an insured risk.

competitive advertising: advertising by individual businesses to increase sales of their own products or services.

complex supply chain: a supply chain that involves more stages than a simple supply chain. There are usually five stages: supplier to agent to wholesaler to retailer to consumer.

compostable packaging: packaging that breaks down and forms organic substances that benefit the soil.

consequential loss (business interruption) insurance: insurance that covers losses that happen as a 'consequence' of another type of risk, such as fire, by providing financial protection to a business where its normal trading is disrupted or stopped.

consumer protection: any means of safeguarding consumers so that they are treated fairly.

consumer: the final user of the product.

consultancy: services and/or advice provided by a professional. The professional providing the services and/or advice is known as a consultant. They will be very knowledgeable and experienced in the area of work. Businesses can pay a lot of money for specialist consultancy services.

contactless card: a debit, credit or gift card that can be used to make payments without having to touch a card reader. Users tap the card over the top of the reader and the payment is made using the card details read by the card reader.

container transport: use of standardised boxes (or containers) to move goods using more than one mode of transport, such as by sea and rail.

containerisation: an integrated transport system using standard-sized containers that can be moved from one method of transport to another.

contract manufacturing: where a manufacturer contracts with another business for the production of components or products. It is a form of outsourcing.

cooperative: a type of business owned by its members.

cost of sales: cost of producing the goods/services, such as raw materials, or the cost of buying the goods from outside the business for resale.

costs: the money that the business has to pay out to run the business. They are the expenses incurred by a business to produce and/or sell its goods and services.

coupons: documents that can be used in part-payment of a future purchase of the product.

courier: a business or person who delivers parcels on behalf of another business or individual in the supply chain.

cover note: a document, produced more quickly than the more detailed insurance policy, that is evidence that a customer is insured.

credit card: a plastic card that is used to obtain goods and services without making payment at the time of the purchase. It can also be used to obtain cash.

credit note: a receipt given to a customer who has returned goods, been overcharged, received goods not ordered or received damaged goods.

credit transfer: method of payment allowing the direct transfer of money from one bank account to another using electronic means.

crowdfunding: funds for a new business venture come from lots of individuals called sponsors who each provide a small amount of the money.

currency: a country's system of money used to buy and sell goods and services.

current account: a type of bank account that provides the account holder with a variety of services including methods of payment, deposit services and possibly an overdraft facility.

current assets: the assets that a business owns for less than a year.

current liabilities: the debts that a business has for less than a year

customs authority: An organisation that is responsible for controlling a country's imports and exports, collecting trade statistics, preventing smuggling and collecting tariffs.

customs duty: a type of taxation that the consumer must pay on imported goods.

customs union: a group of countries where there is free trade between member countries and an external tariff against goods from outside the group.

data analytics: the collection, organisation and interpretation of data to find useful information, such as patterns or trends in the data, from which conclusions can be drawn and informed decisions can be made.

debenture: a fixed interest long-term loan to a company repayable at a set date.

debit card: a plastic card issued by a bank. It can be used to make immediate payment for goods and services up to an agreed limit.

debt factoring: selling the debts owed to a business to another organisation. This other organisation will provide a lump sum based on the total of the invoices sold, and will then collect the debts.

deficit Balance of Trade: when the value of a country's visible exports is less than the value of its visible imports.

delivery note: a copy of the invoice sent with the goods to the buyer. It is signed by the buyer when the buyer receives the goods.

digital advertising media: types of media that use digital methods to advertise products, services, brand or business to customers.

digital billboard: advertising screen that can digitally display images and/or videos.

direct debit: a bank service that enables variable amounts to be paid from a bank account at varying times, when requested by the creditor.

direct mail: personally addressed advertising, including catalogues and leaflets sent by post.

director: a person who runs the business on behalf of the shareholders/owners. They are usually responsible for a specific area or function within the business.

disposing: getting rid of something that is no longer needed by throwing it away.

distribution channel: the path that the product takes from the initial producer to the final customer. The distribution channel is made up of all of the businesses involved in movement of a good or service to the final customer.

dividend: a share of the profits paid to shareholders to reward them for investing in the business.

documentary credit (letter of credit): a letter issued by a bank and sent to another bank, usually in a different country, which acts as a guarantee for payment to be made to the specified person. Documentary credit is also known as a letter of credit.

document of title: a formal commercial document that proves ownership of goods.

domestic supply chain: a network of businesses and/or people based in the same country who support the production of a product and delivering it to the consumer.

downstream operations: activities that support the process of distributing the products from the producer/manufacturer to the consumer.

dropshipping: a business model that allows the retailer to sell its products online without needing to own or operate the physical location where those products are stored and processed.

dumping: occurs when a product is exported at much lower prices than it charges in its home country.

eco-friendly products: products made using natural or recycled materials and that have a lower environmental impact throughout their life cycle.

ecommerce: the buying and selling of goods and/or services over the internet/websites. The term is short for electronic commerce.

economically sustainable communities: communities that have adequate financial resources to survive and operate in the future.

economies of scale: as a business operates on a larger scale it will benefit from cost savings. The average cost of producing the product will reduce as the number of products increases.

efficiency: achieving a task or goal with no waste or effort. It is about producing more output from less inputs (i.e. resources).

electronic point of sale (EPOS): a computerised system of monitoring stock, recording sales and taking payments.

electronic transfer: method of payment allowing the direct transfer of money using electronic means without the need for paper-based or face to face transactions.

email: method of communication to most places in the world using computers, smartphones and the internet.

email marketing: when businesses send emails to consumers to promote their products or services.

embargo: a ban on the import of a product, the export of a product or any trading with a particular country.

employer's liability insurance: insurance that protects a business against claims resulting from accidents or injuries to employees at work.

employment laws: laws that affect the treatment of employees in the workplace. The laws may affect the terms of employment.

enquiry: formal request for information about the goods and services offered by the seller.

enterprise: a business managed by one or more individuals who can take the initiative to make decisions and take calculated risks.

entrepôt trade: the re-export trade, when a country exports goods that it previously imported without changing them.

entrepreneur: an owner that sets up a new business.

entrepreneurship: setting up a new business.

environmental impact: the effect human activity has on the environment.

errors and omissions excepted (E&OE): a statement printed at the bottom of a commercial document. If an error is made on the commercial document, the seller reserves the right to correct the error.

ethics: doing the 'right' thing. It is about the moral behaviour of individuals and managers when operating a business and making business decisions. Ethics focuses on exceeding the legal minimum, i.e., the standard required by law in the country.

excess: part of a claim for loss that is funded by the insured and not paid by the insurer.

exchange rate: the price of one country's currency expressed in terms of another country's currency.

expenses: the costs of running the business, e.g., insurance, wages and salaries.

exporter: a business that exports goods or services.

export: a good or service produced in one country but sold to a customer based in another country.

extended credit: the sale of goods or services using credit. The buyer becomes the owner as soon as the transaction is made.

extractive industries: industries that involve removing natural resources from the ground.

face-to-face communication: when two or more people physically see and interact with one another.

factor: a type of agent who has possession of the goods. They bring sellers and buyers of goods together in return for a commission.

fair trade: an agreement that relates to trade between producers in developing countries and businesses in developed countries to ensure that fair prices are paid to the producers.

fast fashion: the production and sale of high-fashion clothing that is cheap to produce and low priced.

Fashion-conscious customers buy the clothing to copy the latest catwalk styles, which change rapidly. Due to the low price, customers can afford to wear the item on a few occasions and then buy a new item to replicate the new catwalk style.

ferry: a ship that carries trucks that drive on and drive off without unloading.

fidelity insurance: insurance that covers a business against losses resulting from theft by an employee.

finance company: a financial organisation that offers hire purchase agreements and collects the payments.

finance: the money put into a business so that it can function.

financial protection: keeping the insured safe from financial losses.

fleet: a group of vehicles owned by the company.

franchise: an arrangement where one business buys the right to operate under the brand name of another business. Franchises are operated in the private sector.

franchisee: the business that has bought the right to operate under the brand name of another business.

franchisor: the business that owns the franchise and grants a licence to the franchisee to operate under its brand name and use its business format in return for a fee.

free ports: geographical areas inside a country where the production and processing and packaging of goods can occur without the requirement to pay any taxes, including on goods.

free samples: small quantities of products given to consumers without charge.

free trade: trading between countries without any customs duties, tariffs or other trade restrictions.

free trade area: an area within which there are no restrictions to trade.

general wholesalers: these wholesalers offer a wide range of goods in large warehouses.

generation of information: information generation relies on three activities – data input, processing and output. These three activities create information that can be used within businesses.

global market: one market where goods and services are sold worldwide.

global supply chain: a network of businesses and/or people based in different countries who support the production of a product and delivering it to the consumer.

globalisation: the development of world trade into a single global market.

goods in transit insurance: insurance that covers the loss or damage of goods while they are being transported.

goods: tangible products that have a physical presence and can be touched.

grants: a sum of money given to a business or individual for a specific purpose. Often the business or individual needs to satisfy certain criteria to receive the money. The money does not have to be repaid.

gross profit margin: a calculation used to show how effectively revenue is turned into gross profit.

gross profit: the profit that is left after cost of sales has been deducted from sales revenue.

guarantee: details of how far a seller will go to back up a product or service. The seller may cover parts and repairs to goods for a certain time period.

hawker: a mobile salesperson who carries the goods they sell using a cart or the back of an animal.

hire purchase: a business makes a deposit and pays regular instalments to a finance company for the purchase of an asset. During the payment period, the business is renting or hiring the asset. When all the payments have been made, the business becomes the owner of the asset.

home trade: the buying and selling of goods and services within the boundaries of a country.

host country: the country where the multinational company locates. The country hosts the multinational company.

import: a good or service produced in one country but bought by a customer in another country.

importer: a business that imports goods or services.

infant industry: an industry that is in the early stages of development within a country.

informal credit: credit given by small-scale retailers to trusted customers.

informative advertising: advertising that provides facts to consumers, e.g., health risks.

in-house production: all tasks/activities are completed internally within the business itself.

instant messaging (IM): text-based communication between two or more people within an internet-based chatroom on smartphones or computers

insurance broker: insurance expert who can advise people that want to buy insurance and put them in contact with insurers.

insurance policy: the contract of insurance setting out the terms of the policy.

insurance premium: the payment(s) that a customer makes to the insurer for the insurance cover.

insurance quotation: a document that tells an applicant for insurance details of the insurance cover and the cost of insuring.

insurance: a way of spreading risk among a group of people or organisations who contribute to a pool or common fund. People obtain financial protection against losses that result from the occurrence of risks such as fire.

insured (the): A customer who buys insurance cover.

insurer: a business that provides insurance cover.

interdependence: where two or more tasks/activities rely on each other. For example, Task 3 cannot be completed until Task 1 and Task 2 are done.

internet of things: describes the growing number of appliances/devices that are connected to the internet. Many homes have a number of smart devices, such as a television, security camera or video doorbell.

interest: money received as a reward for savings or money paid as a cost of lending.

intermediary: a person or business who acts between two parties to try to reach an agreement or complete a task.

international trade: the buying and selling of goods and services outside of the home country to make a profit.

internationals: businesses that buy and/or sell products outside of the home country but have facilities only in their home country.

internet banking: banking online using a bank's website and an individual security number.

invisible exports: services sold to other countries.

invisible imports: services bought from other countries.

invisible trade: the import and export of services.

invoice: the bill sent by the seller giving details of an individual transaction.

itinerant retailer: a retailer with no fixed location that will move location periodically.

kiosk: a small structure with one or more open sides from which items are sold, such as newspapers, tickets or refreshments.

labour intensive: where production relies mainly on labour, i.e., employees.

labour turnover: the rate at which employees leave an employer (and are replaced by new employees) over a period of time. Low labour turnover means that the workforce is stable and many employees are likely to have worked for the business for a long time.

landfill: a site where waste is disposed of by burying it in the ground.

leasing: a method of having the use of assets by renting them rather than buying them.

limited liability: the owners of the business can only lose the amount that they originally invested into the business if the business gets into debt or fails. The owners cannot be forced to sell their personal possessions to pay for the business's debts.

linear economy: a system where resources are extracted to make products that eventually end up as waste and are thrown away.

loan: borrowing of a set amount of money to be paid back to the lender in an agreed amount of time.

local enterprise: a business serving a specific geographic area.

logistics postponement: when part of the process of producing a product is delayed until the customer demand is realised.

logistics: the functional area that plans and fulfils the efficient transportation and storage of goods from the manufacturer/warehouse to the customer.

logo: a graphic or symbol to represent a product or business. A logo is part of the brand.

long-term finance: money available for more than one year.

long-term liabilities: debts that a business has for more than a year.

loss leaders: products sold at a lower price than the cost of making or buying them, with the aim of attracting customers into a shop where they will make other purchases.

manufacturer: the producer of the product.

mark-up: the difference between the unit cost of a product and its selling price.

mcommerce: the buying and selling of goods and/or services using mobile technology, e.g., a mobile phone, mobile app, mobile device or the internet. Mcommerce is short for mobile commerce.

method of appeal: advertising technique designed to associate a product or service with something to which a consumer can relate, such as the use of humour or music in advertisements

misleading advertising: publishing or communicating advertising messages that include a false claim or statement to encourage the sale of a product.

mixed economies: economies with organisations in both the public and private sectors.

mobile advertising: paid advertising that appears on mobile devices such as smartphones and tablets.

mobile app: an application that can be downloaded on to a mobile device such as a smartphone, e.g., a banking services app.

mobile banking: using a mobile device such as a smartphone to carry out banking activities.

mobile wallet: a digital container on a smartphone or other mobile device designed to keep together and use digital versions of payment cards, vouchers, tickets, receipts and loyalty cards.

monopoly: the seller has no competition. They are the sole seller of the product.

moral behaviour: to act according to one's personal values, beliefs and standards.

mortgage: A type of loan used to buy land or property where the loan is secured against the property.

multi-channel advertising: the use more than one advertising medium, such as combining television with newspaper advertising, to advertise the same product, service or brand.

multi-distribution channel: where a retailer sells its products to customers using a range of different methods, e.g. store, website, app.

multinational: operating in several countries. The operations may involve the manufacture and/or selling of products in the various countries.

multinationals: businesses that have a head office in one country with a centralised structure. The business will have operations in other countries such as factories and offices.

nationalised: owned by the state, i.e., government.

natural resources: resources or materials taken from nature, such as sand or stone.

needs: things that a human beings require for survival, such as water and shelter.

negligent: not taking enough care to stop an injury or damage from happening.

niche product: a good or service aimed at a small group of customers within a market.

night safe: a chute in the wall of a bank that enables people to deposit money after banking hours

non-current (fixed) assets: assets that a business owns for more than a year.

occupational immobility: when an employee finds it difficult to change jobs within an industry as the skills are not transferrable between jobs and industries. For instance, a doctor may find it hard to transfer to a job as a vet.

omnichannel: where the retailer aims to offer customers a seamless shopping experience across all channels.

online auction website: where items are sold by auction over the internet. Sellers present the goods for sale on the online auction website, and individuals can bid the price for which they would purchase the product. The product is usually sold to the person who offers the highest bid to buy.

order: a document sent from the buyer to the seller giving details of what the buyer wishes to order. Also known as the purchase order.

ordinary shares: capital for a limited company where the shareholders are part-owners of the company.

outsourced production: when a business hires another business that completes the tasks/activities on behalf of the business that is paying for the outsourcing.

overdraft: a form of flexible borrowing up to an agreed limit using a bank current account.

partnership agreement/deed of partnership: a written document that details the contract between the partners. The partnership agreement includes key information about how the partnership will operate, such as how profits and losses are shared, how decisions are made and the name/purpose of the partnership business.

The document can be referred to for future reference and in the event of disagreement

paying-in slip: a document that is completed by the account holder to accompany money being put into a current account using a bank branch.

pay-per-click advertising (PPC): online advertisements that include a link to a business's website. The business only pays a fee when a person sees the advert and clicks on the link.

pedlar: a mobile salesperson who carries the goods they sell door to door on their own head or back.

persuasive advertising: advertising that aims to persuade people to buy a particular good or service.

phone: a means of communication that enables a conversation to take place without people being visible to one another.

piece rate: where an employee is paid a certain amount for every item produced, e.g., a payment for every pen produced, rather than the time taken to produce them. It is a way of calculating an employee's wages.

place utility: having products available where they are needed by the customers.

point of sale display: a display of products located where customers make the payment for purchases to attract attention and encouraging additional purchases.

policyholder: term used to describe an insured individual or organisation that has taken out insurance cover.

pollution: the release of harmful materials into the environment.

pooling of insurance risk: risk is shared between a group of people or businesses that are all insured.

pop-up advertisements: advertisements that appear in their own window as the user is browsing a website.

poster: a large printed sheet that often contains pictures and is used to promote something in public places.

preference shares: a type of share that pays fixed dividends and is less risky than ordinary shares.

primary industries: industries that extract or obtain natural resources from the earth.

private sector: enterprises in the private sector are owned by individuals or groups of individuals. They are not owned by the state or the government.

privatisation: where an organisation, industry or service transfers from public to private ownership.

producer: the business who manufactures the product.

production: the process of making a good or service.

productivity: the efficiency of the production of goods or services. It can be measured in different ways, e.g. labour productivity measures the amount of goods or services produced per employee.

profit for the year (net profit): the actual profit made by a business. It is calculated by subtracting expenses from gross profit.

profit: the amount of money that a business earns. It is calculated by subtracting the money it has spent from the total income.

proposal form: the application form for insurance completed by the customer.

protectionism: the placing of restrictions, such as quotas, on international trade to make trade more difficult and to protect industries within a country.

public corporations: organisations which are owned by the government/state to provide a specific service but aim to break-even and generate a large proportion of income from fees and/or taxation.

public liability insurance: insurance that protects a business against claims made by members of the public.

public sector: organisations that are owned and controlled by the government. They are state-owned.

quantity utility: ensuring that the right amount of product is available to satisfy the consumers demand.

quantum computing: an area of computing that uses quantum mechanics to solve complex problems faster than a traditional computer.

quaternary activities: industries that provide intellectual and knowledge-based products.

quota: a limit on the amount of a product that is allowed to be imported into a country in a year.

quotation: a reply to a potential buyer giving details of goods and services requested in an enquiry.

receipt: a document showing that payment has been made.

recycling: reusing resources to produce something else.

reducing: using less and/or avoiding the use natural resources where possible.

regional distribution centre (RDC): a large warehouse for storing products bought by a business to allocate between branches in the region.

regulations: a rule or law that a business must follow. The regulations govern trade activities between businesses based in different countries.

renewable resources: resources that can be used more than once, e.g. wind and solar power.

resale marketplace: a digital marketplace where consumers can buy and sell unwanted products that have been previously purchased.

research and development (R&D): describes the process of innovating new products to introduce to the market.

retailer: a person or business who buys products from a manufacturer or wholesaler to sell on to consumers.

retained profit: profit kept back for use in the business and not paid out to the owners or shareholders as dividends.

reusing: finding new uses for materials in their original form rather than disposing after use.

revenue (turnover): the money received from selling goods or services.

risk assessment: a careful study that aims to identify things that might go wrong and judge what the impact might be.

royalty fee: the share of profits made by the franchisee that is paid each year to the franchisor.

salary: a payment to employees that does not vary according to the number of hours worked or their output. A salary is usually an annual amount which is divided into twelve equal monthly instalments that the employee receives for their work each month.

sale and leaseback: A way of raising finance by selling an asset and then renting back the same asset.

sales period: a specific time period, such as a few days or weeks, when a business reduces its prices or provides other special offers for customers.

sales promotion: the use of short-term sales techniques to bring products to the attention of the consumers to increase demand for a product or service.

sales: the amount of goods or services sold.

savings account: a bank account that allows the account holder to deposit money for a period of time and earn interest.

scommerce: the buying and selling of goods and/or services using social media channels. The term is short for social commerce.

search engine optimisation: techniques to make it more likely that a particular website will appear at or near the top of the results list from an internet search.

search engines: computer programs, such as Google, Bing and Yahoo, that help people to find specific websites or information online.

seasonal demand: goods produced all the year round for which there is demand only at certain times of the year, e.g. greetings cards for Chinese New Year.

seasonal production: goods produced at certain times of year, e.g. fruit.

secondary industries: industries that convert natural resources/raw materials into finished goods.

security: an asset that is used to secure a loan, where the lender may take the security in payment if the borrower is unable to repay the loan.

self-financing: finance provided from within the business.

self-service: the customer's selected goods are scanned and paid for by the customer themselves on unstaffed electronic tills.

self-sufficient: able to satisfy one's basic needs themselves without the help of anyone else.

services: intangible products with no physical identity. They are unable to be stored for later use and cannot be touched.

shares: a security that represents the fraction of ownership that the shareholder has in a company. The holder of a share is a known as a shareholder.

shareholder: a person who owns shares in a company by investing money. They become an owner by buying a share in the company.

short-term finance: money available for a short period, such as up to one year.

sidebar advertisements: advertisements placed vertically at the side of a webpage to attract the attention of the user.

signboards: large display boards, such as signs in a shop, train station or school.

simple supply chain: a supply chain that involves three stages: supplier to manufacturer to consumer.

small-scale retailer: a retailer selling goods and/or services from one outlet, branch or base.

social media advertising: using social media channels to promote a product, service or brand to consumers.

social media influencers: people that use social media to create content that affects others, perhaps encouraging them to think a certain way or buy a particular product.

social media: online communication channels, such as Facebook, that allow users to create, share and exchange information, pictures and videos.

sole trader: a business owned and run by one person.

sorting: arranging items systematically into specific groups.

special offers: price discounts or cost-effective opportunities for customers, such as 'buy one, get one free' (often known as BOGOF) promotions.

specialist wholesalers: these wholesalers stock a specific type of good such as electrical items.

specialisation: where people focus on what they do best. Individuals may concentrate on one task or activity.

sponsorship: businesses making payments or offering other support for an event or team, such as entertainment, sporting, community and charity events.

standard of living: a measure of how wealthy people are and what they can afford to have.

standing order: a bank service that allows the user to pay regular bills at regular intervals after authorisation. It saves remembering payments, such as rent and subscriptions.

start-up business: a business that has just been created. It is only just starting to trade.

statement of account: a document sent at regular intervals to buyers purchasing on credit. It gives details of all the transactions between the buyer and the seller during a trading period and the balance that still needs to be paid.

stock: also known as equity. Stock is the term to describe all of the shares in a company. Units of stock are known as shares.

stock exchange: a place where shares and stocks are bought and sold.

store card: a plastic card provided to customers by a large-scale retailer, through which credit is given (often on a monthly basis).

structural unemployment: a type of unemployment that occurs because there is a mismatch between the skills needed by employers and the skills that employees can offer. Many factors, including technological developments, can mean that the skills needed by employers change, which can make the skills that the employees can offer obsolete.

subscribers: individuals who have agreed to receive emails from a business and have provided the business with their email address.

subsidies: financial assistance offered by national or local government to support economic and social policy.

supply chain management: the organising of all of the stages that products or services must go through until they eventually reach the customers.

supply chain: a network of businesses and/or people who support the production of a product and delivering it to the consumer.

surplus Balance of Trade: when the value of a country's visible exports is greater than the value of its visible imports.

sustainable growth: to grow by meeting the needs of the present without affecting the ability of future generations to meet their own needs.

sustainable logistics: practices and processes aimed at improving the environmental impact of all logistical operations.

sustainable materials: materials that have a limited negative impact on natural resources and people to avoid depleting the environment.

sustainability: the long-term goal of maintaining an ecological balance by avoiding the exhaustion of natural resources.

takeover: the taking of control of a company by purchasing more than half of its shares, i.e., 51% or more, to become the majority shareholder. The majority shareholder has control of all decisions as they have more voting power than other shareholders.

tariff: a type of taxation that an importer must pay on goods brought into a country.

telesales: the selling of goods and services over the telephone.

tertiary activities: industries that are involved in the provision of services.

time utility: providing the consumer with the desired goods at the time when they are required.

trade barrier: a restriction imposed by the government of a country to control international trade.

trade credit: Selling goods and services and expecting payment for them after an agreed period of time.

trade discount: a reduction in the catalogue or list price of a product given to businesses within the same trade.

trade fair: an opportunity for businesses in the same industry to gather and meet each other in one place and promote their goods.

trade journals: specialist magazines used for selling within specialist trades.

trade payables: money owed to suppliers for goods bought on credit.

trade receivables: money owed to a business from its customers who have bought on credit.

trade: the buying and selling of goods and services to earn a profit.

trading bloc: a group of countries that have made a free trade agreement between themselves and have agreed a common external tariff to non-member countries.

traditional advertising media: types of media that use channels that have been in existence for many years, such as print and broadcasting media.

traditional commerce: the buying and selling of goods and/or services at a physical location.

Transport International Routier (TIR): an international customs transit system to move goods in sealed vehicles across the borders of countries without unloading.

transport: the movement of goods, raw materials, equipment and people from one place to another.

transshipment: the movement of goods from one kind of transport, e.g., ship, to another, e.g., road.

tuck shop: a small outlet located within another building, such as a school, that sells a limited range of goods, such as refreshments.

underwriters: people who review a customer's application for insurance cover to determine the risks to the insurer. They then decide whether or not the insurer should accept the insurance application and calculate the premium to be charged.

unit cost: the cost of buying or making one unit of the product.

unlimited liability: the owner(s) of the business are liable for the full debt of the business. If the business gets into debt or fails, the owners may be forced to sell their personal possessions to repay the business's debts.

upstream operations: activities that support the delivery of the materials and/or other resources to the producer/manufacturer.

utilities: services used by the business to be able to operate, e.g. electricity, water, gas, broadband and telephone.

venture capital: finance to a new enterprise from a venture capitalist that specialises in lending to new, high-risk businesses in return for a share of the business.

video advertisements: advertisements that use video rather than images or text.

videoconferencing: a system of linking people in different locations with sound and visuals so that a meeting can take place.

visible exports: goods sold to other countries.

visible imports: goods bought from other countries.

visible trade: the import and export of goods.

voice picking system: a hands-free, paperless system that uses voice prompts to direct workers to specific locations in a warehouse.

voluntary chains: a group of retailers formed by a wholesaler. The group of retailers work together on a non-contractual basis to benefit from economies of scale in advertising and buying.

wage: a payment to employees that varies according to the number of hours worked or their output.

wants: things that people would like to have as they make their lives more pleasant, such as a mobile phone.

warehouse: a large building used to store raw materials or finished products ready for distribution for sale.

waste: unwanted or unusable substances or resources. It is something that is no longer required.

water stewardship: using water in such a manner that is environmentally sustainable and economically beneficial for future generations.

wholesaler: a person or business that buys products in large quantities from suppliers (often the manufacturer of the product) and sells them to retailers and/or other businesses in smaller quantities.

word-of-mouth advertising: personal recommendations from people who have already bought a product or service or from a particular business.

working capital: capital available for the day-to-day running of the business.

Index

Acknowledgements

The authors and publishers acknowledge the following sources of copyright material and are grateful for the permissions granted. While every effort has been made, it has not always been possible to identify the sources of all the material used, or to trace all copyright holders. If any omissions are brought to our notice, we will be happy to include the appropriate acknowledgements on reprinting.

Cambridge International Education copyright material in this publication is reproduced under licence and remains the intellectual property of Cambridge Assessment International Education.

Thanks to the following for permission to reproduce images:

Cover Andriy Onufriyenko/Getty Images; *Inside* **Unit 1** Chris Sattlberger/GI; Richard Drury/GI; D3sign/GI; Oscar Wong/GI; Traimak_Ivan/GI; Monty Rakusen/GI; Maskot/GI; kandhal keshvala/GI; Westend61/GI; Johnny Greig/GI; **Unit 2** Marian/GI; Ezra Bailey/GI; Monty Rakusen/GI; SOPA Images/GI; Mtreasure/GI; Christine Pemberton/LatitudeSt/GI; Narinder Nanu/GI; Maica/GI; Thomas Barwick/GI; Bruce Yuanyue Bi/GI; Rudi_suardi/GI; SolStock/GI; Songsak Rohprasit/GI; Westend61/GI; Tara Moore/GI; Tetiana Radachynska/GI; Busakorn Pongparnit/GI; Westend61/GI; Thomas Barwick/GI; Peepo/GI; Marco VDM/GI; Tara Moore/GI; Tom Werner/GI; Catherine Falls Commercial/GI; Maxxa_Satori/GI; Vadim Sazhniev/GI; D3sign/GI; Oscar Wong/GI; **Unit 3** Insung Jeon/GI; Vincent Pommeyrol/GI; Karl Hendon/GI; Peter Cade/GI; Ake1150sb/GI; Yaorusheng/GI; Bloomberg Creative/GI; **Unit 4** Alan Thornton/GI; DuKai photographer/GI; Ugurhan/GI; Tolga Dogan/GI; F1 Online Rf/GI; Jorg Greuel/GI; Virojt Changyencham/GI; Kmatta/GI; Lebazele/GI; Issarawat Tattong/GI; Comezora/GI; Maskot/GI; **Unit 5** Pawel Libera/GI; PK-Photos/GI; Tek Image/GI; Tom Werner/GI; Grinvalds/GI; Georgijevic/GI; Mangpor_2004/GI; Tom Werner/GI; Xavier Lorenzo/GI; Richard Drury/GI; John Lamb/GI; Douglas Sacha/GI; AleksandarGeorgiev/GI; Xavier Lorenzo/GI; Henrik Sorensen/GI; Peter Dazeley/GI; Westend61/GI; Peter Dazeley/GI; Ligora/GI; Shulz/GI; Extreme-Photographer/GI; Grant Faint/GI; Алексей Белозерский/GI; Drazen/GI; Svetikd/GI; **Unit 6** Timandtim/GI; Piksel/GI; Aleksandr Zubkov/GI; Mikroman6/GI; Jackyenjoyphotography/GI; Oscar Wong/GI; Leon Harris/GI; Laurence Soulez/GI; Krisanapong Detraphiphat/GI; Narvikk/GI; Netrun78/GI; Valdore/GI

Key: GI = Getty Images